Emotion-Focused Therapy
for Depression

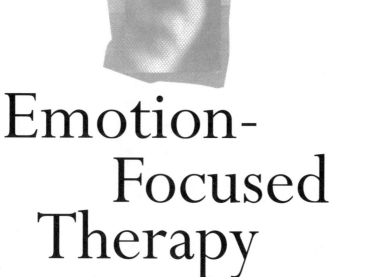

Emotion-Focused Therapy
for Depression

Leslie S. Greenberg and Jeanne C. Watson

American Psychological Association • *Washington, DC*

Published by
American Psychological Association
750 First Street, NE
Washington, DC 20002
www.apa.org

To order
APA Order Department
P.O. Box 92984
Washington, DC 20090-2984
Tel: (800) 374-2721; Direct: (202) 336-5510
Fax: (202) 336-5502; TDD/TTY: (202) 336-6123
Online: www.apa.org/books/
E-mail: order@apa.org

In the U.K., Europe, Africa, and the Middle East, copies may be ordered from
American Psychological Association
3 Henrietta Street
Covent Garden, London
WC2E 8LU England

Typeset in Goudy by Stephen D. McDougal, MD

Printer: Sheridan Books, Ann Arbor, MI
Cover Designer: Naylor Design, Washington, DC
Technical/Production Editors: Gail B. Munroe and Harriet Kaplan

The opinions and statements published are the responsibility of the authors, and such
opinions and statements do not necessarily represent the policies of the American
Psychological Association.

Library of Congress Cataloging-in-Publication Data

Greenberg, Leslie S.
    Emotion-focused therapy for depression / Leslie S. Greenberg and Jeanne C. Watson. —
1st ed.
        p. cm.
    Includes bibliographical references and index.
    ISBN 1-59147-280-6
    1. Depression, Mental—Treatment. 2. Emotions. I. Watson, Jeanne C. II. Title.

    RC537.G723 2005
    616.85'270651—dc22   2005000974

British Library Cataloguing-in-Publication Data
A CIP record is available from the British Library.

Printed in the United States of America
First Edition

To our clients and students,
without whom this book could never have been written.

CONTENTS

Emotion-Focused Therapy

for Depression

1

INTRODUCTION: THE NATURE AND EXPERIENCE OF DEPRESSION AND ITS TREATMENT

Depression is one of the most common and debilitating of the major psychological disorders (Ross, Smith, & Booth, 1997). Clinical depression is characterized by feelings of being discouraged, sad, blue, down, and depleted for a period of weeks or more; the accentuated intensity and extended duration of these everyday experiences define the syndrome. The self becomes organized almost permanently in a depressed state, and resilience is lost. Sometimes the depressed feeling is the prolongation of sadness over a loss or a defeat that lingers seemingly forever. Often agitation and anger accompany clinical depression; anxiety, too, can leave the person feeling insecure and helpless as well as hopeless.

Depression may be experienced as embodied anguish or as physical deadness. The person's sense of his or her own body changes; heaviness sets in, and he or she feels immensely burdened and moves his or her limbs with difficulty. This sensation can progress to the point where depression is as much a sensory disorder as an affective one. The world becomes flat and colorless. People with severe depression no longer feel bitter and hopeless; they simply do not feel.

Depression, according to the fourth edition of the *Diagnostic and Statistical Manual of Mental Disorders* (DSM–IV; American Psychiatric Association, 1994), is recognizable by eight features:

1. depressed mood of at least 2 weeks' duration,
2. loss of pleasure in most activities,
3. significant weight change,
4. disturbed sleep,
5. loss of energy,
6. feelings of worthlessness or guilt,
7. trouble concentrating or making decisions, and
8. thoughts of death.

Depression thus defined is a complex phenomenon. It derives from a number of sources, manifests in a variety of symptoms, may at times be intractable and possibly debilitating, and affects a broad segment of the population.

Various therapeutic interventions have been shown to promote therapeutic change in depression by targeting cognitive, interactional, and neurobiological processes. In this book we suggest that *emotion* is a fundamental aspect of depression and human functioning more generally, that emotional change is a valuable target for therapy, and that a therapy that focuses on emotion is a powerful means of intervention. Empirical studies support this approach and show that deeper emotional processing predicts good outcome and avoidance of relapse. Used as an alternative to or integrated with other approaches, emotion-focused treatment can maximize the effectiveness of therapy and hasten recovery. In the chapters to follow, we demonstrate how emotion-focused therapy is useful in the brief treatment of clients who are moderately depressed.

THE NATURE OF DEPRESSION

Depression is a complex biopsychosocial phenomenon. No single cause can be isolated. When people are depressed, they have disturbances at many levels of functioning. There is clear evidence to suggest that the functioning of neurotransmitters is disturbed in depression, affecting peoples' ability to feel both positive and negative emotions. People who are depressed experience not only a loss of ability to feel interest, pleasure, and joy, but also an increase in sadness, anger, anxiety, and shame. There also is evidence of increased cortisol, a stress hormone, in depression (Thase & Howland, 1995). These changes in physiology influence moods, memory, attention, and behavior.

In addition to neurophysiological and affective disturbances, people with depression have negative cognitions. Their views of self, world, and future are negative. Depression is also characterized by inactivity and social isolation and alienation. All these factors—neurochemical, physiological, affective, cognitive, behavioral, and social—interact in a complex and dynamic manner to constitute depression.

Depression is not a monolithic disorder, but rather an experience that varies greatly from individual to individual and within the same individual from moment to moment and year to year. The diagnosis is an abstraction, subject to definition by the culture in which the individual is embedded. Moreover, there is great variability in how people with depression present themselves. Some are classically depressed, with low mood and loss of energy. But many appear anxious, many are angry, many are abusing substances, and many present with chronic pain conditions or other physical disturbances. Depression seems to affect women more than men (Nolen-Hoeksema, 2001; Piccinelli & Wilkinson, 2000). Some people experience depression as a dramatic change from a previously better state of functioning, but for many depression develops gradually. These differences make it very difficult to develop a single approach to effectively treat all clients. Indeed, it is difficult to conceive of a single theory that could explain chemical changes in the brain, changes in cognition and emotions, differences in men and women, the role of loss, the role of family support, the effect of sunlight, and all the other phenomena associated with depression.

Human beings clearly are nonlinear dynamic systems (Hayes & Strauss, 1998; Thelen & Smith, 1994; van Geert, 1998; Whelton & Greenberg, in press) in whom multiple processes interact continuously in response to a constantly changing environment. It is clear, then, that there are biological, psychological, and social causes of depression, as well as affective, cognitive, and behavioral aspects of the depressive experience (Epstein, 1994). There are both conscious and unconscious sources of depression (Bargh & Chartrand, 1999), as well as multiple levels of processing involved in generating depression (Greenberg & Pascual-Leone, 2001; Teasdale & Barnard, 1993). In addition, personal meanings, will, and choice also are involved in generating depression. It is ultimately the person's broad system of meaning, emanating from his or her depressive self-organization, that is the target of therapy, rather than isolated neurotransmitters, hormones, thoughts, beliefs, behaviors, emotions, or motivations (Mahoney, 1991; Neimeyer & Mahoney, 1995). The dialectical constructivist view of depression we adopt in this book (Greenberg & Pascual-Leone, 1995, 2001; Watson & Greenberg, 1996) incorporates a dynamic systems view of functioning and recognizes multiple sources of experience and meaning. Central to this view is the recognition of clients as active agents in the construction of their depressive experience (Mahoney, 1991; Neimeyer & Mahoney, 1995; Stiles, 1999; Watson & Rennie, 1994) and the mobilization of this agency in changing this experience.

Within this dynamic systems view of self-organization, intervention can and should occur at different levels of the system at different times and with different components of the system in different ways. Psychotherapy research has made clear that all have won and all shall have prizes (Bergin & Garfield, 1996; Hubble, Duncan, & Miller, 1999; Luborsky, Singer, & Luborsky, 1975; Wampold et al., 1997), indicating that many approaches appear to be indistinguishable in terms of their effects. The inability to find treatments that are differentially effective is explained, in part, by the fact that people are complex systems, as well as by the importance of common factors that occur in all treatments (Goldfried, 1991; Norcross, 2002). Each therapeutic approach probably affects the system with some specific change process at a chosen level of the system, whether cognitive, emotional, neuro-chemical, behavioral, or interactional. Any specific effect at one level of the system most likely reverberates throughout the highly interconnected levels of the system. It probably is the specific change factor unique to a particular approach, plus the relational factors common to many approaches, that suc-ceed in producing comparable change in the whole person. Thus, all ap-proaches end up altering the person emotionally, cognitively, behaviorally, and neurochemically.

It is thus important to specify how emotion is involved in depression and to provide methods for working with emotion in depression. To form a maximally effective integrative approach to the treatment of depression, prin-ciples of emotional change that can be used in treatment need to be spelled out to make them available for integration.

In this book we present an emotion-focused approach to the treatment of depression that targets the emotional level of the system. Our emphasis on the emotional process in this approach does not mean that we would not promote cognitive change or that salient neurochemical, behavioral, and interactional processes that would benefit from intervention would escape our attention. Our treatment focuses primarily on intervening at the emo-tional level of the system, because we see this level as highly influential and able to affect the system as a whole in important ways. Emotion influences the biological and neurochemical levels of system functioning, on one hand, and the psychological, cognitive, and behavioral levels, on the other. Emo-tion occurs at the interface between body and mind, constituted by both and influencing both. A therapeutic focus on this critical level of functioning therefore will enhance all treatment approaches.

WHY EMOTION-FOCUSED THERAPY FOR DEPRESSION?

In this book we discuss an emotion-focused approach to the brief treat-ment of clients with moderate depression. We use therapy session excerpts drawn from our depression studies throughout the text to illustrate the therapy process.

In emotion-focused therapy (EFT), promoting emotional processing brings about change by bringing emotion memories into awareness so that they can be symbolized in conscious awareness, exposed to new emotional experience, and reflected on to produce alternative ways of behaving. By labeling experiences stored in implicit memory and becoming aware of their maladaptive emotions, clients are able to differentiate between past and present events, identify their needs in their current situations, and find new ways of realizing those needs. Newly activated adaptive emotions act as antidotes to maladaptive ones and progressively infuse new information into the maladaptive schemes that store painful experience. This process helps generate new meaning and facilitates adaptive resolution of problematic experiences.

Treatment involves first accessing the maladaptive "weak" or "bad" sense of self at the core of depression and the core shame and fear associated with this sense of self. The client must enter into the core maladaptive state to be able to transform it. In emotion-focused therapy, the client cannot truly leave a place until he or she has arrived at it. Once the client enters the maladaptive state, he or she differentiates, elaborates on, and symbolizes it in words with the help of an empathically attuned therapist. Experiencing the maladaptive state and its painful affects in the presence of an empathic other helps break the isolation. The therapist's presence and empathic attunement help soothe the client, the first step in helping him or her regulate and transform core maladaptive states. In addition, the therapist helps the client work to access emotionally based needs and biologically adaptive resources in the personality and to bring these resilient responses into contact with the maladaptive emotions. Access to primary emotions brings adaptive strivings to the fore, promoting the client's resilience and inner sense of direction. Access to alternate emotional responses plus reflection on emotion to create new meaning are key in transforming maladaptive self-organizations.

Comparison With Existing Models

Our approach is offered as an empirically supported alternative to the two major empirically supported psychotherapeutic approaches to the treatment of depression, interpersonal therapy (IPT) and cognitive–behavioral therapy (CBT) and certainly can be integrated with them. IPT contends that depression is caused by interpersonal problems such as grief, interpersonal disputes, role transitions, and interpersonal deficits. Interpersonal therapy involves grieving and accepting the loss of old roles, exploring repetitive patterns in relationships, and reducing social isolation. The emphasis is on dealing with current interpersonal relations (Klerman, Weissman, Rounsaville, & Chevron, 1984). CBT contends that negative thoughts and beliefs about self, world, and future are the key determinants of depression, and therapy involves changing the cognitive content of depressogenic schemata (Beck, Rush, Shaw, & Emery, 1979).

Although interpersonal and cognitive factors clearly are often aspects of depression, EFT focuses on the emotion schematic processes that underlie both of these sets of determinants and views affective processing as an important and fundamental therapeutic target. Changing negative beliefs and interpersonal interactions is important, but in EFT therapists seek to effect permanent change by changing the emotionally based organization of the self. It is not thought or even loss itself that is important in generating depression, but rather the affective memories or emotion schemes evoked by the thought or loss (Greenberg, Elliott, & Foerster, 1990; Greenberg & Paivio, 1997). In EFT therapists treat the underlying emotion-based determinants of depression, rather than focus on the precipitating cause.

People with depression have been found to show an elevated proportion of negative emotion memories of the more distant past (Smith, 1996). Their memories were found to involve not so much the recent life stress that precipitated their depression, but rather emotion memories about earlier life experience. For example, being fired from a job had precipitated a woman's depression, but when her daily experience was tapped, 6 months into the depression, what filled her inner world were emotion memories of her husband's leaving her 10 years previously. This finding supports the idea that the evocation of unresolved emotions and emotion memory is what is important in producing depressive experience.

CBT and EFT are similar in emphasizing change in meaning as important in the treatment of depression. Meaning, beliefs, and thoughts, as CBT suggests, are important in maintaining depression. Self-criticism, perfectionism, and "shoulds" keep the client feeling like a failure. The harder clients try to meet the standards of the critic, the more depleted they become. It is not the cognitive content alone of the perfectionism, however, that the client needs to deal with. It is the affective relationship between parts of the self—the disapproval, dismissal, and contempt—that has to be transformed. EFT works to help clients access more adaptive ways of coping with their feelings of vulnerability and unworthiness to undo the contempt and to promote self-acceptance.

In IPT, role disputes or transitions or severe losses are viewed as precipitating depression. In our view, depression results when a client feels disempowered and unloved and when the self's ability to organize experience in its usual, more hopeful and positive manner is lost. It is not the dispute or the loss alone that produces depression; rather, it is the client's affective response to the dispute or loss that is important. The client feels hopeless and unable to survive the loss or feels humiliated in the dispute and worthless. The evocation of a core insecure self, with its fundamental emotionally based evaluation of threat to its coherence, is at the root of the depression, rather than the interpersonal response produced by it.

EFT and IPT are similar in that both focus on the encouragement of emotion, and as IPT suggests, depression does play itself out in the interpersonal arena. A goal of EFT therapy, similar to IPT and dynamic therapy, is to focus on relationships and to help clients learn to set healthy boundaries so that they are able to merge with others at times of great intimacy but also capable of functioning autonomously when necessary.

General Features of Emotion-Focused Therapy

In EFT (Greenberg, 2002), the lives of human beings are viewed as profoundly shaped and organized by emotional experiences, and emotion itself is considered the creative and organizing force in people's lives. Therapists work to enhance clients' emotional intelligence, which involves the recognition and use of their own and others' emotional states to solve problems and regulate behavior (Salovey & Mayer, 1990). They also focus on helping clients regulate their affect and transform their emotion schematic memory processes. The goal in EFT thus is change in self-organization through increased emotional awareness and regulation, and the use and transformation of emotion.

We have found that EFT for depression works best for clients whose functional impairment is not so great as to completely demobilize them. The clients in our studies (reviewed in the next section) who responded to EFT functioned in their world (i.e., parented, worked, or went to school), although often with difficulty and always with little or no satisfaction. Although all of these clients met criteria for a major depressive disorder, their experiences of depression varied markedly. Some were highly self-critical and felt like failures; others were disappointed in relationships, felt abandoned, and were sad and angry. Others felt empty, confused, and aimless. Yet others were highly afraid and anxious, or angry and agitated, as well as hopeless. Some were highly avoidant, and others worried obsessively; some were openly fragile, and others were highly guarded. Some were concrete and rational in their style of thinking and talking and others very associative and internally focused. In EFT treatment therapists work with the person as a whole, not with a syndrome, and this leads them to pay attention to each client in his or her uniqueness. The EFT approach is therefore first and foremost client centered. Therapists take the whole person into account and are most concerned about forming a supportive, helping relationship in which the focus is on whatever seems most important to the client.

Despite wide variations in clients' experience, all were depressed, and certain depression-related commonalities did exist. They all experienced a type of closing down or withdrawing at the emotional level and a sense of weakness or disempowerment; all felt a defeated sense of self and had difficulty coping with their depressed affect. These clients' ability to put their emotions and subjective experience into words often was not well developed. Many avoided or interrupted their core emotions, being afraid or ashamed of them. They disowned important aspects of their experience. Once they could articulate their inner experience, they experienced either problematic self–self relations, such as self-criticism, shame, and identity issues, or self–other relationship difficulties, such as unresolved issues of loss or anger and feelings of abandonment, isolation, and loss of connection. Notions of what it was to be a competent professional, a good parent, or a good spouse often prevented them from expressing parts of themselves and kept them trapped or invalidated. In their self-critical striving for perfection, many chastised and bullied themselves into passive submissiveness. They often felt deeply discouraged and expressed a high degree of negativity and of disgust and contempt toward themselves. In the search for relational intimacy and connection with others, many clients forfeited expressing what they felt, and to remain connected, they prevented who they were from emerging in relationships or felt deeply anxious about separation or loss. Deep feelings of insecurity, most often related to loss of relationship, left them feeling that they could not survive without the connection or that connection was too dangerous.

Once negative affect was evoked in relation to current circumstance or painful memories, these clients' responses to the painful affect were more harmful than helpful. They deadened to stop feeling, withdrew from others, became overwhelmed by a cascade of self-recrimination, or became outer directed and blamed others. None of these methods of coping with the original feelings of vulnerability, sadness, shame, or fear were adaptive; these attempts to cope led to more depressive experience, rather than less.

Over the course of treatment, EFT for depression helped these clients become more resilient and confirmed their ability to survive. It helped them to reaffirm and re-empower themselves by enabling them to learn to regulate their emotions and contact an emotionally based will to live. It helped them symbolize what they felt and find constructive ways of dealing with their feelings. The therapists promoted change by helping clients clarify their feelings and undo maladaptive ways of responding to painful feelings. Accessing biologically adaptive feelings and needs and allowing them to be fully processed helped clients identify more adaptive forms of responding. As clients approached, contacted, tolerated, regulated, and accepted their emotions, they began to make sense of their experience, and they became empowered by their healthy, more resilient affects. Interpersonal needs were clarified, and assertion was enhanced. As clients accessed their primary emotions and needs and their therapists validated the results of their efforts, the clients gained a sense of self-worth.

Access to their emotions provided these clients with information about the impact of situations on them, gave them information about their reactions to the situations, and organized them to act to attain the adaptive goals that their emotions set as organismic priorities. Once they had symbolized their feelings and needs in awareness, they were able to reflect on themselves and their worlds, integrating their heads and their hearts to cope more adaptively. Many found that the therapist's empathic listening, which confirmed the clients as authentic sources of experience, led them to take themselves seriously and to be more empathic toward themselves. Therapy thus helped these clients regain contact with a more positive and resilient sense of self and promoted a more optimistic sense of mastery and connectedness.

EFT for depression focuses on helping clients regulate their affective functioning by processing their emotional experience in new ways. In this therapy, clients change by accessing alternate emotionally based and resilient self-states in response to situations that previously evoked shame, anxiety, and hopelessness and by using these new more resilient states to combat and transform their depressogenic states. Thus, EFT helps clients clarify what they feel and achieve more resilient self-organizations. These new self-organizations are based on previously inaccessible emotions such as empowering anger at violation, which helps overcome powerlessness; vital sadness at loss, which helps overcome deadening resignation; hope, which helps mobilize the client to overcome hopelessness; and pride and self-worth, which help overcome shame and humiliation.

A principle of EFT is that the way clients process affective information and create meaning changes in different self-states. People change by changing their mode of self-functioning, rather than by staying in the same mode of processing and changing the content of their thoughts in a particular state. It is not by correction of error, logical disputation, or modification of beliefs that enduring change occurs. Instead, real change requires a change in self-organization through the generation of alternative ways of being and seeing. Rather than seeing the world through lenses tinted with sadness, fear, or shame and withdrawing from it, clients begin to approach life with greater acceptance, joy, optimism, and a sense of mastery. They come to replace their negative views of self and dysfunctional beliefs with more adaptive ones not by challenging the validity of beliefs, but by changing their self-organization such that they come to see self, world, and future in a new way. They learn to regulate dysphoric states such as anger or despair by developing or increasing access to self-soothing and self-affirming ways of treating themselves. Greater access to more resilient self-states helps clients combat the depressogenic self-states that generated their feelings of powerlessness, hopelessness, self-contempt, and shame.

The Evidence Base for Emotion-Focused Therapy

Research on an emotion-focused treatment of depression has supported the importance of emotion-focused work. We found that a manualized form of EFT for depression, originally called *process experiential therapy*, was highly effective in treating depression in three separate trials. In these trials, emotion-focused treatment was found to be equally or more effective than a purely relational empathic treatment and a cognitive–behavioral treatment. Both of the treatments with which EFT was compared were themselves also found to be highly effective in reducing depression, but EFT was more effective in reducing interpersonal problems than both and promoted more change in symptoms than the purely relational treatment. EFT was also highly effective in preventing relapse.

In the York I depression study, Greenberg and Watson (1998) compared the effectiveness of process experiential therapy with client-centered therapy in the treatment of 34 adults experiencing major depression. The client-centered treatment emphasized the establishment and maintenance of the client-centered relationship conditions and empathic responding, which are also viewed as a central component of process experiential therapy. The process experiential treatment added to the client-centered treatment the use of specific tasks, in particular systematic evocative unfolding, focusing, and two-chair and empty-chair dialogue. No difference was found between the therapies in reducing depressive symptoms at termination and at 6-month follow-up. Process experiential therapy, however, had superior effects at midtreatment on depression and at termination on the total level of symptoms, self-esteem, and reduction of interpersonal problems. Thus, the addition of these specific tasks at appropriate points in the treatment of depression appeared to hasten and enhance improvement.

In the York II depression study, Goldman, Greenberg, and Angus (in press) replicated the York I study by comparing the effects of client-centered and process experiential therapy on 38 clients with major depressive disorder; they obtained a comparative effect size of +.71 in favor of process experiential therapy. They then combined the York I and II samples to increase the power of detecting differences between treatment groups, particularly at follow-up. Statistically significant differences among treatments were found on all indices of change for the combined sample, with differences maintained at 6- and 18-month follow-up. This finding provides further evidence that the addition of emotion-focused interventions to the foundation of a client-centered relationship improves outcome. In addition, and of great importance, 18-month follow-up showed that the process experiential group was doing distinctly better at follow-up. Survival curves showed that 70% of process experiential clients survived to follow-up—that is, did not relapse—in comparison to a 40% survival rate for those who were in the relationship-alone treatment. Something important seems to have occurred in the process experiential treatment that influenced the probability of relapse.

In a later study, Watson, Gordon, Stermac, Kalogerakos, and Steckley (2003) carried out a randomized clinical trial comparing process experiential and cognitive–behavioral therapies in the treatment of major depression. Sixty-six clients participated in 16 sessions of weekly psychotherapy. Both treatments were effective in improving clients' level of depression, self-esteem, general symptom distress, and dysfunctional attitudes. Clients in process experiential therapy, however, were significantly more self-assertive and less overly accommodating at the end of treatment than clients in the CBT treatment. At the end of treatment, clients in both groups had developed significantly more emotional reflection for solving distressing problems.

Process outcome research on the emotion-focused treatment of depression has shown that both deeper emotional processing late in therapy (Goldman & Greenberg, in press; Pos, Greenberg, Goldman, & Korman, 2003) and higher emotional arousal at midtreatment, coupled with reflection on the aroused emotion, predicted treatment outcomes (Warwar & Greenberg, 2000; Watson & Greenberg, 1996). This finding supports the importance of emotion-focused work as a key change process in treatment.

Emotion-focused therapy, then, appears to work by enhancing emotional processing, which involves helping clients both accept their emotions and make sense of them. The importance of facilitating in-session emotional experience to promote change has become increasingly recognized (Greenberg, 2002; Samoilov & Goldfried, 2000). Reviews of past process outcome studies testing these claims show a strong relationship between in-session emotional experiencing, as measured by the Experiencing Scale (EXP; Klein, Mathieu-Coughlan, & Kiesler, 1986), and therapeutic gain in dynamic, cognitive, and experiential therapies (Castonguay, Goldfried, Wiser, Raue & Hayes, 1996; Orlinsky & Howard, 1986; Silberschatz, Fretter, & Curtis, 1986). This finding suggests that emotional experiencing may be a common factor that helps explain change across approaches.

In our first process outcome study of the York I therapies, the relationship between theme-related depth of experiencing (measured by EXP scores) and outcome was explored. The sample consisted of 35 clients, each of whom received 16 to 20 weeks of either process experiential or client-centered therapy. Depth of experiencing on core themes in the last half of therapy was a significant predictor of a reduction in symptom distress and increase in self-esteem but did not correlate significantly with changes on the Inventory of Interpersonal Problems. Depth of experiencing on core themes also accounted for outcome variance over and above that accounted for by early depth of experiencing and the alliance. Depth of experiencing therefore mediated between any client individual capacity for early experiencing and positive outcome. The client's view of the strength of the early working alliance was shown to predict outcome. However, an increase in depth of emotional experiencing across therapy was shown to contribute 8% to 16% of the outcome variance over and above the alliance. This result suggests that deepening experiencing over therapy is a specific change process that is integral to the alleviation of depression through emotion-focused treatment.

Adams and Greenberg (1996) tracked moment-by-moment client–therapist interactions and found that therapist statements that were high in experiencing influenced client experiencing and that depth of therapist experiential focus predicted outcome. More specifically, if the client was externally focused and the therapist used an intervention that was targeted toward internal experience, the client was more likely to move to a deeper level of experiencing. This study highlights the importance of the therapist's role in deepening client emotional processes. Given that client experiencing predicted outcome and that therapist depth of experiential focus influenced client experiencing and predicted outcome, a path to outcome was established that suggests that therapist depth of experiential focus influences clients' depth of experiencing and that this process relates to outcome.

A study by Pos et al. (2003) suggested that the effect of early emotional processing on outcome was mediated by late emotional processing (*early* and *late* refer to the stage of treatment). In this study *emotional processing* was defined as depth of experiencing on *emotion episodes* (Greenberg & Korman, 1993), or in-session segments in which clients expressed or talked about having experienced an emotion in relation to a real or imagined situation. The depth of experiencing variable thus was rated only for in-session episodes that were explicitly on emotionally laden experience. Depth of experiencing again was found to mediate between capacity for early experiencing and positive outcome. Possessing the capacity for emotional processing early in treatment thus did not guarantee good outcome, nor did entering therapy without this capacity guarantee poor outcome. Therefore, although it is likely an advantage, early emotional processing skill appeared not as critical as the ability to acquire or increase depth of emotional processing throughout therapy. In this study, late emotional processing independently added 21% to the explained variance in reduction in symptoms over and above early alliance and emotional processing.

Warwar (2003) examined emotional arousal at midtherapy and experiencing in the early, middle, and late phases of therapy. Emotional arousal was measured using the Client Emotional Arousal Scale—III (Warwar & Greenberg, 1999a, 1999b). Clients who had higher emotional arousal midtherapy were found to have more change at the end of treatment. In addition, a client's ability to use internal experience to make meaning and solve problems, as measured by EXP, particularly in the late phase of treatment, added to the outcome variance over and above middle-phase emotional arousal. This study thus showed that a combination of emotional arousal and experiencing was a better predictor of outcome than either index alone.

Warwar, Greenberg, and Perepeluk (2003) measured expressed as opposed to experienced emotion and found that client reports of in-session experienced emotional intensity were not related to positive therapeutic change. They described a discrepancy between client reports of in-session experienced emotions and observer reports of expressed emotions based on arousal ratings of videotaped therapy segments. For example, one client reported that she had experienced intense emotional pain in a session, but her level of expressed emotional arousal was judged to be very low.

Greenberg and Pedersen (2001) found that in-session resolution of two core emotion-focused therapeutic tasks predicted outcome at termination and 18-month follow-up and, most importantly, the likelihood of nonrelapse over the follow-up period. These core tasks—resolving splits and resolving unfinished business—involved helping subjects restructure their core emotion schematic memories and responses. These results thus support the hypothesis that deeper emotional processing and emotion schematic restructuring during therapy lead to more enduring change.

Client-centered and process experiential therapy thus have been shown to be effective in alleviating depressive symptoms, with process experiential therapy showing greater effectiveness overall. Regardless of type of treatment, emotional arousal and depth of experiencing were found to predict outcome.

WHAT THIS BOOK CONTAINS

Chapters 2 and 3, in which the role of emotion in human functioning and depression are discussed, respectively, provide the theoretical scaffold of the book. In these chapters we review the psychology and affective neuroscience literature to show that limbic system affective processes play a key role in human functioning and depression. We also offer a dialectical constructivist theory of depression in which a weak or bad self-organization is evoked by experiences of loss, humiliation, or entrapment and in which the self is strengthened by means of a synthesis of preverbal emotional experience with the ongoing verbal symbolization of tacit experience into new identity narratives. Those interested in getting to the therapeutic approach could skip chapters 2 and 3 and return to them later to get the theory.

The next two chapters offer the treatment principles and the intervention framework. In chapter 4 we offer specific principles for emotion assessment and empirically based principles of emotion intervention. Chapter 5 introduces the course of treatment, outlining three major phases—bonding and awareness, evocation and exploration, and transformation.

In the next two chapters we cover the two most fundamental and general processes of the treatment of depression that operate persistently across all phases of the treatment. Chapter 6 focuses on a pivotal element in this therapeutic approach—the creation of a relational bond characterized by presence, empathy, positive regard, and congruence. In chapter 7 we describe a process diagnostic approach to case formulation.

Chapters 8 through 14 then describe the main therapeutic methods. Chapter 8 focuses on the important role of increasing emotional awareness in the first phase of the treatment of depression, and chapter 9 describes specific methods for increasing emotional awareness. Chapter 10 focuses on the role and function of evocation and arousal of emotion in the middle phase of treatment. Chapters 11 and 12 describe specific methods of evoking emotion to be used in this phase.

The book concludes with chapters 13 and 14 on transforming emotion in the last phase of treatment. In chapter 13 we describe the process of generating alternatives by the novel means of changing emotion with emotion, and in chapter 14 we demonstrate the crucial role of reflection on experience in the creation and consolidation of new meaning.

2

EMOTION IN HUMAN FUNCTIONING AND DEPRESSION

I felt before I thought: which is the common lot of man.
—Rousseau (1781/1981, p. 19)

In our view, emotion is foundational to the construction of a sense of self and is a key determinant of self-organization. At the most basic level of functioning, emotions are an adaptive form of information processing and action preparation that orient people to their environment and promote their well-being, disposing them to act on their behalf in a given situation (Frijda, 1986; Greenberg & Paivio, 1997; Greenberg & Safran, 1987; Lang, 1995). According to a number of emotion theories, an important (although not the only) source of emotion at the psychological level is the tacit appraisal of a situation in terms of personal goals, concerns, or needs (Frijda, 1986; Oatley & Jenkins, 1992). *Appraisals* are nonlinguistic evaluations along fundamental survival-oriented dimensions such as goal relevance, uncertainty, danger, novelty, pleasure, or ability to cope (Scherer, 1984). Thus, emotions are important because they inform people that an important need, value, or goal may be advanced or harmed in a situation (Frijda, 1986), and they indicate how individuals appraise themselves and their worlds (Greenberg & Korman, 1993; Lazarus, 1991). Emotions, then, are involved in setting goal priorities (Oatley & Jenkins, 1992) and influence the mode of processing in which people engage (Damasio, 1999, 2003).

Emotions produce biologically based relational action tendencies that result from appraisals of the situation (Frijda, 1986; Greenberg & Korman, 1993; Greenberg & Safran, 1987, 1989; Oatley & Jenkins, 1992). *Action tendency* has been defined as the readiness to act in a particular way so as to establish, maintain, or alter the relationship with one's environment (Arnold, 1984; Frijda, 1986). Different action tendencies correspond to different emotions. For example, fear is associated with the mobilization for flight, whereas anger involves the urge to attack, repel, or break free.

Emotions thus involve a primary meaning system that informs people of the significance of events for their well-being. Emotions also organize people for rapid adaptive action (Frijda, 1986; Izard, 1991; Tomkins, 1968). From birth on, emotion is a primary signaling system that communicates intentions and regulates interaction (Sroufe, 1996). Emotion helps to regulate the interactions of self and others and gives life much of its meaning. Depression, as we will argue, stems from problems in regulating the emotion system.

Recent research has shown that a common earlier view, that emotion is postcognitive, is clearly inadequate (Le Doux, 1996; Zajonc, 2000). Emotion can and often does precede cognition, but more importantly, it makes an integral contribution to information processing in its own right (Forgas, 2000a, 2000b; Greenberg, 2002; Greenberg & Safran, 1987). Neuroscience has shown emotion to be an indispensable foundation for many cognitive processes, particularly for making decisions (Bechera et al., 1995; Damasio, 1994), and changes in emotion lead to changes in modes of cognitive processing. Tucker et al. (2003) recently showed that an evaluative decision begins by recruiting motivational and semantic influences within limbic networks, and these influences appear to shape the development of decisions in various neocortical areas of the brain. Affect, by being so densely interconnected with other brain areas, has a significant influence on decision making. Cognition and emotion are ultimately inextricably linked, so that cognition often works in the service of affective goals, and emotion often is a response to cognition. Emotions, however, set a mode of processing in motion, orienting consciousness to differentially analyze situations for loss, danger, intrusion, violation, novelty, or pleasure. Emotion, in essence, sets problems for reason to solve (Greenberg, 2002; Greenberg & Pascual-Leone, 2001).

Cognition, which has been studied far more extensively than emotion, has been shown to be important in depression. The cognitive triad of negative views of self, world, and the future clearly operates in many cases of depression (Beck, 1996). However, the less extensive but equally important research on the role of emotion in depression has shown that cognition and memory are mood dependent (Blaney, 1986; Forgas, 2000b; Palfai & Salovey, 1993). Forgas (2000a), in his affect infusion model, showed that the infusion of affect into cognition depends on the type of processing that is occurring. When processing is extensive and occurs in ambiguous, open situations, like most interpersonal experiences, affect is most likely to influence the construction of beliefs. By contrast, more controlled processing in clearly defined problem-solving situations is more impervious to affect infusion. Emotion, then, clearly influences cognitions in complex processing situations. Ultimately, it is important to understand the independent contribution of both emotion and cognition in the production of human distress and depression, and it is even more important to understand how they interact in this process. Emotional experience and expression thus clearly involve affect, cognition, and motivation, and at the level of conscious adult experience, emotion and cognition are mutually determining and essentially indivisible.

Recent findings that are important to an understanding of depression illuminate the relationship between positive emotion and psychological resilience. Fredrickson (2001) helped to identify the adaptive function of positive emotions. Positive emotions improve problem solving by making thought processes more flexible, creative, and efficient. The playful creativity associated with emotions like joy and interest motivate people to learn and achieve more than they otherwise would, which helps them to accrue future personal and social resources. She also found that positive emotions build resilience by undoing the effects of negative emotions, a finding that may have relevance for recovery from the effects of depressive self-criticism (Fredrickson, 2001). Furthermore, the neuropsychological research of Davidson (2000a, 2000b) indicated that a tendency toward low positive affect conferred a vulnerability to depression, whereas a stable positive affective style built psychological resilience. The ability to recruit positive emotions in the face of stress appears to be a crucial component of resilience (Davidson, 2000a, 2000b). Hope, for example, is an important aspect of resilience and is important in combating depression.

Evolution, however, has endowed humanity with more so-called negative basic emotions than positive ones to aid survival. An important conclusion to be drawn from an evolutionary point of view is that unpleasant emotions often are useful. Anxiety, anger, sorrow, and regret serve a useful purpose, or they would not exist. Unpleasant feelings draw people's attention to matters important to their well-being and promote adaptive action. However, when unpleasant emotions endure even after the circumstances that evoked them have changed or when these emotions are so intense that they overwhelm or evoke past loss or trauma, they can become depressogenic. Healthy adaptation thus necessitates learning to be aware of, tolerate, regulate, and use negative emotionality (Frijda, 1986; Tomkins, 1962) as well as to enjoy positive emotionality for the benefits it endows (Fredrickson, 1998). Dysfunction in the ability to access and process emotional information, both positive and negative, disconnects people from one of their most adaptive orientation and meaning production systems (Frijda, 1986; Izard, 1991), and this dysfunction is implicated in the affective disorders.

In his book *The Feeling of What Happens*, Damasio (1999) described emotion as so central to human functioning that he attributed the emergence of consciousness itself to emotional awareness. According to Damasio, emotion first and foremost provides information about the status of the body-self in the environment, and knowing springs to life in the story of changes in this status. Feeling, then, is the awareness of the emotional impact of the physical environment on the body, and it is this impact that gives rise to consciousness. In this view, the first narrative thus involves the brain linking a nonverbal account of the self in the process of being modified to its cause. Consciousness comes into being in the creation of this account and is manifest as the feeling of knowing. It is only later that self-reflective consciousness and linguistic representation emerge. The brain thus can be seen to possess two important meaning systems, one based on a sensory motor language and the other based on a symbolic conceptual language. Body talk, then, is intelligent brain talk, and people need to pay attention to "feeling knowledge" to make sense of it with their linguistic conceptual abilities to be able to benefit consciously from its evolutionarily adaptive offerings.

The feeling dimension of emotion thus is an important source of consciousness. The complexity of emotion, however, resides in the fact that emotion includes more than feelings and sensations, which simply arise and are not directed toward anything. Emotion also involves the more intentional components of cognition, evaluation, and motivation, all of which are related to objects or situations. The cognitive component of emotional processing consists of information about situations, whereas the evaluative component consists of an assessment of the personal significance of the information for the individual. The motivational component addresses the individual's needs, wishes, goals, and readiness to act in the situation. Depressed emotional states, such as feeling worthless, desperately inadequate, or unlovable, involve both the feeling and the intentional components. The components are not separate entities, but rather different aspects of a larger whole that we will refer to as an *emotion scheme*.

In his newest book, Damasio (2003) suggested that there are three types of emotion proper that go beyond the more fundamental elements of reflexes, pain and pleasure, and drives and motivations. He identified these as background emotions, primary emotions, and social emotions. He viewed these levels as hierarchically nested within each other, with social emotions at the top incorporating within them responses categorized as primary and background emotions. Thus, for example, the social emotion of disdain incorporates the primary emotion of disgust and the background emotion of distaste, whereas the social emotion of embarrassment builds on the primary emotion of shame and a background feeling of shying away from something. The social emotions add cognitive and social components to the primary emotions. In conclusion, depression is constituted by many components—biological, experiential, cognitive, and social—that build on and complement each other. Depression involves sensory body aspects, like feelings of heaviness; emotions, such as sadness; evaluations, such as "I'm a failure"; and social aspects, such as isolation, and these aspects all interact.

AFFECTIVE NEUROSCIENCE AND DEPRESSION

Recent developments in affective neuroscience suggest that the emotional processing of simple sensory features occurs extremely early in the processing sequence (Forgas, 2000a, 2000b; LeDoux, 1996). Most sensory stimuli are relayed through the thalamus to the amygdala (LeDoux, 1996) and up to the cortex. Information is processed by the amygdala before it is conscious, and people respond emotionally before they think. Le Doux (1996) concluded that there are two different paths for producing emotion. One he called the "low road"; when the amygdala senses danger according to a global apprehension of patterns, it broadcasts an emergency distress signal to brain and body. The other is the slower, "high road," in which the same information is carried through the thalamus to the neocortex, where it is subjected to a more detailed analysis. Because the shorter amygdala pathway transmits signals more than twice as fast as the neocortex route, the thinking brain often cannot intervene in time to stop emotional responses. Thus, the automatic emotional response, be it jumping back from a snake, snapping at an inconsiderate spouse, yelling at a disobedient child, or wanting to sink into the ground from shame, has already occurred before one can stop it.

The autonomy of emotional processing also is highlighted in the work of Ladavas, Cimatti, del Pesce, and Tuozzi (1993) on detecting emotion in subliminal stimuli. These authors argued that the automatic, unconscious process of emotion generation is cognitively impenetrable. They saw emotion as modularly organized and suggested that although the output of emotion modules may be crude and diffuse, the modules become the substrate for further cognitive elaboration, which is highly cognitively penetrable. Such a view of emotion modules seems logical when considering the evolutionary significance of emotional responses: when faced with an unpredictable, dangerous environment, our evolutionary ancestors relied on an automatic and accurate system of identifying "bad" and "good" elements of the environment and quickly forming appropriate actions in response. Öhman and Mineka (2001), for example, proposed an evolutionarily defined fear module. To support this, they cited evidence that the fear response is elicited by stimuli of evolutionary significance (e.g., a snake); such responses are elicited automatically and are free from the influence of cognitive expectancy or instruction.

Rapid stimulus processing by lower evaluative mechanisms predisposes an individual's behavior toward appetitive stimuli and away from aversive stimuli prior to more detailed processing of the stimuli (Cacioppo, 2003). Bargh and Chartrand (1999) commented in an article entitled "The Unbearable Automaticity of Being" that perceived objects or events are immediately and unintentionally classified as good or bad in a manner of milliseconds, and this results in a behavioral predisposition toward or away from the stimulus. Automatic evaluative processes thus prepare people for appropriate responses while the conscious mind is otherwise engaged. As LeDoux (1996) emphasized, the initial "precognitive" perceptual and emotional processing of the low road is highly adaptive because it allows people to respond quickly to important events before complex and time-consuming processing has taken place.

Current evidence suggests that the amygdala has an important role in the generation of negative affect, which may be a special case of its more general role in directing attention and resources to affectively salient stimuli and issuing a call for further processing of stimuli that have potentially major significance for the individual. The amygdala is critical for recruiting and coordinating cortical arousal and vigilant attention. It also is important for optimizing sensory and perceptual processing of stimuli associated with underdetermined contingencies, such as novel, surprising, or ambiguous stimuli, which often are interpreted negatively, especially by people prone to depression (Davis & Whalen, 2001; Holland & Gallagher, 1999; Whalen, 1998).

In addition to the amygdala's central involvement in affect, the right hemisphere has been found to be strongly implicated in the reception and expression of affective states, and there is considerable evidence to support lateralization of subcortical as well as cortical structures (Schore, 2003). Thus, the right amygdala, the right basal ganglia, and the right thalamus all have been shown to mediate emotional and facial processing and fear activation. Evidence from affective neuroscience indicates that there is both implicit (right hemispheric) and explicit (left hemispheric) affect regulation, that implicit forms of affect regulation are central to well-being, and that the neurological effects of neglect and trauma in early life are primarily in the right hemisphere (Schore, 2003).

Philips, Drevets, Rauch, and Lane (2003) suggested that there are two systems involved in the regulation of affective states and emotional behavior. The ventral system, including orbitofrontal and prefrontal cortex, insula, ventral anterior cingulate, and amygdala, is important for the implicit identification of the emotional significance of environmental stimuli and production of affective states. It also is central to the automatic regulation and mediation of autonomic responses to emotional stimuli and contexts accompanying the production of affective states. The dorsal system (dorsolateral prefrontal cortex, nonlimbic dorsal anterior cingulate, hippocampus), is involved in explicit, emotion-labeling tasks and is associated with the verbal components of emotional stimuli. This system is important for the effortful regulation of attention and affective states. According to this work, essential affective self-regulatory processes occur largely at levels below conscious awareness, probably in the orbitofrontal cortex, which takes over amygdala and lower-level right hemispheric functioning for complex processing (Derryberry & Tucker, 1992; Joseph, 1996; Rolls, 1996a, 1996b). The executive regulator of the right brain, the right orbitofrontal cortex, is involved in interoception, or the subjective evaluation of the physiological condition of the body, and the differentiation of an affect associated with a bodily feeling (Craig, 2002). Treatment of problems of automatic affect regulation thus is most effectively approached with a relational form of therapy, rather than a primarily left hemispheric, verbally mediated cognitive form of intervention.

In major depression, both structural and functional abnormalities in the amygdala have been reported. Several recent studies have reported an association between enlargement of amygdala volume and depression (Davidson, Pizzagalli, Nitschke, & Putnam, 2002). Researchers also have reported a positive correlation between amygdalar activation and depression severity or dispositional negative affect in patients with major depressive disorder (Abercrombie et al., 1998; Drevets et al., 1992). After pharmacologically induced remission from depression, amygdalar activation has been observed to decrease to normative values (Drevets, 2001). In light of the pivotal role of the amygdala in recruiting and coordinating vigilant behavior toward stimuli with undetermined contingencies, hyperactivation of the amygdala in major depression may negatively bias the initial evaluation of incoming or emotionally arousing information, a phenomenon clearly observed in depression.

There also is some evidence from affective science that supports the view of depression as a heterogeneous condition rather than a singular phenomenon. Different parts of the brain have been found to be involved in different processes in different depressions (Davidson et al., 2002; Drevets, 1998; Goodwin, 1996; Kennedy, Javanmard, & Vaccarino, 1997). Depression appears to comprise different affective processes that are not yet clearly understood. The anxiety, agitation, and deadness of depression all have their own affective basis. In a similar way, the responses of perfectionism versus avoidance versus dependence may all reflect different neurological substrates. Mayberg, Lewis, Regenold, and Wagner (1994) implicated selective dysfunction of paralimbic brain regions in patients with clinical depression, supporting the concept of specific neural systems that regulate mood. Mayberg et al. concluded that recognition of these regional abnormalities may have clinical utility in both the diagnosis and treatment of depression.

The examination of subtypes or specific symptoms of depression thus may be more informative than investigating the syndrome as a whole. This conclusion is evident in a study (Brody et al., 2001) that found that a serotonin reuptake inhibitor, paroxetine, significantly normalized the ventral frontal metabolism and alleviated depression in a subset of patients with anxiety, sadness, and psychomotor retardation as the primary presenting symptoms. This finding implies that specific symptoms of depression can be targeted with medications intended to produce precise regional brain changes. Attending to these different styles and implementing specific interventions to ameliorate and change them is central to EFT.

Evidence also suggests a link between amygdalar activation and both memory consolidation and acquisition of long-term declarative knowledge about emotionally salient information (Davidson et al., 2002). Increased amygdalar activation during depressive episodes may favor the emergence of rumination based on increased availability of emotionally negative memories (Drevets, 2001). There are individual differences in amygdala activation at baseline (Schaefer et al., 2000), as well as in response to challenge (see Davidson & Irwin, 1999), and these differences are important in individuals' vulnerabilities to depression and other disorders. Hyperactivation of the amygdala in depression is more likely associated with the fearlike and anxiety components of the symptoms than with the sad mood and anhedonia. Excessive activation of the amygdala in patients with depression may also be associated with hypervigilance in some depressions, particularly toward threat-related cues, and to anger and irritability in other depressions. These responses then further exacerbate some of the other symptoms of depression.

Amygdalar influence on the prefrontal cortex (PFC) also is of great importance in depression. Davidson (2000a, 2000b) argued that in the affective domain, the PFC implements affect-guided anticipatory processes. The PFC plays a crucial role in the representation and attainment of goals. The amygdala, however, has extensive projections to the cortex, both enabling and biasing cortical processing as a function of the early evaluation of a stimulus as affectively salient. The amygdala therefore influences goal representation and attainment. Left-sided PFC regions are particularly involved in approach-related appetitive goals, whereas right-sided PFC regions are involved in goals that require behavioral inhibition. Davidson et al. (2002) argued that abnormalities in PFC function would be expected to compromise goal instantiation in people with depression. Left-sided hypoactivation would result in deficits specifically in pre–goal attainment forms of positive affect, whereas right-sided hyperactivation would result in excessive behavioral inhibition and anticipatory anxiety.

In a line of research on anger, Harmon-Jones, Vaughn-Scott, Mohr, Sigelman, and Harmon-Jones (2004) found that left frontal activity was increased and right frontal activity decreased by a verbal insult but that high levels of sympathy for the person delivering the insult eliminated this effect. They concluded that the experience of sympathy for the other person was important in reducing angry approach tendencies and that left frontal activity is a stronger indicator of approach in anger than self-reported anger.

The amygdala, as well as being activated automatically, also receives inputs from the cortex, allowing for conscious processing to affect emotionality. A second, more conscious form of emotional processing that involves complex perceptions and concepts received from the cortex begins to operate, but often only after the emotional brain (the amygdala) has provided a more immediate "intuitive" appraisal from the initial input. Davidson (2000a) reported that hypoactivation in regions of the PFC with which the amygdala is interconnected may result in a decrease in the regulatory influence on the amygdala and result in prolonged amygdala activation in response to challenge; this process might be expressed phenomenologically as perseveration of negative affect and rumination. Mayberg et al. (1999) found that the experience of sadness activated limbic areas but simultaneously deactivated cortical regions known to mediate attentional processing, resulting in changes in awareness of the environment and impaired attention. People whose depression was in remission, however, showed suppression of limbic activation and increased cortical activation. The authors concluded that the interaction of these areas is important in interventions and is crucial in mood regulation. They suggested that remission of depression may rely not on change in either cortical or limbic areas alone, but on a reconfiguration of their interaction, either through bottom-up (limbic–cortical) or top-down (cortical–limbic) interventions.

It is our contention that depression sets in when rapid emotional schematic memories based on the limbic system and the responses of shame, sadness, fear, or anxiety associated with them are activated. The individual with depression is unable to regulate these emotions, and there is an absence of positive affective experiences, either currently or in the past, to help modulate the depressive experience. The automatic and rapid responses of shame, anxiety, and sadness strongly influence the person's self-organization and mode of processing. Once a person enters a depressogenic affective state, all kinds of physiological and cognitive processes ensue. The amygdala-influenced emotional evaluation and responses in reaction to failure and loss appear to be extraordinarily difficult to extinguish, especially when they are accompanied by hypoactivation of the left prefrontal cortex and hyperactivation of the right prefrontal cortex; the individual becomes less able to seek out pleasurable experiences to offset the negative emotion and is behaviorally inhibited (LeDoux, 1996). Therefore, the challenge of any effective psychotherapy, whether for depression, anxiety, or trauma, is to help the client to more effectively regulate his or her levels of emotional arousal and develop alternative ways of behaving that promote the experience of more positive emotions and less behavioral inhibition. Schore (2003), in his psycho-neurobiological approach, suggested the need for relational soothing interventions rather than verbally mediated interventions to regulate affective intensity.

In addition, individuals can be helped to encode intense emotional experiences in verbal memory to help ameliorate their level of arousal. It is probable that the symbolic processing of intense emotional experience restructures the emotion system so that the individual no longer reacts to current situations and reminders of past experience with the intensity of past feelings of abandonment, powerlessness, and humiliation. A neuroimaging study (Rauch et al., 1996) showed that when people relive traumatic experiences, they have decreased activation of Broca's area and increased activation of the limbic system in the right hemisphere of the brain. This finding suggests that when people are reliving intense experiences, they have great difficulty putting the experience into words. In fact, relatively increased activation of the right hemisphere compared with the left implies that when people relive traumatic emotional experiences, they are imbedded in the experience—they have a flashback experience—but they lack the capacity to analyze what is going on in words and in space and time.

Evidence also is mounting showing that the amygdala to some degree can be modulated by certain types of cognitive tasks, such as labeling stimuli (Hariri, Mattay, Tessitore, Fera, & Weinberger, 2003). Recent neuroimaging evidence has shown that when individuals are instructed to regulate their emotional response, a conscious effort to do so can modulate amygdala activation. Rating of one's emotional responses is associated with decreased activity of the amygdala compared to passive viewing of emotional stimuli (Lange et al., 2003; Phan et al., 2003; S. F. Taylor, Phan, Decker, & Liberzon, 2003). Decreased amygdala activation to emotional stimuli can result from the use of cognitive reappraisal strategies (Ochsner, Bunge, Gross, & Gabrieli, 2002), and amygdala activation can be enhanced by an instruction to maintain one's emotional state (Schaefer et al., 2002).

Lane et al. (1998) identified a number of paralimbic and neocortical areas that participate in the experience of background feelings and in focal attention to feelings, whereas others have implicated the anterior cingulate cortex in inhibiting sexual arousal related to amygdala activation (Beauregard, Levesque, & Bourgouin, 2001), in relaxation (Critchley, Melmed, Featherstone, Mathias, & Dolan, 2001), and in accurate monitoring and modulation of somatic states. These findings are of great importance to psychotherapy as they reveal that automatic emotional responses can be modulated by awareness and certain prefrontal activity. Evidence on prefrontal activity in the brain and on cognitive processing in regulating emotion suggests that awareness, attention, labeling, reappraisal, and meaning making are more important than reasoning or decision making in regulating emotion.

Not all individuals are able to rationally dispute intense feelings, and alternative strategies may be required for people in the throes of limbic activation. Support for this observation comes from studies on skin conductance and amygdala activation. Certain autonomic responses that are known to be modulated by the amygdala, such as the skin conductance response (Mangina & Beuzeron-Mangina, 1996), are unaffected by information that the possibility of shock associated with a stimulus is zero. In other words, conditioned responses (such as skin conduction) to stimuli persist despite full access to the knowledge that the contingency has been dissolved (Hugdahl & Öhman, 1977). Evidence is mounting on the importance of nonverbal relational factors in soothing arousal and influencing the more nonverbal right hemisphere both in infant development and in trauma (Schore, 2003), indicating that interpersonal soothing often is superior to reasoning in producing calm.

EMOTION-FOCUSED THERAPY
AND AFFECTIVE NEUROSCIENCE

A review of affective neuroscience thus indicates that relational empathy, awareness, labeling, reappraisal, and meaning making all can help modulate amygdala arousal. In addition, amygdala-generated experience can be transformed by the activation of alternate hemispheric processes and alternate states that promote approach or positive feelings to help transform depressogenic withdrawal and negative emotions. Emotion-focused therapy focuses on providing an empathic relationship; helping clients make sense of emotional experience to regulate the rapid-acting, automatic emotion system; and transforming maladaptive emotional states by the activation of alternate, adaptive emotion states.

When a person who is depressed perceives a threat, this activates in-wired, basic evaluations and fixed physiological and motor sequences. In response to danger, the startle reflex and various expressions of the fight, flight, or freeze response are activated (Cacioppo, 2003). In response to loss, humiliation, and entrapment, in-wired affective–psychomotor programs of mourning, withdrawal, and defeat are activated (Gilbert, 2004). Panksepp (2001) suggested that the most basic tendencies for which in-wired evaluations and affective motor programs exist in animals are those for seeking, rage, fear, lust, care, panic, and play. Other affect theorists have proposed six to nine basic affective programs, including anger, sadness, fear, disgust, surprise/interest, and excitement/joy (Ekman & Friesen, 1975; Tomkins, 1962). The degree to which these automatic, basic responses can be inhibited depends in part on a person's relative level of emotional arousal, which in turn depends on the activation of brain stem arousal centers. Under ordinary conditions, people can regulate their anger or irritation or ignore the sensation of hunger or sexual arousal, even while the appropriate physiological processes associated with these states, such as increased blood pressure, secretion of saliva, and contraction of stomach muscles, continue. Higher (neocortical) top-down levels of processing can, and often do, override, steer, or interrupt the lower levels or interfere with emotional and sensorimotor processing.

Much adult activity is based on top-down processing, where higher cortical areas act as a conscious control center. People often hover above their somatic and sensory experiences, knowing they are there, but not allowing them to dominate their actions. Under ordinary conditions, consciousness allows people to achieve balance and to control the production of emotion and regulate body states. This type of top-down processing also can produce emotion without activation of the amygdala (Teasdale et al., 1999). These more cognitively generated emotions, however, are more complex social feelings that are at the top of the hierarchy of emotion, and they are more dependent on conscious processing.

Rapid, amygdala-based responses of fear and anger are activated automatically and strongly influence the person's subsequent mode of processing and decision making. Rapid and intense feelings, such as the shame and sadness so central in depression, also are activated in such a fashion. These emotions are not easily regulated by top-down processing. The emotional brain serves as a "smoke detector" that interprets whether incoming sensory information is a threat to safety or identity or a loss. It is involved in forming and activating emotional memories in response to particular sensations, such as sounds and images, that have become associated with threats to self and loss.

Memory is very important in the generation of emotion. Two different memory systems have been found to be involved in intense emotional experiences. One is an autobiographical memory system that is verbal and serves a social function—communication of one's experiences to others. The other memory system, which often is referred to as *implicit memory*, is more influenced by the amygdala and other subcortical areas and contains the sensory and emotional imprints of particular events that determine the value that people attach to those imprints (Van der Kolk & van der Hart, 1991). It is important to work with both these systems in therapy. Subcortical areas of the brain involved in implicit memory that are not under conscious control and have no linguistic representation have a different way of remembering than the higher levels of the brain in the prefrontal cortex. Under ordinary conditions, the two memory systems are harmoniously integrated. Under conditions of intense arousal, however, the limbic system produces emotions and sensations that can contradict a person's attitudes and beliefs.

In EFT the therapist works both with automatic, amygdala-based emotions and memories and with their verbal representation. EFT provides an empathic relationship and facilitates clients' putting intense emotional experiences into words, thereby modulating amygdala activation. This approach is in contrast to those that attempt to dampen emotional responses and rely on top-down techniques to manage emotions and sensations, which are viewed as unwanted disruptions of "normal" functioning that need to be harnessed by reason or controlled. Conceptual processing that focuses on inhibiting unpleasant sensations and emotions rather than on processing them to completion does not facilitate working them through and integrating them. Some clients need to spend time embedded in an empathic relationship and becoming aware of, labeling, and understanding their emotional responses before they can turn attention to modulating these responses. EFT uses the more bottom-up processing strategies to enable clients to regulate affect.

In bottom-up experiential processing, clients experience being in an empathically attuned environment that in itself reduces arousal, and this aids them in becoming aware of and tracking the sequence of physical sensations and impulses (sensorimotor processes) as they progress through the body (Perls, Hefferline, & Goodman, 1951). They become aware, or mindful, of their experience (Greenberg, 2002; Greenberg & Safran, 1987; Kabat-Zinn, 1990; Kennedy-Moore & Watson, 1999). Therapists help clients temporarily disregard top-down thoughts and focus on bodily sensations and impulses until they resolve or crystallize into clear meanings (Gendlin, 1996). It is through labeling and symbolizing their experience that clients come to more clearly understand its meaning. Once clients have clearly articulated these meanings, they are in a position to reflect on and evaluate their appropriateness, expression, and fit with current goals and needs (Kennedy-Moore & Watson, 1999; Watson & Greenberg, 1996). The bottom-up element of the process consists of clients learning to observe and follow the unassimilated sensorimotor reactions that are activated in the present. Awareness and processing of bodily felt experience is a central focus in the EFT of depression.

Relational soothing and bottom-up processing, by themselves, do not resolve all psychological problems, but they are an essential element of emotion regulation and optimal functioning. In EFT the client initially is directed within an empathic relational context to track and articulate sensorimotor experience while consciously inhibiting content and analytical or interpretive thinking, so that unassimilated sensory and affective experience can be verbalized and recoded in linguistic memory, along with the experience of relational safety. In this way clients gradually assimilate their experience. Awareness, as opposed to avoidance, of internal states allows feelings to become known and to be used as guides for action. Such awareness is necessary if clients are to respond adaptively to current situations and manage their lives satisfactorily. By being aware of and tolerating their feelings and sensations, clients have new options for solving problems that allow them to react less automatically and to find better ways to adapt.

Emotion Schemes

Neuroscientists like Damasio (1994) have argued that the formation of systematic connections between categories of objects and situations, on the one hand, and primitive, preorganized emotions, on the other, leads the maturing human to be capable of emotion experience that is automatic. This automatic experience is of a higher order than the amygdala responses in that it is more organized. Much adult emotional experience is of this higher order, generated by learned, idiosyncratic schemes that serve to generate emotional experience and responses and help the individual to anticipate future outcomes. This higher-level synthesis of a variety of levels of processing produces *emotion schemes* (Oatley, 1992; J. Pascual-Leone, 1991) and *emotion schematic memory* (Leventhal, 1984). In our model, we see the emotion scheme as central (Greenberg & Paivio, 1997; Greenberg, Rice, & Elliott, 1993), and we see depressive emotion schematic processing as the main target of intervention in EFT of depression.

Emotion schemes are formed in the following manner: Humans continuously filter, interpret, transform, and derive meaning out of incoming sensory input, which may come from inside the body (e.g., muscular or visceral activity, chemical reactions, breathing, and fatigue) or from the environment (e.g., images, tactile sensations, scents, sounds). These sensations are interpreted and attached to other sensations, configurations, and a larger scheme of meaning. A basic task of the human mind is to evaluate the significance of all incoming information and integrate it into a unified cognitive affective meaning. Emotion schematic memory is formed in this way as the mind rapidly scans millions of possible connections and associations to create a coherent interpretation about their existential relevance. The mind also needs to create a response that not only produces internal satisfaction, but also is in harmony with the demands and expectations of the environment. All this input and output is represented in the mind through the flow of neural activity across various spatially distributed circuits. These circuits become functionally linked. They cluster information into categories, extract general properties, form contrasts, and construct responses. The resultant neural activity becomes a schematic structure that, when activated, creates a cascade of sensorimotor and representational processes that are at the heart of the flow of experience.

Once formed, emotion schemes produce complex bodily felt feelings and action tendencies. These responses are no longer a result of purely innate emotional responses to specific cues, like anger at violation or fear at threat, but of acquired responses based on lived emotional experience. With development, emotional experience, rather than being governed simply by biologically and evolutionarily based, amygdala-driven affect motor programs, is produced by highly differentiated structures that have been refined through experience and bound by culture into schemata or organized units in memory. Thus, over time, with healthy development, the innate response of joy at a human facial configuration becomes differentiated into feelings of pleasure with a specific caretaker and contributes to the development of basic trust. Feeling an emotion involves experiencing body changes in relation to and integrated with the evoking object or situation and one's past emotional learning.

The emotion scheme, then, is a response-producing, internal organization that synthesizes a variety of levels and types of information, including sensorimotor stimuli, emotion memory, and conceptual-level information. In contrast to a cognitive schema, the emotion scheme is a structure that includes a large component of nonverbal and affective experience. It represents an integration of people's biology and experience in that it is the prod-

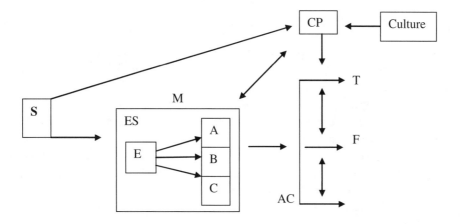

Figure 2.1. Sequence of emotion responses to a stimulus. A = affective experience; AC = actions; B = behavioral disposition; C = cognitive semantic processing; CP = conceptual processing; E = evaluation; ES = emotion schematic processing; F = feelings; M = mode of processing; S = stimulus; T = thoughts.

uct of people's synthesis of their coding of their own emotional experience in situations with a representation of the evoking situational cues and with subsequent learned beliefs or rules governing this experience. This activity all operates automatically, outside of awareness (Greenberg et al., 1993; Greenberg & Safran, 1987).

Thus, in a simplified model of functioning, shown in Figure 2.1, we suggest for simplicity the following sequence: A stimulus (S) rapidly evokes a basic evaluation (E) influenced by evolution and experience (learning). This sets off automatic emotion schematic processing (ES), which produces the ABCs of existence: a sensory aspect that produces affective experience (A), a motoric aspect that produces behavior in the form of a disposition to act (B), and a cognitive semantic aspect that provides basic meaning (C). Emotion schematic processing determines the mode of processing and this interacts with top-down conceptual processing (CP), influenced mainly by culture, which is activated more slowly, and analyzes the situation in greater detail in a particular way influenced by the emotion schematic mode of processing. These sources interact to produce conscious thoughts (T), feelings (F), and actions (AC), which all interact to influence each other. We do not believe this process really follows the simple linear sequences as we have depicted; we have presented the process as a sequential model for ease of representation. Rather, we see the self as a dynamic, self-organizing system in which its processes all interact in circular, simultaneous, and reverberating ways.

To simplify even further, we propose that in the sequence generating depression, a stimulus (S) evokes tacit emotion schematic processing that involves a core evaluation in relation to a need that in turn produces affect

(A). This sets conceptual processing in motion. Thus, fundamental evaluations of novelty, threat, violation, loss or isolation, intrusion, and pleasure evoke fundamental affects of excitement, fear, anger, sadness, disgust, and joy respectively. These affects influence the conceptual processing that follows. The messages from the emotional brain to the prefrontal cortex prepare it for analyzing whether there is novelty, danger, attack, loss, and so on. In people who are depressed, the fundamental evaluation is often one of diminishment and humiliation or insecurity and anxiety, and this evaluation leads to dysfunctional beliefs and negative thoughts and to the secondary bad feelings they produce. In EFT the fundamental evaluation and the mode of processing imbued with affect are the targets of change. To change this emotion schematic processing, the core emotion needs to be brought into awareness, and an affective antidote needs to be provided.

The emotion schemes that form the foundation of the self themselves are integrated affective–behavioral–cognitive structures. Much emotion, as we have seen, involves automatic appraisals of situations in relation to one's well-being. These appraisals are essentially implicit nonlinguistic cognitive–perceptual evaluations regarding what is good or bad for the self. These schemes, however, are far from being purely cognitive structures. The nonlinguistic appraisals are made in reference to underlying goals, needs, and concerns, which are the motivational components of emotions. *Motivation* has been defined as the disposition to desire the occurrence or nonoccurrence of a situation (Frijda, 1986). Thus, needs, goals, and concerns are represented internally as standards against which situations are evaluated. If the appraisal of the situation and the need or concern are sufficiently mismatched, a negative emotion follows, with its attendant action tendency and sensory response. The action tendency organizes the individual to act in a way conducive to attaining or safeguarding a goal or need. The sensory response informs the person that what is occurring is important and needs attention. In depression, the predominant evaluation is that goals cannot be achieved and needs are not being met, and the person is left feeling hopeless and powerless to attain desired goals.

Attention

The involvement of focal attention seems to be a requirement for the processing of automatic emotional information into explicit memory. People who are depressed often are avoidant and focus not on their core emotions, but rather on their symptomatic feelings. The process of coding experience in consciousness often does not occur in their lives, because experience occurs so quickly and there is too much to process, or because the symbolization may be impaired in unresolved states of high intensity. In a study that evaluated the effects of attention to feelings on affective well-being, Lischetzke and Eid (2003) found that individuals who were able to regulate their moods felt better after attending to their emotions but that disregulated people felt worse, highlighting the importance of the therapeutic relationship in helping people with depression to resolve negative emotional states.

Use of focal, focused attention to attend to bodily felt feelings, to images of the past, and to painful experience previously avoided is a central method in EFT in making the implicit explicit and in helping construct new experience. As James (1890) first noted, one's experience is what one agrees to attend to. Helping clients focus their attention on aspects of their representations of past experiences helps them create the opportunity for further processing of emotionally stored information. One of the main targets of intervention in emotion-focused therapy thus is the client's attentional allocation. The therapist can influence both what the client attends to and how much attention is available for processing. What is attended to influences what one experiences, as well as the attributions one makes.

The therapeutic use of focusing of attention on different levels of processing, including images, emotions, bodily sensations, global linguistic statements, and perceptions generated from recollections, is a unique and important change process in the emotion-focused approach to the treatment of depression. The arational, nonlinear focus of attention on different levels of information produces new information processing configurations in the brain. This therapeutic strategy can lead to the formation of new schemes by new associations of various elements. As Hebb (1949) suggested, neurons that fire together wire together. Emotion appears to be intricately interwoven with the brain's capacity for integration and self-regulation, and activating emotion appears to stimulate the neural networks and lead to connections that would not be made rationally. Within the setting of a secure, empathic therapeutic relationship, such a multifocal process fosters the creation of new memory associations. This new combination of elements may be essential for the consolidation and resolution of unresolved memories or painful experience. This therapeutic process often leads to the integration of emotional experience that had previously been isolated because it was overwhelming.

EMOTIONAL DYSFUNCTION IN DEPRESSION

Although it is important to recognize the adaptive function of emotion, it is clear that given that emotions reflect experience, they can become maladaptive responses to situations. Emotions become maladaptive through learning and socialization and are especially vulnerable to failures early in the dyadic regulation of affect. In addition, affect repertoires do show innate individual differences. Some people's affect systems are more sensitive or more intense than others'. From birth onward, interpersonal processes provide crucial meaning and the context for sensations and emotions. If children are well cared for, they associate their body signals of distress with various ways of feeling better. They thereby learn to use their own body signals and emotions as guides for action. They internalize the soothing of their caretakers, and their body experience reflects the quality of these early caregiving experiences. This awareness remains at the very foundation of their consciousness, and people continuously try to understand the meaning of their sensations and make sense of their emotions.

In our view, affect regulation is important in depression. Problems with emotion modulation lead to depressive moods and to reliance on maladaptive actions. People who suffered traumatic losses or were abused or neglected as children, and therefore did not have the opportunity to experience being involved in a healthy affect-regulating relationship, lose the capacity for effective regulation of their emotional states. This inability to regulate their emotions leaves people hypersensitive to unpleasant experiences, and their own affective experience is perceived as an existential threat. In an attempt to counteract their negative feelings, such people may engage in pathological forms of self-soothing or self-control, including self-mutilation, bingeing, starving, or ingesting alcohol and drugs to self-medicate. All of these dysfunctional means of coping need to be focused on in different ways in treatment.

We have observed that in the majority of clients in our studies, some significant form of past trauma was involved. Many of the ubiquitous depressive experiences of feeling abandoned, humiliated, trapped, and powerless in childhood can be seen as "small t" traumas (Shapiro, 1995, 2001). An underlying cause of many adult-related depressions may be found in intense early experiences of being humiliated and abused, or feeling trapped or abandoned, with the resulting experience of powerlessness and fear. In these experiences, an intense emotion related to the person's sense of self—one that could not be fully processed at the time it was experienced—remains etched in memory and has a lasting effect. Being ostracized and humiliated in childhood, especially repeatedly, evokes shame, and this shame stimulates fears of survival. Loss, fear of abandonment, lack of love, or experiences of defeat similarly arouse fears of survival of the self as one knows it. Any event that threatens coherence of the self-identity and attachment security can cause these experiences to be stored as signifying danger. A sense of threat, coupled with a sense of humiliation, powerlessness, and defeat, can result in depression. These feelings and experiences likely contribute to the hyperactivation of the amygdala and to the asymmetrical functioning of the prefrontal cortex. Thus, people who are subjected to negative emotional states may lack the experiences that would enable them to recruit positive emotions in the face of stress. All these factors compromise their resilience and make them more vulnerable to depression.

As people mature, they develop an ever-greater capacity to create meaningful associations with specific physical sensations. They develop capacities to soothe themselves and to prevent the emergence of anxiety. However, when the physical sensations are associated with extreme shame or fear that was not soothed, people may be unable to regulate them adaptively. These sensations were never associated with possible solutions, so when they are experienced in the present, people react with fear or dread or shut down emotionally in an effort to ignore or push the sensations away. In depression, the core maladaptive schemes produce sensations of deadness, powerlessness, shrinking, withdrawing, bleakness, pain, and emptiness. People cope with these dreaded sensations in maladaptive ways that maintain their depression. In addition to trying to deaden and distract themselves, people who are depressed also withdraw and isolate themselves, sleep more than necessary, and become less active in an effort to stop the sensations. This demobilization worsens their depression. People also develop different styles of adapting to traumatic circumstances; some develop perfectionistic styles of coping, whereas others become more avoidant and yet others dependent. EFT thus focuses on the different affective and coping styles that are involved in different types of depression for different people.

The lack of differentiation between the somatic emotional response to past and present is pivotal to maladaptive emotional responding in trauma-based depression. For instance, if a man who was verbally and physically abused by his father all through childhood is not able to process these experiences, the physical sensations of powerlessness and shame in response to violation and humiliation that were previously appropriate to the situation are schematically stored, ready to be activated. As an adult, any experience of powerlessness or shame resembling his childhood experience can bring up the same physiological feelings and color the present perception of reality. He may experience the same feelings, leaving him unable to assert himself, walk away, set boundaries, or evoke any of the more positive, resilient reactions of a healthy adult to unfair treatment. The past becomes repeated in the present, and because of the responses embedded within the scheme, the client cannot assert himself. Although he may attempt to gain cognitive control or insight, he has no ability to choose his autonomic responses in the present. They are biochemically and physiologically dictated by his stored affective responses to past events.

In EFT, activating maladaptive core experiences is the first step in bringing about change in depressive emotional experience in therapy. Core experiences of powerlessness, abandonment, or humiliation and the self-contempt and shame underlying the depressive hopelessness need to be transformed by accessing adaptive feelings such as healthy grieving for what was missed, which reopens the capacity for love and closeness, or by accessing adaptive anger at maltreatment, which opens the path to pride and self-worth. These adaptive emotions need to be attended to and validated and then used to vitalize a more resilient sense of self to help transform the person's maladaptive affects and to explicitly challenge maladaptive beliefs. In this way, new self-experience and new perceptions are integrated with the existing negative ones to consolidate a new self-organization (Greenberg, 2002; Greenberg & Paivio, 1997).

3

DEPRESSION: A DIALECTICAL CONSTRUCTIVIST VIEW

Emotions make things matter.

—Frijda (1986, p. 5)

In this chapter we lay out our general dialectical constructivist model of functioning and apply it more specifically to depression.

A DIALECTICAL CONSTRUCTIVIST MODEL: INTEGRATING BIOLOGY AND CULTURE

As well as having emotions, people also live in a constant process of making sense of those emotions. We have proposed a dialectical constructivist view of human functioning to explain this process (Greenberg & Pascual-Leone, 1995, 2001; Greenberg, Rice, & Elliott, 1993; Guidano, 1991, 1995a, 1995b; Mahoney, 1991; Neimeyer & Mahoney, 1995; J. Pascual-Leone, 1987, 1990, 1991; Watson & Greenberg, 1996; Watson & Rennie, 1994). In our view, the self is a multiprocess, multilevel organization emerging from the dialectical interaction of many component elements. The highest-level dialectic, the one of most concern to psychotherapists, is the dialectic that generates meaning. This dialectic involves ongoing, moment-by-moment implicit experience and higher-level, explicit, reflexive processes that interpret, order, and explain elementary experiential processes. Affectively toned, preverbal, preconscious processing is seen as a major source of self-experience and is itself generated by many dialectical processes at many different levels. Articulating, organizing, and ordering this experience in language into a coherent narrative is the other major element that also involves many underlying dialectical processes. This view suggests that two-way communication occurs between the implicit and explicit systems and constitutes a dialogic self (Hermans, 1996).

Human beings, in our view, function as dynamic systems that integrate many dialectical processes at many different levels, from neurochemical to conscious and conceptual (Mahoney, 1991; J. Pascual-Leone, 1987, 1990, 1991; J. Pascual-Leone & Johnson, 2004), and this integration results in affect and cognition being inextricably intertwined. Individuals thus constantly create the self they are about to become by synthesizing biologically based information and culturally acquired learning. Although biology and culture may occasionally conflict, they are not inherently antagonistic to one another. Rather, they are both necessary streams of a dialectical synthesis, and people live most viably by managing to integrate inner and outer, biological and social, emotional and rational.

Figure 3.1 illustrates how two main streams feed conscious experience. One, coming from within, is affective in nature; the other, coming from without, is cultural in nature. In addition, both streams themselves are in constant interaction with others and with the environment in a dialogic process of meaning construction. The internal affective stream, based mainly on biology, provides the building blocks for a person's basic self-organization. Over time, this level is influenced by cultural practices (such as culturally determined child-rearing practices) and by learning and experience and is organized into schemes based on emotion experienced in situations. These schemes become the primary generators of experience. At any one time, a person is organized by a tacit synthesis of a number of these emotion schemes into one of many possible self-organizations, such as vulnerable, withdrawn, open, or good humored. This tacit organization provides "the feeling of what happens," or a bodily felt sense of who one is. Conscious experience results when this implicit feeling is attended to and symbolized explicitly.

When the self-organized experience is both symbolized (usually in words) and reflected on, meaning is created. The symbolic, linguistic process is acquired by learning from culture and is informed by narrative, myth, and cultural symbols. Meaning, narrative, and identity are constructed by reflecting on experience, making sense of it, and explaining it to oneself in an ongoing dialectical interaction between symbol and bodily felt experience (Gendlin, 1962). The client thus is an active constructor of meaning.

A model of the stages of emotional processing depicting how awareness and expression of emotional experience are generated helps elaborate the dialectical meaning-making process (Kennedy-Moore & Watson, 1999). In

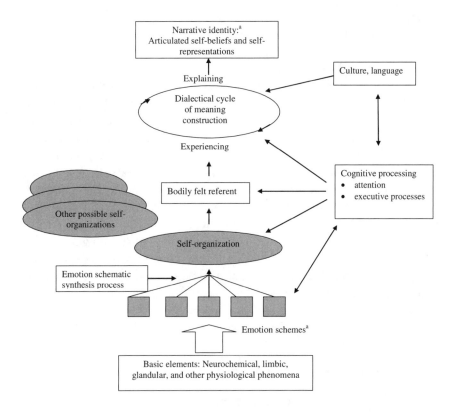

Figure 3.1. The dialectical construction of the self.
[a]These are also influenced by interactions with others, making self-construction both an intrapersonal and interpersonal process.

this five-step model, the first two steps involve the initial prereflective reaction and the conscious perception of the aroused response—the bodily felt side of the dialectic. The next three steps involve the labeling and interpretation of the response, the evaluation of the response, and the perceived context for expression—the more conceptual and socially influenced side of the dialectic. This model indicates the complex interaction of automatically generated emotion and deliberate reflection in the creation of both experience and expression.

The initial prereflective reaction entails the perception of the stimulus, including the preconscious cognitive and emotional processing and the accompanying physiological changes. Typically this perception is experienced as some level of arousal indicating that something requires attention. The conscious perception of the response usually follows as the person becomes aware of his or her aroused affective response, which leads to the third step of labeling the response. Labeling the arousal response depends on both internal and external situational cues to determine the nature of the response. The person subsequently evaluates his or her response in terms of whether it is valid and acceptable or not; the person's values and beliefs about what is important or desirable influence this evaluation. Finally, the person evaluates the social context for the expression of the emotion to determine whether its expression will be supported.

In our view, symbol and bodily felt referent thus interact to carry meaning forward, and newly symbolized experience is organized in different ways to construct new views. Attending to and discovering the preconceptual elements of experience influence the process of meaning construction. New experiential elements come from many sources—from within, from memory, and sometimes from without—to influence constructions. People thus are viewed as constantly striving to make sense of their preconceptual experience by symbolizing it, explaining it, and putting it into narrative form. Preconceptual tacit meaning carries implications and acts to constrain, but it does not fully determine meaning. Rather, it is synthesized with conceptual, explicit meaning to form explanations constrained by experiencing (Greenberg & Pascual-Leone, 1995, 2001). Blocks and rigidities in the emotional meaning construction process are part of the cause of depression, because they prevent emotion from being processed.

Dysfunction can arise through various mechanisms, including the following:

- through the particular meanings and narrative created (meaning creation),
- from incongruence between what is reflectively symbolized and the range of experienced possibilities (disclaimed or unsymbolized experience),
- from the type of experience that is generated by the schematic syntheses formed on the basis of prior experience (learning), and
- from problematic shifts between a plurality of self-organizations or lack of fit or integration between them (conflict and splits).

CONSTRUCTING THE SELF

In our view, the self, first and foremost, is a *process*, not a structure (Elliott, Watson, Goldman, & Greenberg, 2004; Greenberg & Pascual-Leone, 1995; Whelton & Greenberg, 2001). People are dynamic self-organizing systems, and the self emerges in the moment as a synthesis of inside and outside influences. There is no permanent, hierarchical organization, topped by an executive "Self" or single ruling "I." Instead, at different times, different voices or aspects, functioning heterarchically, act to construct a sense of coherence or unity by integrating different aspects of emotional experiencing in a given situation and across time (through memory). The momentary self is something closer to the result of a chorus of jazz singers in which the different voices sing improvisationally, sometimes in unison, sometimes in harmony, sometimes in counterpoint, and sometimes in dissonance. The result is an emergent property that arises in the moment.

Although there is no such thing as a "true self," from a dialectical constructivist perspective there is such a thing as a "true self-experience" (Fosha, 2000, 2004). These are moments of experience when intellectualization, disclaiming, interruptions, and avoidances are no longer operating, and the client is having a deep and meaningful emotional experience that makes things significant in his or her life. These experiential moments often occur with the accessing of core emotions or during moments of deep connection with others. They are moments when, subjectively, the client feels in some fundamental way that what is being experienced is real and deep and true. The client then signifies this as an experience of his or her true self, even if he or she is having this experience for the first time. Clients say such things as "I'm able to be myself" and "I'm discovering who I truly am." These moments of true experience are as much a construction and a statement of value as a discovery of who the client truly is. They are a declaration of who the client determines himself or herself to be.

In a dialectical constructivist, process view of functioning, stability is seen as arising from repeated constructions of the same state from multiple constituent elements. People are viewed as stabilizing around characteristic self-organizations that are unique constellations of emotion and cognition that are constructed afresh each time. These are attractor states in dynamic system terms (Whelton & Greenberg, 2001). These characteristic organizations impart character to the person and are responsible for the more enduring aspects of personality. Adding or subtracting elements from the process of construction, however, can alter these traits, making character change possible. These traits in essence are organized attempts to minimize unpleasant affect, maximize positive affect, and allow for a socially appropriate degree of expression of emotion (Magai & Haviland-Jones, 2002). These organizations also act as selective filters for the intake of information and involve a set of strategies for dealing with affectively relevant goals.

Emotion Schematic Processing

The emotion schematic system is seen as the central catalyst of self-organization, and therefore of depressive self-organization, and is ultimately the road to the cure of depression. As shown in Figure 3.1, experience and performance are not generated by a single emotion scheme or by a single level of processing. Rather, they are generated by a tacit synthesis of a number of schemes that are coactivated and that coapply. These schemes are synthesized to configure a response to a situation with the help of other mental operations like attention, executive processes, and reflection, which boost and interrupt the application of certain schemes (Greenberg & Pascual-Leone, 1995, 2001; J. Pascual-Leone, 1990, 1991). For simplicity, we will refer to the complex synthesis process, in which a number of coactivated emotion schemes coapply to produce a unified sense of self in relation to the world, as the *emotion schematic process*. The experiential state of the self at any one moment will be referred to as the *self-organization*. In depression, the self is organized experientially as unlovable or worthless and helpless or incompetent because of the activation of emotion schematic memories of crucial losses, humiliation, or failure in prior experience. These emotion memories are evoked in response to current losses or failures and cause the self to lose resilience and collapse into powerlessness. This state is symbolized as feeling hopeless and often as worthless or anxiously insecure. In addition to possessing biologically based depression-generating meaning and expressive systems, individuals also are active agents constantly constructing meaning, thereby creating the depressed self they are about to become.

The Narrative Self

A level of organization of self that is higher than the schematically based self-organization (i.e., the feeling of who one is) can be referred to as a *narrative identity* (Greenberg & Angus, 2004; Whelton & Greenberg, 2001). This identity involves the integration of accumulated experience and of various self-representations into a coherent story or narrative. Identity cannot be understood outside of this narrative. To assume coherence and meaning, human lives must be "emplotted" in a story. In this process, people organize events into a narrative discourse such that disparate actions and experiences of their lives are formed into a coherent narrative. These stories are influenced by the different cultures, which have complex rules about the form meaningful narratives can take.

The stories that people tell to explain who they are emerge in a dialectical interaction between the experiencing and the explaining aspects of self-functioning. At core, the self is embodied, but a body needs a story to act meaningfully; to relate past and future; and to situate dreams, goals, regrets, plans, lost opportunities, hopes, and all the stuff of a truly human life (Whelton & Greenberg, 2001). Life is inherently a story, the structure of which we make explicit when we reflect on our past and our possible future. Given that the self experientially is a set of complex self-organizations in constant flux, the creation of the self-narrative is crucial to the establishment of a stable identity (Greenberg & Angus, 2004). Schematic emotional memories of repeated life events, what Philippot and Schaefer (2001) termed *generic autobiographical memories*, appear to play an important role in the narrative. Generic schematic memories that capture a theme or recurrent self-organization across situations, such as "dinnertimes were like walking on eggshells," are associated with more affective arousal. Access to these memories as well as to episodic memories of highly significant moments are important aspects of emotion-focused treatment of depression. A preliminary study of clients' external narratives (when they were talking about what happened to them) found that clients who experienced good outcomes narrated significantly more generic autobiographical memories in therapy sessions than did clients with poor outcomes (Rotondi-Trevisan, Angus, & Greenberg, 2004).

What a dialectical constructivist view suggests, then, is that the many voices that compose the self are given coherence in the stories that people tell to account for themselves. Narrative thus is one pole of the dialectic. Coherence also is achieved in the body, which irreducibly situates the self in the environment (Damasio, 1999; Gendlin, 1996; Mahoney, 1991). This other pole, the intricate network of bodily, sensorimotor, and affective subsystems whose information is organized and synthesized by memory into experientially available self-states, is fundamental to embodied human experience. All emotions are thus storied, and all personal stories are shaped by—emplotted within—the trajectory of emergent emotion themes (Greenberg & Angus, 2004). It is often the narrative of the rise and fall of emotion themes—and the conflicting desires, intentions, goals, and purposes they represent—that provides the connective thread that weaves together disparate experiences and events to create a meaningful and coherent whole—a storied experience. Essentially, narratives weave sequences of emotions into coherent stories.

The task of emotion-focused therapy (EFT) is to help clients form new emotion schematic memories that lead to new responses and to the narrative consolidation of these changes. This form of transformation is not the same as simply "telling" a new story. It consists rather of "living" a new story—of physically experiencing new possibilities and having new experiences that contradict previous ones and stimulate flexible responding.

AN EMOTION-FOCUSED THERAPY THEORY OF DEPRESSION

Within a dialectical constructivist view, depression is an emotional disorder of the self and involves a loss of the self's sense of vitality and ability to organize resiliently. Instead of experiencing themselves as strong, vital, and joyful, people with depression experience themselves as weak, damaged, and blameworthy and react to setbacks with significant loss of self-esteem. The self is organized as hopeless, helpless, incompetent, and insecure because of the activation of emotion schematic memories of crucial losses, failures, humiliation, or neglect. These generic memories come from people's experiences of certain feelings earlier in their lives, often in their formative years. Once activated, these emotion-based self-organizations impair people's capacity both to process and to regulate their emotional experiences in the present. The goal of therapy is to restore the spontaneity of the self's ability to function and to access and support the existing resources of the personality to enable these to transform the depressive self-organization.

Within the process view of the self proposed earlier in this chapter, depression is a form of self-organization designed to regulate the self and a response to cope with a perceived situation. The symptoms of depression are both an expression of vitality and an attempt to close down that vitality. The depressive self-regulation has some positive aspects. It can be inventive in expressing a person's uniqueness and creative aspects of his or her self-functioning, and it has some significance in evolutionary survival. Initially, depression was probably an adaptive response to overwhelming loss, powerlessness, or defeat (Gilbert, 1998). The low mood, hopelessness, and even sense of worthlessness in some way help the person cope with situations experienced as overwhelming by proclaiming defeat and warding off further attack. Depression thus is the self's creative adjustment in a difficult situation (Perls, Hefferline, & Goodman, 1951).

Depression thus acts as a creative adjustment to the activation of painful affective states that the person feels unable to regulate; often these states emerge in relationships with others, particularly the states of shame-based worthlessness and anxiety-based insecurity. When these affective states cannot be accepted, processed, and regulated, a sense of depressive hopelessness results. During depressive episodes, people often do not have access to their core painful affects. They are not in contact with their core shame, anxiety, sadness, or anger, and they are not aware of the voices in them that disclaim and avoid their internal experience. Rather, they feel globally distressed, lack motivation, and feel they cannot get anything done. They are not aware that their malaise is exacerbated by their inability to discriminate and process their core emotions.

Developmental Precursors of Adult Depression: Depression in Adolescents

Harter (1998) developed a model of the development of depression in adolescents in which self-worth and affect were found to correlate highly with depression. Building on an earlier, overly simple model that suggested that cognitions were the primary cause of depression, she developed a more complex model in which self-worth, affect, and general hopelessness were found to be a composite indicator of risk for depression in adolescents. Her research identified two adequacy/competency domains and two social support domains important in predicting depression. The first cluster in the adequacy/competency domain was concerned more with peers and involved physical appearance, peer likeability, and athletic competence, and the second was more concerned with parental approval and involved scholastic competence and behavioral conduct (i.e., conforming to rules and norms). The two social support domains were peer support and parental support. High risk for depression arose from an interaction between a sense of inadequacy in peer-salient competencies in Domain 1 and lack of peer support in Domain 2 and between inadequacy in parent-salient competencies in domain 1 and lack of parental support in Domain 2. Thus, an interaction between feelings of inadequacy and lack of support from people perceived as involved with that competency were found to increase risk for depression in adolescence. Adolescents who felt unpopular, physically unattractive, or athletically incompetent and who had no peer support were at risk for depression, as were those who were not succeeding academically or in their conduct and who felt unsupported by their parents.

Harter (1998) reported that a model in which there is a direct path from depressed affect to self-worth fitted the data just as well as an earlier model in which the path led from self-worth to depressed affect. A bidirectional model was confirmed by interview data that revealed that many adolescents experienced depressive affect prior to low self-worth. Many researchers and therapists alike have fallen victim to the notion that cognition takes precedence over emotion in depression, espousing the view that the cognitive judgments inherent in self-worth precede depressive affect. However, it has become clear to us and others that the directionality of these links varies depending on the particular emotions and cognitions in question (e.g., primary vs. secondary or instrumental emotions, conscious vs. unconscious cognitive processes) as well as on particular developmental and individual difference factors (Greenberg, 2002; Leventhal & Scherer, 1987). A more complex understanding of the psychological processes in depression is called for.

In Harter's (1998) sample of students who experienced low self-worth leading to depressed affect, physical appearance was the most prevalent reason given for negative self-evaluation. For those who reported that depressed affect preceded low self-worth, rejection and interpersonal conflict were among the main causes cited. From the students' reports, it appeared that both a sense of inadequacy and the actual loss of significant others or loss of their approval typically resulted in depressive reactions. For those whose loss of self-worth resulted from self-criticism, it appears that the person's self-critical self-organization needs to become the target of treatment. For those in whom depressed affect led to low self-worth, it appears that treatment should focus more on their conflictual or nongratifying relationships with significant others.

These adolescents also reported experiencing depression as a combination or blend of anger and sadness (Harter, 1998). Eighty percent of the sample selected sadness and anger as the two emotions that they most typically experienced when they were depressed. One depressed adolescent lamented that she felt sad because other people had hurt her but that she also felt angry at them for not caring and for rejecting her. Thus, in depression, sadness, typically over the loss of a significant other, is generally accompanied by anger at being abandoned or unfairly treated. Thirty-nine percent of the adolescents in the total sample reported anger toward others, whereas 40% reported anger toward both others and the self. The results suggest that there may be at least two important patterns of depression in adolescents. In the first, there is profound sadness in combination with anger toward others. In the second, sadness is accompanied by anger directed toward others as well as toward the self.

Depression in Adults

Depression in adults seems to build on the feelings of inadequacy and lack of support laid down in adolescence. It appears, however, that a developmental shift in the affective domain takes place between adolescence and adulthood, in that shame emerges as important in adult depression. Adults seem to assume more responsibility for their role in negative social interactions and become more self-critical, especially if they have had a lack of support growing up. They therefore experience more shame or are more able to articulate it. Like adolescents, adults experience anger toward others but are less likely to express it; adults seem to have developed stronger defenses or inhibitions against the display of angry or aggressive impulses toward others. Several researchers have reported suppressed anger and hostility in adults with depression (Biaggio & Godwin, 1987; E. Frank, Carpenter, & Kupfer, 1988; Riley, Treiber, & Woods, 1989). In addition to shame, depressed adults who experienced loss or neglect as children carry the insecurity of abandonment and experience a lot of fear.

Depression in adults has been found to result from three major types of life event stressors: loss, humiliation, and entrapment (Brown, Harris, & Hepworth, 1995; Kendler, Hettema, Butera, Gardner, & Prescott, 2003). Loss, long viewed as a major precipitator of depression, was described as a diminution of a sense of connectedness or well-being, including a real or realistically imagined loss of a person, material possession, health, respect, employment, or cherished idea about self or a close tie. Humiliation was defined as feeling devalued in relation to others or to a core sense of self, usually with an element of rejection or a sense of role failure. Entrapment was viewed as an ongoing circumstance of marked difficulty of at least 6 months' duration that the person could reasonably expect to get worse, with little or no possibility of resolution being achieved as a result of anything that might reasonably be done.

Gilbert (1992) suggested that entrapment in unrewarding environments or inability to escape from hostile or abusive others may be more depressogenic than loss. Gilbert and Allan (1998) found that feeling defeated by life, perceptions of entrapment, and escape motivation were all significantly associated with depression. When a strong aversive emotion is coupled with an inability to escape, depressive demobilization results. A similar process of defeat occurs in loss, in which the failure is one of not being able to reach the lost object but also being unable to let go of the need for connection or closeness. Kendler et al. (2003) found that loss and humiliation were the main antecedents of pure depression, with entrapment and loss being a better predictor of mixed depression and anxiety.

Thus, depression often occurs when people feel disempowered and lose their sense of resilience and mastery. However, as Gilbert (1992) noted, it is important to recognize that although feelings of worthlessness and failure are central features in the majority of depressions, they are not present in all clients with depression. Powerlessness from loss of control over important resources, even without feelings of personal worthlessness and negative self-views, may be sufficient in some people to precipitate depression. For example, people can become depressed when someone they love leaves, or when they are downsized and unable to find another job, or when affected with disease or loss of limb. In these situations, they may not blame themselves, but they may still become depressed. It is the core affective state of powerlessness that is key in many depressions. People with depression have lost the ability to tolerate and process their core affective experience of sadness and anger; instead, a sense of powerlessness prevails. They lose spontaneity and their access to inner resources, and they shut down, become passive, and lose the ability to respond to setbacks in more hopeful, agentic, and resilient ways.

Affect Regulation in Depression

In adult life, although failure and isolation, and the loss of status or connection that follows, can precipitate depression, ultimately it is the self's inability to regulate its own affective response to these stresses that is important in precipitating and maintaining depression and its concomitant sense of low self-worth. Early life experiences of loss, humiliation, or entrapment (or traumatic experience of this type in later life) handicap people in their ability to process emotional experience and lead to the construction of dysfunctional emotion schemes, the emotion scheme being the central catalyst of emotion-based self-organizations. Experiences of powerlessness, rejection, loss, and lack of support, especially early in life, often result in emotions becoming overwhelming, and these experiences become encoded in emotion schemes. Major depressive disorders often co-occur with anxiety disorders, making anxiety and helplessness, in addition to shame and hopelessness, important emotion schematic aspects of the insecure self that is at the core of depression. The sadness and neediness experienced by the childhood sense of loss and deprivation are experienced as personal inadequacy. Current disappointments, rejections, or slights are experienced as confirmation of inadequacy and damage. Intense feelings of self-contempt and shame for the damaged self, as well as basic anxiety and dependence, form the maladaptive affective core of depression; sadness at loss and anger at violation, adequately processed and supported, form the adaptive core. Whatever the antecedents, empowerment and reconnection appear to be the antidote. Reviving the capacity to feel adaptive anger and sadness is key to overcoming depression and powerlessness.

The secure self, in our view, is formed primarily through the dyadic regulation of affect, and failure in this leads to an insecure sense of self (Fosha, 2000; Schore, 2003; Siegel, 2003; Stern, 1995; Trevarthen, 2000). The infant enters the world with a set of core adaptive affects that need to be regulated in interaction, and failures in dyadic regulation of these affects lead to a weakened sense of self. Parental neglect and abuse, emotional as well as physical, including threat, humiliation, and criticism, leave the developing self in danger and powerless to respond and increase the person's vulnerability to depression. Schore (2003) pointed out that how caretakers treat infants affects how the infants' brains mature and their ability to self-soothe.

In addition to the ability to regulate emotion, how a child experiences the emotions of others toward the self becomes the foundation for self-experiences and ultimately for the views of self embedded in emotion schemes. A secure sense of self and a view of "I am a lovable person" is the result of many experiences of having felt love from others (Gilbert, 2003). By contrast, a child who is sexually abused stores in memory experiences of fear and disgust, which become experiences of "I am disgusting and bad." Tomkins (1962) argued that shame and other self-conscious emotions are laid down in memory as scenes and images of self in relationships. People then come to live in their own minds according to how others have treated them. Beliefs about the self, then, are based on emotional memories, coded via the fast-track limbic pathways, that inform the cortically higher systems that construct a self-identity. This is how a client comes to say, "I know my body is not really disgusting and my husband is not dangerous, but each time he approaches me with sexual intentions I feel disgusting and afraid."

Childhood maltreatment is a significant source of affective disregulation, the construction of dysfunctional schemes, and subsequent depression. Because the primary source of safety and comfort is at the same time dangerous and a source of fear and humiliation, the inability to be protected or soothed by the caretaker results in unbearable states of anxiety and aloneness. Pathogenic fear and shame, and possibly rage, result. An empty sense of the self as unlovable, bad, defective, worthless, and helpless is formed. The self experiences despair, helplessness, and hopelessness. There also can be a sense of fragmentation, a feeling of falling apart, and an inability to regulate one's own affect. The formation of a vulnerable powerless sense of self and difficulties in affect regulation, however, can result from an experience other than an ongoing lack of empathic attunement from caretakers; they also can result from intense emotional experiences of loss, humiliation, or entrapment at any point in life that do not receive adequate responses such as validation, amelioration, care, soothing, and comfort or from random experiences of abuse or trauma in which one feels alone, violated, afraid, and powerless. Difficulties with affect regulation may result, and maladaptive ways of coping with painful affect may develop.

The Weak and Bad Self-Organizations

In the dialectical constructivist view, the self is modular in nature, and different self-aspects tend to form around particular psychological states and emotions reflected in both inner experiencing and in behavior. These partial selves are not reified structures, but rather dynamic self-organizing systems that emerge as different voices in the personality. They are not permanent, fixed "true" parts of the self; rather, each part continuously constructs itself by integrating many inputs. Further, each self-aspect contains much more than any one explicit description can capture. These self-organizations, based on the synthesis of emotion schemes, are like "voices" in the person (Elliott & Greenberg, 1997; Stiles, 1999), sometimes speaking alone, but often speaking along with other voices, either in unison or in contradiction. It is vital that therapists recognize and respect this multiplicity of self-organizations or voices, because they are an important source of growth and creative adaptation. They also can be a source of dysfunction.

On the basis of our clinical observation, it appears that depression occurs if a person's weak or bad self-organization is triggered or when it becomes the dominant organization. This self-organization, as we have said, is more than a negative view of self, others, and the world and more than interpersonal disruptions, although all of these are important. Rather, the weak or bad self-organization involves the evocation of powerless, predominantly shame- and fear-based experience and dysfunctional ways of coping with the emotion generated. The problem of depression thus arises from how affect is evoked, dealt with, and regulated. Intense shame, based on a fundamental evaluation of diminishment, is evoked by perceived failure, whereas ruptures in relationship evoke an evaluation of abandonment or isolation and the overwhelming anxiety of basic insecurity in more dependent personalities. These affective experiences lead to the activation of an emotion schematic-based self-organization of oneself as depressed, defeated, powerless, ashamed, worthless, and unloved. The person's dysfunctional way of coping with these feelings by means of avoidance and withdrawal exacerbates the depression. Depression thus sets in when an emotional sense of some combination of feeling unloved, humiliated, trapped, and powerless dominates and the person is unable to mobilize alternative responses.

Some theorists have distinguished between dependent-type depressions and perfectionistic type depressions (Blatt, 1974). Dependent-type depressions result if people's life experience has left them with an unloved and weak sense of self from poor attachment relationships and losses. As a result, they are more vulnerable to interpersonal loss and abandonment, feel basically insecure, and withdraw from relationships (Blatt, 1974, 2004). Their voiced experience is "I cannot survive alone" or "I am alone and unloved." In contrast, perfectionistic type depressions occur if people have been subject to high demands and low interpersonal support or bad treatment and have not formed a competent sense of self. These people are harshly judgmental, view themselves as bad and worthless, and feel contempt for themselves. The self then feels ashamed and attempts to shut down feeling. This process produces the self-critical types of depression associated with perfectionism that have been found to be somewhat intractable to brief treatment (Blatt, 2004). The experience is voiced as "I am not good enough" or "I am worthless." In therapy the self-critical, shame-based organization and the anxious dependent self-organization often are highly intertwined, but they sometimes do emerge discretely as momentary states of core shame or core anxiety.

Self- and Other-Oriented Themes in Depression

To more fully understand the different types of depression, we conducted a qualitative study of the postsession and posttherapy reports of 72 clients and their therapists in the York studies of EFT for depression. This study revealed two major therapeutic metathemes with a variety of subthemes. The different subthemes represent, in narrative form, the different types of self-organizations that were worked on in therapy. The two major themes, labeled as self-oriented and other-oriented, and the subthemes are described briefly in the sections that follow (Goldman, 1997; Kagan, 2003). Each client could have more than one theme and more than one subtheme running through the therapy. Most clients had themes in both the self and other domains and had both self-critical and abandonment subthemes.

Self-Oriented Themes

Self-oriented themes were concerned with intrapersonal issues of self-worth and self-acceptance. These themes fitted Blatt's (1974) descriptions of self-critical depressions and involved a sense of the self as bad (Greenberg & Paivio, 1997). Negative fixation on the self, characterized by self-blame, self-contempt, and self-doubt, figured prominently. There also was a marked concern either with negative affective states (e.g., I am in pain, I am angry, I am fearful, I am ashamed) or blockages in the ability to feel at all (e.g., I feel inhibited about my anger, I am frightened of my weakness, I am angry about being sad). This cluster involved perfectionism, and people reported having extremely high standards for performance across domains, a fear of failure, and a concern over making mistakes.

Grounded theory analysis of 36 client and therapist postsession reports on what occurred in the therapy sessions filled in after every session, yielded four categories around the self-oriented theme: self-criticism, shutdown, lack of direction, and helplessness (Kagan, 2003). With three exceptions, every person in this study had at least one theme around the self. Self-criticism was the most prevalent self-oriented theme category (92%), followed by shutdown (47%). Almost all clients therefore experienced and worked on self-criticism in the therapy sessions.

Four types of self-criticism in turn were identified:

1. *compare and despair*, or feelings of inferiority to others;
2. *too sensitive or needy*, or self-criticism of the need for affiliation;
3. *internalized "shoulds" and unacceptable feelings*, or failure to reach expectations or ideals or having feelings that were not acceptable; and
4. *unworthy*, or a view of the self as unlovable, undesirable, or not good enough.

In a difference qualitative study of self-criticism transcripts of two-chair dialogues (Whelton & Greenberg, in press; Whelton & Henkelman, 2002), the following eight categorical clusters describe how the critic acted: demanding and giving orders; exhorting and preaching; explaining and excusing; inducing fear and anxiety; concern, protection, and support; describing; exploring and puzzling; and self-attacking and condemning.

Other-Oriented Themes

The second major theme was clustered around high need for the approval, acceptance, and affection of significant others. This category mapped onto the dependent-type depressions in the literature (Blatt, 1974), which we have referred to as the *weak me* self (Greenberg & Paivio, 1997). In such depressions there is a stress on the actions and feelings of others and a high external locus of responsibility for the feeling states of the client (e.g., my children ignore me, I feel left out or unappreciated, I need unconditional love). Clients with other-oriented themes spent a lot of time in therapy talking about their feelings in relation to other people in their lives, their losses, their abandonments, the perceived expectations others had of them, and their frustrations around not having the kinds of relationships they wanted in their lives. They often felt they had missed love or that others demanded a great deal of them. They feared they would be rejected, punished, and judged harshly if they did not meet the expectations of others. They often appeared to seek approval and felt they could not say no, lest they risk the rejection and disapproval of significant others.

All of the 36 clients had other-oriented themes. Four types of other-oriented themes emerged from the analysis: abandonment or rejection, isolation, loss, and blame (Kagan, 2003). Abandonment or rejection experiences figured prominently in the 36 depression cases studied, constituting 83% of the other-oriented themes, followed by isolation (31%). The two main subcategories of abandonment or rejection were approval seeking and self-critical abandonment. Approval-seeking abandonment in turn broke down into two subtypes, caretaking and pleasing.

Many clients had mixed-theme depressions involving both self- and other-oriented themes. Some of this mixed group of clients reported a high degree of concern around both rejection and the expectations of others, on one hand, and self-worth and self-acceptance, on the other. Other clients demonstrated a high self-oriented need for achievement and success along with a strong desire for affiliation, belonging, and acceptance by others. Such individuals thus had elements of both self-critical depression and dependent depression. This finding shows that the self-critical, shame-based organization and the anxious dependent self-organization often are highly intertwined.

In our view, depression appears to be formed at the boundary between self and other. In this study, only three clients (8%) had only self- or only other-oriented themes. Nearly all depressions thus appear to involve a combination of themes involving both self and other. The evidence, however, points to fear of abandonment or rejection as the core category around which the vast majority of depressions in this study clustered. Even the clients who presented with a highly self-critical component to their depression had abandonment concerns. Many self-critical clients eventually revealed that the need to be perfect at all times, always be strong, or never fail was prompted by a need to be loved and a belief that only skill, mastery, and perfection would earn them the love they needed. Self-criticism was the most common self-theme category (92%), manifested in all but three of the 36 cases in this study. In the majority of cases, self-criticism was paired with abandonment or rejection, making self-criticism and fear of abandonment or rejection the most common shared thematic pairing (75%). Self-criticism was found alongside many of the other themes around the self and others and appeared to function as an amplifier of existing themes, combining with and intensifying such themes as lack of direction, shutdown, helplessness, isolation, and loss.

It may be that the two "styles" of depression—introjective (self-oriented, perfectionistic) and anaclitic (dependent, helpless, approval seeking)—are indicative of different methods for dealing with the threats of abandonment and rejection (Blatt, 2004). For some people, the best line of defense against rejection is a good offence, albeit against the self, which manifests as self-criticism. Although introjective depression ostensibly involves unrealistically high standards and intense needs for achievement, it is germane to inquire about the deeper reason for such behaviors. It is clear that perfectionism is not a goal in itself but acts as a kind of insurance against a feared outcome, such as abandonment. The perfectionistic clients in this study spoke of needing to care for others, appear perfect, always be strong, and never show anger as being the necessary conditions of being connected to or valued by others. Often, deeper examination of an introjective depression reveals the anaclitic depressive themes beneath it. Self-criticism thus may best be understood as an attempt to cope with feelings of dependency, the need to be loved, and attachment needs, rather than as a totally different character subset with unique vulnerabilities to depression.

Emotion Schemes and Depression

In our model the core depressogenic weak or bad self-organization is activated by a current emotional experience of loss, humiliation, or entrapment. It is, in our view, the tacit emotional meaning of an event, rather than thoughts or beliefs alone or expectations of others' responses to the self, that governs functioning. When people experience a depressogenic life event, feelings of being unloved, lonely, sad, disappointed, angry, powerless, and ashamed may be activated. We hypothesize that it is these experiences that act as major triggers of a core experience of self as deeply inadequate or insecure. The emotion-cued basic evaluation, based on emotion memories and tacit organizations of experience of prior vulnerabilities, begins the process of defeat setting in. The self evaluates itself as diminished, unlovable, abandoned, or unable to survive alone. As a result, the self is no longer organized in terms of strengths and resources but rather around a sense of powerlessness, inadequacy, and insecurity. Resilience is lost as the person experiences shame, anxiety, and powerlessness and a sense of the self as weak or bad. In response to loss, humiliation, or failure, depression-prone people lose their resilience and give up. Indeed, many theories of depression capture the essence of a "failed struggle" at the onset of depression that occurs when an individual who at first is invigorated to pursue a goal becomes demobilized when these efforts fail. Attachment theorists have observed that despair follows protest (Bowlby, 1980), whereas in learned helplessness theory, an animal that makes invigorated attempts to escape can become demobilized when it fails to do so (Seligman, 1975).

As shown in Figure 3.2, in response to an event, often a major life stress or the person's apprehension of loss or failure generates an adaptive emotion of, say, sadness and distress at loss. This emotion, with its attendant tendency to seek comfort and solace, is the primary emotional response. However, in people prone to depression, we hypothesize that this initial adaptive emotional reaction to setback evokes a schematic prototype of related emotional experiences stored in memory that produce a fundamental evaluation of diminishment or abandonment that accompanied earlier experiences of sadness and loss (Smith, 1996). This scheme then comes to govern the person's mode of processing. The evocation of maladaptive emotion occurs because memories are stored at emotion addresses, and in this case sadness evokes sad memories and their attendant unresolved emotions. The activation of core maladaptive emotion schemes by the initial primary adaptive emotion is central in the production of both a lasting set of negative cognitions and a hopeless sense of self characteristic of depression. The maladaptive emotion sche-

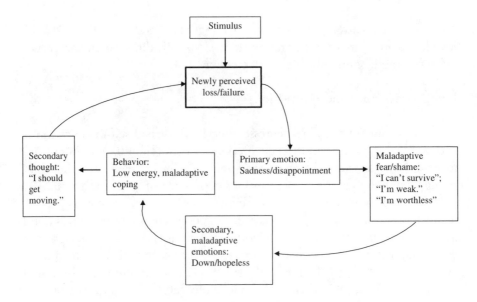

Figure 3.2. Emotion schematic cycle of responses to loss leading to depression.

matic memory process produces the maladaptive pathogenic emotions of shame, fear, and anxiety. Thus, feeling sad or distressed in response to a loss or failure evokes the depressive state of core shame and fear and the weak or bad defeated sense of self formed from the person's previous life experiences. Once this response is activated, the person feels worthless, unloved, abandoned, alone, and empty. A core sense of powerlessness and of feeling defeated, stuck, and trapped prevails.

Thus, it is the person's emotional reaction to a present situation that activates maladaptive emotion schemes and a depressogenic self-organization that we refer to as *voices* in the personality. This maladaptive state often includes introjected negative evaluations, such as "I'm worthless," and self-contempt. The activation of the powerless, trapped sense produces a secondary emotional response of hopelessness, resignation, and the enduring depression.

Thus, people with depression, in response to challenges, organize automatically in a nonresilient manner and then expect to lose and to be put down or shamed. Escape appears blocked, and the person feels guilty, fearful, and inferior. Depression-prone people then react to their own submission by feeling weak, inferior, blocked, and trapped by virtue of having given up or submitted (Gilbert, 2004). These feelings result in their secondary hopelessness. When people have had experiences of overcoming obstacles or have discovered islands of hope in their prior struggles, they are far more resilient. Nondepressogenic resilient responses involve assertion and anger in the face of obstacles or setbacks, and these responses can result in a sense of personal control or the ability to accept defeat and let go of the goal. In addition, if nondepressogenic people take flight, they feel relieved at escaping, or they accept compromises and do not feel bad about giving in or giving up. If an individual can accept defeat and move on, depression may be mild and relatively short lived. It is when individuals are defeated but cannot let go and move on or change their goals and aspirations that serious depression is more likely. Helping clients let go of or change goals thus becomes an important goal in EFT for depression.

All these elements—the negative evaluative voice, the primary shame or fear, the weak or bad sense of self, and the secondary hopelessness—are synthesized into the complex depressed "bad feeling," with its resulting lethargy and inactivity. The process of depression also involves an escalatory process of self-criticism. The person begins chastising himself or herself for being depressed, and this may result in attempts to "coach" the self, more and more coercively and disparagingly, on how to "snap out of it." This, in turn, produces further experience of failure or unworthiness, which further evokes emotion schemes related to failure and loss. This is a type of secondary depression. In addition, maladaptive coping ensues. People withdraw from social interaction, self-medicate, and try to escape the bad feelings.

People's ways of coping with distressing emotion thus becomes an important part of the depression itself. Rather than dealing with the core painful affect, people demobilize, withdraw from others, and avoid dealing with situations. They feel hopeless, chastise themselves for how they feel, and therefore do nothing. Part of people's reason for avoidance may be learned helplessness because of failed prior attempts to have their needs met, or they may not have learned alternative responses to help them feel better. They may try to find ways to dull the pain that can be more problematic. They may automatically interrupt their emotions and experience confusion, causing a general malaise to set in. They sleep, distract, and use substances to escape the pain. To the extent that particular defensive, coping, or behavioral strategies become associated with the regulation of aversive affective states, they become automatic maladaptive solutions to emotional problems. Coping strategies such as avoidance, distraction, or deadening are a form of procedural knowledge that is activated as soon as a particular emotion is experienced. People automatically attempt to suppress and distract themselves from their emotions. They isolate themselves from others, thereby robbing themselves of social support.

In summary, then, our model of depression suggests that it is the activation and synthesis of core emotion-linked depressogenic schemes, and the inability to cope with the expression they produce, that lead to depressed self-organizations (Greenberg, Elliott, & Foerster, 1990; Paivio & Greenberg, 1998). Schematically generated depressive experience is then symbolized in awareness as negative beliefs about self, other, and world and is experienced as feelings of fear of abandonment, basic insecurity, and shame and behaviorally as an inability to go on. In response to painful core affects and self-experience, people also institute dysfunctional coping strategies such as avoidance, deadening, incomplete processing of their feelings, and withdrawal, thus exacerbating the depression.

Depressogenic emotion schemes based on loss, humiliation, and entrapment store emotional experience in primitive forms. When situations occur in the present with features that resemble those earlier experiences, then the depressogenic schemes may be activated and, once activated, influence current perceptions and experience. Depression-prone people become overwhelmed by their negative affect, and their ways of trying to regulate their emotions lead to difficulties (Kennedy-Moore & Watson, 1999). Their intense responses of despair and hopelessness to their own core emotional states of vulnerability, as well as their inability to cope with their emotions, are important parts of their depression, and both the core state and the maladaptive coping need to be dealt with in therapy.

The Emotions in Depression

Though it is common to hear people say, "I'm feeling depressed," depression is not an emotion. Sadness, disappointment, fear, and shame are. Depression is a syndrome, and often avoidance of core emotion is an aspect of this syndrome. People with depression fear their core feelings. Women most often disown their anger and men their sadness and vulnerabilities. Instead of the normal fluctuations of happiness, sadness, disappointment, anger, and desire, some people with depression feel a kind of gray monotone.

What are these painful and dreaded emotions that people with depression feel trapped in and try to avoid? In the study described in the preceding section (Kagan, 2003), four general emotion clusters emerged as the categories that best described the emotions most clients focused on in therapy for depression: shame or guilt, fear or anxiety, sadness, and anger. There were no depression stories that did not feature at least one of these emotional categories. This finding supports the view that emotion is an integral part of all depression narratives. Many clients focused on more than one emotion in their treatment. The frequency of emotional themes of the 36 therapies was as follows: anger, 66%; shame or guilt, 56%; fear or anxiety, 50%; and sadness, 39%. These themes are discussed in the sections that follow.

Shame and Guilt

Clients with depression frequently express feelings of shame. Shame is an especially painful emotion because it is the one most closely associated with personal identity. In shame, the self is felt to be defective. The experience of shame causes the self to curl up and retreat into itself. Core feelings of shame are deeply painful and clients often avoid them in seeking to minimize their pain. Resolution of the problem of shame lies in acceptance and strengthening of the self. The therapist must strive to facilitate self-acceptance through protracted immersion in the depths of the client's shame and validation of the client's identity.

Although guilt was the focus of most of Freudian psychoanalytic theory and treatment of depression, shame seems to be more intimately connected with depression and at the core of the most damaging depressions. Clients feel guilt about things they do or don't do, but they feel shame about who they are. In shame, people experience themselves as unworthy, uncouth, repulsive, or stupid. As Tomkins (1962) first pointed out, although sadness or distress is the affect of suffering and fear is the anticipation of one's end, shame is the affect of indignity, defeat, transgression, and alienation. And as painful as are sadness or distress and anxiety or fear, shame strikes deepest into the human heart. Shame is felt as an inner torment, a sickness of the soul that one cannot escape by leaving. It does not matter whether the humiliated person has been shamed by derisive laughter or whether the mocking is internal; in either event, the person feels naked, rejected, contemptible, alienated, and lacking in dignity or worth.

Shame is the emotion of low self-esteem and is the core feeling that has to be unearthed and combated in many people with a self-critical depression. Such people often appear to feel inferior to others, less attractive and different. Wanting to sink into the ground is regarded as one of the typical action tendencies of shame. Shame is a central organizing emotion that can be incorporated into people's personalities in different ways. When people feel shame, they experience being diminished in the eyes of the other and believe that they have evoked or will evoke negative feelings, contempt, ridicule, disgust, or disinterest in others. As a consequence, they do not wish to form relationships; they disengage, actively reject the self, or even attack the self. When shame is internalized, people treat themselves with the contempt with which they have been treated, and they make similar evaluations of themselves as were made of them (Gilbert, 1998). People who have heightened internalized shame hate themselves. These individuals feel very internally persecuted, find it difficult to trust a therapist, and will often dismiss the therapist's reassuring efforts. In the extreme, they may have beliefs such as "I am bad at the core of me" or "if you knew the real me, you wouldn't want to look at me."

Shame is closely related to contempt. Shame is most generally and most effectively induced by contempt expressed by a social partner, be it parent, peer, or intimate other. Contempt can vary in intensity from a milder shame-inducing contempt to an annihilating sense of contempt and disgust in which the tendency is to get rid of or expunge the offending object. If that object is the self, this leads to an annihilating internal agency. We will deal further with work on self-criticism in chapter 11.

People develop different ways of dealing with shame, and these become material for therapeutic exploration. Sometimes people learn as children to fight back and to get angry to counter the parent's contempt, often expressing contempt back to the parent. Or the parent's contempt may be internalized, such that one part of the self has contempt for another part of the self. So part of the self is contemptuous and condemning and another part ashamed. Contempt for the self is often coupled with contempt for others. In other people the shame is so integrated into the core sense of self that the self feels ashamed without any signs of contempt for self or others. Shame also often is mixed with other emotions. Shame and anger appear to be dynamically linked. Shame often activates anger at the other in whose eyes one feels shamed. Other emotions also often become activators of shame because shame becomes associated with emotional expressions that once were shamed. Thus, there is shame at one's own anger or at one's vulnerability.

In our qualitative study of 36 clients with depression, shame appeared frequently in therapy and seemed always to be a maladaptive emotion. Fifteen of the 36 clients had a strong explicit theme of shame running through their stories, and for many others shame about the self ran through the dominant self-critical and abandonment themes, although it was not the most prevalent or explicit emotion. Clients expressed shame around not being "good enough" and around being vulnerable, "weak," or "different." Three categories of shame worked on in therapy were differentiated: core shame, societal shame, and self-shame.

Core shame, based on worthlessness, involved a pervasive sense of shame that was a legacy of abuse. For example, Anne experienced core shame and felt that she was not worth loving. Ever since she was a child, she reported, no one ever cared for her. She received the message from significant others, "You are rotten, you are dirt," and she internalized it. She described herself as having "no inner strength," and she despaired of ever finding any. A childhood mental disability led another client, Brian, to feel that he was inferior, and Deirdre had core shame about her body; she felt that she was a disgusting blob and that people only wanted to get away from her.

Societal shame was based on humiliation, such as the shame one feels at losing a high-paying job or getting divorced. These clients felt shamed in the eyes of others. For example, Steven presented in therapy after having lost his job and his sense of identity. He experienced both his unemployment and his subsequent depression as shaming. Sandy also experienced a type of socially based shame regarding her alcoholic husband; she felt ashamed of her life with her alcoholic husband, and so she hid it from others. She felt that her choice of two alcoholic husbands reflected badly on her, and she felt shame over her poor judgment.

Self-shame was more internal and reflected a failure to live up to one's own standards. For example, Raymond experienced shame that was more internally based. He felt that he was a disappointment, and so he avoided his feelings. He was ashamed of himself for avoiding his core feelings, but the experience of shame was so painful that he was trapped in a shame cycle that involved avoiding and judging. To numb himself, Raymond drank, which impaired his ability to act wisely on his own behalf, leading him to experience even more shame. He was failing himself. Teresa, another client, had internalized the parental message that "something is wrong with her," and she felt a sense of shame around not being "normal." She also felt "cheap" around her brothers, who had abused her sexually and contributed to her confusion about love.

Guilt has different origins than shame. Guilt comes from feelings of obligation, failure to meet standards, and duty directed toward others. Guilt can be depicted as a sense of having failed to meet the expectations of others or as being overly responsible for the well-being of others. If people have a strict moral code and fail or slip up, they may feel guilty. Guilt, in moderation, serves a societal purpose. But in depression, a lot of self-denial and self-sacrifice often stem from guilt. Guilt about feeling angry, desiring revenge, or experiencing seductive or sexual impulses is also important in some depressions. When, for example, the submissive wife of a bullying husband felt angry at him, she automatically interrupted the feelings and did not allow herself to experience her anger. If her anger was brought to awareness, she felt guilty about it. She ended up depressed.

People also have desires or wishes they are not explicitly aware of, but still they feel guilty. When people deny their sexual feelings or their anger, they still feel guilty about their unacceptable impulses. It is interesting to note that all cases of shame or guilt were found to involve self-criticisms and that shame and guilt often co-occurred.

Clients in this study expressed guilt primarily for failing to achieve personally important goals, failing to act in ways they deemed appropriate in relationships, or being selfish, or they felt guilt induced by the expectations of others. Clients in our sample most often felt guilty about seeking to meet their own needs or having pleasure, believing they had to sacrifice these to attend to others. For example, Helen felt guilty about breaking off her relationship with her boyfriend, even though she was not happy with him and he was not meeting her needs. She had a sense that she "ought" to have sacrificed her own needs in deference to the needs of others needier than herself. She often found herself acting as an advocate for people in need and "collecting wounded birds." Caring for herself caused Helen to feel guilty. Another client, Melissa, felt guilt around her ambivalence about being the responsible, dependable caregiver. She felt guilty that part of her wanted to run off and escape all responsibilities and be free.

Fear or Anxiety

When shame or guilt was not the core emotion in depression, then anxiety or fear, in the form of basic insecurity, was. Anxiety in depression is generated by a core insecure and vulnerable sense of self that is chronically activated in interpersonal situations of loss of connection. It is this holistic, multicomponent, bodily felt sense of self as ineffective and unprotected that requires therapeutic attention and needs to be changed. It is important in working with this primary insecurity to recognize the existence of other possible self-organizations, in particular to recognize the hidden self-aspect in which resilient resources reside. Clients often refer to a hidden, essential part of themselves that consists of their adaptive wants and needs for survival and well-being (Greenberg & Paivio, 1997). Through negative learning experiences, this essential part of the self has withdrawn for protection but comes out in a safe environment and is available as an inner resource when seen and validated. When this part is contacted, adaptive longings for connection, freedom, and spontaneity arise. Emotionally focused interventions support the emergence of this essential self-organization to foster the development of a stronger and more secure sense of self.

Fear and anxiety formed a prevalent emotional category in our study, found in half of the cases (18 out of 36). As with all of the categories of emotion in this study, there was no "one size fits all" fear. The 36 clients expressed a variety of fears that were sorted into five subcategories:

1. *Fear of rejection or judgment* blocked clients from expressing themselves and taking the risks they needed to take to have authentic self-regard.
2. *Maladaptive core fears* clustered around a sense of the world as being a bad and frightening place.
3. *Fear of repeating family patterns* involved fear of repeating emotional experiences like being in a cold relationship or doing to one's children what was done to one.
4. *Fear of change* involved feeling stuck or unable to make changes because of fear.
5. Finally, *fear of feelings* involved the covering up of more primary, adaptive emotions that needed to be unearthed to facilitate emotional change.

Fears of abandonment or rejection and fear of failure blocked clients from expressing themselves and taking the risks they wanted to take. For example, Michael was afraid of failing to achieve societal and parental expectations and had difficulty staying in touch with his own internal values.

Some maladaptive core fears clearly were the result of an emotional legacy from a difficult childhood. These kinds of fears clustered around a sense of the world as being bad and of oneself as being maltreated. Clients felt unsupported by the universe and worried that the bottom could drop out of their world at any moment. From an early age, for example, Melissa experienced her parents as needy and insecure, and she felt she could never go to them for comfort. As a result, she felt that she needed to control everything around her to compensate for her anxiety and foreboding that the world "would come crashing down on her." She described herself as feeling "fearful, cautious, trapped, and stifled." In the case of Peter, a childhood of abuse from his violent father had colored his view of himself and the world and led him to expect that "bad things will happen" to him. Peter was particularly fearful of anger, because he identified it as synonymous with "father." His childhood experiences left him fearful of expressing or experiencing intense feelings. He recalled being told not to cry when his father beat him. In therapy, Peter realized that his current sense of doom paralleled his early feelings with his father. He had a sense of grief around his lost childhood and a lack of faith in ever being happy. His fear of anger and confrontation had the effect of escalating his anger, so Peter was learning how to accept and express his anger more constructively instead of shutting down in fear.

Some clients feared repeating the past. For Brenda, her experience of debilitating anxiety was connected with her fear of being in a cold, emotionless relationship like her parents had. She was angry with her family and frightened that she would become like them. Janice, a woman with children of her own, was fearful that she would recreate her familial experience of abandonment if she acted on her desires to be more carefree, adventurous, and self-nurturing. Fear of change ran through many depression stories. Bill, a divorced man with children, entered therapy feeling stuck and unable to make any changes because of fear, a remnant of his childhood experience of instability and turmoil. He said he had retreated into a "safety cocoon" to shield himself from his parents' arguments at the dinner table.

Sadness

Depression is often confused with sadness, and feelings of sadness are present in most depressions. However, sadness is not depression. The human proclivity for attachment predisposes people to sadness when attachments are severed. There is the acute sadness of sudden loss and the chronic sadness of mourning a past loss. Feelings of sadness occupy a continuum from nostalgia to full-blown despair. Sadness can be an adaptive emotion, alerting a person to loss and encouraging him or her to attend to the grief process. Sadness can also be secondary, masking other, more threatening emotions such as anger, fear, or shame. Sadness is less defended against than anger, although many clients fault themselves for being sad or feeling depressed, and this can result in secondary depression. When clients cry, the tears can come from different places in their psyche. They may be shedding tears of self-pity, crying crocodile tears, or choking on unacknowledged hurts and old wounds. It is the latter that therapists try to access in therapy.

Sadness was a core emotion theme in 39% of the cases in our sample. In half of these cases, sadness was found alongside anger; the two tend to be linked. The expression of anger often opens up into sadness, and the expression of sadness can be anger in disguise. In clients with depression who defended against anger because they feared its destructiveness or believed it could lead to abandonment, sadness often was the predominantly expressed emotion.

The categories of sadness identified were lamenting unmet needs; remorse; the current loss of relationships, hopes, or ideals; and unresolved grief. *Lamenting unmet needs and disappointment* involved voicing feelings of disappointment around not getting one's needs met. *Remorse* focused on injuries people had inflicted on others or pain they had suffered themselves. Remorse presented as a type of sadness combined with guilt and involved the wish to undo previous actions. *Current loss* involved a present-day loss of hopes, ideals, status, or relationship. *Unresolved grief* featured a sadness derived from unresolved feelings about a person who had died. This grief involved anger, pain about not being loved, and shame and fear from abuse.

Many clients entered therapy voicing feelings of disappointment around not getting their needs met. For example, Sharon expressed a sense of having had her "deepest hopes and needs crushed and disappointed." Teresa reported that she was "tired and feels like giving up" because she had so much sadness over parental neglect and not getting her needs met by her family. In the case of Greg, what first presented as anger toward his mother and her "barracuda-like" behavior opened up into sadness around having never been acknowledged by his mother and sadness around his unmet childhood needs. Grieving what was missing was helpful for all these clients.

Several clients reported feelings of remorse around pain they had inflicted on others or had suffered themselves. Remorse presented as a type of sadness combined with guilt and wishes to undo previous actions. John expressed a deep sadness around the ending of his marriage and painful feelings of remorse around unintentionally hurting his ex-wife. Another client, Ellis, cited feelings of remorse and sadness around his ex-wife.

For many clients, depression was precipitated by a present-day loss of hopes, ideals, status, or relationship. The sadness they felt was related to a feeling of loss. Glenda illustrated the theme of sadness as loss in her depression story, which involved her feelings of sadness around the ending of her marriage, which triggered her lifelong fear of abandonment. Another client, Jennifer, experienced sadness around the ending of her relationship and the loss of her sense of direction. She processed the sadness around her losses in therapy and eventually came to accept her feelings and recognize them as part of a healing process.

Finally, several depression stories featured sadness derived from unresolved grief. Linda felt a lot of grief around the death of her mother and needed to grieve the vision of the family she never had. She also grieved the death of her father while simultaneously processing her anger toward him. Leslie carried a great sense of pain and grief around not feeling loved by her parents, who separated with seemingly little concern about the effect it would have on her. She worked through and came to accept that it was not that she was unlovable but that her parents were inadequate as people and as parents. All of these clients evoked, processed, and worked through their sadness.

The sadness sometimes itself was the change, and at other times it led to change in view of self, other, and world.

Anger

Anger is a particularly troubling emotion for many people with depression. Anger, like all other emotions, is neither good nor bad in itself; it is just an innate response to frustration and violation. Anger can be used for many worthwhile purposes. It is the fuel that feeds people's desire for justice, what makes them want to see wrongs put right. Anger is a feeling that tells people that they need to protect themselves from harm. Anger can be protective and constructive, but it can also be destructive. What frightens some people is the feeling that anger can run amok. Anger is not aggressive behavior or violence; anger is an emotion. Violence is a behavior and involves choice and learning. Anger cannot be escaped, but clients can learn to make it safe and even to use it for productive ends. Practicing assertive communication and behavior helps make sure that one expresses anger constructively and does not hurt others. As clients develop assertive skills, they find that they feel less aggrieved and isolated and thus have less to be angry about.

Men are often socialized to ignore their feelings and to dissociate themselves from any feelings except for sexual and angry feelings. If a sense of hopelessness, worthlessness, or powerlessness creeps in, men feel only a vague sense of vulnerability. Lacking skills to deal with these feelings because they have learned to think and do rather than feel and experience, men shut down their feelings. Feelings, however, cry out for expression, and men often deal with them in the only way they know how—with anger and destructive behavior. They can be angry at others or engage in self-destructive behavior such as excessive drinking or health-endangering behaviors. Anger, then, is often an expression of depression in men. Whereas women often are more intrapunitive and able to acknowledge their sadness and distress, men tend to act out and express anger when depressed, a pattern that is not exclusive to men but is more prevalent in them.

Although irritability and anger can be symptoms of some depressions, many depressions are characterized by a lack of anger. The failure to be able to use anger or act assertively to get one's own way (or agree to some compromise) not only confirms one to be in a powerless, subordinate position, but also increases the desire to escape. Research has shown that anger suppression is significantly correlated with feelings of entrapment and wishes for escape (Allan & Gilbert, 2002). Although excessive anger expression is associated with poorer health and poorer social relationships than mild to moderate expression (Broman & Johnson, 1988), it has also been found that anger inhibition, submissive behavior, and poor assertiveness, especially emotional distress at expressing assertive behaviors, are linked with depression (Akhavan, 2001; Harmon Jones et al., 2002). The evidence seems clear that many clients who are depressed experience heightened anger that is not expressed. Anger is often a first affective response to having a path to a goal blocked, but if the person feels trapped and the anger has no effect, then anger becomes resignation. Thus, being able to remobilize anger is very helpful in undoing depression, because the demobilization of anger results in powerlessness.

Anger was the most predominant emotional theme in the 36 cases of depression in our study (Kagan, 2003). Anger featured in 66% of the depression narratives. Four subtypes of anger were discovered within our data: *resentment and frustration, boundary violation, fear of anger,* and *blaming anger. Resentment* is a feeling of bitter anger about a situation in the past, accompanied by a sense of frustration at being powerless to express this hostility overtly. The key point in resentment is the sense of not having been able to express anger directly. *Boundary violation* anger is a response to being violated or abused in some way. Often clients who experienced childhood sexual abuse carried this type of anger. *Fear of anger* often came from having experienced or witnessed violent abuse. *Blaming anger* involved other-directed anger. Self-criticism was paired with anger in 22 of the 24 anger cases and often occurred alongside sadness.

One client, Judith, entered therapy feeling resentment and frustration. She was burdened with feelings of responsibility for everyone and everything. She had lived her entire life doing what others wished because she did not want to "rock the boat." She stifled her anger for fear that she would hurt others, but she felt perpetually misunderstood and disrespected. Another woman, Janice, felt she was "breaking under pressure of trying to be all things to everybody." As a result of this constant pressure, she felt angry about having to put her needs aside all the time, a pattern learned very early in her family of origin.

A commonly shared variant of resentment-type anger was frustration around being blocked from expressing one's true feelings or needs. Many therapists reported that their clients expressed these resentments in their sessions. For example, Amy felt she could not express her needs and wants to others, and she was frustrated by this. She often felt that she put others' needs ahead of her own. She had a lot of anger toward her father, but she was afraid to acknowledge it because of the potential consequences. Another client, Sharon, entered therapy claiming that she "had no outlet for her emotions, and that they collected inside her like a reservoir that pulls her down over time and makes her negative about herself."

Boundary violation anger was a response to being violated or abused in some way. Often clients who had experienced childhood sexual abuse carried this type of anger. Less extreme forms of childhood injury also produced a feeling of being violated. One client, Monica, wanted to let go of her anger toward her father, but she felt a sense of hopelessness around ever getting him to acknowledge the damage he had caused. She held a lot of anger toward her parents for not being very loving. In another case, Andrea had anger over childhood sexual abuse. However, she was in conflict about the expression of that anger and angry with herself for not being able to prevent the abuse.

Some clients in the sample evidenced fear of anger because of past experiences of violence. For example, Peter was raised by a violent, abusive father and grew up fearful of anger. Peter was uncomfortable with anger, but he wanted to learn how to deal with anger constructively instead of suppressing it. He saw anger as a sign that he was "writing off" someone and cutting him or her out of his life. Peter had a lot of inner conflict around his anger toward his ex-wife and her boyfriend, but he stopped himself from feeling, because feelings were threatening to him. Through his therapy, Peter came to see that his fear of confrontations made his anger grow.

Blaming anger could be directed outward or inward. Craig blamed his ex-wife for destroying his life and doesn't feel he can forgive her. He also blames his parents for his childhood and feels cheated by the lack of support he received. Craig also blames himself that he is so unhappy.

Emotions, and specifically anger, sadness, fear, and shame, play a central role in depression. As we have seen, each emotion is embedded with a significant narrative, and narratives provide the scaffold that sequences emotions into coherent stories. The major narratives are ones of a "weak" fear-based self, dependent on others for approval and acceptance, and a "bad" shame-based self lacking in self-worth and self-acceptance for failing to meet perfectionistic standards. The following chapters address how to work with these emotions and stories to help transform them into more resilient self-experience.

4

PRINCIPLES OF WORKING WITH EMOTION IN DEPRESSION

This is the greatest paradox: The emotions cannot be trusted, yet it is they that tell us the greatest truths.
　　　　　　　　　　　　　　—Paraphrased from Don Herold, comedian

In working with the emotions in depression, it is important to make distinctions between different types of emotional experience and expression that require different types of in-session intervention. In addition, it is important to have a set of principles for guiding intervention. We outline these principles in this chapter.

We have emphasized the importance of engaging in process diagnosis and of differentiating between primary and secondary emotions and between emotional experience that is adaptive and maladaptive (Greenberg & Safran, 1987; Greenberg, Rice, & Elliott, 1993; Greenberg & Paivio, 1997). In addition to these process diagnoses, several other global process distinctions need to be made in assessing emotional experience and expression:

- whether an emotion is a new expression that involves the freeing up of blocked emotion or an old, stale expression that involves the repetition of emotion too freely expressed. The fresh expression of previously overinhibited sadness or anger in depression is generally helpful, whereas the venting of too often expressed, stale anger or sadness neither is therapeutic nor leads to a reduction in expression.

- whether the emotion being experienced and expressed is a sign of distress or is a sign of the process of resolving distress (Kennedy-Moore & Watson, 1999). For example, weeping when feeling overwhelmed and unable to cope is a sign of depression and is to be distinguished from weeping as part of a healthy grieving process that may relieve depression.
- whether emotion is over- or undercontrolled. Depressed clients with overregulated emotion need evocative work, and clients with undercontrolled emotion need regulation work (Greenberg, 2002).
- whether the client can or cannot regulate the intensity of his or her emotions.

PRINCIPLES OF EMOTION ASSESSMENT

Primary emotions in depression are the depressed person's most fundamental, direct, initial, rapid reactions to a situation, like being immediately sad at a loss or angry at a violation. Primary feelings are fundamental states in that they are irreducible to any other feeling. (The terms *emotion* and *feeling* are used synonymously in this book.) Primary feelings can be acknowledged, or they can be unacknowledged or out of awareness. *Secondary emotions* in depression are responses that are secondary to other more primary internal processes and may be protections (defenses) against these, such as feeling hopeless when faced with an obstacle or angry at suffering a loss. These are learned reactions to an underlying process. Secondary emotions can be responses to prior thoughts, prior feelings, or a prior sequence of thoughts or feelings, or they can be emotions about emotions. Sequences such as feeling angry in response to feeling hurt or feeling afraid or guilty about feeling angry occur often in depression. Secondary emotions need to be explored to get at their more primary generators. Most depressive symptoms of hopelessness, helplessness, and despair are secondary emotions.

Instrumental feelings are emotional behavior patterns that people have learned to use to influence or manipulate. In other words, instrumental feelings are an overlearned feeling–thinking–expressing complex that a person knows serves some purpose, like dominance or security. For example, an angry–helpless reaction can help a person control others and avoid taking risks and responsibility. These feeling behaviors are often depressed people's way of indicating their distress and involving other people. For example, some people with depression complain when they feel sad, whereas others talk in a way that invites the other person to come and rescue or nurture them. These are ways of coping and of surviving a situation. Although the instrumental feelings appear to overlap with secondary feelings, instrumental feelings are more a part of the person's personality and are a recognizable part of a person's character.

The next crucial distinction to be made is between primary emotions that are adaptive, which are accessed for their useful information, and primary emotions that are maladaptive, which need to be transformed. Awareness of adaptive primary emotions provides access to good information that promotes orientation to the world and problem solving. Thus, accessing the healthy anger at unfairness that underlies the powerlessness of some depressions promotes adaptation, and accessing the shame and sadness at loss of esteem that underlies rage can promote attachment in place of destructiveness. Maladaptive emotional responses are responses that are a function of learning and survival. At the heart of maladaptive emotional responses in depression are deep-seated fears, such as fear of abandonment, fear of closeness, fear of annihilation, and deep feelings of shame at being defective, unworthy, or despicable. The maladaptive responses were once adaptive responses developed as a survival strategy in reaction to fears of loss, destruction of self, or humiliation and neglect in childhood or early adult experiences (e.g., fear at the danger of approaching a harmful attachment figure, shame to protect from overexposing the self to lack of support or recognition).

Maladaptive primary emotions are old, familiar feelings that occur repeatedly and do not change. In depression these are feelings such as a core sense of loneliness, sadness, abandonment, or wretched worthlessness or recurrent feelings of shameful inadequacy; these maladaptive emotions can plague people all their lives. Maladaptive emotions do not provide adaptive information to guide action. They also do not change in response to changing circumstances, and when expressed, they do not provide adaptive directions for solving problems. Rather, they leave the person feeling stuck, hopeless, helpless, and in despair. Some of the self-related maladaptive emotions prevalent in depression are shame, self-disgust, and self-hatred and feelings of unworthiness, inadequacy, inferiority, unlovability, being not good enough, embarrassment, unattractiveness, vulnerability, and insecurity. These emotions and feelings generally are accompanied by such thoughts as "I'm lazy," "I'm losing it," "I'm no good," "I can't cope," "It's my fault," "I'm a failure," "I'm different," "I'm no good," "I'm incompetent," "I'm unlovable," and "I can't survive on my own." It does not help simply to get in touch with these feelings; they must be replaced or transformed.

Other-related maladaptive emotions are rage, hair-trigger anger, fear, and lack of trust. Maladaptive emotions appear predominantly as fear- or shame-based feelings. Maladaptive emotions may involve a blend of a number of emotions, but generally the emotions are maladaptive for the self because they include a threat to the self represented by fear or shame (A. Pascual-Leone & Greenberg, 2004). Thus, therapists often see fear- or shame-based sadness as a maladaptive emotion blend. Maladaptive emotions that are more externally focused and are socially maladaptive generally include some form of destructive anger.

Another discrimination to make is whether a primary emotion is a core emotion related to a core concern (Fosha, 2000, 2004). A primary emotion is the very first emotion a person has, based on a currently operating concern, whereas a secondary emotion occurs later and obscures a primary emotion. A core primary emotion, however, is one that is at the core of a client's problem and is related to a core need or concern that is not being met; fear of abandonment or shame at diminishment might be at the core of a depression. A core emotion may not necessarily be being felt at the moment. Rather, it is a more enduring part of the person that influences his or her personality. The concept of core is more of a structural than a phenomenological construct. Whereas *primary*, *secondary*, and *instrumental* refer to what is experienced directly in the moment, *core* refers to enduring emotions and needs that currently may be out of awareness and not experienced but still are an important underlying aspect of the client's depression.

Thus, a core emotion of, say, anger or shame can be contrasted with a secondary, reactive emotion like hopelessness or anxiety that is not at the core of the problem or the self but is more characteristic of the person's reaction to what is currently occurring. An emotional reaction like hopelessness or anxiety, although often secondary at a particular moment, can be a primary emotion if it is being experienced freshly in the moment in response to the person's current concern (i.e., it is primary but not core). Thus, a client whose husband had died a number of years previously had been trying ever since to be a strong person—mother to her children, daughter to her parents, successful career woman, and breadwinner. In an early session, she arrived at a feeling that it was all too much, and she felt hopeless and helpless for the first time in therapy. She began to cry and, facing her defeat for the first time, she said, "With all that has happened, it's just too much, I can't keep going, something has to change, I just can't continue carrying all this—but I don't know what can change." She was in that moment experiencing a primary emotion of hopelessness, but this was not the core emotion underlying her depression. For this client, the sadness of unresolved grief for her husband was the core emotion underlying her depression, and her core need was for support. Facing her loss, grieving, and seeking support were important in alleviating her depression.

These distinctions between the different types of emotion guide intervention. Primary emotions need to be accessed for their adaptive information and capacity to organize action, whereas maladaptive emotions need to be regulated and transformed. Secondary emotions need to be regulated by exploring them to access their primary cognitive or emotional generators. Emotion-focused therapy (EFT), therefore, involves accessing primary adaptive emotions to symbolize their adaptive information and evoking maladaptive emotions to make them amenable to change by exposing them to new information and experience. When therapists are working with secondary anger, it is important first to validate the client's feelings of anger and to understand and help them express their anger to help access the underlying feelings of sadness. As clients learn how their secondary experience obscures their primary experience, their growing awareness will help them identify the underlying feelings more quickly. There is generally a good reason why someone needs to express anger instead of fear, but rather than take this means of protection away, it is more effective and caring to understand how and why people react as they do.

When working with secondary feelings, some useful questions therapists can ask clients to help them identify their primary feelings are as follows:

- What did you feel first in the situation?
- Were there any other feelings underneath?
- Did you have other feelings that you did not show at the time?
- What is this feeling a reaction to?
- What impact did the event first have on you?
- How did it affect you in the moment?
- What did it lead you to want to do?

In addition, therapists can ask themselves, Is there something more here? Is there a deeper feeling? Is this a symptom of something else? Is there something underneath leading to this feeling?

In general, the most helpful way to work with instrumental emotion is to increase the client's awareness that the emotional expression is being used to achieve an aim and to help him or her discover its function. For example, with one client, who seemed to feel anger at everything that occurred, it was helpful for her to become aware of her style of expressing. After a while, it became clear that angry expression was part of her way of surviving. It kept people away, it allowed her to be angry, and it allowed her to express distress. It also helped her to avoid reflecting on what was happening, both inside herself and in her environment. The client was caught in a never-ending anger–complaint cycle, and the therapist helped her focus on this cycle in the therapy session in relation to her complaints about what was happening both outside the session and in the session. The therapist observed that this client, if asked questions about other topics in the midst of being angry, was able to stop showing this feeling and start talking about the other things; this was a marker that indicated that the client could tolerate a focus on her instrumental use of emotion because the instrumental feeling state was within her control. Questions therapists can ask clients in working with instrumental feelings are as follows:

- Is this a style of expression?
- Does this feeling serve a purpose?

- What does it do for you?
- What would other people say is your most common expression that you use to get something from them?
- What is it you are trying to get when you express that?

Questions therapists can ask themselves to help identify the primary experience include

- Is this a primary experience, or is my client avoiding, deflecting, or denying a feeling?
- Is my client protecting?
- Can this client access his or her core experience?
- Does this client feel entitled to have his or her experience?
- Are this client's primary feelings over- or underregulated?

Questions therapists can ask themselves to help identify maladaptive feelings are

- Is this feeling useful?
- Is the client stuck in the feeling?
- Is the client a victim of the feeling?
- Is the client feeling overwhelmed by the emotion?
- Is the client overreacting?
- Is this a feeling related to another time or place?
- Is the client unaware or having a problem with regulating feeling?
- Is the client feeling bad about himself or herself?

We offer these lists of questions in an attempt to make explicit the implicit processing in the therapist, rather than as a recommendation that the therapist sit in therapy and ponder these questions. The therapist does not assume that he or she is an expert who can assess the client's experience. Rather, the therapist is fully present and in contact with the client and is open to sensing that there is a deeper feeling present or that this feeling is at the core. Assumptions about what the client is feeling, however, are always held lightly and only guide the therapist's next moment to help clients explore and come to what is right for them.

MEASURING PRODUCTIVE AND UNPRODUCTIVE EMOTIONAL EXPERIENCE IN SESSIONS

In our efforts to rate, from videotapes of therapy sessions, whether an emotion was primary, secondary, or instrumental and adaptive or maladaptive, we found it difficult to establish reliability on small segments of sessions (2–4 minutes). We did, however, find that it was possible to rate reliably whether an episode of emotion was therapeutically productive or unproductive. We developed the Productivity Scale (Greenberg, Auszra, & Herrmann, 2004) to differentiate between productive and nonproductive emotional states in therapy, and we found that the presence of productive emotions clearly predicted therapeutic outcome in an intensive analysis of eight clients with depression (Auszra, Herrmann, & Greenberg, 2004).

An emotional state that is being experienced in the present is productive when it is either (a) a primary adaptive emotion being processed in such a way that the adaptive information it entails can be extracted and used or (b) a primary maladaptive emotion being processed in such a way that it either has the potential to be transformed into a more adaptive emotion or is currently in the process of transformation. To be productive, the emotional state has to be primary, because secondary and instrumental emotions neither grant access to underlying maladaptive emotion schemes nor contain adaptive information concerning the significance of events to the well-being of the organism. An emotional state thus is considered to be therapeutically productive when a client experiences a primary core emotion in an aware and contactful manner and without being stuck in it. In addition, to be therapeutically productive the emotion needs to be relevant to a central therapeutic theme.

In terms of this definition, a client is contactfully aware when he or she takes responsibility for the felt emotion (does not take stance of a victim) and is not overwhelmed by the emotion. The client thus does not attribute responsibility for felt emotions to external sources, nor does he or she attribute responsibility for the resolution of a problematic situation to external sources. For example, when expressing anger, the client does not merely blame the other, or when expressing hurt, the client does not focus only on external factors responsible for his or her situation. In addition, a client is not making contact with an emotion in an aware manner if the emotion is overwhelming, if the client is not able to regulate it adequately, or if the client is dissociating; in such cases the emotion lacks any information value for the client. An emotion is not overwhelming when a working distance from the feeling is created and the client can gain information from the feeling or be moved by it.

A client is "stuck" if he or she experiences a primary maladaptive emotion persistently in the same manner, such that the manner of experiencing and emotional awareness do not progress. A maladaptive primary emotion that occurs in therapy is stuck if it is a repetitive response to the same evoking situation (e.g., anger against abusive father), a repeated similar response to different evoking situations (e.g., anger when criticized by parent, partner, coworker), or constitutes a general style of emotional reaction and is characteristic for that client (e.g., helplessness as a general response to all kinds of challenges). The maladaptive primary emotion is stuck or blocked if the client shows no improvement in his or her ability to tolerate it better (e.g., the

TABLE 4.1
Markers of Productive and Unproductive Emotions

Productive	Unproductive
Primary adaptive emotion is productive if in present awareness.	Conceptual talking about feelings.
Primary maladaptive emotion is productive if being processed in present awareness in a contactful manner.	Avoided, dreaded, or suppressed.
Client experiences self as agent rather than victim of the feeling.	Client experiences self as victim.
Emotion is not overwhelming.	Emotion is overwhelming.
Emotion is not stuck or blocked.	Emotion is stuck.

client repeatedly says "I can't take it" or "It's too overwhelming"), regulate it better (e.g., when a certain emotion is experienced, the client consistently and automatically experiences high arousal, and often transitions between low and high arousal are abrupt), or accept it better (the client repeatedly rejects the felt emotion—"I don't want to be angry" or "I hate being in this state"). In addition, emotional awareness does not develop (i.e., the emotion does not differentiate into more complex feelings or meanings or into a sequence of other feelings and meanings) when a maladaptive emotion is stuck. Table 4.1 summarizes the markers of productive and unproductive emotions.

PRINCIPLES OF EMOTION-FOCUSED THERAPY FOR DEPRESSION

EFT relies on four major empirically supported principles for enhancing emotion processing. The principles are embedded within an overarching framework that emphasizes emotional and social support as important in the promotion of change and especially important in the treatment of depression. In therapy, emotional and social support is operationalized as the provision of a relationship characterized by attunement to affect, validation of experience, and empathic responsiveness. Outside therapy, it involves encouraging the acquisition of interpersonal emotional support characterized by listening, validating relationships and instrumental support when needed. Emotional support inside therapy is the foundation for the therapeutic effectiveness of the following four emotion processing principles: (a) increasing awareness of emotion, (b) enhancing emotion regulation, (c) reflecting on emotion, and (d) transforming emotion. These four principles act as a general guide for working with emotion. They are the foundation for the different goals of emotion-focused intervention and indicate how to work with different types of emotion at different times.

Emotion Awareness

The first and most general goal in EFT for depression is to promote emotional awareness. Clients' ability to articulate what they are experiencing in their inner world is a central focus of EFT for depression. The therapist works with clients to help them approach, tolerate, and regulate, as well as transform, their emotions. Acceptance of emotional experience, as opposed to avoidance, is the first step in awareness work. Emotional awareness appears crucial to emotional development. To the extent that clients attend more to internal and external emotion cues, the cognitive processing of this information will contribute to problem solving and development. Attention to an emotional experience necessarily precedes and facilitates the description of that experience using language or other representational modes. This in turn contributes to the further elaboration and refinement of the schemata used for processing emotional information in the future. Levitt, Brown, Orsillo, and Barlow (in press) recently showed that acceptance of emotion leads to quicker recovery than its suppression.

Awareness involves a form of dual processing consisting of both detachment from and actual experiencing of current experience—a form of experiencing the experience. Awareness thus involves both the detachment of mindfulness and a type of jumping into the stream of experience so that one is both observing and touching the ongoing experience simultaneously.

With clients who are overregulated, intervention should guide them to both be mindful of their experience and to fully feel their visceral emotion in a progressive way all at the same time. Overregulators find it tempting to remain mindful of their experience without fully experiencing it. At a certain point, they have to stop simply observing and jump in to acquaint themselves with their experience. Therapists need to help these clients both observe and experience what they are doing, and each of these aspects of awareness may be useful at different times or for different clients.

For underregulators of emotion, who are consistently flooded by more than they can handle, therapy needs to concentrate on helping them develop coping skills or learn to better use the ones they have, so the more detached form of awareness promoted by mindfulness is helpful. Therapists should keep in mind that clients with borderline disorders do not have internal capacities to self-soothe; helping fragile clients self-soothe will be discussed more fully in the Emotion Regulation section that follows.

The goal in the treatment of depression is for clients to become aware of their primary emotions and eventually to access primary adaptive emotions. In depression, these adaptive emotions generally are anger at violation or unfairness and sadness at loss. Primary adaptive emotions also include the more pleasurable states of joy, compassion, and calm. Core shame and worthlessness and deep anxiety and insecurity, the dreaded states that clients generally seek to avoid, often block access to adaptive states, and helping clients acknowledge these feelings and process them is a major task of EFT.

Increased emotional awareness helps undo depression in a variety of ways. Becoming aware of and symbolizing emotional experience in words provides access to both the adaptive information and the action tendency in the emotion. Awareness helps people make sense of their experience and promotes their ability to assimilate this experience into their ongoing self-narratives. Emotional awareness is not *thinking* about the feeling; it involves *feeling* the feeling in awareness. Only when emotion is fully felt does its articulation in language become an important component of its awareness. A further related benefit of symbolization in awareness, as suggested by Rimé, Finkenauer, Luminet, Zech, and Philippot (1998), is that it allows for emotional sharing. They found that the subjects in their sample shared most emotional experiences with others, and they suggested that this sharing promotes access to social support, contributes to the construction and consolidation of memories of important self-relevant events, and enhances the processing and completion of emotional memories.

Once the client has accepted a core emotion, rather than avoided it, the therapist then helps the client use or transform the emotion. The client learns how to accept and use the adaptive emotions they become aware of to improve coping. The therapist helps clients to make sense of what their emotion is telling them and to identify the goal, need, or concern the emotion is organizing them to attain. Adaptive emotion is used both to inform and to move. Maladaptive emotion, on the other hand, is acknowledged to make it accessible to new input.

As the client progresses in therapy, the goal is to move to higher levels of emotional awareness. Levels of emotional awareness (LEAS), a tool developed by Lane and associates (Lane, Quinlan, Schwartz, Walker, & Zeitlin, 1990; Lane & Schwartz, 1992), measures five levels of emotional awareness: physical sensations, action tendencies, single emotions, blends of emotion, and blends of blends of emotional experience (i.e., the capacity to appreciate complexity in the experiences of self and other). Lane and Schwartz (1992) discussed emotional understanding in psychotherapy as a developmental process that begins when clients enter therapy with simplistic understandings of emotions. Most commonly, a client will report "just feeling bad" or "feeling it in my stomach." In the initial sessions, therapists need to work to increase clients' awareness of bodily sensations, comfort with these sensations, and flexibility in responding to these sensations. Body awareness in psychotherapy has taken a number of forms, including mindfulness training (Kabat-Zinn, 1990; Linehan, 1993; Orsillo, Roemer, & Barlow, in press; Segal, Williams, & Teasdale, 2002), focusing (Gendlin, 1996), and progressive muscle relaxation (D. A. Bernstein, Borkovec, & Hazlett-Stevens, 2000).

The fundamental processes involved in the cognitive elaboration of emotion addressed by LEAS are the dynamic interactions between becoming aware of phenomenal experience, establishing a representation of it, elaborating that representation (e.g., identifying the source of the emotional response), and integrating it with other emotions and cognitive processes. LEAS scores have been found to correlate significantly with self-restraint and impulse control (Barrett, Lane, Sechrest, & Schwartz, 2000). This finding, replicated in independent samples, indicates that greater emotional awareness is associated with greater self-reported impulse control. High LEAS scores have also been associated with better recognition of emotion in others in both purely verbal and purely nonverbal tasks (Lane et al., 1996; Lane, Shapiro, Sechrest, & Riedel, 1998).

Salovey, Mayer, Goldman, Turvey, and Palfai (1995) found that individual differences in emotional awareness predicted recovery of positive mood and decrements in ruminative thoughts following a distressing stimulus. Individuals who reported that they were "usually very clear about their feelings" were more likely to recover a positive mood after a distressing event, even after controlling for depression, neuroticism, adjustment, and mood. Furthermore, after a distressing event individuals who reported being very clear about their feelings experienced a significant decline in ruminative thought over time compared with those who were typically unclear about their feelings.

Emotional arousal and the promotion of emotional processing (Foa & Kozak, 1986; Greenberg & Safran, 1984, 1987) are important aspects of the emotion awareness process. Emotional processing has been measured as either increased or decreased emotional responding resulting from exposure to both a fear state and to information inconsistent with the activated cognitive–affective fear structure (Foa & Kozak, 1986). A long line of evidence on the effectiveness of exposure to previously avoided feelings of fear supports its use in dealing with trauma and other anxiety-based disorders (Foa & Jaycox, 1999). Habituation helps clients overcome their avoidance and approach what they had fearfully avoided. By facing dreaded feelings and finding that they survive, clients increase their sense of control and become more able to acknowledge painful emotions (Daldrup, Engle, Holiman, & Beutler, 1994; Greenberg & Bolger, 2001; Williams, Stiles, & Shapiro, 1999).

Emotional processing in our view, however, involves more than exposure alone. It involves a set of steps of cognitive–affective processing that has long been defined in experiential therapy as the *deepening of experience* (Klein, Mathieu-Coughlan, & Kiesler, 1986). In this process, first clients must approach bodily felt feeling by attending to the emotional experience. Then they must allow and tolerate being in live contact with their emotions. These two stages are somewhat consistent with the more behavioral notions of exposure. From the experiential perspective, however, approach, arousal, and tolerance of emotional experience are necessary but not sufficient. Optimum emotional processing involves the integration of cognition and affect (Greenberg, 2002; Greenberg & Pascual-Leone, 1995; Greenberg & Safran, 1987).

Once they achieve contact with their emotional experience, clients must also cognitively orient to that experience as information and then explore and make sense of it (Pos, Greenberg, Goldman, & Korman, 2003). This process includes exploring beliefs relating to experienced emotion, giving voice to emotional experience, and identifying needs that can motivate change in personal meanings and beliefs. If such exploration occurs, new emotional reactions and new meanings potentially emerge, which then subsequently may be integrated into and change existing cognitive–affective meaning structures (Greenberg & Safran, 1987). Emotional processing thus involves overcoming avoidance, approaching awareness, tolerating arousal of emotion, exploring and reflecting on emotion, and creating new meaning. This processing has been shown to predict outcome in psychotherapy for depression (Castonguay, Goldfried, Wiser, Raue, & Hayes, 1996; Goldman & Greenberg, in press; Pos et al., 2003).

Emotion awareness and experience need to be promoted, then, as a baseline skill in the treatment of depression. With emotionally overcontrolled or constricted clients, the therapist can encourage a persistent focus on the client's here-and-now, moment-by-moment reactions to what is being talked about to help him or her develop this skill. Therapists need to encourage clients to become aware of their feelings, their bodily sensations, and their current emotion. Here-and-now awareness of bodily felt feelings can lead to awareness of other feelings that were not in the client's immediate awareness. For clients with depression, this focus will lead to awareness of previously unacknowledged emotions of anger, sadness, fear, and shame. These emotions need not only to be aroused and tolerated, but also to be symbolized and explored, both for the useful information they provide and to identify whether they have any maladaptive aspects.

Emotional expression has recently been shown to be a unique aspect of emotional processing that predicts adjustment to breast cancer (Stanton et al., 2000). Women who coped with cancer through expressing emotion had fewer medical appointments, enhanced physical health and vigor, and decreased distress compared to those low in expression. Expressive coping was also related to increased quality of life for those who perceived their social environment to be highly receptive. Analyses suggested that expressive coping enhanced the pursuit of goals but that this was mediated by hope. Those who at study entry were higher in hope (i.e., who had a stronger sense of agency and ability to make plans to attain goals) had more success in coming to adaptive resolution of complex emotions through expressive coping than those with less hope. Expressive coping may help one attend to and clarify central concerns and may promote the pursuit of goals. Emotional arousal, awareness, and in some situations expression, therefore, appear to be therapeutic aspects of emotional processing when dealing with loss and fear involved in depression.

Becoming aware of feelings requires some very specific microprocesses involving elements of feeling that must be present in awareness for the client to be considered fully in touch with the experience of his or her emotion. These elements are the stimulus situation, the physiological arousal and sensation, the symbol or cognitive label, the mobilization of impulse or action tendency, and the need. Any or all of these elements may be missing from the client's awareness for reasons ranging from avoidance to lack of information. For example, a more histrionic client might report high levels of physiological arousal but be unable to cognitively symbolize the emotion she is experiencing. This block to cognitive clarity would be the target of therapeutic intervention. On the other hand, a narcissistic client who can declare what he is feeling and what he would like to do to the person who has offended him might be in a cold, detached state of avoidance of the visceral experience of his feeling. For this client, attending to the arousal and sensation would help him become aware of the emotion.

The assessment of what elements are missing guides the process of emotional awareness intervention in a systematic way. The goal is to help clients be aware of all five elements. The process of becoming consciously aware of emotional responses, in itself, has a physiological effect that is self-regulatory. Thus, allowing oneself to experience emotional distress and then attending to the emotion can lead to a process of change (Greenberg, 2002).

Emotion Regulation

The second principle of emotional processing involves the regulation of emotion. *Emotion regulation* refers to the processes by which people influence which emotions they have, when they have them, and, most importantly, how they experience and express these emotions. The self-regulation of emotion is usually defined in terms of the conscious regulation of emotion and the set of control processes by which people voluntarily control when, where, and how they experience their emotions. Cicchetti, Ackerman, and Izard (1995) stressed that a central component of emotion regulation is the "intercoordination of the emotions and cognitive systems" (p. 4). Cognition about emotion is an essential aspect of the conscious regulation of emotion. For example, reappraisal has been found to help regulate emotion better than suppression (Gross, 2002). Thus, the creation of new meaning can help one gain a greater sense of control or view things in a new way, and this helps regulate emotion. Emotional regulation also describes the ability of the cognitive system to gain information from the emotion system (Cicchetti et al., 1995).

As noted in chapter 2, LeDoux (1996), Damasio (1994), and Davidson (2000a) showed that the prefrontal cortex is connected to and can influence the amygdala. But the emphasis on changing the way we feel by consciously changing the way we think is a result of the current dominance of cognitive views in psychology. As we have said, evidence from affective neuroscience indicates that there are both implicit (right hemispheric) and explicit (left hemispheric) affect regulation (Schore, 2003) and that in more fragile clients, a deficit in the more implicit forms of the regulation of emotional intensity is the problem. Essential affective self-regulatory processes occur largely at levels below conscious awareness, probably in the orbitofrontal cortex, which takes over amygdala and lower-level right hemispheric functioning in more complex processing (Derryberry & Tucker, 1992; Joseph, 1996; Rolls, 1996a, 1996b). Implicit affect regulation that occurs through right hemispheric processes is not verbally mediated and is most directly affected by relational and emotional communication through facial expression, vocal quality, and eye contact.

Rather than adopting a conventional two-factor view of emotion regulation, in which one system is seen as generating emotion and another system as subsequently regulating emotion, we see emotion regulation as an integral aspect of the generation of emotion and coterminus with it (Campos, Frankel, & Camras, 2004). Regulation, therefore, is not easily achieved through the cognitive system alone. Helping clients find ways consciously or purposively to cope with their emotions, however, often is a first therapeutic step for clients who are highly distressed.

Important questions in the treatment of depression are what emotions are to be regulated and how. Emotions that require regulation in depression generally include secondary emotions such as despair and hopelessness and primary maladaptive emotions such as the shame or anxiety of basic insecurity or panic. Overwhelming grief or hair-trigger anger also may need to be regulated. The ability to down-regulate emotional arousal is clearly important to be able to work effectively in a job. In addition, the ability to contain one's anger or grief, especially in a public setting, is an important aspect of emotion regulation, as is the ability to calm one's anxieties and modulate one's shame.

Emotion regulation in depression involves not only the restraint of certain emotions, but also the maintenance and enhancement of other emotions; up-regulation also can be helpful. Accentuating pleasant experience and accessing suppressed, unpleasant, or negative emotional experience are important in therapy. For example, a depressed client who is feeling numb may learn that listening to a sad piece of music will help activate sad feelings, allowing him or her to become unstuck. In addition, the ability to communicate negative emotions to others to work through these emotions is often helpful in alleviating depression.

In depression, two of the most important regulation skills clients can develop are the more explicit procedure of taking an observer's stance to get a working distance from overwhelming despair and hopelessness and the development of more implicit self-soothing capacities to calm and comfort core anxieties and humiliation and regulate general level of arousal. In depression, the secondary experience of dread and hopelessness from ruminating about failures or emotional injuries often initially needs regulation. Rather than dwelling on these experiences, the client needs to be able to access positive experience and interpersonal or intrapersonal support.

Soothing comes interpersonally in the form of empathic attunement and responsiveness to affect and through acceptance and validation by another person. Being able to soothe the self develops initially by internalization of the soothing functions of the protective other (Stern, 1985, 1995). Clients with underregulated affect also have been shown to benefit both from validation and from learning emotion regulation and distress tolerance skills (Linehan, 1993). The provision of a safe, validating, supportive, and empathic environment helps soothe automatically generated underregulated distress (Bohart & Greenberg, 1997), helps clients internalize the soothing of the therapist, and strengthens the self of clients with depression. Emotion regulation skills useful in treating depression involve such things as mindfully identifying and labeling emotions; establishing a working distance from hopelessness or worthlessness; increasing positive emotions such as joy or hope; reducing vulnerability to overwhelming fear, shame, and hopelessness; and learning techniques for self-soothing, breathing, and avoiding distraction from rumination.

Forms of meditative practice and self-acceptance often are helpful in achieving a working distance from the overwhelming core maladaptive emotions of shame and vulnerability. The ability to regulate breathing and to observe emotions and let them come and go are important processes to help regulate many types of emotional distress. Mindfulness treatments have been shown to be effective in treating generalized anxiety disorders and panic (Kabat-Zinn et al., 1992), chronic pain (Kabat-Zinn, Lipworth, & Burney, 1985), and prevention of relapse in depression (Teasdale et al., 2000). In addition, it is helpful to guide disregulated clients to be mindful of what is going on outside of their immediate internal emotional experience by redirecting their attention to the external environment. Being aware of their body in contact with the chair, the look on the therapist's face, or the light coming in through the window helps them become more present and less disregulated.

Physiological soothing involves activation of the parasympathetic nervous system to regulate heart rate, breathing, and other sympathetic functions that speed up under stress. At the more deliberate levels, promoting clients' abilities to receive and be compassionate about their emerging painful emotional experience helps them tolerate emotion and self-soothe. In this process, clients also can use their higher brain centers to consciously recognize the depressogenic messages sent from the lower level and then act to calm the activation by using coping self-talk and other conscious strategies for self-calming.

Skills for deliberate emotion regulation relevant to depression and the attendant anxiety can be promoted through psychoeducation. Teaching clients that hopelessness is often secondary to a more core feeling that needs to be acknowledged and that depression and anxiety often arise because of avoidance of a core emotion prepares them to face the core emotion. Therapists can teach clients that it is important to label emotions for their informational value to better understand the motivational information involved in emotions. Lists of emotions and their corresponding motivational information and other aids can help clients learn to identify, label, and differentiate various primary emotional experiences. Clients also can be encouraged to write narratively about their depressive experiences and to record emotions, physical symptoms, thoughts, and behaviors involved in these episodes.

For highly fragile personality-disordered clients, such as those with borderline disorders, building implicit or automatic emotion regulation capacities over time is important. Directly experiencing aroused affect being soothed by relational or nonverbal means—a more right hemispheric process (Schore, 2003)—is one of the best ways to build the internal capacity for self-soothing. Although the primary therapeutic goal for fragile clients is to be able to automatically regulate the intensity of their affective arousal so it does not become overwhelming, initially deliberate behavioral and cognitive forms of regulation—a more left hemispheric process—are useful for clients who feel out of control. Thus, taking a warm bath to calm down (sensory regulation) or learning to distract or take a time out when angry (cognitive–behavioral regulation) can improve coping.

Depressed clients with personality disorders and borderline functioning most of all need to develop their automatic affect-regulation abilities to be able to calm their overwhelming anxiety and the intensity of their feelings. Development of these abilities comes primarily through a good emotional bond with a responsive therapist. The therapist and client dyadically regulate affective arousal by successfully negotiating state transitions. The process of re-experiencing positive affect following negative experience helps the client learn that negative affect can be endured and transformed.

In depression, amygdala-based emotional arousal of threat, loss, and humiliation needs to be approached, allowed, and accepted rather than avoided or controlled. It appears that acknowledging, allowing, and tolerating emotion are an important aspect of helping to regulate it and help clients develop compassion or empathy for themselves. Individuals can provide this soothing of emotion to themselves reflexively through internal agency (e.g., through diaphragmatic breathing, relaxation, development of self-empathy and compassion, self-talk), or another person may provide it. Often, however, a relationship with an attuned other is essential in developing affect regulation.

Reflecting on Emotion

What people make of their emotional experience makes them who they are. In addition to the informational value of emotion awareness, symbolizing emotion in awareness promotes reflection on experience to create new meaning, and this helps people develop new narratives to explain their experience (Greenberg & Pascual-Leone, 1995; Guidano, 1995a, 1995b; Pennebaker, 1990; Watson & Greenberg, 1996; Whelton & Greenberg, 2001). For example, symbolizing traumatic emotion memories in words helps promote their assimilation into a client's ongoing self-narrative (Van der Kolk, 1994). Putting emotion into words thus allows previously unsymbolized experience in emotion memory to be assimilated into people's conscious, conceptual understandings of self and world where it can be organized into a coherent story. Pennebaker and colleagues showed the positive effects of writing about emotional experience on autonomic nervous system activity, immune functioning, and physical and emotional health (e.g., Pennebaker, 1990, 1995). Pennebaker (1995) concluded that through language, individuals are able to organize, structure, and ultimately assimilate both their emotional experiences and the events that provoked the emotions. In addition, once they put emotions into words, people are able to reflect on what they are feeling, create new meanings, and evaluate their own emotional experience.

Within the field of consciousness research, a distinction is made between phenomenal and reflective awareness. *Phenomenal awareness* refers to the actual content of consciousness (focal attention to feelings and background feelings), whereas *reflective awareness* involves attending to or performing a cognitive operation on the contents of conscious experience (Farthing, 1992). Reflective awareness, or *metacognition*, requires the creation of a representation of experience, and this representation will affect how future emotional information is interpreted and experienced. Reflective awareness is a fundamental skill required for successful psychotherapy and is a key goal of treatment.

Both insight and reframing of emotional experience have long been viewed as ways to change emotion. We present it as an important, but not the only, or even the major, way to achieve emotional change. J. Frank (1963) did much valuable work in his search for common factors in different theories of psychotherapy, basing his work around the concept that every person has his or her own unique "assumptive world" consisting of the current totality of experience, both conscious and unconscious. This concept highlighted the role of meaning frameworks in the determination of experience. The role in psychotherapy of people's capacity for conscious awareness of the processes and contents of their own mind and for reason and insight to shed light on unconscious motivations has been substantial, from the beginnings of psychoanalysis right up to the present day. Although the subject matters of Freud's (1915/1957, 1923/1961) theory and technique of psychoanalysis were unconscious motivations and repressed affect, the methods through which these were addressed were highly cognitive and interpretative. The express aim was to have the client achieve conscious insight into the roots of his or her psychic disturbance.

Insight was one of the first processes of change in psychotherapy ever proposed. Awareness and insight are often conflated, but they differ in important ways. Becoming aware of an emotion, such as when acknowledging an experience of feeling angry or sad in a bodily felt way or symbolizing the sounds and smells of a highly charged emotional event from the past, differs significantly from reflexively making meaning or narrating an experience. The latter involves explanation, which is more than symbolization. Thus, the narrative that a client forms of why a relationship ended is very different from the actual experience of the loss of the relationship. Once the client recognizes that he or she is sad about a loss, the way he or she explains the loss is very important and will greatly influence his or her emotional state. An explanation involving rejection because of personal failings will lead to shame. An explanation involving a mutual lack of compatibility, on the other hand, will provoke feelings only of loss.

Similarly, acknowledging anger at not getting what one wants in a relationship is one step in an emotional change process. Understanding this anger or explaining it as a function of the other's inability to live up to one's high standards will lead to one reaction, whereas explaining it as one's own overly high need to be appreciated will have very different experiential and relational impacts. Thus, how the client understands his or her emotions conceptually and the story in which these emotions are embedded influence what the emotions come to mean to the client. There is a vast empirical literature on the influence of attributions and cognition in general on emotion and on depression (Abramson, Seligman, & Teasdale, 1978; D. D. Clarke & Blake, 1997), and these all attest to the importance of reflecting on emotion. Many therapists have written on the importance of changing clients' assumptive frameworks in therapy (Beck, 1983; J. Frank, 1963; Frankl, 1959).

Basic to this view is that the self is represented in memory as a dynamic and complex system of cognitive structures (self-schemata). These are constructed through interaction with the environment, and they function out of conscious awareness to organize and process self-relevant information, generate meaning, and serve as the interpretive framework that links individual emotional and behavioral responses with events in the external world. Self-schemata influence one's perception of, interpretation of, and response to social information (Bargh, 1982); regulate behavior and mood; and influence the processes by which people make judgments about self and others (Markus & Wurf, 1987). Research also indicates that individuals high in self-complexity (i.e., with many diverse and clearly articulated self-conceptions) show less resistance to feedback that challenges the established self-view and less emotional reactivity to stressful life events than low-complexity individuals (Linville, 1985, 1987). Stein and Markus (1994, 1996) maintained that self-conceptions play a crucial role in promoting or hindering the process of adaptation and argued that it is the way in which self-schemata are organized that allows for flexibility and adaptiveness in emotional and behavioral responding.

The self is strongly implicated in the development of depression. Beck (1996) argued that change in depressive affect requires interventions that focus primarily on the negative content (e.g., images, thoughts) of self-schemata. Blatt (1974, 2004), on the other hand, proposed that self-reflectivity, the capacity to tolerate and integrate affective experiences, and a sense of agency are critical in the development of one's sense of self. He suggested that distortions in all three aspects of the self are integral to the experiences of dependency and self-criticalness of people with depression and that both types of experiences must be attended to in the treatment of depression.

In a similar vein, experiential and constructivist psychotherapies maintain that depression is the function of one's inability or failure to process and make sense of internal experience (Greenberg, Watson, & Lietaer, 1998; Guidano, 1995a, 1995b; Neimeyer & Mahoney, 1995; Rogers, 1959; Toukmanian, 1992). They contend that change in self-conceptions entails schematic transformations that emerge from the act of reflecting on and restructuring self-relevant information, rather than from change in schematic content alone (Guidano, 1991, 1995a, 1995b; Mahoney, 1991, 1995; Neimeyer & Mahoney, 1995; Toukmanian, 1990, 1992). Clients come to therapy with locked-in, rigid self-perceptions that constrain the generation of alternative perspectives for adaptive responding. Because change occurs at the level of clients' inferential or meaning-making processes, therapy must help clients learn to engage in more flexible and productive modes of processing so that habitual forms of experiential constructions can be modified (Toukmanian, 1992, 1996). This process creates a means by which self-schemata are further differentiated and reorganized, leading to the creation of new meanings, a fuller and more differentiated sense of the *I* and *me*, greater flexibility in construals of self and self in relation to others, and increased adaptiveness in everyday functioning (Guidano, 1991).

Transforming Emotion

The final principle of emotional processing involves the transformation of one emotion by accessing another. This principle is used to help transform core maladaptive emotions. Although emotions can be transformed by the more traditional means of experiencing and expressing them to completion (habituation) or through reflecting on them to gain new understanding (insight or reframing), we have found another process to be more important: the process of *one emotion changing into another emotion*. This novel principle suggests that a maladaptive emotional state can be transformed best by undoing it with another more adaptive emotional state. The coactivation of the more adaptive emotion along with or in response to the maladaptive emotion helps transform the maladaptive emotion. This principle suggests that clients can undo their maladaptive depressive emotional state, such as fear-based insecurity or shame-based worthlessness, by accessing other, more adaptive emotions, such as anger or sadness. It also suggests that developing the ability to link negative and positive emotional states and to make transitions between these emotions is an important part of therapeutic change. As different states are coactivated over time, the more adaptive emotion, together with its attendant needs, action tendencies, and meanings, fuses with the maladaptive emotional state and helps transform it.

Spinoza (1675/1967) was the first to note that emotion is needed to change emotion. He proposed that "an emotion cannot be restrained nor removed unless by an opposed and stronger emotion" (p. 195). Reason clearly is seldom sufficient to change automatic emergency-based emotional responses. Darwin (1897/1998), on jumping back from the strike of a glassed-in snake, noted that he had approached it with the determination not to start back, but that his will and reason were powerless against the imagination of a danger that he had never even experienced. Rather than reason with emotion, one needs to replace one emotion with another. As Shakespeare observed, "one fire burns out another's burning; one pain is lessen'd by another's anguish" (*Romeo & Juliet*, Act 1, Scene 2). Guidano (1991) similarly noted that "while thinking usually changes thoughts, only feeling can change emotions" (p. 61).

Different types of empirical evidence support this principle of transforming emotion by replacing a problematic emotion with competing emotional responses. Parrott and Sabini (1990) reported evidence of mood-incongruent recall as a form of mood regulation. They found that mood repair occurs when people recall events that counteract both sad and happy moods and that this process occurs without awareness. In a further interesting line of investigation, positive emotions have been found to undo lingering negative emotions (Fredrickson, 2001; Fredrickson & Levenson, 1998). The basic observation is that key components of positive emotions are incompatible with negative emotions. Fredrickson (2001) suggested that by broadening a client's momentary thought–action repertoire, a positive emotion may loosen the hold that a negative emotion has on his or her mind. The experiences of joy and contentment were found to produce faster cardiovascular recovery from negative emotions than a neutral experience. These results suggest that positive emotions fuel psychological resilience. A further study by Tugade and Fredrickson (2000) found that resilient individuals cope by recruiting positive emotions to regulate negative emotional experiences. They found that these individuals manifested a physiological bounce back that helped them to return to cardiovascular baseline more quickly.

In a study of dealing with self-criticism, Whelton and Greenberg (in press) found that people who were more vulnerable to depression showed more self-contempt but also less resilience in response to self-criticism than people less vulnerable to depression. The less vulnerable people were able to recruit positive emotional resources like pride and anger to combat the depressogenic contempt and negative cognitions. In other words, resilient people, after a distressing experience, appear to generate a positive feeling, often through imagery or memory, to soothe themselves, and they can combat negative feelings and views of self in this more resilient state. Accessing a positive emotional state therefore helps them counteract the effect of a negative emotional state. These studies together indicate that emotion can be used to change emotion and that positive affect does regulate negative feelings.

Davidson (2000a, 2000b) suggested that the right hemispheric, withdrawal-related negative affect system can be transformed by activation of the approach system in the left prefrontal cortex. He defined *resilience* as the maintenance of high levels of positive affect and well-being in the face of adversity, and he emphasized that it is not that resilient people do not feel negative affect; what characterizes resilience is that the negative affect does not persist. Levenson (1992) reviewed research that indicates that specific emotions are associated with specific patterns of autonomic nervous system activity, providing evidence that different emotions change one's physiology differentially. Emotion also has been shown to be differentially transformed by people's differing capacity to self-generate imagery to replace unwanted, automatically generated emotions with more desirable imagery scripts (Derryberry & Reed, 1996), suggesting the importance of individual differences in this domain.

Bad feelings thus appear to be able to be replaced by happy feelings, not in a simple manner (i.e., by trying to "look on the bright side"), but by the evocation of meaningfully embodied alternate experience to undo the negative feeling. For example, in grief, laughter has been found to be a predictor of recovery; being able to remember the happy times and to experience joy help provide an antidote to sadness (Bonanno & Keltner, 1997). Warmth and affection, similarly, often are an antidote to anxiety. In depression, a protest-filled, submissive sense of worthlessness can be transformed therapeutically by guiding clients to the desire that drives their protest—a desire to be free of their cages and to access their feelings of joy and excitement for life. Isen (1999) hypothesized that at least some of the positive effect of happy feelings depends on the effects of the neurotransmitters involved in the emotion of joy on the specific parts of the brain that influence purposive thinking; Isen cited the growing evidence that positive affect enhances flexibility, problem solving, and sociability.

Fredrickson (2001) also demonstrated how positive emotions serve to broaden and build strategies that enhance problem solving. Positive emotions such as joy, interest, pride, and love broaden people's momentary thought–action repertoires, which in turn serves to build their enduring resources to cope with life. In addition, research on mood-congruent judgment has shown that moods affect thinking (Mayer & Hanson, 1995). Good moods lead to optimism; bad moods, to pessimism. Shifts in mood lead to shifts in thinking and have clearly been shown to lead to different kinds of reasoning (Palfai & Salovey, 1993).

In a different line of research on the effect of motor expression on experience, Berkowitz (2000) reported a study on the effect of muscular action on mood. Subjects who had talked about an angering incident while making a tightly clenched first reported having stronger angry feelings, whereas fist clenching led to a reduction in sadness when talking about a saddening incident. This indicates that motor expression may intensify congruent emotions but dampen other emotions. Thus, it appears that even the muscular expressions of one emotion can change another emotion. In addition, in line with the James–Lange theory (James, 1890), Flack, Laird, and Cavallaro (1999b) demonstrated that adopting the facial, postural, and vocal expressions of an emotion increased the experience of the emotion, whether or not subjects are aware of what emotion they are expressing. The experience of an emotion to some degree can thus be induced or intensified by putting one's body into its expression. It is interesting to note that there are individual differences in this capacity, with those who are more body sensitive showing this tendency to a greater degree.

A more general line of research in social psychology on the effects of role-playing on attitude change also supports the idea that performing actions in a role brings people's experience and attitudes in line with the role (Zimbardo, Ebbesen, & Malasch, 1997). Thus, role-playing can transform what is at first not real into something real, just as saying something can lead to believing it (Myers, 1996). Thus, a possible way to evoke another emotion is to have clients role-play its expression. As they express an emotion, it will change their experience toward the expression.

In psychotherapy research, music has been found to be helpful in evoking alternate emotions and to be even more helpful than imagery for changing emotion (Kerr, Walsh, & Marshall, 2001). Right frontal electroencephalogram (EEG) activation normally associated with sad affect was shifted toward symmetry by both massage and music (Field, 1998; Jones, Field, Fox, Davalos, & Gomez, 2001). Shifts to more positive mood, or at least to symmetry between sad and happy affect, were accompanied by shifts from right to left frontal EEG activation in both mothers and children (Fields, 1998).

In a final line of research on emotional expression in EFT for depression (Greenberg & Watson, 1998), we found clinically interesting patterns of change in emotions. Korman (1998) demonstrated that good- and poor-outcome cases were discriminated by the degree that emotions changed over therapy. Intensive analyses of small samples of clients in this treatment for depression revealed how emotions changed. The results of our single-case investigations combined with the larger group studies relating emotional arousal and change to outcome (Korman, 1998; Warwar & Greenberg, 2000) indicated that emotional arousal in midtreatment predicted outcome and that the decrease of one emotion plus the increase of another emotion occurred to a significantly greater extent in good- than in poor-outcome cases. In a number of the good outcomes, reduction of shame and fear were found with increases in sadness and anger.

In the intensive analysis of one random sample of 4 good- and 4 poor-outcome clients from the larger pool of 34 clients with depression, expression of fear in therapy sessions on the core theme of view of self were reduced over therapy in all four of the good-outcome cases (Avagyan, 2001); there was no comparable change in the poor-outcome cases. The emotions that replaced fear differed by case. For example, in one good-outcome case, fear of failure was replaced by anger at midtreatment; in another, fear of rejection was replaced with sadness in the late phase. In the given therapeutic context, anger and sadness were judged as more adaptive than fear. In contrasting poor-outcome cases, fears of failure or rejection remained throughout and were never replaced or reorganized by the emergence of other emotions.

In another small sample, other patterns of replacing emotion with emotion appeared (Florence, 2001). For example, in one case, the three most dominant emotions expressed in the early phase (in relation to all emotions in that phase) were fear/anxiety (28%), shame/guilt (28%), and hopeless/helpless (17%). Dominant emotions in the middle phase were sadness (43%), pain/hurt (29%), and anger/resentment (10%). In the late phase, fear/anxiety (16%), pain/hurt (13%), joy/excitement (13%), and contentment/calm/relief (13%) were the most dominant emotions. In other cases, a dominant emotion of shame in the early phase was replaced with anger or joy in later phases, and in others dominant emotions of fear or sadness were replaced with anger. In the poor-outcome cases, this transformation of frequency of experienced emotion and the replacement of one emotion by another was not readily traceable. The overall lower level of emotional arousal achieved in poor-outcome cases was also noticeable. It appears that lack of arousal precluded emotional processing, and this seemed to leave client and therapist stuck in the early problematic feeling states.

Another set of single-case studies on clients from this population of clients with depression investigated the process of assimilating unwanted experience into awareness (Honos-Webb, Stiles, Greenberg, & Goldman, 1998; Honos-Webb, Surko, Stiles, & Greenberg, 1999). These studies showed that change in therapy occurred by replacing a dominant maladaptive voice in the personality that was warding off emotional experience with a more emotionally adaptive voice that allowed the emotion to be assimilated. Notable in these studies were the idiosyncratic patterns of emotional transformation; which emotions replaced which were unique to each client.

This principle of changing emotion with emotion goes beyond ideas of catharsis or exposure and habituation, in that the maladaptive feeling is not purged or simply attenuated. Rather, another feeling is used to transform or undo it. In these instances, emotional change occurs by activating incompatible, more adaptive experience to replace or transform the old responses. Clinical observation and research suggest that emotional transformation occurs by a process of dialectical synthesis of opposing schemes. When opposing schemes are coactivated, they synthesize compatible elements from the coactivated schemes to form new higher-level schemes, just as in development, when schemes for standing and falling in a toddler are dynamically synthesized into a higher-level scheme for walking (Greenberg & Pascual-Leone, 1995; J. Pascual-Leone, 1991). Thus, in therapy, maladaptive fear once aroused can be transformed by the more boundary-establishing emotions of adaptive anger or disgust or by the softer feelings of compassion or forgiveness. Similarly, maladaptive anger can be undone by adaptive sadness. Maladaptive shame can be replaced by accessing anger at violation, self-comforting feelings, and pride and self-worth. Thus, the tendency to shrink into the ground in shame is replaced by a thrusting-forward tendency in newly accessed anger at violation. Withdrawal emotions from one side of the brain are replaced with approach emotions from another part of the brain, or vice versa (Davidson, 2000a, 2000b). Once the alternate emotion has been accessed, it fuses with the original state, transforming it over time.

WHEN TO FOCUS ON EMOTION AND WHEN TO REGULATE

Another important aspect of emotion regulation is learning when to introspectively deepen attention to one's emotional experience and when this may be counterproductive. Clients who are depressed can be either over- or underregulated. The goal in sessions with different clients and at different moments clearly differs. Criteria for when to focus on, go into, deepen, and explore emotion and when to regulate emotion are important. It is helpful to think about an intensity–clarity continuum and to work with clients to help them identify a point at which emotion gets to be too disorganizing, overwhelming, and confusing, at which point it needs to be regulated. It is useful to focus on and explore emotion, but when the client reaches the point of disregulation (e.g., shows signs of dissociating, becomes numb, has anxiety tingling down the arms, starts to blank out), the amygdala is hijacking thinking and problem solving, and the client would benefit from regulation.

The first and foremost criterion for facilitating more emotion is a relational bond sufficient to contain the emotion that will be facilitated and agreement and collaboration to explore emotion. The therapist needs to assess the client's capacity to tolerate anxiety and feelings and the kind of avoidance and interruptive processes he or she uses. The main tasks of treatment should be consistent with what the therapist understands to be the client's emotional capacity. Because standard diagnostic systems such as the

Diagnostic and Statistical Manual of Mental Disorders do not assess emotional capacity, they are not useful in this regard. Two people can have similar clusters of symptoms on Axis I and Axis II but have quite different emotional capacities.

In general, avoidance of emotion is an indicator for increasing emotion awareness. When clients are obviously feeling something and interrupting it or when they avoid by intellectualizing or deflecting and distracting, it is potentially therapeutic to help them approach their emotions. Clients who become hopeless when they avoid sadness or anger benefit from greater emotional awareness and better access to their own emotion-based action tendencies. Facing the feelings stored in emotion memory and putting the emotions into words can help clients who need to reprocess traumatic experience. Therapists should help clients feel feelings directly when the alliance is high and the avoidance is low. When avoidance is moderate to high and the client becomes tense (e.g., striated muscles, interrupted expression), work needs to focus more on awareness of avoidance and interruptive processes than on the emotion itself. When clients become flat, somatize, or become slightly confused when they approach emotion, therapists need to use a form of graded approach to emotion to build the client's capacity to tolerate anxiety and feelings.

A counterindication to facilitating the evocation of emotion is that the therapeutic relationship cannot yet support it because the client lacks the perception of safety. Emotions should not be evoked until trust has been established and the therapist has sufficient knowledge of the client and his or her circumstances. The strongest counterindicator for increasing emotional arousal is that the client becomes overwhelmed by emotion and becomes disorganized. When clients are extremely fragile (e.g., cannot tolerate any emotion without starting to lose a sense of themselves or start projecting their feelings and thoughts onto others), they need regulating, soothing, and integrating processes to build structure and develop a capacity to tolerate first anxiety and later deeper emotions and feelings. A previous history of aggression or of being unable to cope also is a strong counterindicator for evoking anger or vulnerable feelings. Emotional arousal also is generally counterindicated for clients who engage in destructive coping. If they use substances to self-medicate, binge, or engage in self-harm to deal with distress, it is not advisable to activate distress until they have learned better coping skills.

5

THE COURSE OF TREATMENT IN EMOTION-FOCUSED THERAPY

Experience is knowledge, everything else is information.

—Anonymous

Emotion-focused therapy (EFT) can be seen as operating according to two overarching principles: facilitating a therapeutic relationship and promoting therapeutic work. These principles, which Greenberg, Rice, and Elliott (1993) initially laid out in an earlier manualized variant of EFT called *process experiential therapy*, operate throughout the different phases of therapy. Facilitating a therapeutic relationship works according to three subprinciples: empathic attunement, bonding, and task collaboration. The empathic attunement principle emphasizes the therapist's presence and moment-by-moment attunement to the client's shifting affective experience. The focus of this principle is the therapist's state and perceptual process; it is the client's affective experience that the therapist attends to and is in contact with. The bonding principle emphasizes the expression or communication of what is understood. The therapist throughout conveys empathy, acceptance, and genuineness. Task collaboration, the third relational principle, emphasizes moment-by-moment and overall collaboration on the goals and tasks of therapy.

Promoting therapeutic work also operates according to three subprinciples: differential experiential processing, growth and choice, and task completion. Differential experiential processing refers to the different modes of processing and different tasks that need to be promoted at different times to promote deeper experiencing in the client. At one time a therapist may promote an internal focus; at another, the active expression of a feeling; at another, making sense of emotion; and at yet another, interpersonal connection. The tasks of attending, experiential search, active expression, interpersonal contact, and self-reflection are just some of the different modes of processing that therapists might promote. In addition, different tasks are engaged in at different markers of different types of emotional processing problems. Thus, for example, when a client experiences unfinished business, the therapist suggests an empty-chair dialogue; at another time, when a client is not attending to a bodily felt sense, the therapist uses focusing.

Growth and choice, which privilege client self-determination, is the next work subprinciple. The therapist supports the client's potential and motivation for self-determination, mature interdependence, mastery, and self-development. Growth is promoted first through a process of listening carefully for the client's strengths and internal resources and helping the client to explore the growing edge of his or her experience and focus on possibilities. Encouraging the client to make in-session decisions about the goals, tasks, and activities of therapy and sharing control also facilitate choice and self-determination.

The final principle is task completion. This principle promotes thematic attention to completion of a task that has been initiated if it is consistent with the client's goals. When the task is experienced as contrary to the client's goals, the therapist resorts to following the moment-by-moment process to become more attuned with the client's goals. Adopting these principles leads to a style of following and guiding clients' moment-by-moment experience.

In the most general terms, therapy is built on a genuinely prizing empathic relationship and on the therapist being highly present with, respectful toward, and responsive to the client's experience. At the same time, therapists assume that it is useful to guide the client's emotional processing in different ways at different times. The optimal situation in this approach is an active collaboration between client and therapist, with each feeling neither led nor simply followed by the other. Instead, the ideal is an easy sense of coexploration. When disjunction or disagreement occurs, the client is viewed as the expert on his or her own experience, and the therapist always defers to the client's experience. Thus, therapist interventions are offered in a nonimposing, tentative manner as conjectures, perspectives, "experiments," or offers, rather than as expert pronouncements, lectures, or statements of truth.

The combination of relationship and task-oriented styles of intervening in EFT leads to a creative tension that makes it possible to combine the benefits of both styles while softening the disadvantages of each. The therapist constantly monitors the state of the therapeutic alliance and the current therapeutic tasks to judge the best balance of active stimulation with responsive attunement. The relationship always takes precedence over the pursuit of a task. Buber (1958) wrote that a compassionate human face, when unadorned by pretence, role, or assumption of superiority, offers more hope to another than the most sophisticated psychological techniques. Although the therapist may be an expert in the possible therapeutic steps that might be facilitative, the therapist must present himself or herself as a compassionate human being who is a facilitator of client experience. Meaning thus arises from a coconstructive process, rather than arrival at some therapist-predetermined reality.

Following these principles, we have come to view the therapist as an *emotion coach* (Greenberg, 2002). Coaching entails both acceptance and change (Linehan, 1993); the therapist promotes awareness and acceptance of emotional experience and coaches clients in finding new ways of processing emotion. Following provides acceptance, whereas guiding introduces novelty and the possibility of change. Guiding provides direction for exploration not by suggesting what content clients should focus on or by interpreting the meaning of their experience, but rather by guiding the type of processing in which they engage.

Coaching clients with depression to become aware of their emotions involves helping them verbally label emotions while they are being felt, helping them accept the emotion, and talking with clients about what it is like to experience an emotion. It also involves facilitating new ways of processing the emotion and guiding clients in ways of soothing or regulating the emotion. In addition, coaching clients who are depressed involves facilitating the use of adaptive emotions, usually anger and sadness, to guide action and transform maladaptive emotions, usually fear, shame, or anger. It is important to note that clients often cannot simply be taught new strategies conceptually for dealing with difficult emotions; rather, clients require experiential facilitation to engage in the new process, and only later does the therapist explicitly teach the client what to do. For example, accessing anger or a need or goal may be very helpful in overcoming the sense of depressive hopelessness or defeat. However, explicitly teaching clients that this is what they should do is not nearly as helpful as interpersonally facilitating this access by asking them, at the right time, in the right way, what it is they feel or need.

To guide the therapeutic relationship and work, we have developed a context-sensitive approach to case formulation to help promote the development of a focus for brief treatments. Case formulation relies on process diagnosis, development of a focus, and theme development, rather than on person or syndrome diagnosis. In a process-oriented approach to treatment, case formulation is an ongoing process, as sensitive to the moment and the in-session context as it is to an understanding of the person as a case. This responsiveness is required both to maintain a respectful relationship and to be consistent with the view that clients are active agents who are in flux and constantly creating meaning. Clients are dynamic, self-organizing systems entering different self-organizations at different times. The state the client is in at the moment and his or her current narrative are more determining of his or her experience and possibility than any conceptualization of a more enduring pattern or reified self-concept that may be constructed early in treatment. Therefore, in a process diagnostic approach, the therapist maintains a continual focus on the client's current state of mind and current cognitive–affective problem states. The therapist's main concern is to follow the client's process and to identify core pain and markers of current emotional concerns, rather than to formulate a picture of the client's enduring personality or character or a core pattern. A collaborative focus and a coherent theme develop from a focus on current experience and exploration of particular experiences to their edges, rather than on establishing patterns of experience and behavior across situations in the world.

PHASES OF EMOTION-FOCUSED THERAPY FOR DEPRESSION

EFT for depression comprises three major phases. The first phase, bonding and awareness, is followed by the middle phase of evocation and exploration. Finally, therapy concludes with a transformation phase that involves constructing alternatives through generating new emotions and reflecting to create new meaning. The phases and steps, described in detail in the paragraphs that follow, guide implementation of EFT's two major principles— facilitating the therapeutic relationship and promoting therapeutic work.

The first and foundational phase of the treatment, the bonding and awareness phase, has three main goals: to promote a trusting relational bond, to promote the client's emotional awareness, and to collaboratively establish an initial focus for treatment. Work on these goals continues throughout therapy. Once a safe working environment and an alliance to work on emotional awareness are established and an initial focus on aspects of experience that are generating the depression has been formed, the transition to the second phase takes place.

The second phase, evocation and exploration of emotionally laden material, is what most clearly characterizes EFT as an experiential approach to therapy. In this phase it is crucial that clients experience in the session what they are talking about and that focal concerns are felt experientially, not just known intellectually. To promote experience, therapists must assess clients' internal and external supports for making contact with their experience and their capacity to contain and process what they contact. If supports are insufficient, therapists must help clients develop the resources and capacity to process their experience.

EFT works on the basic principle that clients cannot leave a place (i.e., change an emotional experience) until they have arrived (i.e., fully experienced the emotion). Clients therefore need to reclaim disowned experience before they can be changed by it or change it. In this process, it is not that clients simply discover things they did not know, but rather that they experience in a bodily manner aspects of themselves they have not consciously felt or may have previously disclaimed (Greenberg & van Balen, 1998). It is this reowning of experience that makes EFT an experiential therapy. Therapists help clients experience what they are talking about so that clients can become aware of their feelings and the impact of events. In this way, clients can clearly and impactfully experience the message or significance of their feelings and later use, transform, and reflect on their feelings to create new meaning. In this phase therapists offer their expertise as process facilitators with knowledge of how to help clients arrive at and process what they feel at their core. To do this effectively, therapists need to be able to collaboratively establish a sufficiently supportive environment. The goal in the evocation phase is to help clients experience their core vulnerabilities by accessing core maladaptive schemes in the session. This phase involves a dual focus on facilitating access to internal and external supports to promote contact with previously disclaimed experience and helping clients not to interrupt and prevent their experience from entering their awareness.

Phase 3 involves transformation. As clients leave the place they arrived at in Phase 2, the emphasis shifts to the construction of alternative ways of responding emotionally, cognitively, and behaviorally by accessing new internal resources in the form of adaptive emotional responses and by making sense of experience in new ways. The shift to this phase occurs when the emotional experience at the core of the problem has been evoked in the session, reclaimed, and its origins or generators explored. In the transformation phase, the therapist offers process expertise to help focus the client on ways of accessing new adaptive emotional responses and to facilitate the client's construction of new meaning. The client generates new experience both by accessing his or her emotions and amending his or her narratives; in this way a new lived story, as well as a new told story, emerge. It is during the transformation phase that the dialectical process of making sense of newly synthesized experience is most evident in producing change. Clients consolidate new meaning and generate new explanations and narratives that help them make sense of the changes in their experience of themselves and the world.

The three phases generally overlap, are often interactive in nature, and can repeat themselves as new issues arise. The client sequence of forming a trusting bond and increasing emotional awareness, evoking or re-evoking experience rather than simply talking about it, developing new emotional responses, and creating new meaning are the fundamental processes of EFT

TABLE 5.1
Steps in the Phases of Treatment

Phase	Step
1. Bonding and awareness	1. Attend to, empathize with, and validate client's feelings and current sense of self. 2. Provide a rationale for working with emotion. 3. Promote awareness of internal experience. 4. Establish a collaborative focus.
2. Evocation and exploration	1. Establish support. 2. Evoke and arouse problematic feelings. 3. Undo interruptions. 4. Help client access primary emotions or core maladaptive emotion schemes.
3. Transformation	1. Help client generate new emotional responses to transform core maladaptive schemes. 2. Promote reflection to make sense of experience. 3. Validate new feelings and support an emerging sense of self.

for depression. Throughout therapy the client is seen as an agent who is the expert on his or her own experience. The therapist is seen as offering process expertise that can help to guide and facilitate the client's movement toward his or her goals.

The three phases of bonding and awareness, evocation and exploration, and transformation can be divided into step sequences, as summarized in Table 5.1. These phases and the steps within them are more overlapping than linear in sequence. Thus, for example, the first phase, bonding and awareness, continues throughout treatment into the final phase. Exploration and reflection, too, are fairly continuous throughout treatment, but evocation and generation of alternative emotions, although they may occur at any point, are generally found more frequently toward the later part of therapy.

Phase 1: Bonding and Awareness

During Phase 1, bonding and awareness, the therapist

- attends to, empathizes with, and validates the client's feelings and current sense of self;
- provides a rationale for working with emotion;
- promotes awareness of internal experience; and
- establishes a collaborative focus.

Attend to, Empathize With, and Validate the Client's Feelings

Clients throughout treatment need a facilitating environment in which to engage in the EFT process. They need a safe and validating relationship in which to sort out their feelings and an accepting and soothing relationship to help them regulate their emotions. Talking with the therapist helps clients sort out which feelings are healthy and useful and which are problematic and need change. Clients need their therapists to validate and strengthen their emerging new feelings and new sense of themselves. Recognition from others is one of the crucial components in a new sense of a valued self and is an important ingredient in overcoming the core sense of worthlessness or abandonment in depression.

In the initial stages of therapy, the goals are to make contact with the client and to establish a warm, empathic, and collaborative bond. Clients with depression often feel very isolated and hopeless, and highly attentive listening helps the client to feel understood, relax, and focus internally. The therapist therefore immediately begins to attend to the client's underlying internal experience and becomes empathically attuned to the client's feelings. From the start the client is implicitly being trained, by the therapist's consistent empathic focuses on the client's internal experience, to attend to this internal experience. Therapists in this phase convey understanding, acknowledge the client's pain, validate his or her struggles, and focus on the emotional impact of events in the client's life. By the therapist's attentive listening, presence, and caring, and by the attitude conveyed by the therapist's face, body, hands, and eyes that validates the client's specialness, the client comes to feel seen, valued, and respected and is thereby more inclined to trust and be open. By attending to the client's core humanness and expressing unconditional confidence in the client's strengths and capacity for growth, the therapist helps reveal the client's uniqueness and strength. When someone sees the possibility of growth in another being, this possibility is stimulated.

The deeply held therapeutic attitude of empathy and positive regard and a focus on strengths and resources help create an emotional bond of trust and respect and help develop the safe environment and a secure base for the exploration that will take place as the therapy progresses. In addition to creating a bond, the therapist provides a rationale, right from the start, for the goal of accessing and becoming aware of underlying feelings and needs involved in the depression. If the client's emotions are underregulated, the therapist provides a rationale for the goal of finding better ways of coping with feelings that seem overwhelming.

The therapist provides education on the view that feelings provide important information about how people react to situations and that it is important for clients to clarify what their emotions are telling them. The therapist places strong emphasis from the start on clients' need to validate and accept the pain they feel. When clients come to therapy, they do so because they are suffering and feel some form of pain—they often feel that something in their life or inside of them is broken. To create an emotional bond and sense of collaboration, the therapist must quickly and surely grasp the nature of the client's enduring pain. Once the client has articulated this pain, his or her sense of isolation is broken. The client feels a sense of relief that the pain has been described, that someone understands, and that he or she now is not so alone in the struggle. Hope is created, and agreement to work on resolving the chronic enduring pain creates an alliance spurred by this hope. Resolving the articulated enduring pain becomes the goal of treatment and the basis for the working alliance.

Provide a Rationale for Working With Emotion

It is necessary, in the early phase of therapy, that the therapist explicitly provide a rationale for working with emotion and reach an agreement with the client on goals for treatment. For clients who recognize that their emotions are the source of their distress, the importance of focusing on emotion is self-evident; for others, working with emotions is a totally new way of viewing problems. First, the therapist gives the general rationale that emotions provide information about one's reactions to situations and about central concerns and that awareness of these emotions and the ability to deal with them and their message are central to healthy functioning. The therapist tells the client in a respectful, conversational way that lack of awareness, suppression, and disregulation can lead to distress and highlights the relationship between depressive symptoms such as hopelessness and rumination and avoidance of underlying emotions.

As treatment progresses, the therapist provides more specific aspects of the rationale. When, for example, the therapist feels it is necessary to explicitly direct a client to attend to his or her internal experience, the therapist can explain that the client's body is telling him or her something about how he or she reacted and that it is important to receive that message. When the client interrupts a feeling in the moment, the therapist brings the client's attention to the interruption and discusses the difficulties produced by the client's fear and avoidance of emotion. The therapist offers rationales in as individualized a form as possible relevant to the shared understandings of the client's unique problems. The general rationale the therapist conveys is that feelings are adaptive guides to action, provide information about reactions, need to be acknowledged and reflected on, and, if dysfunctional, need to be transformed.

Within initial sessions, therapists also might provide some education to clients about depression and its treatment so that clients are oriented to the goals of the treatment and the manner in which it will be conducted. It is important both to obtain clients' collaboration with EFT's aim to work on emotions and to help clients see how this work relates to their own goals for treatment. When relevant, in this early phase the therapist educates the client on the importance of and skills to achieve emotion regulation. By discussing their experiences of mood disturbances, clients can begin to see how their unprocessed underlying emotional experience relates to episodes of depression and anxiety. This realization helps the therapist provide an experience-near rationale for focusing on underlying emotions. Likewise, exploring the developmental origins of their depressions helps clients gain a better understanding of how they came to have this condition. They then can begin to recognize that certain emotional reactions that they have had repeatedly over time, such as feelings of abandonment or shame, are involved in their depression.

Along with a rationale, psychoeducation within sessions can be helpful in giving clients a framework and preparing them for later transformation. We favor an experientially based approach to psychoeducation in which education is tailored to the client's state and given only when the client is in a teachable moment. For example, when a client interrupts anger and feels resigned, the therapist might comment that suppressing anger can lead to hopelessness and depression. Or a therapist might suggest to clients in moments of desperation that they can learn to regulate their distress first by checking their breathing and then by trying to articulate the threat in words. Thus, the therapist might say something like, "Try saying, 'I won't survive,' and then breathe into that, and then ask yourself, 'What do I need to do to help myself feel more secure?'"

Awareness of Internal Experience

From the very first session, therapist responses focus clients on mindful awareness of their internal experience. Therapists repeatedly reiterate the importance of focusing on the client's internal world and, most centrally, on the client's current emotional experience. Problems are defined in feeling terms. The therapist directs the client to attend to the bodily felt sense of what he or she is talking about with the ultimate goal of accessing the core emotion scheme that generates personal meaning. Such a focus eventually helps clients attend to, overcome avoidance of, acknowledge, and fully experience their own painful feelings and emotional meanings in the safety of the therapeutic environment. Once these feelings are out in the open, the client can differentiate, clarify, and understand his or her experience and, in collaboration with the therapist, modify dysfunctional processes. He or she can then access alternate needs, goals, and concerns and bring internal resources to bear to promote change.

Some clients are extremely externally focused, and helping them contact their feelings can be challenging. The therapist can bring a persistent, gentle pressure to focus on current internal experience first through empathic responding and emotion inquiries, and later by guiding the client's attention to internal experience. The therapist thus consistently encourages the client to become aware of his or her internal experience and to develop mindfulness (Kabat-Zinn, 1990; Perls, Hefferline, & Goodman, 1951). Later, process directives like suggesting that the client repeat key phrases that stimulate emotion in the session can be used to intensify experience and make it more vivid. A balance needs to be struck between allowing clients to tell their story and tracking their reactions, on one hand, and explicitly directing their attention internally, on the other. Questions used throughout therapy include, What are you aware of as you say this? What is happening in your body? What is it like inside right now?

Using empathic exploratory responses and emotion awareness questions, the therapist works to help clients approach, tolerate, regulate, and accept their emotional experience. Acceptance of emotional experience, as opposed to its avoidance, is an important step in emotion awareness work. Once the client accepts rather than avoids the emotion, the therapist then helps the client use the emotion by making sense of what the emotion is telling them and identifying the goal, need, or concern it is organizing them to attain. Emotion is used both to inform and to move.

Because the best way to move out of an emotional state often is to go through it (Hunt, 1998), therapists help clients first to arrive at their emotions, and later they help them construct new responses, leave or transform maladaptive emotional states, and move on. Therapists also help clients who feel overwhelmed by their emotions to develop affect regulation skills that help them cope with these states. Helping clients arrive at, accept, and regulate their feelings involves helping them do the following:

- become mindfully aware of their emotions;
- accept, tolerate, and allow their emotional experience (for over-regulated clients) or develop emotion regulation skills to tolerate emotion (for underregulated clients);
- label and describe their feelings in words to aid problem solving and lower arousal levels; and
- identify their primary and core feelings in a situation (Greenberg, 2002).

EFT is essentially an exploratory process. Both client and therapist spend a lot of time attending to and symbolizing the idiosyncratic meaning of experience. The therapist does not try to use a predetermined notion of what is causing the problem or focus on particular feelings or thoughts viewed as being at the root of depression. Rather, together client and therapist attempt to articulate the client's unique experience. This painstaking form of coconstructive exploration ensures that together they capture the real quality of the client's feelings and meanings. This very particular and idiosyncratic rendering of the client's subjectivity enables him or her to evoke experience as well as to understand it. For example, this type of exploration of the client's subjective experience may reveal not just that the client is sad, but that it is a desperate, abandoned feeling captured in the words "I feel like a motherless child." In another client the exploratory process may reveal that this sadness has a hopeless quality of "what's the use" or an explosive sense of loss. The collaborative attempt to capture and differentiate the client's bodily felt feeling clarifies and creates meaning for the client where previously there was confusion and doubt.

At any one moment there is more available to awareness than the client is currently symbolizing, and exploration of the vague edges of consciousness will yield new information. Exploration then involves concentration of attention on internal experience in an attempt to clearly symbolize felt meanings that are at the edge of awareness but currently not fully in awareness and then reflection on these meanings. Identification of feeling and meaning is quite problematic for many clients. They might become aware of tightness in their jaws and chests or a knot in their stomachs without being able to symbolize what they are feeling. They also might mislabel an experience, for example, by labeling a feeling *anger* when it would more authentically be labeled *anxiety* or *dread*. Attending to and accurately symbolizing the experience requires mindful concentration and a process of experientially searching one's internal experience until one captures what one is feeling or understands the idiosyncratic meaning of the experience. Empathic responding to client experience is one of the best ways to help clarify it and create new meaning. Clients also can be encouraged to write narratives about their depressive experiences and to record separately their emotions, physical symptoms, thoughts, and behaviors involved in these episodes in emotion diaries (Greenberg, 2002). Clients can also be encouraged to practice mindful awareness of emotion as homework.

Clients who are overwhelmed by their emotions benefit from learning emotion regulation skills that increase their ability to tolerate and use their emotions without resorting to control strategies such as avoidance or worry. Early sessions may need to focus on development of somatic awareness to help clients become more aware of their bodily reactions to emotions without interrupting them. Increased understanding of emotional experience and regulation and strategies for regulating emotions and getting needs met in social and intimate relationships and at work also may need to be focused on.

The aim with clients who are punitive and neglectful of themselves or rejecting of others is to try to help them to be more accepting, compassionate, and nurturing of themselves. First, the therapist's empathic, responsive attitude models a way of being with clients that they can internalize. Second, therapists can teach their clients the importance of focusing and becoming aware of their inner experience as a guide to their needs and actions. Other ways therapists can encourage different behavior is by asking their clients how they might respond to someone else in a similar plight or to ask them to think of ways they could be more compassionate and self-nurturing—for example, by giving themselves special food treats, pampering themselves with warm baths, setting aside time to refresh themselves, seeking out more social support, or engaging in fun activities. Clients can also be asked to imagine being compassionate with themselves; a guided imagery task can help them do this. Recognizing their limits is another way therapists can help clients take care of themselves; clients who are depressed often need help to say no to the demands they make of themselves and that others make of them. Being attuned to their bodily reactions and feelings will help clients be more sensitive to feeling tired and drained and more aware that they need to rest. Therapists encourage clients to respect these feelings and allow them to guide their actions.

Establish a Focus

Establishing a focus can be seen as the case formulation aspect of EFT. A defining feature of emotion-focused intervention is that it is process diagnostic (Greenberg et al., 1993) rather than person diagnostic. Thus, the therapist considers the client's manner of processing, in-session markers of problematic emotional states, and coevolving therapeutic themes in developing a focus. Although the client has been diagnosed as depressed, this diagnosis in itself does not give a lot of information as to what the focus of treatment will be. This focus should reflect the underlying determinants of this client's depression and the collaborative development of an understanding of the client's core pain.

The therapist attends to a variety of different markers at different levels of client processing as they emerge. Markers are client statements or behaviors that alert therapists to various aspects of clients' functioning that might need attention. It is these that guide intervention, more than a diagnosis or an explicit case formulation (Goldman & Greenberg, 1997). The client's presently felt experience indicates what the difficulty is and indicates whether problem determinants are currently accessible and amenable to intervention. The early establishment of a focus and the discussion of generating conditions of the depression act only as a broad framework to initially focus exploration. The focus is always subject to change and development, and process diagnosis of in-session problem states is a means of focusing each session.

Therapists work with a variety of markers at different levels. Beginning in the first session, the first level a therapist attends to is the client's moment-by-moment manner of processing. These initial markers include the micromarkers of client vocal quality, depth of experiencing, and degree of emotional arousal, and the therapist assesses the presence of these markers by being attuned to both the client's language and his or her nonverbal behavior. Of particular importance is the assessment of the client's degree of engagement and distance from his or her own moment-by-moment experiencing. In addition, markers of the client's more characteristic style are also important. These markers reveal important general aspects of how clients treat themselves and others and can be gleaned from clients' accounts of their attachment histories and descriptions of their interactions with others and with themselves.

The next level of processing that therapists attend to involves the types of cognitive–affective problem states the client enters. The emergence of task markers identifies particular in-session cognitive–affective problems such as conflict splits or problematic reactions that indicate that the client is in a particular state and is ready to engage in specific therapeutic interventions or tasks.

A final level of processing to which therapists attend, and one that always is in the background, is that of content and theme. Therapists and clients develop over time a shared view of the underlying determinants of the depression, and this shared view provides the collaborative focus and the key themes of treatment. The focus generally emerges by Sessions 3 to 5 in a 16- to 20-session therapy. If the focus has not emerged by then, therapist and client should pay explicit attention to establishing a focus.

These different levels of processing together constitute a sequence of comprehension. First, therapists attend carefully to clients' moment-by-moment process in the session and to how clients are engaging in the work of processing their emotional experiencing. Second, they listen to clients' life histories to identify their characteristic ways of being with themselves and others. Third, therapists listen for markers of specific cognitive–affective tasks or problem states, and finally and throughout, therapists listen for the client's main underlying problems to emerge. Thus, EFT therapists pull together information from multiple levels in working with their clients. Therapists are sensitized by theories of determinants of depression (e.g., self-criticism, dependence, loss, unresolved anger, powerlessness), but these theories are useful tools that provide perspective, not definitive determinants. Thus, therapists seek to understand clients in their own terms, and each understanding of the client is held tentatively and is open to reformulation and change as more exploration takes place. Treatment is driven not by a theory of the causes of depression, but rather by listening, using empathy, following the client's process, and identifying markers; the therapist's sense of the determinants of the depression is built from the ground up using the client as a constant touchstone for what is true. Treatments therefore are custom-made for each client.

Identifying and articulating the problematic cognitive–affective processes underlying and generating the depression and the symptomatic experience is a collaborative effort between therapist and client. The establishment of agreement on the determinants of the client's depression helps alliance development in that it implicitly suggests that the goal of treatment is to resolve this issue. Sometimes this agreement is implicit or so clear that no explicit goals are discussed. Sometimes the establishment of a validating relationship itself is the goal. For clients who are unable to focus inward and be aware of their experience, the very ability to attend to their emotions and make sense of them may become the focus of treatment. In general, however, the therapist and client establish an explicit agreement that treatment goals involve addressing the underlying determinants of the depression. Thus, a focus and a goal for a client with depression might be to acknowledge and stand up to his overly hostile inner critic that produces feelings of inadequacy. For a client with low self-esteem, the focus and goal might be to become more aware of and more clearly able to express her feelings and needs. For a dependent client, the focus and goal might be to assertively express and resolve resentment at feeling dominated by a spouse. For an anxious client, it might be to develop a means of self-soothing and self-support and for another to restructure a deep fear of abandonment and insecurity based on trauma or losses in the past.

In developing a focus for therapy, it is important that a shift in session content take place from talking about the client's symptoms and reactions to situations toward exploring the client's agency in the creation of the problematic experience. The realization that current experience is not inevitable but in some fashion is constructed by the way the client regulates affect and constructs meaning is at the essence of taking personal responsibility. Moving from avoiding internal experience or blaming others to focusing on and exploring the internal generators of one's own reactions is central in developing awareness of agency in the creation of experience. Thus, it is important to help the client move from "It devastated me" or "It made me feel angry" to questioning, "What is occurring in me that leads to these reactions?"

The focus thus becomes one of taking responsibility for one's agency in the construction of one's personal reality (Neimeyer & Mahoney, 1995). The therapist needs to help the client take responsibility, in a nonblaming fashion, in a context of exploring a problem. Therapists do not give a message to clients that they are responsible for their own distress, but rather a collaborative effort emerges of inquiry into how the client's psychological processes contribute to the distress. The message is, "Let's explore what happens in you that leads to this feeling."

Awareness of agency fosters a sense of control over experience and a healthy detachment from certain types of experience. Becoming mindfully aware that one is, for example, an agent who is thinking self-critical thoughts is far different from believing the thought and being overwhelmed by its implications. Thus, when clients are able to say "I'm aware of 'thinking' I'm a failure" or "I make myself feel guilty," they are adopting quite a different stance to their experience than when they say "I am a failure" or "I am guilty." Therapist statements such as "So, you feel bad when you criticize yourself for falling short" or "So, it's when you get the feeling 'I won't be able to survive' that you begin to panic" highlight sequences and client agency in the creation of their experience. The subtle emphasis on agency and personal responsibility in these interventions begins to help clients experience that they are agents in the creation of their experience and that rather than being passive victims, they have some control over their experience. The focus of therapy then shifts to helping clients mindfully explore their role in the creation of their experience.

Phase 2: Evocation and Exploration

During the evocation and exploration phase, the therapist

- establishes support for contacting emotions,
- evokes and arouses problematic feelings,
- undoes interruptions, and
- helps the client access primary emotions.

Establishing Support for Contacting Emotions

Therapists need to assess client readiness for evocation and to ensure that the client has sufficient internal support before evoking a painful emotion. For some clients, the primary focus often needs to be on building supports for promoting contact with their emotions. Some clients dissociate, avoid their feelings, or become very tense at the prospect of encountering their feelings. If the therapist notices that a client has begun to glaze over or tense up, he or she might suggest that the client breathe deeply, put his or her feet on the ground, or feel grounded in the chair. If the client seems to be dissociating slightly (i.e., "spacing out"), the therapist can suggest that the client look at the therapist or describe what he or she sees in the room to promote a sense of connection with the therapist or with present reality. Before evocation and arousal take place, the therapist can help the client practice establishing ways of soothing himself or herself or imagining going to a safe place if things get too difficult.

Two deficits that prevent a client from experiencing emotion are anxiety about inner feelings and lack of ability to name an emotional experience. In the case of anxiety about inner feelings, a type of graded exposure or desensitization process is most useful in helping clients develop the support they need to approach and tolerate their emotions. It is important not to push clients too hard to face what they dread, because this simply increases their self-protective efforts. The goal in EFT is to melt defensive and protective barriers, not tear them down. This is done by providing empathic support and helping clients become aware of their blocks. In the presence of skill deficits in naming emotion, such as in alexithymia, therapists need to help these clients become aware that they lack the ability to name emotions and then to provide tasks, such as keeping a diary or a daily log of emotions, to help them begin to develop this ability (Greenberg, 2002). Often these techniques do not work with these clients, and therapists need to be extraempathic and even more sensitively attuned so that they can help these clients articulate their inner experience.

With more fragile clients who have not developed a strong sense of self or boundaries between self and other, the development of awareness and evocation of emotion is more of a long-term objective. Promoting access to experience and asking feeling-oriented questions are pointless, because these clients have yet to develop an awareness of their internal world and first need to develop internal supports for deeper experience. With fragile clients the relationship is seen as the point of therapeutic departure. Thus, a more relational form of work needs to be followed in which the process of contact with the therapist becomes the focus before any evocation takes place. In addition, with clients who have experienced trauma or who are at risk of suicide or self-harm, external safety issues need to be dealt with as the first order of business before any type of internal exploration or evocation is attempted.

Problems in the relationship between client and therapist are a potential source of shaming for clients and need to be addressed to help clients develop support for emotional awareness and to enable new experience and learning. Therapists need to be highly aware of their own impact on clients' momentary experience, focusing on disruptions in relational contact as both a source of shaming of the client but also of discovery and an opportunity for new experience.

Evoking and Arousing Problematic Feelings

To change depressive experience, the client needs to evoke the experience in the session. The therapist therefore attends to process cues in the present moment to best intensify and evoke experience and core memories. To maintain the alliance in this most painful phase of treatment, the client needs to agree that it is valuable to open up painful experience and that the tasks undertaken to access the bad feelings and the pain are relevant (Bordin, 1979; Horvath & Greenberg, 1994; Watson & Greenberg, 1994, 1996). How and which depressed feelings are activated in the session depends on the therapist's process diagnostic assessment of the client's specific generating conditions (e.g., despairing hopelessness, anxious helplessness, resignation, emptiness). Work on evoking experience also involves work on awareness of avoidance and interruption of emotional experience, which will be discussed in the next step.

The therapist can use stimulating methods in this phase to vivify the client's experience. Bringing alive the experience of hopelessness, for example, may involve the use of a two-chair dialogue in which one part is a "doom caster" and the other part the hopeless experience induced by this. Evoking emotion involves either attending to features of the client's experience like a sigh, a shrug, or a statement of resignation to amplify them or using a more expressive method like a self–self or a self–other dialogue. The therapist might ask the client to engage in a two-chair dialogue and to express in the critic chair what they do to themselves to make themselves feel that they are worthless or that there is no hope. By actively saying to themselves "You are worthless" or "Nothing will ever change" and elaborating on these self-statements, clients begin to activate the feeling of hopelessness in the session. Once a client's emotional experience of hopelessness has been evoked, he or she is able to access the information that constitutes this experience in a "hot" fashion.

In general, it is a secondary or reactive feeling that is first evoked, often the feeling the client wants to be rid of, like hopelessness, despair, or resignation. This state then is explored to get at deeper, more primary feelings, such as shame, anxiety, or resentment, the blocking of which is leading to the experience of the secondary bad feeling. In the evocation process emotional meaning also is explored, symbolized, and reflected on. This newly created meaning in turn feeds back and activates further emotion schemes or moderates the existing ones. Thus, "I feel hopeless" transforms into "I feel empty, like I'm nothing unless someone approves of me," and then the core shame-based sense of inadequacy is accessed. Once this core emotion scheme of worthlessness is activated, it is more amenable to new input and change, right then. When clients begin sessions by talking about what has been bothering them and recounting a past episode, the goal for the session is to get in touch with the part of that story that is most alive for the client in the moment and to re-evoke the experience being talked about. Change occurs most effectively when the emotion scheme generating the experience is accessed and reflected on in the session.

Many techniques can be used to bring the emotional experience alive—empathic responding, focusing, and imagery, in addition to psychodramatic enactments. Use of imagery, metaphoric language, and empathic conjectures that move beyond the surface, closer to implicit feelings, are very helpful in evoking feelings. For example, therapists may ask clients who are out of touch with their emotional experience and just talking about their external situations to attend to their bodily sensations in the situation. Or they may ask clients who are talking about feeling like failures to imagine a specific situation or interaction that triggered this feeling to help promote more differentiated exploration of the feelings and thoughts in the situation. Alternatively, the therapist can observe that as the client talks, there seem to be tears behind the laughter, or the therapist can ask, "How does it feel now, as you talk about this?" or respond with "That's the part that still hurts or bothers you." Gestalt experiments, both structured and created to suit the moment, are often the most powerful means of evoking experience; the therapist asks the client to do something in the session and then to focus on the experience created.

In the case of depressed clients whose emotions are underregulated, the goal is to regulate, rather than further arouse, the already overaroused bad feeling. For example, clients who are feeling very hopeless may weep about how hopeless everything is, and those who are excessively blaming may fume in rage. The therapist can propose techniques such as breathing to reduce arousal, taking an observer's stance and describing sensations, or identifying the cognitions generating the feelings to help the client regulate the over-aroused emotion and establish a good working distance from it. Once the secondary reactions are regulated, the primary emotion becomes more accessible. Mindless explosions or venting of emotion is not the goal of the evocation phase; rather, experiencing the full impact of the emotion and symbolizing it in awareness are encouraged to facilitate lowered arousal levels and the creation of new meaning and courses of action.

Undoing Interruptions

Exploring and overcoming blocks to emotion, avoidance, and interruptive processes is an important subtask of EFT of depression. Facing what is dreaded can be threatening, but collaboration for this purpose provides safety and minimizes the development of opposition, misalliances, or treatment impasses.

The client's means of preventing or interrupting his or her emerging experience come into focus as they emerge in the moment. As client and therapist begin to work on evoking emotional experience, blocks to experience emerge, or they may already be observable in the client's manner and narrative process. The therapist then needs to focus on the interruptive process itself and to help clients become aware of and experience how they interrupt their feelings or needs. As blocks to experience emerge in the session, therapists ask clients first to become aware that they are interrupting, then to identify how they do this, and finally to become aware of the feelings or needs that they have interrupted. Blocks include the extremes of dissociation and numbness, as well as the changing of topics to avoid feeling and tears that are felt but stifled.

Fear and dread of emotion often is a major issue. One client, for example, was afraid that if he got angry or sad, he would fall apart. As he explored this in therapy, it became clear that his mother often had humiliated him for showing emotion. This client had to work through the cognitive (catastrophic expectations), physical (squeezing his jaw), and behavioral (changing the topic) ways of stopping himself from feeling, including his imagined humiliation and fear of falling apart, to help him overcome the block. Asking clients who are blocking to enact their interruptive processes can help bring these processes to awareness and vivify them.

The experimental method of trying something in the session to see what the client experiences helps bring to the surface his or her ways of preventing completion of the task and methods of avoiding experience. Two-chair enactments often are helpful in working with self-interruption. Clients enact the interruptive processes and dramatize them to experience themselves as agents of the interruptive process. This awareness of agency increases the probability that the client will choose to stop the process or, if it is totally automated, to work on becoming more aware of it. After some time, enacting the interruptive process and becoming aware of how he or she interrupts experience helps the client evoke the suppressed emotion and access the unmet need.

Therapists in training often ask how to deal with clients who are blocked. Often the most important factor is the empathic relationship. It is through safety and support over time that blocks come to dissolve. In EFT of depression, the therapist seeks to be closely attuned to the core growth-oriented part of the client. It is through this experience of personal safety and the therapist's close attunement to clients' possibilities that clients often are able to undo interruptions, let down their protective barriers, and access a core affective experience. The therapist's timing in trying to access emotion also is important. It is crucial to dig where the ground is soft and to begin to evoke emotion only when it clearly is being felt or is near the surface but is being interrupted. Then, to help the emotion flow into expression, the therapist can provide an appropriately timed empathic capturing of the feeling in a form that clearly conveys that he or she is on the client's side, such as "I know how much that can hurt" or "How discarded that must have made you feel" or "No wonder you feel so afraid."

Helping the Client Access Primary Emotions

The goal of the evocation and exploration is to access new primary experience as a basis for reorganization of the self. The client needs to unpack and explore the feelings that are evoked to get at the primary feelings. In depression, the first evoked bad feelings, as we have said, often are secondary reactions, feelings of hopelessness, despair, or resignation. These are themselves made up of complex cognitive–affective sequences. The goal, once these feelings are evoked, is to slow down and unpack the generating sequences, to differentiate feelings, and to get at underlying primary emotions and associated automatic perceptions and appraisals and, finally, at the client's needs. Appropriate adaptive emotional responses are generally energizing or self-soothing because they guide and protect. Thus, adaptive anger involves a buildup of energy to aid in overcoming obstacles. Adaptive sadness allows for withdrawal and recuperation or reaching out for comfort, leaving one calm and able to contact the world and act. This unpacking and differentiating is facilitated by the therapist's empathic understanding and empathic exploration and through the client's process of enacting different aspects of the self.

Interventions used to facilitate client exploration always involve a balance between process directiveness and empathic responding (Greenberg et al., 1993). Intervention is guided by ongoing attunement to client processes and subtleties of expression. In the process of exploring their experience, clients may recall concrete moments, re-experience aspects of past events, or move in and out of dialogues between parts of the self or between the self and others. As the process evolves, a client often begins to see or experience things in a new way and to realize that a self-criticism is an old parental message, that a feeling of being judged by others is an attribution of one's own self-criticism onto them, or that an experience of unresolved anger or grief resolves and unmet needs become clear (Greenberg et al., 1993).

Therapists in the evocation and exploration phase predominantly focus on helping clients take ownership of their core experience. The new core feeling arrived at is either a primary adaptive emotion or the maladaptive emotional experience generated by a core dysfunctional emotion scheme. A major shift occurs at this point in the treatment of depression. The client now is no longer focused on depressive symptoms or hopelessness; rather, he or she has either connected with adaptive responses or is grappling with the core issues, such as feeling worthless or basically insecure, that have resulted in the depression. Clients then have to have help in trusting their adaptive inner voice or dealing with internalized contempt; with annihilating internal voices; with earlier experiences of abandonment, humiliation, or trauma; or with feelings of being unloved and unlovable.

Once a core primary emotion is aroused, if the client tolerates it, it follows its own course, involving a natural rising and falling off of intensity. Decrease in intensity allows for reflection. Arousal also leads to associations and results in the activation of many new schemes, especially when attention is explicitly focused on the task of making sense of the aroused emotion. Thus, it is the combination of arousing, symbolizing, and reflecting that carries forward the process of meaning construction and that ultimately leads to the generation of alternatives to the maladaptive aspects of experience. Once experience is evoked, one feeling follows another in a process of allowing, expressing, symbolizing, and completing one emotion, which then allows for the emergence of a new emotion or felt meaning. Thus, the fear or sadness at the base of a client's depression, once it has been expressed, symbolized, and differentiated, is often followed by newly emerging anger. In other clients, anger may be followed by sadness or shame, resentment by appreciation, hate by love, and aversion by desire.

The goal of EFT is for the client to acknowledge and experience previously avoided or nonsymbolized primary adaptive emotion and needs. It is not only the experience of primary emotion per se, but also the accessing of the needs, goals, and concerns and the action tendencies associated with them, that is important. Thus, by acknowledging the sadness of a loss underlying a depression, a client may experience a longing to be cared for and grieve the loss, or a maltreated client, by experiencing anger at being robbed of dignity, may assert boundaries. The need and action tendency associated with the primary emotion lead to adaptive action. It is by shifting the experience to the primary emotion and using it as a resource that client change occurs. In some cases change occurs simply because a client accesses underlying anger and reorganizes to assert boundaries or another client accesses sadness, grieves a loss, and organizes to withdraw and to recover or reaches out for comfort and support. Contacting the need and realizing the action tendency provide motivation and direction for change and an alternative way of responding. Action replaces resignation, and motivated desire replaces hopelessness.

In many instances during this step, however, it is complex maladaptive emotion schematic experience that is accessed at the core of the depression, rather than unexpressed primary adaptive emotions such as sadness or anger. The complexity in the process of change lies in distinguishing between adaptive and maladaptive core experience. Once clients have arrived at a core experience, they need to decide whether it is a healthy experience. If it seems like the core emotion will enhance their well-being, then they can stay with this experience and be guided by the information it provides. If, however, they decide that this core emotion will not enhance them or their intimate bonds, it is maladaptive. When clients, in dialogue with their therapists, decide that they cannot trust the feelings at which they have arrived as a source of good information, then they need to transform the feeling.

Core schemes that are maladaptive result in feelings such as powerlessness or invisibility or a deep sense of woundedness, shame, insecurity, worthlessness, or being unloved or unlovable. These feelings are accessed as being at the core of the secondary bad feeling of depressive hopelessness. Core depressive experiences often relate either to worthlessness or to anxious dependence. At the core of the self-critical depression is a feeling that one is worthless, a failure, and bad, and at the core of a dependent depression is a feeling of fragile insecurity and of being unable to hold together without support. These feelings are generated by the core weak and bad depressive self-schemes. In these instances, the client must access the primary maladaptive feelings of worthlessness, weakness, or insecurity to be able to achieve change. What is curative is the ability first to symbolize these feelings of worthlessness or weakness and then to access alternate adaptive self-schemes. The generation of alternate schemes is based on accessing adaptive feelings and needs that get activated in response to the currently experienced emotional distress. The client's response to his or her own symbolized distress is adaptive, and accessing it provides a life-giving resource.

A professionally available psychotherapy film allows comparison of the emphasis in EFT on accessing core emotion with those of other approaches (Shostrom, 1986). In this film, a recently divorced man with depression was seen in both cognitive–behavioral therapy (CBT) by Beck (1996) and interpersonal dynamic therapy by Strupp (Strupp & Binder, 1984), both developers of their approaches. The client talked about how depressed he would get on Saturday afternoon when he was alone at home with nothing to do. He talked about the loneliness he felt and his belief that nobody liked him. In EFT, this state of loneliness, loss, and humiliation (related to being a friendless only child of alcoholic parents) would become the focus of treatment even in the first session. In CBT with Beck, the validity of the belief that "no one cares about me" became the focus. We, however, see the belief as state dependent, produced by the emotion of schematically produced loneliness and vulnerability. In EFT beliefs are not given primacy as causes or change agents in depression, but rather are viewed as articulations of core affective states. That is, beliefs generally are viewed as the verbalization of stored perceptions of sensory experience. The formulated belief and language itself are not the cause of depressive experience, in this view, but rather are the articulation in words of implicit emotion schematic experience. Beliefs can certainly contribute to and maintain negative affect, but they are not the cause of the primary affect. Beliefs are an articulation in language and a narrative-type explanation of a complex bodily felt experience, rather than the cause of it.

In the film, Richard's belief that no one cares about him articulates some aspect of his sense of loneliness and loss of love and produces secondary feelings of sadness and rejection. EFT therapists would view the depressive loneliness as produced by the stimulus-cued, automatic evocation of an affective state of loneliness built up from years of experience of feelings of loneliness and being unloved that are stored in Richard's emotion schematic memory. It is not whether the belief is true or not that is at issue in EFT, but rather whether it is useful or adaptive. It is clear that in Richard's case the belief was not useful. So EFT therapists would not dispute the belief or compare it to the evidence for its validity. Rather, they would view this belief as maladaptive and work not to disprove the belief, but instead to generate alternative emotional states and different modes of processing that are more functional. Cognitive–behavioral theory proposes working in the domain of truth and validity. EFT proposes working in domains of value and functionality, of what is good for one and useful.

The dynamic interpersonal approach exemplified in Strupp's sessions with Richard viewed Richard's problematic interpersonal responses—that is, his not being able to reach out or his aggressive interactions with others—as the source of the depression and the focal target of change. EFT therapists instead would focus directly on accessing Richard's core affective experience of a lonely, abandoned child, which is affecting his interpersonal behavior and transforming it. Although this might become a focus in interpersonal therapy, it is not conceptualized as being the underlying determinant of depression, as it is in EFT.

Once the client has experienced and symbolized the feeling of worthlessness or insecurity, the elements of the dysfunctional beliefs or expectancies embedded in the maladaptive emotion scheme become accessible to articulation. In the aroused state the most meaningful elements of the state-dependent beliefs are obtained in their deepest and most essential form. Now they can be articulated and conceptualized in the emotional meaning context in which they operate. This hot cognition thus is obtained in a truly felt manner and is not just a conceptual statement made without any emotional investment. The belief representing the core emotion scheme is made more easily accessible for articulation through emotional arousal and is more amenable to the input of new information and experience and thereby to change (Greenberg & Safran, 1987).

The client's articulation "I see myself in certain ways" is a very important aspect of articulating the belief representing the core emotion scheme. This disembedding from one's view and getting a metaperspective on oneself and the world open one up for change. Once the client has articulated a belief, the therapist does not challenge the belief but rather reflects it, holding it up for further inspection. Such beliefs are not necessarily about the self; they can also be about anticipated interpersonal experience or expectations. They can involve such expectations as "I will be rejected if I reach out" or "If others know who I really am, they will judge me or reject me." These beliefs have been described as maladaptive interpersonal cycles, and they contain in them the relevant needs, such as the need to be close, to be in control, or to be admired. Emotions and the schemes formed around them include cognitions, relational action tendencies, and needs, so the way they are articulated in language can be described in terms of their belief component, their feeling component, or their need component or in terms of the relationship between the components or between the components and other people.

Identifying maladaptive feelings helps clients articulate the destructive beliefs and the unmet needs that form a part of them. Maladaptive feelings are almost always accompanied by thoughts that are hostile to self or blaming of others. Depressogenic thought processes and beliefs need to be identified if they are to be overcome. Beliefs such as "I am worthless" or "I can't survive on my own" often accompany or help articulate a complex maladaptive feeling state. It is not that the belief always is sitting there in clients' heads, articulated in language, nor is it that these beliefs cause the problem. Rather, beliefs are a way of representing the emotional problem in language. They are an aspect of a narrative that articulates the felt and lived experience. When they are conscious and occur as repeated thoughts, they help maintain and intensify the depressive feeling states. Thus, thinking "I am a failure" or "I can't cope" intensifies the very states that produce these thoughts.

Clients often experience these beliefs as a negative voice in their head. Many learned this harsh internal voice through previous maltreatment by others, and it is destructive of the healthy self. Internalized hostility and contempt often lead to vicious self-attacks that leave clients stuck in their unhealthy feeling. To change the contempt, the destructive beliefs, and the totality of the experience they represent, clients must first articulate the beliefs in words. This articulation, called a *belief statement,* gives clients something to hold onto in dealing with these feelings and identifying what needs to be changed. EFT involves changing articulated beliefs not primarily by confronting their rationality or their validity, but by accessing alternate emotions and self-views that challenge the usefulness of the destructive beliefs and allow alternate beliefs to become accessible.

Beliefs thus are language-based representations of core emotion schemes that need to be changed. Putting the beliefs in words allows clients to discuss, reinspect, and challenge them. Accessing maladaptive feelings and identifying destructive thoughts and beliefs facilitate change both by providing access to the state that needs to be exposed to new experience and by paradoxically stimulating the mobilization of a healthier self-organization by a type of opponent process mechanism. Self-states often are closely connected to their opposites.

Phase 3: Transformation

In this phase the therapist

- helps the client generate new emotional responses to transform core maladaptive schemes,
- encourages reflection to make sense of experience, and
- validates new feelings and supports an emerging sense of self.

Generating New Emotional Responses

The first step in transformation involves helping clients access their opposing internal emotional resources and use these to transform the maladaptive emotion and challenge the dysfunctional beliefs. Once the client has been helped to arrive at and experience a core primary emotion, the therapist and client together evaluate if the emotion is an adaptive or maladaptive response to the current situation. Often this is self-evident; for example, when someone feels worthless or disgusting, it is clear this response is not useful or desirable. In cases when it is less clear, as with anger at feeling slighted or feelings of helplessness, client and therapist together explore if the feeling is maladaptive and possibly based on a psychological wound or trauma of some kind from the past, in which case the pain may need to be processed further to promote change. If the emotion arrived at underlying the depression is healthy, such as unexpressed anger or sadness, this adaptive emotion is used as a guide to action. If it is a core maladaptive emotion, such as shame or fear, it needs to be changed.

Part of clarifying that an emotion is maladaptive is identifying the negative voice and beliefs associated with it. The therapist does not challenge the negative voices in the personality or try to have the client reason with them. Rather, the therapist helps the client access an alternative, more adaptive self-organization to challenge the maladaptive state; together, they empower a new voice. The new voice, representing new possibilities, comes from within, from a new emotional state accessed in the session. The focus then becomes the generation of new possibilities within the personality by forming and relying on alternate self-organizations that the client constructs from newly accessed healthy emotional responses and needs. Therapists encourage clients to use these newly accessed resources to transform the maladaptive emotions and to challenge the destructive thoughts in their maladaptive emotional states. Clients can access new emotion by attending to subdominant emotions that they currently express but have not experienced fully and by attending to their needs (Greenberg, 2002). Further means of accessing healthy emotion are covered in chapter 13.

When clients experience the primary maladaptive feeling of shame and worthlessness and are able to symbolize it and realize that this is what they feel (rather than avoid it), they can begin to gain some reflective mastery over the feelings. With the realization and articulation of this core feeling, the desire to be rid of it and the need to feel acceptable become much more accessible, and the client begins to feel more strongly that he or she deserves to have the need to decrease suffering met. This sense of entitlement to one's need to be valued or accepted occurs especially in an empathic, validating, and supportive therapeutic environment. Clients are more able to be empathic toward themselves when they are both actually experiencing their suffering and receiving empathy and compassion from another. They simultaneously need to experience their distress and to step back sufficiently to see themselves, as well as to empathize with themselves, symbolize their experience, and reflect on their own pain and suffering. Once they have stepped back to view themselves, they have already begun reorganizing. They are more aware. Now they are ready, with the therapist's help, to let go of the bad feeling and construct new alternative responses to the situation that will help transform the old responses. Now they can let go of the shame and attend to the anger at having been shamed. Then they are in a position to access the need for protection of the more resilient sense of self and to stand up for or protect the self. By developing this alternate, more assertive self-organization and symbolizing it in words, a new voice emerges to challenge the old voice.

Emergence of new feelings results in the establishment of new needs and goals. To meet these new needs and goals, the client must access new resources. Working with emotion does not mean focusing only on emotion, but also focusing on motivation and goals. People are highly motivated, and they want to create possibilities as well as satisfy unmet needs. Helping clarify needs and wants helps clients establish a new path. The core of the change process involves the client's accessing inner strengths on the basis of adaptive primary emotional experience and directing attention to emergent, alternate, emotionally based needs and goals. Generating alternative responses in EFT thus is based on transforming emotion by both letting go of maladaptive emotion and changing emotion with emotion.

As we have seen in this process, clients transform maladaptive emotion states by becoming aware of them, by fully experiencing them, and by accessing other more adaptive emotions. In time, the more adaptive emotion transforms the maladaptive emotion by integrating with it to form a new scheme.

Reflecting on experience and symbolizing the new lived experience in words help to strengthen the formation of new schemes.

As part of this process the dysfunctional belief, which has been accessed through emotional arousal and symbolized in an emotionally rich context, is challenged from within by the newly accessed, voiced, and validated need or goal and by the additional resources mobilized by this need. Thus, the therapist helps the client access the need to be loved or recognized that is at the core of a feeling of worthlessness and supports the use of this need in combating the client's belief that he or she is worthless or unlovable. The client learns to say, for example, "I needed support, not criticism; I deserved more. I was only a child. I needed love."

The therapist supports the emergence of internal strengths, competence, and internal resources to combat negative cognitions and core maladaptive schemes. A client's internal support—that is, self-compassion and self-soothing capacities—also is evoked in response to his or her symbolization of distress and recognition of the core feeling and need, helping to regulate hopelessness, anxiety, or isolation. But key to change in the client is recontacting his or her core sense of vitality and the will to live. Once clients connect with their strengths, they then are able to provide themselves the support they did not obtain from others, and they begin to assert themselves and challenge self-denigrating or invalidating beliefs about the self or catastrophic assumptions concerning separation and abandonment. The combination of awareness of the belief, letting go of the bad feeling, and access to new needs, goals, and internal resources, plus the therapist's support and validation, provides the client with the strength to combat dysfunctional beliefs.

EFT thus involves exposing clients' unhealthy emotions at the core of their depression to more resilient internal experiences. Helping clients access their feelings of healthy sadness or anger exposes their fear and shame to new input. The maladaptive feelings and the shrinking action tendencies begin to be replaced with thrusting forward, reaching out, or recuperative tendencies, and their self-critical views of themselves as bad or worthless are challenged by the sense of worth accessed in healthier emotional states. Clients are thereby helped to integrate all parts of their experience into a new sense of self and to feel more self-accepting.

Clients change continually in light of emerging goals and opportunities. Once they feel their shame at being maltreated or their fear of rejection, they also can contact their need to be valued. With their attention shifted to the new goal of being valued, they set themselves a new problem to solve—how to feel valued. When clients discover that they can do something about their feelings, they can then prepare to solve their problems. Motivated both by their healthy aversion to pain and by their need for mastery, human contact, comfort, and safety, clients mobilize new resources to better cope. In this process, they help an alternate, healthier part of themselves to surface that they then can use to challenge and change some of their core unhealthy feelings, beliefs, and hostile thoughts. The newness in this process comes from within, by accessing previously unacknowledged healthy feelings and needs, and from without, by the affective attunement and confirmation of an empathic other.

At times clients also need to get some distance from emotions that overwhelm them. For the process of changing emotion with emotion to work, clients have to be able to name their emotions, evaluate them, and identify the negative voice. When clients are overwhelmed by their emotions, they cannot do this. With such clients therapists need to help them create a working distance by teaching and facilitating emotion regulation skills. Particularly helpful are learning to breathe properly and taking an observer's stance on the experience, which enables them to note that they are having the experience, rather than simply being in the experience.

Homework also can be useful in promoting and consolidating transformation. Homework is used in EFT predominantly to promote emotion awareness, regulation, reflection, and transformation of emotion. The main purpose of homework in emotion-based therapy is to consolidate and reinforce in-session changes that have taken place through practice outside the session. Practice enhances learning, and in-session change needs to be fully integrated (Goldfried & Davison, 1994). Thus, once clients have become aware of something such as awareness of a new feeling or of a critical voice, therapists ask them to practice being aware of this during the week. Clients who have gone through a significant transformation in a session such as the softening of a critical voice or the mobilization of an unmet need can practice being compassionate to themselves or asserting their needs during the week to fully integrate these changes.

Encouraging Reflection

New meaning is created by reflecting on experience to make sense of it and developing a new verbalized narrative of how the transformational experience fits or changes the client's identity. The new lived experience is consolidated in a new told story. The client constructs alternate meanings, develops a narrative of resilience, and explores the implications of this new self-validating view. The goals are now to clarify an experientially based nondepressed story about oneself, one's past, and one's future that is based on a sense of self-worth and strength and to promote actions based on the new realizations. In creating new meaning, clients reflect on their experience, often make connections between elements of their lives, change their views of themselves or their history, and state intentions and the desire to attain a feeling of greater connection and mastery in their lives. For example, a client who began with a narrative of failure and inability ends with a narrative of strength. Many of the women in our research began with stories of disempowerment and being silenced and ended up feeling empowered and finding their own voice.

Reflection and the creation of meaning are ongoing throughout treatment and continue beyond any single emotionally laden episode of treatment, but clients often refer back to such episodes and to core metaphors that arose in them. Thus, experientially based metaphors such as being "alone in a vast field," "in a glass cage," "at sea in a rudderless boat," or "thrown on a trash heap" become symbols of problems, whereas "rising out of a pit" or "being able to stand firm" or "to freshly see again" are metaphors that capture emergence, development, and the creation of new meanings and solutions.

Self-experience is now reorganized in such a way that the client is able to symbolize and organize emotional experience in terms of a new, more resilient view of self. Thus, the self is no longer judged as a failure, or separation from an attachment object is no longer perceived as dangerous to self. Both one's view of self and world and one's experience of being in the world change.

Supporting and Validating an Emerging Sense of Self

When a more confident, assertive, accepting sense of self emerges and the client reflects on this, the therapist acknowledges and validates this sense and helps the client to link this to life outside of therapy and to solve problems. The newly found sense of self-validation is used as a base for action in the world. After the client has experienced a shift in emotional process and has reorganized, the therapist and client collaborate in proposing actions that could consolidate the change. Frequently these possibilities emerge spontaneously. If not, the therapist promotes new ways of coping and encourages clients to connect with others rather than withdraw, to take risks, and to try new things. Expression, rather than depression, is encouraged. The therapist also might engage in experiential teaching to cognitively consolidate changes in perspective. Thus, the therapist might underscore how at moments of desperation, focusing internally and symbolizing one's experience to oneself, such as saying, "I feel devastated," can help the client gain a sense of mastery. Or the client may realize how putting himself or herself in the center of the experience and becoming an active agent of it rather than a passive victim helps to regulate an experience. Homework is useful for consolidating this insight as well.

6

THE THERAPEUTIC RELATIONSHIP

In this chapter we look at the role of the therapeutic relationship in emotion-focused therapy (EFT) for depression. We focus on both the client's and the therapist's contributions to the relationship. The two essential foci of an optimal therapeutic environment in EFT are (a) the relationship as an affect-regulating bond characterized by the therapist's presence and provision of empathy, positive regard, and congruence and (b) the facilitation of specific modes of emotional processing and experiencing at particular times. The result is a style of relating that involves a combination of following and leading that embodies all of the Rogerian relational qualities, and emphasizes empathic attunement to affect (Rogers, 1965).

Empathy has been established as one of three empirically supported aspects of the relationship, one that correlates highly with outcome ($r = .317$; Bohart, Elliott, Greenberg, & Watson, 2002; Watson, 2001). Deficits in empathy and emotional connection between infants and their caretakers have been found to affect areas of right brain development involved in empathy and compassion. When the client makes an empathic connection with the therapist, the client's brain centers are affected, and new possibilities open up for him or her. In addition, the Rogerian components of acceptance and congruence not only create an optimal therapeutic environment in which clients feel safe to fully engage in the process of self-exploration and new learning, but also contribute to clients' affect regulation by providing inter-personal soothing. Over time, the client internalizes this interpersonal regu-lation of affect into self-soothing, which is the capacity to regulate one's own inner states. These optimal therapeutic relational qualities thus facilitate the dyadic regulation of emotion through provision of safety, security, and con-nection, breaking the client's sense of isolation, confirming self-experience, and promoting both self-empathy and self-exploration. The establishment of an empathic connection between therapist and client begins in phase 1 and influences the remaining steps and phases of treatment.

Therapists first create a warm, safe, and validating climate through their way of being with the client. One of the central elements of this way of being is the affective climate created by facial, vocal, gestural, and postural cues. The emotional climate has to do with the total attitude of the therapist, who communicates his or her perceptiveness and attunement to the client through verbal expressions, body posture, and vocal and facial expression. It is clear that the therapist's overall attitude, not only his or her techniques, influ-ences the client's responses and the way the client experiences and expresses his or her feelings in the therapeutic relationship. The therapist who con-veys genuine interest, acceptance, caring, compassion, and joy and who avoids anger, contempt, disgust, and fear creates the environment for a secure emo-tional bond. The classic film series *Three Approaches to Psychotherapy* (Shostrom, 1965) shows the psychologists Rogers, Perls, and Ellis providing therapy sessions to a woman, Gloria. A recent analysis by Magai and Haviland-Jones (2002) studied the emotional climate that each of the therapists cre-ated. In their behavior in the film, in their theories, and more generally in their personalities and personal lives, the therapists expressed and focused on very different emotions. Rogers focused on interest, joy, and shame. Perls focused on contempt and fear, and Ellis on anger and fear. The therapists' facial expression of emotion and their vocal quality clearly set very different emotional climates and are aspects of their ways of being.

Clients' right hemispheres respond to therapists' microaffective com-munication as well as to their words, and all of these influence clients' pro-cesses of dynamic self-organization. In addition to the categorical emotions expressed by the therapist, such as interest, anger, sadness, fear, and shame, the vitality aspects of the therapists' emotional expression, such as rhythm, cadence, and energy, are also important in affective attunement. Therapists' facial communication of emotion is one of the central aspects of the emo-tional climate. As Levinas (1998) argued, seeing the face of the other evokes experience in the viewer. The face is a powerful, if ambiguous, text from which much is read, and facial expression is a central aspect of relational attunement. People have been shown to read facial affect automatically at incredibly high speed, especially affects, such as anger and fear, that have implications for survival. Childhood abuse has been shown to affect the ac-curacy of interpretation of facial cues and to lead to the overattribution of hostility to others' facial expressions. Clients thus learn some of who they are and how acceptable they are from the facial expressions of their therapists, which evoke in them certain feelings.

Pacing is another of the more crucial influences on emotional climate. The therapist's tone, energy, rhythm, and cadence need to be appropriate to the emotion being worked with. A slow, soothing tone and manner are crucial when the client is accessing core vulnerable emotions such as sadness, whereas an encouraging, more energetic tone is helpful in supporting the more boundary-setting emotions of anger and disgust.

Clients see their experience reflected in the therapist's face and manner of response. If clients see understanding on the therapist's face and hear a validating response, they are helped to acknowledge that they do experience and that they are able to communicate their feelings. They experience that their feelings have an impact not only on themselves, but also on others, which in turn has an impact on them. Put more simply, a client feels, "Oh, you get it, you get me, and I get you too!" For example, when clients are experiencing grief or sadness, therapists respond to clients' pain in different ways. Therapists' faces register pain, their eyes may tear, they lean in and listen closely (these are right brain–to–right brain communications; Schore, 2003). To bring this experience into the room even further and help solidify it with the client, therapists might ask clients what it is like to share these feelings with them, how they experience the therapist, or what their sense of the therapist is in the moment. The therapist also might ask what the client sees in his or her face and how this makes the client feel. Therapists may also share with their clients their own sense of feeling close to them as clients share their feelings. This communication validates the client's ability to be with these feelings and to also let the therapist into the experience. In this way, therapists deepen the dyadic experience (Fosha, 2004).

In addition to providing a safe and responsive emotional climate attuned to clients' feelings, therapists facilitate different types of processing and also use specific interventions that have been found to help clients resolve particular cognitive–affective problems—for example, directing attention inward when the client is externally oriented, promoting dialogues between parts of self to facilitate integration, facilitating a broader view of a significant other with empty-chair work, focusing on an unclear felt sense, and evocatively unfolding to promote an understanding of problematic reactions.

Balancing the receptive and the deepening aspects of the therapeutic relationship can pose some special challenges with clients experiencing depression. Clients may have difficulty focusing on their bodily felt experience. Such clients may be so disconnected from the flow of their inner experience that all they are aware of is the chronic sense of heaviness, listlessness, and apathy so characteristic of the depressed state. Other clients may have been so neglected as children that they have neither the language to describe their subjective experience nor the skills to attend inwardly to the emotional impact of events. To these clients, therapists who focus on their inner experiencing and affective states are speaking a foreign language. Patience is required of therapists as these clients learn the vocabulary and skills to enable them to work effectively in EFT and subsequently to focus on their own experience in the world at large.

People with depression can be very sensitive to criticism and susceptible to feelings of failure. As a result, some clients experience feelings of shame, inadequacy, or failure when their therapists ask them to focus on their feelings or propose a task to help them move beyond a passive sense of powerlessness or to overcome a past sense of victimization. Therapist attempts to promote an internal focus or exploration of the client's own contribution to particular problems can be experienced as shaming and create a sense of failure in clients who feel overly responsible or who blame themselves for their intense feelings of hopelessness and despair. Therapists need to be especially sensitive to their clients' responses to their formulations and suggestions.

Numerous studies have shown that in addition to empathy, a positive therapeutic alliance is associated with good outcome (Horvath & Greenberg, 1994; Safran & Muran, 1998). The development of collaboration has been established as an important aspect of the therapeutic relationship. Thus, in addition to creating the emotional climate that secures a warm, trusting bond, it is important to foster and nurture a collaborative alliance throughout the course of therapy. The alliance reflects three important aspects of therapeutic work: the bond, or the feelings the participants have toward each other; the extent to which they agree on the goals of therapy; and the ways in which they go about meeting those goals (Bordin, 1979).

There are a number of ways to develop and maintain the therapeutic alliance. The first of these involves introducing clients to the process of therapy (Watson & Greenberg, 1995). At this level, therapists define the relationship in terms of confidentiality, boundaries, timing, and structure of the sessions and convey that the primary focus of treatment is the client's concerns. The therapist's central intention with this introduction is to help clients open up and reveal their inner thoughts, feelings, and fears—in other words, to risk being vulnerable with their therapists in the hope that together they can come to a better understanding of clients' inner and outer worlds and effect meaningful change that will ameliorate their sense of despair. Unless this exploratory goal is adequately negotiated between the parties, the therapy will likely end prematurely or be bogged down.

Once this introductory phase has been successfully negotiated, therapists and clients enter the working phase of therapy. The relational tasks that are important during this phase include provision of a rationale for and agreement to engage in the specific processing tasks that best fit with the formulation of the client's problems and the agreed-on goals in therapy. The implementation of experiential tasks poses unique problems for clients with depression. An important goal in EFT is to foster dialogue between clients' inner reflective selves and their experiencing selves. However, both of these aspects of functioning are impaired in depression. With depression, clients lose the ability both to experience and to stand back from their experience to examine it reflectively. As a result, therapists work to stimulate experience and to foster clients' ability to attend to, observe, and reflect on their inner experiencing.

Another potential difficulty with the therapeutic alliance during the early and middle phases of therapy is a discrepancy between the therapist's and the client's view of the client. Therapists see clients as active agents in life in general and in the therapy process specifically. However, clients who are depressed see themselves as passive victims, as swamped by their feelings, and as having little or no control over the process. Moreover, their lack of energy and general malaise can frustrate therapists who work really hard to promote a shift in their clients' mood. Together, therapists and clients jointly create a positive or negative therapeutic environment.

THERAPIST CONTRIBUTION TO THE ALLIANCE

In the 1940s and 1950s, Rogers articulated the therapist's contribution to therapy by emphasizing the importance of empathy, acceptance, and regard as essential elements in creating an environment in which clients feel safe to explore their experiences (Rogers, 1957, 1959). He suggested that therapists need to

> create a warm, safe, non-judgmental environment, to respond with deep understanding of the client's emotional experience, to set limits on behavior but not on attitudes and feelings, and for the therapist to withhold from probing, blaming, interpreting, reassuring, or persuading. (quoted in Bozarth & Wilkins, 2001, p. ii)

In this way the therapist can best contribute to the creation of a positive therapeutic alliance. A recent study that looked at clients being treated for depression in cognitive–behavioral and process experiential psychotherapy found that clients' perceptions of the relationship conditions were highly correlated with their ratings of the therapeutic alliance in both approaches (Watson & Geller, 2005). In addition, their perception of the relationship was associated with changes in level of self-esteem and self-report of interpersonal difficulties, whereas therapists' acceptance of their clients was predictive of changes in depression.

We briefly discuss each of the therapist attitudes—presence, congruence, empathy, and acceptance—in turn in the sections that follow. We discuss each separately, as if it were distinct from the others, but it is probably more accurate to see them as part of a single therapeutic way of trying to be fully present with and understand another (Geller & Greenberg, 2002). Without being fully present, it is not possible to communicate healing empathy. Although it is possible to empathize with another person without necessarily feeling accepting, this would be cold, clinical empathy. In a similar way, although it is possible for therapists to intentionally convey that they understand clients and care for them, if this is insincere, therapists risk appearing artificial, and clients are unlikely to trust such therapists with the most precious and vulnerable aspects of their psyche.

Presence

To establish a positive alliance, it is important for therapists to be present with their clients. Therapeutic presence involves, among other qualities, being receptive and sensitive to the client's moment-by-moment, changing experience, being fully immersed in the moment, feeling a sense of expansion and spaciousness, and being with and for the client (Geller & Greenberg, 2002). The kind of presence that seems to be therapeutic is the state of awareness of moment-by-moment emotional reactions, as well as thoughts and perceptions, occurring in the client, in the therapist, and between them in the therapeutic relationship. Therapists need to let go of their own specific concerns (e.g., the quarrel with their spouse, the falling value of the dollar, an upcoming vacation) and truly show up in the session. To be present for clients is to empty oneself, to clear a space so as to be able to listen clearly in the moment to the narratives and problems that clients bring. Therapists need to see their clients' faces and hear their voices. It is through the therapist's undivided and focused attention that the client feels prized and is able to clearly discern his or her own concerns and difficulties. By giving clients their full attention, therapists are able to more fully resonate with clients' feelings and experience of events and to provide the level of empathic responding that will be most optimal at different points during the session.

Being present allows for the type of attunement that keeps the contact between the two people alive and allows the interaction to unfold in a smooth and flowing manner. Implicit understandings and intentions that fit with the other person's last moment guide much of what both parties do moment-by-moment in therapy. When a therapist's response does not fit the client's experience, there is a disjunction and a potential rupture in the smooth cocreated experience. The dyad must negotiate any pending rupture either implicitly, by self-correcting and refitting their responses to each other, or explicitly, by articulating intentions, feelings, and needs and renegotiating the next step. This type of continued presence results in the smooth, seamless interaction of true dialogue. Dialogue of this type often leads to heightened moments of meeting, or what Buber (1958) referred to as "I–Thou" contact. In these moments, people share living through an emotional experience together. An intersubjective experience is lived while it is occurring: It is a shared experience of attending to and experiencing the same thing at the same time and knowing that the other is coexperiencing the same thing. Each experiences something of the other's experience and knows that this is occurring. This shared experience creates a strong bond, a sense of togetherness that breaks any sense of existential isolation and promotes trust and openness. It also is a lived moment of experience that remains indelibly stamped in memory. These moments produce therapeutic change in clients' sense of self and way of relating.

Congruence

Congruence, or authenticity, can at an initial level of analysis be broken into two separate components (Lietaer, 1993): (a) awareness of one's own internal experience and (b) transparency, or the willingness to communicate to the other person what is going on within. To be facilitatively congruent, therapists need also to be committed to understanding and respecting their clients. They need to operate both with a genuine desire not to have power over their clients and with a belief in the therapeutic importance of accepting their clients' experience as valid. Finally, they need to be fully present and in contact with their clients as well as themselves. These intentions both precede being facilitatively congruent and are themselves important aspects of therapeutic congruence.

The communicative aspects of congruence involve the ability to translate intrapersonal experience into certain types of interpersonal responses that are consistent with certain implicit intentions (Greenberg & Geller, 2001). The deeper-level intentions include, in addition to valuing and understanding the other, the intention to facilitate the other's development, to be accepting and noncritical of the other, to confirm the other's experience, to focus on the other's strengths, and above all to do the other no harm. These intentions are what determine whether congruence is therapeutic. If, for example, one had a genuine desire to harm, being congruent would not be therapeutic.

Being aware of one's own flow of internal experience and connecting with the essence of one's feeling is a central component of congruence and is the easiest aspect of the concept to endorse as universally therapeutic. In our view, it always is therapeutic for therapists to be aware of their own feelings and reactions, because this awareness orients them and helps them be interpersonally clear and trustworthy. This inner awareness and contact naturally flow from the experience of therapeutic presence.

The case of transparency, or the communication component of congruence, is much more complicated than the self-awareness component. Being facilitatively transparent involves many interpersonal skills (Greenberg & Geller, 2001). This component involves the ability not only to express what one truly feels, but also to express it in a way that is facilitative. *Transparency* thus is a global term for a complex set of interpersonal skills embedded within a set of therapeutic attitudes. These skills depend on three factors: first, on therapist attitudes; second, on certain processes such as facilitativeness, discipline, and comprehensiveness; and third, on the interpersonal stance of the therapist.

First, and probably most important, congruent responses need always to be communicated nonjudgmentally. In life, clearly, one can be congruently destructive; one can congruently attack or even murder. This obviously is not what we mean by the term *congruence* in therapy, because the term is really qualified tacitly by a number of other beliefs and views. We thus find it helpful to use the words *facilitative* or *therapeutic* to qualify the word *congruent*.

Second, therapeutic genuineness also means being transparent in a disciplined manner. Therapists need first to be aware of their deepest level of experience, and this may take time and reflection. Next, they need to be clear about their intention for sharing their experience—that it is for the client or the relationship, and not for themselves. It is also always important for therapists to be sensitive to the timing of disclosure and to whether clients are open to or too vulnerable to receive what the therapist has to offer. Discipline thus involves restraint in communicating what the therapist is feeling and taking the time to make sure, for example, that what the client is expressing is a core or primary feeling, rather than a secondary feeling. Another qualifying concept that helps to clarify the transparency aspect of congruence is comprehensiveness, by which we mean "saying all of it." The therapist expresses not only the central or focal aspect that is being felt, but also the metaexperience—what he or she feels about what he or she is feeling and communicating. Thus, a therapist who says that he or she feels irritated or bored is not saying all of it. Therapists need also to communicate their concern about this potentially hurting their clients and to express that they are communicating this out of a wish to clarify and improve a connection, not destroy it; this is the meaning of "saying all of it."

Interpersonal stance is the third factor. Congruent interaction can be examined in terms of the interactional stance therapists take in relation to a circumplex grid of interpersonal interactions (Benjamin, 1996). This grid is based on the two major dimensions of autonomy–control and closeness–affiliation. Consistent with interpersonal theory, this grid outlines a set of complementary responses that fit each other and that interactionally "pull" for each other. Thus, attack pulls for defensiveness or withdrawal, and affirmation pulls for disclosure and revelation. The skill of congruent responding involves not reacting in a complementary fashion to a negative interpersonal pull of the client, like recoiling when attacked, but rather acting in such a way as to pull for a more therapeutically productive response from the client, such as clear expression. This would be achieved by an empathic, understanding response to an attack, rather than recoil.

A response from an affirming stance is likely to be facilitative. Affirmation is the baseline response in supportive therapies and pulls for trust and disclosure. But what can a therapist do when he or she is not feeling affirming, but is feeling angry, critical, and rejecting and cannot get past this feeling to something more affiliative? A facilitatively congruent interactional response involves first connecting with the fundamental attitudes or intentions of being helpful, understanding, valuing, respecting, and being nonintrusive or nondominant. This connection will lead the therapist to express these feelings as disclosures. If the interpersonal stance of disclosing the difficult feeling is adopted, rather than the complementary stances of attacking, rejecting, or seducing, then this congruent response is more likely to be facilitative. It is not the content of the disclosure that is the central issue in being facilitative; rather, it is the interpersonal stance of disclosure *in a facilitative way* that is important. What is congruent is the feeling of wanting to disclose in the service of facilitating and the action of disclosing.

The different ways of being facilitatively congruent in dealing with different classes of difficult feeling thus are to some degree specifiable. They all involve adopting a position of disclosing. Expressing a feeling that could be perceived as negative in a stance that is disclosing, rather than in the stance that usually accompanies that feeling, will help make it facilitative. Disclosure implicitly or explicitly involves willingness to or an interest in exploring with the other what one is disclosing. For example, when they feel attacked or angry, therapists do not attack the other, but rather disclose that they are feeling attacked or angry. They do not use blaming, "you" language. Rather, they take responsibility for their feelings and use "I" language to disclose what they are feeling. Above all, they do not go into one-up, escalatory positions in this communication, but rather openly disclose feelings of fear, anger, or hurt. When the therapist experiences nonaffiliative, rejecting feelings or loss of interest in the client's experience, the interactional skill involves being able to disclose this in the context of communicating congruently that the therapist does not wish to feel this. Or therapists can disclose these feelings as problems getting in the way and that they are trying to repair so that they will be able to feel more understanding of and closer to the client. The key in communicating what could be perceived as negative feelings in a congruently facilitative way is to communicate in a nondominant, affiliative, disclosing way.

For example, a very fragile and explosive client once told a therapist in an intense encounter that she feared and hated the therapist because he was so phony and acted so presumptuously in assuming that he understood what she felt. She said that she saw him as a leech trying to suck her emotional life out of her and that although he professed good intentions, he was really out to destroy her. Under the relentless attack, the therapist told her that he felt afraid of her anger. Tears came to his eyes as he told her how hurt he felt, without blame or recrimination, and without an explicit power- or control-related intention to get her to stop—just a disclosure of what it felt like inside for him in that moment. This disclosure led to a change in the interaction and pulled from the client some of her concern for the therapist.

Empathy

Unless therapists are empathically attuned to clients' feelings and meanings, they are not able to perceive their clients' goals or work with them to identify tasks that might be helpful in the realization of those goals. With clients with depression, the role of empathy and acceptance is particularly important. In addition to being essential to the development of the facilitative working relationship, empathy is an important means of helping clients regulate their affect. Having the therapist be attuned to and convey an understanding both verbally and nonverbally (e.g., facially) of a client's inner affective state provides the experience, for the first time, that one's affective state can be seen and shared by another. This is crucial in helping clients consolidate themselves as a self both separate and connected. Empathy from the therapist also helps clients become aware of and symbolize their own experience. Empathic responding by therapists helps clients become aware of their emotional experience, label it in awareness, and modulate it so that it is not overwhelming or muted excessively so that its message is lost. Empathic understanding responses and empathic affirmations amplify the client's experience so that it can be apprehended more clearly, whereas evocative reflections and empathic conjectures facilitate its differentiation, modulation, and evaluation. Empathic exploration facilitates the client's turning inward to explore and unpack his or her inner subjective worldviews and feelings about events. Therapists gently and tentatively accompany their clients as they try to articulate their inner experience. The sense of companionship and unity that emerges from this common endeavor helps to forge a therapeutic bond and assists the therapist in correctly identifying the goals of treatment. Empathic exploration is not only an important task by itself because it facilitates clients' awareness and differentiation of their inner experience; it is fundamental to the development of a productive working alliance.

Empathy also highlights the subjectivity of clients' perceptions and experience. Therapists highlight clients' role in constructing their experience by emphasizing the subjectivity of their perceptions and construals of reality. For example, the use of the word *seems* in phrases like "It seems so hopeless" suggests that the depressogenic construal is a subjective state that is open to reformulation and may be time limited. As Troeml-Ploetz (1980) observed, therapists' reflections of clients' current states and self-expressions act as paradoxical interventions that imply alternative views. For example, a therapist intervention that validates a client's view that the world seems black, as opposed to one that contradicts the client's view, has the paradoxical effect of making the client realize that it is not all black. Thus, therapists' reflections help to activate clients' reflective processes and encourage them to evaluate and examine the representativeness of the words they are choosing to label their experience and the completeness of their narratives.

Acceptance

Warmth, compassion, openness, and respect toward the client and his or her experience, as well as caring for the client as a separate person with permission to have his or her own feelings and experiences, are all crucial aspects of therapy. The sense that another is accepting and can be trusted, to the extent that one perceives the other as congruent and sincere, is very important to the sense that one is valued and liked by the other. Acceptance by another affirms one's existence and fosters a sense of belonging and participation, because it simultaneously allows one to accept one's own experience. By being accepting of their clients, therapists provide a climate in which clients can become aware of their experience and can integrate and process it in ways that can facilitate their developing new modes of being. Acceptance of experience does not mean that the therapist evaluates it as good; rather, it is a type of acknowledgment that this is what the client is experiencing in the moment, that the experience is what it is.

Acceptance also involves unconditional confidence in the inner core of possibility within the client. By sensing their therapists' unconditional acceptance of their experience, clients lose their preoccupation with their therapists, and their energy becomes available to turn inward and contact their own experience. Reduction of interpersonal anxiety leads to capacity for tolerance of more intrapersonal anxiety. Clients are able to face and accept more of their experience with the unconditional acceptance of another. Acceptance seems to be particularly important in the treatment of depression. A recent study of the relationship conditions found that of all the conditions, clients' postsession report of therapists' acceptance was most predictive of a decline in depression (Watson & Geller, 2005).

Relation Difficulties With Clients With Depression

It is easy to be present and embody the attitudes of acceptance, empathy, and congruence when clients are easy to work with, are focused on and share their inner subjective experience, are self-motivated, and seem responsive to the interventions. However, it can be harder to maintain these attitudes when therapists experience clients as resistant to their efforts or somehow unable to respond to their attempts to help them with their feelings of despair and hopelessness. Some therapists may fear being bogged down by their clients' feelings of depression. They may feel frustrated by their clients' fogginess or difficulty clearly presenting what they are experiencing. Some therapists may feel scared and overwhelmed by the depth of their clients' despair; they may be so anxious that they focus rigidly on whether their clients are likely to self-harm and forestall any articulation or expression of their clients' pain. These therapists may work hard to try to cheer up their clients and to shift their mood by being overly reassuring or by problem solving for them. All of these feelings are quite natural; however, they need to be carefully monitored and regulated because they can leave the client feeling criticized, invalidated, and disempowered. Although the end goal is to help clients shift their mood and attain a more hopeful and optimistic perspective, it is important to provide a facilitative emotional climate and the optimal conditions of empathy, acceptance, and congruence.

When they experience clients as resistant, therapists need to be less focused on their own agendas and more open to their clients. At these times it is better for therapists to let go of their objectives and once again try to be fully present and connect with their clients' subjective experience. This openness will help them reach a better understanding of what their clients' objectives are and how to achieve them together. It helps at these times to try a number of alternative ways of proceeding to find the one that fits best with clients' style, objectives, and current problems. Like their clients, therapists too need to be able to curb their own inner critic and the voices that contribute to their feeling ineffectual and like a failure when clients do not respond as anticipated. Therapists can soothe their own anxiety when things are not going well by using emotion regulation strategies such as imagining a safe place, good connections with others, use of soothing self-talk, and a focus on feeling compassion, receptiveness, and acceptance of their clients' difficulties.

CLIENT CONTRIBUTIONS TO THE ALLIANCE

Most of the research on what constitutes a good alliance has focused on therapist and client in-session behavior (Henry, Schacht, & Strupp, 1990; Horvath & Greenberg, 1994; Safran & Muran, 1998). Other research has looked at client demographic characteristics and attachment patterns in the development of the alliance (Beutler, Harwood, Alimohamed, & Malik, 2002). More recently Kwan, Watson, and Stermac (2000) looked at the attitudes clients with depression held about therapy. Clients reported on their perceptions of the potential helpfulness of therapy, the amount of social support they expected to receive, and the possible negative consequences that might ensue as a result of being in therapy. They found that when clients with depression entered therapy with an open, trusting stance toward their therapists and toward their own experience, they developed more positive alliances with their therapists. In contrast, clients who were skeptical about the benefits of therapy, who feared a loss of social support and approval, and who felt ashamed formed poorer alliances with their therapists and were more likely to drop out. Thus, clients who enter therapy with a collaborative mindset are predisposed to establish positive alliances with their therapists. These clients see treatment as useful, expect to benefit, are trusting about the services they will receive, and work more easily in therapy, in sharp contrast to clients who enter therapy feeling skeptical, ashamed, or otherwise unable to engage in therapy.

Blocks to Engagement

Clients may have one or more of five main problems in becoming engaged in the process of therapy:

1. They feel ashamed.
2. They are skeptical about the process.
3. They are overly passive.
4. They have difficulty constructing narratives and accessing memories.
5. They have difficulty exploring their feelings.

Concern about the methods used, the length of therapy, and reluctance to explore feelings can occur at any time in therapy. The following sections describe these relational problems and how they are addressed in EFT.

Shame

Many clients enter therapy feeling ashamed and defeated, a state that is associated with most depressions. Therapists need to be particularly alert to cues that clients are feeling ashamed and demoralized. Sometimes this state is communicated in their body language—for example, downcast eyes or slumped posture. At other times this state is more covert and less obvious; clients may have difficulty talking about the details of their lives; they may try to entertain the therapist, maintaining a gloss to divert attention from the deeper sense of defeat and shame they are experiencing. Western culture has very ambivalent attitudes toward help seeking and especially toward psychotherapy. Many cultures, including some Asian cultures, have beliefs that may induce shame in seeking and being involved in therapy. There is still a stigma attached to seeking psychotherapy in many cultures and subcultures. The act of seeking help, although it can indicate that one is taking charge and trying to find solutions to current difficulties in functioning, also puts one in a one-down position in relation to the helper and others who appear to be able to live independently without assistance.

Therapists try to be sensitive to clients' feelings of shame by respecting their autonomy and by minimizing the power imbalance between therapist and client. Clients are encouraged to be active in therapy as they explore their experience and begin to examine the sources of their depression. They are viewed as experts on their own experiences. Moreover, therapists' acceptance and communication of a nonjudgmental stance are vital to help clients overcome their sense of failure at needing help. For some clients, the experience of being in therapy can alter these feelings toward needing help. For example, instead of loss of social support, many clients find that family and friends in fact rally to their aid when they know that they are seeking outside assistance; this may be true in the workplace and in other social contexts as well. In this way clients' expectations of how others will react are disconfirmed.

This may not always be the case, however, and clients who see their social relationships as jeopardized as a result of being in therapy may choose to withdraw rather than face the losses or turbulence that might ensue. These clients may be viewed as being in the precontemplation stage of engaging in therapy (Prochaska, DiClemente, & Norcross, 1992). Resolving clients' ambivalence about being in therapy and about revealing hidden aspects of the self may involve exploring these issues empathically so that clients can seriously weigh the benefits and consequences of remaining in or leaving therapy. The method used will depend on how early these feelings emerge and on the overall quality of the alliance. For clients who are more deferent, therapists might suggest a two-chair dialogue to work on their ambivalence. However, if these strains appear early in therapy and the client is more resistant, then a less directive, more exploratory approach that helps the client actively make a decision about the preferred course of action might be more helpful.

Skepticism

Some clients express their reluctance to engage as well as a general distrust of the process through skepticism about the procedures, and a few may express skepticism about the process itself. Some clients may be operating with an alternative worldview that sees their problems in primarily physiological terms, and thus they may not be open to psychological processes. Others may question the therapist's focus on their feelings, believing that talking about feelings will not be useful, especially when they cause so much pain. Other clients may see no benefit in talking to anybody. Clients concerned about the length of therapy, especially of brief treatments, may question whether they can be treated successfully in such a short time. Yet others may believe treatment will last too long, thinking that a session or two should be all they need to feel better again.

Clients sometimes deliberately refrain from expressing their emotions in therapy because they judge their feelings to be overwhelming, wrong, or shameful; this is frequently an issue at the beginning of therapy. Clients may be reluctant to focus on their feelings and fearful of the consequences of doing so. Psychotherapy research shows the importance of having clients and therapists agree on the specific goals and interventions to be used in therapy (Horvath & Greenberg, 1994), so it is important to provide a safe, nonthreatening context for clients to express their emotions. For those clients for whom an accepting environment is insufficient, it may be important to address their negative attitudes toward emotion before implementing any techniques aimed at increasing emotional expression.

Emotion-focused therapists are very careful not to ride roughshod over clients' emotion expression–related beliefs, especially when they do not match therapists' own beliefs on the value of focusing on emotion. Clients' negative attitudes toward emotion may be deeply rooted in their sense of identity and based on powerful experiences or highly meaningful family or cultural values. Simply dismissing these beliefs or forcing clients to act in a way that is contrary to their values may impede the development of a good working alliance and is unlikely to lead to a positive outcome in therapy. When clients have negative attitudes toward emotion, therapists can help them to articulate their personal goals and values concerning emotional behavior. Making these beliefs explicit gives clients the opportunity to re-examine and perhaps revise them. Empathic exploration and two-chair dialogues may be useful in helping such clients explore their beliefs. Psychoeducation is also useful; informing clients about research and clinical observations on the benefits of emotion may be very helpful in resolving their negative attitudes toward the value of focusing on emotion.

Client skepticism needs to be addressed before therapy can proceed. For some clients, it may be sufficient to give them a theoretical framework that helps them see the potential benefits of working with emotions in therapy or discussing their problems with someone else. However, EFT therapists need to be careful not to invalidate their clients' concerns by being too persuasive. It is a delicate balancing act to provide a rationale for the treatment while respecting clients' autonomy and freedom of choice. If skepticism persists, it might be more beneficial to explore clients' reluctance in greater depth so that therapists can understand it better and clients can have the opportunity to examine their beliefs and fears before deciding whether to commit themselves more fully to the process of EFT.

Passivity

Some clients with depression present as overly passive, dependent, or negativistic and unable to assume responsibility for the therapy. These clients seem to hope that the therapist will cure them without their having to be actively engaged in the process. Typically such clients do not think about what has been discussed between sessions and do not actively engage in understanding their depression or looking for ways to ameliorate it. They do not seem to know how to actively engage in the process. They have difficulty being reflective and are unable to see how their behavior contributes to their problems. They have a tendency to be somewhat impulsive in an attempt to find easy solutions. With these clients, it is important for the therapist to try to help them become more reflective. Homework assignments can involve asking clients to try to observe their behaviors and reactions to note when they seem excessive or puzzling and to bring these observations in for exploration. Asking them to keep emotion logs or diaries can be helpful (Greenberg, 2002). Therapists need to work hard to help clients formulate questions about their experiencing that they can then track together to try to promote greater reflexivity and agency.

Difficulty Constructing Narratives

Some clients have difficulty talking about the details of their lives, whereas others may not have easy access to early memories. Clients with depression often observe that it is like wandering lost in a fog. They feel disconnected from the world around them; they have limited attention spans and difficulty concentrating, and they feel unable to think clearly. These clients may be so withdrawn from the flow of daily living, even from work or other attachments, that they do not have much to share about their lives. They may also have difficulty constructing narratives or stories about their lives because they have few memories of the past and few autobiographical memories; this is very likely in clients who were neglected as children or who have experienced some other type of trauma. Such clients often have tremendous difficulty trying to link their feelings to specific events; they might say that there is no reason for them to feel the way they do. These clients seem to lack an inner barometer of what is good or beneficial for them, a deficit that is often exacerbated by their feelings of depression.

Clients with depression who have difficulty constructing narratives or providing the therapist with accounts of their past and current life may have difficulty in short-term therapy and may need longer-term therapy to learn to become aware of their feelings and express them. Therapists must be especially patient with these clients; it is easy to feel frustrated and stuck with them. These clients may appear obdurate and difficult, with the result that the therapist may feel that he or she is caught in a power struggle. For example, when a 47-year-old man who was a single child was asked about his childhood memories or his most painful early feelings, he could not recall or recount anything. All he could say was that his parents fed and clothed him well and that he liked reading comics. He answered all inquiries about how he felt by saying that he was either fine or frustrated. Therapists work at viewing such clients' difficulties sympathetically and try to let go of their own agenda for clients to respond in certain ways to the treatment.

To assist these clients with the task of therapy, therapists are highly attuned to their clients' nonverbal behaviors and facial expressions. These may be quite muted and fleeting but nonetheless can provide clues to what is happening within clients at different times and when different topics are discussed. It is often useful for therapists to use conjectural empathy based on clients' body posture and facial expressions as well as whatever content they do provide to help these clients become aware of and label their feelings. In addition, it may be important to heighten clients' sensations and work with visual imagery to try to make their experiences more alive and available in the moment. In working with the client discussed in the preceding paragraph, his therapist continued to encourage him to symbolize his feelings. With the help of an emotion diary, he was able to recall childhood memories of loneliness and not fitting in and gradually was able to say that he felt sad and angry. During the course of therapy, his live-in girlfriend moved out, and he was able to say he felt lonely and discarded. This reflection allowed him to identify and label his need for her, which led him to reach out to her. She was very responsive to his approach and his increased self-disclosure of his feelings for her.

Difficulty Exploring Feelings

Many clients are unable to articulate what they are feeling. *Alexithymia* has been proposed as a term to describe an inability to put words to one's feelings. For some clients this may be a skills deficit; for others, their mistrust of others or of their own perceptions and feelings may make them reluctant to talk about them publicly in a therapeutic setting. Therapists may be alerted to clients' lack of awareness of their emotional experience when they do not refer to feelings at all in their narratives. These clients may talk about what is happening in their lives but pay little attention to the impact of events on them and to their own inner responses to events. They may talk in well-modulated, rhythmical tones, as if they were presenting a well-rehearsed speech or chatting to a friend. They are not immediately in touch with their feelings; instead, they seem distant from them and appear to be talking about them rather than experiencing or expressing them in the moment. In contrast, when clients are in touch with their feelings, their voices are focused inward and are soft and hesitant, with ragged pauses and emphasis in unexpected places (Rice & Kerr, 1986). Their language is often poignant and vivid so that there is a sense of immediacy and aliveness.

Clients' difficulties with expressing feelings can stem from difficulties understanding feelings because of limited emotional processing skills, blocked emotional awareness, negative attitudes toward emotion, or limited understanding of their emotional experience. Many clients with depression have difficulty attending to their feelings and lack the skills required to label and interpret them. Often these clients have lost touch with the flow of inner emotional experience because they have become stuck in chronic states of depression. Although some clients may find it relatively easy to listen to their inner subjective experience and be quite adroit at rendering it in words, others may be quite lost and able to focus only on physiological signs and symptoms, such as a general sense of malaise or heaviness. These clients often say things like "I don't know how I feel" or "I don't have the words." They may appear confused when asked how they feel about something. Their focus of attention is on the outside world (Leijssen, 1996, 1998; Polster & Polster, 1973). A number of techniques can be helpful in enhancing clients' emotional processing skills, including focusing, empathic responding (especially evocative responses), highlighting clients' nonverbal behavior, and assigning homework exercises to identify problematic situations and related thoughts and feelings.

It is difficult to help clients explore their feelings when they are actively trying to block them from awareness. Weston (2005) found that clients with depression often were aware of trying actively to interrupt or prevent an experience from emerging in the session. Avoidant clients, however, often are not consciously aware of their feelings because these feelings are so threatening. With avoidant clients it is particularly important to provide conditions of safety so that they can begin to confront the painful feelings that they are trying to keep out of awareness. If these clients are able to express their feelings in a safe and supportive environment, they may come to see their feelings as painful but bearable. This realization will make them more comfortable and committed to working in an experiential mode with less need to avoid their feelings.

Clients' nonverbal behaviors and their presentations in the session can alert therapists to emotional blocking. For instance, clients might quickly change topics when approaching emotionally charged material, or they might suddenly "freeze up" while discussing certain emotionally laden events or problems. Rhythmic, "chatty" speech, which makes clients sound like newscasters reporting well-rehearsed material, can also be a sign of emotional blocking (Rice, Koke, Greenberg, & Wagstaff, 1979). Clients also may have difficulty exploring their feelings because they have limited knowledge or understanding of their emotional experience: When clients are confused or uncertain about how they are feeling, therapists can suggest focusing, asking clients to attend to their inner experiencing and identify the main feeling or issue that is of concern. Therapists may alternatively use evocative or exploratory reflections to help clients get in touch with their inner experience.

RELATIONSHIP REPAIR

When the relationship becomes derailed, therapists can engage in metacommunication either to clarify the nature of the tasks and goals or to discuss the relationship more generally (Watson & Greenberg, 1995; Watson & Rennie, 1994). Therapist congruence is especially important. Clients may benefit from knowing how their therapist is experiencing them, and they may request specific feedback from their therapist about some aspect of the interaction. Clients with abuse histories may be working to correct their reality testing in a different interpersonal environment with their therapists.

Tears or strains in the alliance need to be attended to and repaired if therapy is to progress. The therapist needs to inquire into client signs of dissatisfaction, hostility, or withdrawal in a congruent, nonblaming manner

(Safran & Muran, 1998; Watson & Greenberg, 1995). The goal is to listen to and understand the client's feelings and concerns about the therapist or the therapy and not to get into defending the therapist's prior actions. Defensive responses are likely to increase the rupture or leave the client feeling criticized. The goal is to empathically understand prior empathic failures. For such clients, this experience of having their feelings of being misunderstood by the other understood and responded to breaks their sense of isolation and provides a strong healing experience. The process of being understood allows the hope to emerge that one's concerns can be acknowledged and understood.

7

CASE FORMULATION FOR DEPRESSION

This chapter explains the role and nature of case formulation in emotion-focused therapy (EFT) for depression. Case formulation is based on client processes, as opposed to the specific content of their narratives (Goldman & Greenberg, 1997). Formulation is a complex process that continually seeks to integrate information from a number of different levels regarding the clients' immediate experience in the session. When treating clients for depression, therapists integrate the following levels of information about their functioning:

- the manner in which they process their affective experience moment by moment in the session and regulate that affect,
- their life histories and early attachment experiences,
- the specific issues that they bring to each session, and
- their moment-to-moment verbal and nonverbal behavior in the session.

Process is privileged over content, and process diagnosis is privileged over person diagnosis. In EFT, therapists explicitly attend to in-session markers of client processing difficulties and intervene to facilitate productive processing. Therapists develop ways of conceptualizing their clients' problems on the basis of particular in-session states so that they are able to choose among different interventions that suit these states. They also remain centered in the present and responsive to clients' moment-by-moment experience, as well as mindful of the background of their clients' context and past experience.

Case formulation is an ongoing process. To facilitate the development of the therapeutic relationship and the goals and tasks of therapy, therapists attend to client markers of characteristic style and their ways of processing their experience throughout the phases of treatment to provide emotion-focused interventions relevant to their clients' concerns. It is important to be open to new information as each new phase of the treatment is introduced to ensure a continued good fit.

Case formulation is useful to help orient therapists to salient aspects of clients' experiencing that may be important to explore. Research indicates that client-centered therapists who are unable to help clients structure their sessions to effectively explore experiential questions are more likely to have poor outcomes (Watson, Enright, Kalogerakos, & Greenberg, 1998). Thus, it is important that therapists know when and how to be maximally responsive to their clients. Developing case formulations helps therapists organize information, form blueprints of their clients' experiences, direct attention, and determine the focus of the session on the basis of what is salient for the client moment to moment.

In EFT, case formulation has an orienting function that is always balanced with the client's sense of its fit. By alerting therapists to the poignant, difficult parts of clients' experiences that need to be processed, case formulation helps structure the session. However, therapists hold case formulations tentatively and are constantly open to revising them according to new information and input from the client. Case formulations of underlying determinants of the depression or of core themes or tasks take a back seat to clients' immediate and more pressing concerns, unless it becomes obvious that the two are linked and can easily be explored together with the client's agreement.

Phenomenological and experientially oriented approaches have regarded case formulation as unnecessary because of concern that therapists would become overly invested in certain theories and ideas at the expense of genuine and empathic contact with their clients (Rogers, 1965). According to these approaches, a priori assumptions about the client would leave therapists insufficiently open to clients' unique experiences in the moment and to a view of clients as the experts on their experience. However, the approach Rogers advocated presupposes that all clients can immediately and automatically engage in experiential exploration, which research has shown not to be the case (Klein, Mathieu-Coughlan, & Kiesler, 1986). Moreover, it is clear that in good-outcome cases, therapists actively work with their clients to resolve specific issues. Therapists do not respond to everything the client says with equal attention; rather, they choose to focus on different aspects of the client's experience at different times. To facilitate understanding, it is important to explicate the tacit knowledge that directs therapists' attention and helps them to actively collaborate with their clients to ensure positive outcomes, even as they remain focused in the present and trusting of their clients' experiences.

DEVELOPING A FOCUS

In brief EFT, case formulation is helpful in facilitating the development of a focus and fitting the therapeutic tasks to the client's goals to establish a productive working alliance (Elliott, Watson, Goldman, & Greenberg, 2004; Watson & Bohart, 2001). The following eight steps have been identified to guide clinicians in case formulation and development of a focus in EFT. Steps 3 through 5 are best viewed as occurring concurrently.

1. Identify the presenting problem and a focus for the treatment in collaboration with clients.
2. Listen to and explore clients' narratives about their presenting problems.
3. Gather information about clients' early attachment identity-related histories and current relationships.
4. Identify the painful aspects of clients' experience.
5. Observe clients' style of processing emotional material.
6. Identify the intrapersonal and interpersonal issues that are contributing to clients' pain.
7. Confirm this understanding with clients and suggest tasks that will facilitate resolution of the painful issues.
8. Attend and respond to clients' moment-by-moment processing in the session to guide interventions.

Therapists attend to different client markers during the different steps to help them develop a formulation of clients' difficulties and a focus of treatment. These include markers of clients' emotional processing style (Step 5), markers of their characteristic styles of responding (Step 6), task markers (Step 7), and micromarkers (Step 8). Any formulation is held tentatively and is constantly checked with the client for relevance and fit, with clients' moment-by-moment processing in the session remaining the ultimate guide. It is important that therapists frame their interventions in a manner that is relevant to their clients' goals and objectives and that there is agreement about the behaviors and interactions that are contributing to the clients' depression.

An EFT approach to therapy gives priority to the client's moment-by-moment experiencing rather than formulations about the source of his or her dysfunction. It is assumed that a focus on current experience will reveal both the processes underlying dysfunction as well as how these are used to create meaning (Goldman & Greenberg, 1997). In tracking the client's experience moment by moment, an emotionally salient context is created in which the most relevant material will emerge along with its emotional significance. The most distinguishing aspects of an EFT approach to case formulation are the therapist's attention to the meaning and poignancy of clients' utterances and the identification of affective problem markers and tasks to facilitate the development of a focus on clients' core maladaptive schemes.

Identifying the Presenting Problem and Gathering Information

The first steps in developing a case formulation involve the identification of the presenting problem, exploring clients' narratives of their current life situation and problems, and gathering information about childhood experiences with caretakers. Clients initially present with symptoms of depression, but for EFT therapy to be successful, the presenting problem needs to be understood in terms of clients' narratives about their environmental and relational contexts so that the sources of clients' pain and the painful ways they treat themselves can be identified and changed. Therapists need to explore clients' narratives about their presenting problems to understand how the clients perceive them and to gather information about clients' current life circumstances, relationships, identity, and attachment histories.

Identifying the Pain

To formulate cases successfully, therapists develop a pain compass that acts as an emotional tracking device for following their clients. Pain or other intense affects are the cues that alert therapists to potentially beneficial areas of exploration; clients' moment-by-moment experience and current life circumstances help therapists determine relevant areas and questions for exploration in the here and now. Therapists' primary objective is to access information that is emotionally alive. To work successfully, therapists need to use emotional processing tasks that fit with clients' goals and ways of processing material. Thus, formulations are useful to help therapists determine what they need to do to be maximally responsive to their clients and to negotiate the goals and tasks of therapy so that there is synergy between the participants.

To develop a pain compass, therapists listen for what is most poignant in clients' presentations. They also immediately begin to flag the painful life events their clients have endured. Painful events provide clues about the sources of important emotion schemes that clients may have formed about themselves and others and provide therapists with an understanding of clients' sources of pain and vulnerability. A number of themes recur in the attachment histories of clients with longstanding chronic depression or multiple episodes, including loss, rejection, humiliation, and conflict. Clients who experience recurrent or chronic depression often report the loss of a caregiver at an early age followed by poor emotional and social support and emotional and physical abuse or neglect by caregivers. In less severe cases, for clients who have not experienced chronic or multiple episodes of depression, current life circumstances can bring on the condition by leaving them feeling powerless and defeated by events and seriously challenging their sense of competency. Clients may alternatively become depressed as a result of interpersonal conflict that they find wearing and are unable to resolve. Other clients feel trapped in their relationships and life situations because their values make it difficult for them to leave, they are reluctant to violate the expectations of significant others, or they lack the material, psychological, or physical resources to successfully disengage from a difficult situation.

For example, Penny was a young mother in her early 30s. When she came to see the therapist, she was feeling trapped in her marriage. Her husband was emotionally abusive and experienced severe depression. Penny had married early to escape a difficult home situation. Her father was an alcoholic and neglectful of the family, and her mother, who had severe mood swings, was very self-centered and demanding of Penny, who had sacrificed most of her childhood and adolescence to care for her parents and siblings. Penny was experiencing depression and anxiety when she came to therapy. She felt that she was "dying" in her marriage and that the conflict was bad for her son. However, she had strong religious views and did not feel that she could separate, nor did she think she could cope financially because she was unemployed and very much wanted to be a full-time mother for her son. As the therapist learned more about Penny and her life situation, it became clear that she often invalidated her thoughts and feelings and had great difficulty setting limits with people around her. Client and therapist agreed to work on helping Penny be more assertive within her marriage to see if that would improve the situation and to work with her conflict about leaving her husband to see whether she could resolve it satisfactorily.

Observing Clients' Manner and Style of Emotional Processing

As therapists listen to clients' narratives, they attend to how the clients process their emotional experience. They assess clients' emotional processing strengths and deficits and attend to how aware clients are of their emotional experience, the labels they use, their evaluations of their emotional experience, whether they are overwhelmed or distant from their emotional experience, and whether their emotional expression fits the evoking situations.

Whether clients are aware of their emotional experience is evident in how expressive they are in the session, both verbally and nonverbally. When clients are aware of their emotions, they express them in words and refer to their emotional states. Otherwise, they may reveal their emotions through nonverbal behaviors like crying, laughing, or fidgeting. In contrast, when clients are not aware of their emotions, they make no reference to them. Their behavior and responses are determined by values that are dictated by their culture, significant others, and society at large. The focus of their narratives is usually external, involving descriptions of events and the actions of other people. Clients who are aware of their emotional experience are able to differentiate the various nuances of their emotions; for example, they are able to differentiate hot rage from cold punitive anger or wistful sadness from deep regret.

Clients may have problems modulating their emotional experience. Some do not have enough distance from their emotions and are overwhelmed or flooded by their experience. They may feel that they are the victims of their feelings and may be unable to achieve sufficient distance from them to be able to use the information they provide in a constructive way. Other clients are so distant from their feelings that their experience is stifled and totally out of awareness. Clients should ideally reach a stage when they are able to move fluidly and easily through different emotional reactions elicited by different situations and interactions with others (Mahoney, 1991; Rogers, 1959).

Penny was at times quite distant and at others flooded by her emotional reactions to situations. It was very difficult for her to register the moment-to-moment effects of interactions, partly because her attention was so focused on the other person that she ignored and did not process her own feelings. However, at other times she could be very sensitive and easily hurt; she would be overcome by the intensity of the emotion and unable to modulate it. It became clear that Penny needed help to focus on her own feelings and to express them to herself and others. An important part of the therapy was to help Penny attend to her emotional experience in the session and in her interactions with others and to help her modulate those reactions when they became too intense and overwhelming.

By identifying the deficits in clients' emotional processing style, therapists are able to decide how best to work with clients. For example, if a client's feelings are out of awareness, therapists work actively to heighten them through responding empathically, gently teaching clients to turn inward to try to represent their experience in words, or using more evocative techniques and active expression tasks. For clients who have suppressed their emotional experience because caregivers did not attend to it or because others actively invalidated it, the primary task of therapy may be to help them articulate their early memories and emotional experience so as to consciously represent the attendant emotion schemes that may be driving their behavior in the present. Clients for whom the primary task is to articulate the pain and attendant emotional memories from earlier experiences may be resistant to the active expression tasks or other directive interventions that focus on their construals or cognitions. These clients require patience of their therapists and adequate feelings of safety in the therapeutic relationship so that they feel able to access their emotional experience. Therapists may encourage these clients to focus on their bodily reactions and physical sensations before having them become more emotionally aroused in the session. Therapists may also set up some parameters for safety so that clients have a way of stopping the exploration of difficult emotional material. For example, therapists may reassure clients that they can stop at any time if the experience becomes too overwhelming.

For some clients, the major task of therapy may be the articulation of their preverbal emotional experience. For clients whose early attachment histories were disrupted or very difficult, memories of the early experience may need to be reconstructed and processed in order for them to come to terms with how they view themselves. For example, Penny had great difficulty initially naming her experience and understanding the sources of her problem. She feared rejection and put others' needs before her own. As she began to explore her current life situation and the ways in which she treated herself, she began to explore her early childhood environment. After a particularly intense session, she had an image of herself as an infant tossed on a garbage heap. At first she was taken aback by the image, but as she worked with it with the therapist, it became clear that this was her experience of herself within her family from very early on. Naming her early experience and symbolizing it was an important watershed in therapy, and she was thereafter able to commit to caring for herself. She began to see how this emotion scheme constructed early in life influenced her actions and led her to expect that others would find her unlovable and reject her. Subsequently, she worked to develop behaviors and relationships that were life enhancing as opposed to negating.

Therapists observe the types and varieties of coping strategies that clients use to modulate their affect. Clients often lack coping strategies that would enable them to modulate their affect as the need arises. The strategies people typically use when they are flooded by emotional experience or are experiencing aversive emotional reactions have been classified as behavioral (e.g., going for a run, doing housework) or cognitive (e.g., thinking about the problem and ways of solving it), engaged (e.g., becoming aware of the feelings, actively reflecting on the meaning and significance of their feelings) or disengaged (e.g., going to a movie, engaging in distracting behaviors), relying on self (e.g., looking to the self to soothe the feelings) or others (e.g., reaching out to others when distressed), and long term or short term. People learn these strategies from caregivers as ways of dealing with distress and as a means of soothing negative feelings and reactions.

Clients who have chronic depression may not have these skills. Early environments of abuse and neglect do not provide clients with an album of happy memories to call on when feeling distressed, nor is it likely that their caretakers were able to show them how to distract and soothe themselves when they were overcome by negative emotions. Clients with depression often are disengaged from their experience, are unable to turn to others for support, and typically use long-term rather than the short-term strategies. For example, clients who are depressed tend to avoid problematic situations when they arise and often forget to return to difficult issues later, feeling too hopeless and ineffective to change them. There is also a tendency for clients who are depressed to ruminate for long periods of time and experience great difficulty in repairing their mood.

Once clients' coping strategies become clear, it is easier to know which responses and behaviors to address in the session. For example, if it becomes clear that a client engages in invalidation, the therapist might look for markers of self-interruption in the session or use empathy to validate and support the client's feelings within the session. Other tasks that might be appropriate include two-chair work, to make clients more conscious of how they invalidate themselves and help develop alternative behaviors, and possibly empty-chair work with the significant other who invalidated and dismissed their feelings when they were children, to help them reprocess the events and engage in alternative interpersonal behaviors.

Identifying Clients' Intrapersonal and Interpersonal Issues

Markers of clients' characteristic styles of responding reveal how clients typically treat themselves and others and help therapists understand their manner of processing (Elliott et al., 2004; Watson & Bohart, 2001). These interaction patterns are usually manifest in clients' life histories and narratives of how others treat them and how they treat themselves. Therapists develop an understanding of clients' characteristic styles as they listen to their early experiences with caregivers and interactions with significant others in their lives. Clients' histories provide important clues to emotionally salient material and illuminate the treatment clients have received from others, as well as how they may be treating themselves. Early experiences of powerlessness, loss, and rejection often lead to sadness and neediness, which are experienced as evidence of personal inadequacy and inherent unlovableness, and to self-contempt and self-esteem vulnerability.

For example, a client who as a young boy experienced the loss of a caretaker followed by inadequate emotional and psychological support or who was emotionally and physically abused as a child may need to learn how to treat himself or herself in more positive and self-nurturing ways. Clients who were not provided with models of positive self-nurturing behaviors consequently are unable to accept themselves; to listen to and be empathic to their experience; and to love, nurture, and protect themselves. Instead, these clients often engage in controlling, punitive, harsh, invalidating, and neglectful behaviors toward themselves and may allow others to treat them in a similar fashion. Other clients may experience conflict around their right to feel anger, may feel self-critical of their own weakness or need for others, or may elevate others while they diminish themselves.

The information that therapists learn about clients' early life histories and interpersonal relationships provides a backdrop to the session and a context for clients' current concerns. Therapists form tentative hypotheses that will be either borne out or not as the process unfolds. They form a conceptual framework for understanding the clients' pain and the intra- and interpersonal interactions that might be contributing to their depression. Clients' life histories are the store of knowledge that therapists draw on to guide their responses in sessions, especially when they have to choose between competing responses or when they are trying to structure the session and focus the client.

Penny's characteristic way of treating herself was to neglect herself and take care of everybody else. She had grown up with parents who were emotionally unavailable and inadequate in providing for their children's physical needs. From an early age Penny learned to ignore her feelings and to focus on everybody else in an attempt to maintain some sort of order at home. Subsequently in her marriage, Penny once again subjugated her own needs to care for a difficult and demanding husband. She was aware that she felt stifled and unable to express her needs to others or have them met. She wanted to work on these issues in therapy, and she agreed that they were contributing to her depression.

Working With Specific Tasks

The hallmark of EFT is the attention paid to specific in-session tasks. These tasks follow from the identification of specific markers that indicate unresolved cognitive–affective problems. As they listen to clients' narratives, therapists ask themselves what specific in-session behaviors are contributing to their client's depressions. The focus on specific client statements is partly influenced by therapists' understanding of the painful and difficult aspects of clients' experiences that have been inadequately processed. For example, her therapist was particularly aware that Penny's attention was directed outward, so they agreed early on that it would be good for her to learn how to focus inward. Subsequently they used two-chair tasks to work with her self-interruptions, which prevented her from knowing her experience in the moment, as well as her invalidating and critical way of treating herself. As they worked, it became clear that she had unfinished business with her parents, so they did some empty-chair work to help her establish clearer boundaries and set limits with significant people in her life. In-session tasks are discussed in more detail in chapters 11 and 12.

Two major classes of markers for specific tasks involve interpersonal issues and self–self relations. Interpersonal markers are statements that alert therapists to difficulties clients are having in their present or past interpersonal relationships. These markers usually indicate that the client has unresolved needs and feelings toward a significant other and often emerge when clients have experienced loss, neglect, or abuse. Tasks that can be used to successfully resolve these problem states are empty-chair work and empathic exploration.

The self-markers indicate how clients treat themselves and process emotion. Typically, clients with depression are either neglectful of themselves and their experience or are controlling and punitive with themselves. Neglectful self-statements are those that indicate that clients do not know what they are feeling or have difficulty focusing on their feelings. Other self-markers are evident when clients dismiss and downplay what happens to them or assume an external focus and omit any references to how they were feeling about the events that they are recounting. For example, Beth came from a large family. She was a very bright child but had not received much support and attention from her parents, who were uneducated and overwhelmed with the demands of providing for a large family. Beth had dropped out of university and had become a sales clerk in a large department store. In her spare time, she had written a novel. She came to see a therapist because of intense depression after her novel had been rejected for publication. She felt that her life was washed up in part because she had failed to establish a long-term relationship and have children, and she did not feel that she had any career prospects. It soon became clear that Beth was not in touch with her feelings. She often was unaware of what she felt and expressed confusion when asked. She preferred to remain very analytical about the events in her life and continually tried to prove how she had failed. The primary focus of treatment was to help Beth become more aware of her feelings through tasks like focusing and empathic exploration and to help her evoke and explore her experience so that she could represent it in words and begin to get a sense of her own needs and goals and work out ways to realize them.

Controlling and punitive self-markers include statements that indicate that clients are being self-critical, placing excessive demands on themselves to fulfill obligations, invalidating their feelings, and interrupting their experience; these markers are discussed in the following paragraphs. In addition, focusing on the needs of others and engaging in self-harm like not eating, abusing alcohol, or cutting themselves are other self-markers that indicate the need for specific in-session tasks.

Self-critical statements are easy to spot. Clients refer to themselves as failures or as inadequate in some way. Sometimes self-critical markers are not immediately apparent but can be elicited if the therapist asks clients to note what they are saying to themselves to contribute to their depression. Occasionally therapists can sense that clients are being self-critical if they are defensive in their interactions. With self-criticisms, the primary task is to help clients become aware of their negative statements and to realize how painful they are by using two-chair work. If clients become aware of the link between their self-statements and consequent feelings of sadness and despair, they are often able to recognize that they need to stop the behavior and solicit support and validation instead, at which point clients and therapists can begin to work on constructing alternative behavioral responses.

Some clients make coercive self-statements, which indicate that they place excessive demands on themselves to meet certain standards and the expectations of others. Typically these clients are more in tune with external standards and the needs of others than they are with themselves. Burnout or depression occur when the self becomes depleted and exhausted and is unable to meet the continuous and unrelenting demands these clients make of themselves.

When clients are invalidating their feelings, they often say things like, "What difference does it make?" or "I shouldn't feel like that" or "It's not important how I feel." By invalidating their feelings, clients lose touch with what they need. As they continue to deaden their reactions, they sink into a state of defeat and despondency as they give up on understanding or realizing their own goals and objectives. For example, a client who experienced neglect as a child had a tendency to constrain his emotional expression. After observing his self-restraint, his therapist became particularly attuned to statements that indicated that he was silencing himself or not expressing himself clearly to others. The therapist suggested two-chair work to help the client become more aware of how he was processing his emotions and the negative impact that type of processing had on him.

Some clients deliberately interrupt their experience so that it remains out of awareness. These clients often do not finish their sentences, space out in the session, and easily lose their train of thought. They may freeze and go silent and may be very reluctant to engage in exploration. They may change the topic often or be easily diverted by sights and sounds outside of the therapy room. The primary objective of the therapist when these behaviors occur is to help clients become aware of how they are interrupting their experience and the subjective impact of that behavior on themselves.

Attending to Moment-by-Moment Processing

Micromarkers are the verbal and nonverbal behaviors that clients express during the session that alert therapists to their moment-by-moment processing and enable therapists to adjust their interventions to be maximally responsive to clients. Therapists are attuned to the quality of clients' descriptions, the words they use, and their style of speech. Micromarkers also provide a gauge of how much clients are in touch with their inner experience and the status of the working alliance. For example, Penny would often end her sentences by saying, "Well, what do I know?" She was able to very clearly describe the events in her life and talk about what her husband was doing, but she seldom referred to her own feelings and needs. She would often berate herself for being selfish. These served as cues to her therapist that she tended to dismiss her own experience and that she was very self-critical. Initially, her fast rate of speech and thin, reedy vocal quality, which indicate anxiety as well as an external focus, cued the therapist that she needed help to turn her attention inward using empathic tasks and focusing.

Verbal Markers

Therapists work to distill the nuances in clients' descriptions by paying particular attention to the different shades of meaning implied by their descriptions of events to get a full understanding of their clients' experience. The objective is to carefully unpack the client's unique and idiosyncratic perspective on events so as to gain insight into the personal significance of the events. Therapists help clients differentiate their feelings, for example, by working to understand whether their clients are sad and disappointed or sad and relieved when a relationship ends.

Therapists listen for what is poignant in clients' stories to track their pain. Poignancy is the criterion that a therapist uses to decide where to focus an intervention, because it is likely to lead to material that is emotionally alive and personally significant for the client. Thus, if the client says he or she feels confused about an interaction and that it left him or her bruised and out of sorts, the therapist would attend to the sense of being bruised, as opposed to the confusion. The former connotes pain, whereas the latter indicates a more intellectual activity as clients struggle to understand.

The way clients describe their experience can be an important clue as to whether they are in touch with their emotions or not. Language that is abstract or relies on clichés is usually a good indication that clients are disengaged from their experience. When clients are actively engaged in representing their inner experience, they tend to use more idiosyncratic and vivid language and metaphors to convey descriptions and meanings. For example, one client describing a quarrel with a friend might merely say, "We had a disagreement," whereas another might say, "Ted really upset me yesterday— he was irritated and quite dismissive of my ideas, and I was left silenced and confused by his reaction." The latter description gives one a clearer sense of how the client felt and perceived the interaction, whereas the former statement is unclear about what happened, what the client's perceptions were, and how he or she responded.

Reports of intense emotions or reactions are usually good clues that clients need to process certain experiences or that certain issues are problematic. After responding with empathic understanding to their clients' feelings, therapists may then attempt to facilitate clients' exploration of their reactions using empathic explorations. For example, if a client found himself "flying off the handle," an empathic response with an emotion inquiry might be, "It just felt that there was no other way of responding right then, you just felt so enraged. What was happening?" This response is empathic, conveying the client's sense of the situation, and it also opens up the possibility that there might be an alternative way of responding and helps to focus the client's attention on his response and the situation so that they can be examined in more depth.

Similarly, if a client is constantly talking about her emotional reactions but leaves the details hazy, it is important to ask her to provide a better sense of the situation so that she and the therapist can understand it better. Empathic exploration helps both therapists and clients ground clients' reactions in real events so that their patterns of responding become clear and can be examined more fully. To facilitate the full processing of an emotion, therapists try to ensure that all five components of emotions are processed, including the stimulus situation, the meaning, the sensory feeling, the action tendency, and the need or concern.

Another way therapists can identify emotionally salient material is to ask themselves whether clients are speaking from the head or the heart. When therapists are trying to heighten clients' awareness of their feelings or evoke affective experience in the session, they deliberately avoid focusing on clients' analytical and rational statements in favor of statements that reveal clients' inner subjective experience. However, if a client is reprocessing an experience or reflecting on a response, then it is appropriate to follow the client's more conceptual track as long as it is accompanied by a sense of deep exploration and re-examination.

Therapists are very aware when their clients' descriptions seem rehearsed and carefully packaged. Rehearsed descriptions often appear in the narratives of clients with depression as accounts of the numerous ways in which they have failed or descriptions of how hopeless things are. Because an important objective is to help clients out of repetitive thinking grooves, therapists begin to help clients to get more in touch with their affective reactions, to see the events in their lives differently, and to reconsider their assumptions. In rehearsed description speech is fluid, as in a prepared speech. In contrast, when engaged in deep reflection, clients' speech is seldom fluid and smooth; rather, it is ragged as they stop to explore and try to express their thoughts and feelings in new ways.

At times, clients may ramble, which indicates that they are unable to focus their explorations. Clients who are out of touch with their inner experience and actively trying to avoid their feelings may ramble. Clients with depression may be quite afraid of focusing on their feelings of despair and hopelessness, uncertain that they can ever feel differently. These clients may come up with various theories to explain their behavior without being able to turn their attention inward and undertake a more focused inner exploration. When clients begin to ramble, therapists can gently and patiently work to refocus their attention on their inner experience and help them label it so that they can see that experiences and feelings can shift and change as they attend to and process them in awareness.

Nonverbal Markers

Therapists are highly attuned to the pauses in clients' speech. Pauses often indicate that clients are engaged and are searching for a new way to represent their experience or considering new perspectives. Sometimes, however, a pause after a therapist response can indicate disagreement or a difficulty with the way in which therapy is progressing. These types of pauses are important to attend to because they provide a reading on the quality of the alliance and the need for further clarification.

Another clue that clients may be having difficulty expressing their emotions is when their expressed feelings and behavior are incongruous. Ambiguous expression can take a variety of forms, such as mixed signals, expressions of which the sender is not aware, or expression that creates an unintended impression. For example, clients may recount very traumatic or sad material while smiling or display signs of anxiety in the session but deny feeling uncomfortable. The key characteristic of ambiguous expression is that clients are not able to convey the desired emotional message to others.

When working with clients who have difficulty getting in touch with their emotional experience, therapists pay close attention to clients' nonverbal behavior and note when their eyes and body language are downcast or when their eyes tear up even as they maintain a more rational and unemotional front. When therapists observe signs of incongruence either in dialogue in the session or in clients' descriptions of what is happening to them, therapists might empathically communicate their observations to their clients and try to explore what is happening. The client may be experiencing a conflict, may lack skills, or may even have unfinished business that needs to be resolved. Therapists seek first to explore the ambiguity to understand what is occurring inside the client. They then help clients understand their feelings more clearly using techniques for enhancing emotional processing skills such as empathic affirmation, empathic exploration, empathic conjectures, two-chair work, and systematic evocative unfolding. When clients can accurately label and interpret their feelings, they are better able to communicate these feelings clearly to others and are less likely to have poorly understood feelings leak out in socially detrimental ways.

An important nonverbal micromarker is client vocal quality. Rice, Koke, Greenberg, and Wagstaff (1979) identified four types of voice quality—external, focused, limited, and emotional—that provide information on the type of processing activity that the client is engaged in during the session. External voice has a rehearsed quality, and focused voice indicates that clients are actively searching and trying to put things together in new ways. Limited voice has a thin, reedy quality that suggests that clients are anxious about engaging in psychotherapy, whereas emotional voice is an indication that clients are actively expressing their emotions in the session. Therapists ideally listen for focused voice, which helps pinpoint the salient and important aspects of clients' experiences that they are trying to reconfigure. When treating depression, it is also important to pay attention to emotional voice and to facilitate clients' expression of their feelings, because the free expression of sadness, grief, anger, and resentment is often constricted with depression.

CASE EXAMPLES

In EFT, therapists attend to multiple markers. They weave together information from clients' histories, emotional processing style, and current behavior to help identify statements that are most pertinent to clients' presenting problems. The choice of task depends on the clients' current emotional processing in the session and its relevance to salient and painful aspects of the clients' experiencing.

For example Jane, a 28-year-old artist, presented for therapy because she was feeling very depressed. Her primary complaints when she entered therapy were that she was unable to meet her work commitments and was experiencing difficulties in her marriage. She was initially frustrated at her inability to be disciplined and organize her time better. She had diminished libido and little desire to be sexually engaged with her husband. It became clear early on that Jane was quite self-critical and assumed that much of what went wrong was her fault. She tended to gloss over her feelings, speaking rapidly and often dismissing the painful aspects of her experience. Initially the therapist focused on Jane's self-criticism about her work to help her be less punishing toward herself and then shifted to interpersonal tasks as Jane focused on her distress about her loss of interest in sex and her feelings of neglect and abandonment as a child. When Jane was 4 years old, her mother died, and 2 years later, her father became severely ill; Jane was cared for by her older adolescent sister. Jane needed the opportunity to attend to and symbolize her inner experience because this had not been possible when she was a child; instead, in an attempt to cope she stuffed her feelings down and invalidated them. Her style of emotional processing was evident in her speech. When she presented for treatment, she spoke with a limited voice. As treatment progressed, she became more focused and self-assertive as she began to voice and assert her own needs.

Another client, David, was a middle-aged professional who had recently lost his job and came to therapy because he was feeling quite depressed. His marriage was rocky, and he was beginning to doubt his abilities and talents. During the first session he told the therapist that emotional expression had been actively discouraged in his family and that the children were expected to be rational and self-disciplined. He had learned early to shut off his emotions so as to keep them out of awareness. Although this strategy had worked well for him in his life to date, he found that he was unable to control his depression since being laid off.

The therapist observed that he often interrupted his emotional experience. First, she asked him to slow down and attend to his inner experience, to become aware of his body and its sensations and of his emotions. Next, the therapist helped him find the appropriate labels for his experience. This search for labels allowed the client to get in touch with his deep sadness and sense of unworthiness since losing his job. He felt diminished at home because he was no longer the breadwinner, and he feared that his wife no longer found him useful and attractive. The therapist introduced two-chair tasks to change his self-criticism and some empty-chair work with his parents to help change his interpersonal style of relating.

As he became more assertive and self-accepting, and with some encouragement from his therapist, he was able to approach his wife to check out how she felt about him and the situation. He was relieved to learn that in fact she was very supportive and not at all distressed that she was carrying the financial load of the family for the time being. She was primarily concerned about his mood and the fact that he seemed to have become withdrawn and to have lost interest in her. He began to confide in her more, and their sense of intimacy and closeness increased. In the meantime, in therapy the client began to explore his career options and realized that in spite of his regret at losing his position with its accompanying status and financial security, he felt relief. He got in touch with the stress that he had felt in his previous position, and as he acknowledged the negative impact of his previous job, he began to see its loss as an opportunity for him to do something that was more meaningful and satisfying. He became less depressed and successfully pursued an alternative career.

In EFT, therapists use multiple sources of information to be maximally responsive and attuned to their clients' experience in the session. Although their primary focus is on clients' immediate processing in the session, therapists integrate how clients process their emotional experience in the session with information from clients' case histories to understand the painful and poignant aspects of clients' experiences and to develop a sense of how clients treat themselves and others. As therapists develop a focus and a theme for treatment, they establish agreement with clients about the causes of their depression and ways of working with it in EFT. Agreement between therapist and client about the sources of distress and on ways of working with it is essential to the successful implementation of different tasks and the resolution of clients' feelings of depression.

8

BONDING, AWARENESS, AND COLLABORATION

Emotion-focused therapists work to promote several different processes to help clients resolve depression. The bonding and awareness phase is the initial and foundational phase of treatment. There are three important subgoals during this phase: to create a trusting relational bond, to promote the client's emotional awareness, and to establish a collaborative focus on the generating conditions of his or her depression.

The phases of treatment described in chapter 5 are presented as a set of sequential steps; however, they do not necessarily occur in a linear fashion. The activities of bonding and awareness, evocation and exploration, and transformation are interwoven throughout the therapeutic process and are recapitulated and augmented as other processes occur; however, some processes are emphasized or highlighted over the others at different phases of therapy, as we have indicated. Although bonding and awareness are typically focused on in the early stages of treatment, awareness can be heightened after periods of arousal and reflection, and the emotional bond between therapist and client develops throughout treatment. In a similar way, although reflection and the consolidation of new meaning are typically the focus in the third phase of therapy, clients are reflecting in the first phase as they become aware of their emotions and of their different ways of construing their experience.

As we outlined in chapter 3, emotional expression can be viewed as involving five important steps in emotional processing: the initial prereflective reaction, the conscious perception of the aroused response, the labeling and interpretation of the response, the evaluation of the response, and the perceived context for expression (Kennedy-Moore & Watson, 1999). Clients with depression usually have lost touch with the full range of their emotional experiencing. They are no longer informed by their initial prereflective reactions to events because everything is overshadowed by the black cloud of their depression. Their mood is predominantly negative and low, so they are not aware of the nuances of their feelings. As a result, the flow of experience is interrupted, and clients lose touch with their surroundings. They feel stuck. Even though awareness of feelings can be painful, clients need to become aware of their feelings before they can change them.

An important goal in an emotion-focused therapy (EFT) for depression is to help clients become aware of their feelings in the moment. At first, this may entail having them become more aware of the nuances of their depression so that they can become aware of slight variations in how they feel and begin to attend more closely to moments when their feelings change. As they begin to attend more closely to their feelings, clients may become aware of other reactions and feelings that they had overlooked when they processed all the events in their lives through the primary lens of their depression.

CREATING A BOND

The importance of the relationship in facilitating the tasks of therapy was discussed in chapter 6. However, it is important to re-emphasize that the creation of a bond characterized by warmth, empathy, and respect is central to the later emotion work. Bond creation is the major task in the first three to five sessions. It is an important part of building the initial alliance and continues to be important throughout treatment. The emotional climate set by the therapist in the early sessions strongly influences what will follow. Creating an emotion-friendly environment is important to help clients access and focus on their painful feelings. If clients are initially slow or reluctant to disclose their feelings in the early sessions, therapists may explicitly encourage them to express their feelings in the session and be highly supportive and empathic toward their experiences as they emerge.

At the beginning of treatment, therapists accept clients' experiences as they are presented. They do not attempt to challenge their clients' views, nor do they suggest alternative responses. Instead, as therapists convey their understanding and concern for their clients, they begin to build an understanding of their clients' functioning and ways of processing their experience. In this initial phase of treatment, therapists work to provide empathy and support for clients' feelings of despair. During this phase it is important to help clients feel validated so that they can reveal the depth and extent of their feelings without fear of criticism or of being shamed. More importantly, therapists at this phase do not convey the message that clients' feelings need to change or that their feelings are invalid or mistaken. The primary objective is to make clients feel safe and accepted so that they can martial the resources to begin to reflect on their current state and generate alternatives.

The primary objectives at this time thus are to help clients feel safe and understood and to facilitate self-disclosure. In conjunction with developing a bond, therapists work to have clients articulate their feelings and focus on their inner experience. If clients are to open up and reveal vulnerable aspects of their subjective selves, they need to feel safe and to know that they will be understood. The trust and support that develop between the participants help clients to share painful aspects of their experience that may be difficult to talk about and share with another. The process of revealing self to an understanding and supportive other contributes to the development of a therapeutic bond, which in turn facilitates and enhances the emotion work that follows. The bond is strengthened as clients begin to become more aware and experience the relief and benefits of exploring their experience.

Clients with depression in particular need to feel safe and accepted because they are very sensitive to criticism and feel bad and worthless in their depressed state. However, because they are less attuned to the flow of their experience and the impact of their environments, they can be slow to perceive their therapists' caring and support. Therapists therefore provide a lot of empathy and validation at the beginning of treatment to provide a supportive and safe environment, to build a trusting bond, and to create a facilitative environment for exploration. Therapists need to acknowledge the depths of clients' pain and validate it, rather than try to talk them out of their feelings of hopelessness. By empathizing with and acknowledging how badly their clients feel and how hopeless things seem right now, therapists provide needed validation and support for clients so that they can begin to look for alternative ways of viewing their experience.

Therapists strive to create an environment in which clients with depression can express their pain and vulnerability without fear of being evaluated. These clients are often encouraged to "cheer up" by well-meaning friends and family, so the opportunity to share the full intensity of their feelings of despair in therapy and to feel recognized and validated can be experienced as a tremendous relief when they realize they no longer have to put up a front and cover up how badly they feel. The objective at this juncture is not to push for exploration, but rather to give clients space to fully express their fragile, weak sense of themselves. Therapists are nonintrusive and work with clients to help them open up their experience and express it in words. In this way, therapists convey that an important task for clients with depression is to become aware of and to articulate their pain as part of attending to and processing their emotional experience. During this time therapists are also identifying how clients are processing their emotions as they gather information to assist with case formulation.

PROMOTING AWARENESS

Gestalt theorists conceived of awareness as forming a figure against a background or as configuring reality or experience into a conscious form. There are two basic modes of attention and awareness, an analytic mode and a synthetic mode, used to differentiate and to integrate experience, respectively. Both of these processes are important in the creation of meaning. There also are two levels of awareness: One level is associated with immediate awareness and experience of phenomena, and the other results from reflection on experience. Therapists encourage their clients first to become aware of their phenomenal experience, including their sensations, their emotions, and the meaning that situations and events have for them. In therapy, awareness of emotion is central to change. Having emotional experience informs people that something matters to them, and becoming aware of feelings tells people that they are experiencing events. The reflective level of awareness derives from viewing one's experience from an observer's perspective. Clients become aware of the links among events, their reactions, and other people, as well as the specific meanings that situations have for them, by reflecting on their experiences and forming narratives to explain them. This reflective process is described more fully in chapter 13; in this chapter we are primarily concerned with the process of making clients more aware of their immediate experience, sensation, feelings, and meanings that arise spontaneously in the present.

As the initial sessions proceed and as clients talk about their week, about their symptoms of depression, or about past events, therapists constantly attend to clients' present emotional experience and respond empathically to it. Thus, when a client says, "I feel so bad, I can't get going in the morning," the therapist empathically understands this but also attempts to catch the underlying feeling—maybe of hopelessness or of irritation—and to empathically explore it. If the client begins feeling deeply hopeless and weepy, the therapist validates the client's pain and reflects an understanding of how hard it is to keep going when it feels (for example) like there is no fuel left inside. Statements that both validate and focus on clients' subjective experience also help to begin the process of evoking emotional experience in the session. When therapists reflect how hard it must be, tears may well up in clients' eyes, and they may begin to open up about their experience, or they may visibly suppress their experience. The therapist thus begins to see clients' core concerns and internal struggles in both what clients are feeling and how they respond to their experience. The expression or suppression of emotional experience in the session reveals how clients process their emotions and provides important markers of current cognitive–affective processing difficulties. When emotions emerge in a session, they are a red flag signalling "This is important to my well-being" and that a need of central concern is being activated. The therapist attuned to emotion will view the emergence of emotion as an opportunity for intimacy in the therapeutic relationship and will approach the client's experience, move closer to it, and validate it. The therapist can move closer to and validate an expression of pain by saying, "Of course it hurts deeply when you say this" and can validate a suppression of feeling by saying, "It's really hard to feel those things. It's safer right now to hold them at bay."

Initially the therapist invites the client to speak and to reflect on and organize his or her experience into some form of narrative or explanation. Speaking and disclosing constitute the core of the therapy process, because it is from this base—the client's text—that the client and therapist, by reflecting on what the client says, deepen the experience of what is being told. Through their conversation, they both come to read more into what is happening and see more aspects of what is occurring. The therapist's first task therefore is to create a climate in which the client can speak. The basic relational attitudes described by client-centered therapy help achieve this.

At first, clients may not take up the therapist's invitation to share and explore their emotions and experience. Rather, they enter therapy seeking answers from an expert. They come with questions and with an attitude of asking, or they want reassurance from the therapist, or they want to continue to try to solve problems in familiar and unsuccessful ways. They may try to use logic or intellectualize their experience. In the beginning of therapy, clients generally talk about their depressive symptoms and events and do not explore their feelings, nor do they raise questions about their internal experience. They look toward the therapist for direction and answers. They explain to the therapist things about their lives; they want to talk about their complaints, about their fatigue, about their symptoms of depression. They want to discuss with the therapist what can be done about these problems, and they ask the therapist, implicitly or explicitly, to cure their depression. In summary, clients want the therapist to give them the solution for their depression and psychological problems.

At some point, however, often because of the safe relational environment, therapists' empathic responses, and the establishment of a good working alliance, clients make an important step forward. They begin to initiate and speak by themselves about themselves in a more exploratory way, rather than waiting for questions or asking for guidance. The client then is willing, at least to a minimal degree, to engage in a process of increasing awareness and self-exploration. This is the moment that EFT becomes possible. The shift from an external to an internal focus marks the first step in a deepening of the experiential process. Now that the process of therapy has begun, methods of increasing awareness are most useful.

Clients in EFT learn to attend to both their inner experience, including body sensations and feelings, and their outer experience, including the people in their lives and the events that occur. An important task for clients is to learn to differentiate between the inner and outer worlds and to be able to integrate the information from both to form new gestalts. Differentiating facets of self, other, and world is very helpful in teasing out and coming to understand what one is feeling. By differentiating their experience, clients can move from "I feel bad" to, for example, "I feel unfairly treated and humiliated by the way he discarded me for someone else." This articulation allows clients then to explore the nature of the injury to themselves and all its implications on different levels. It helps clients define the nature of their problems and opens up paths for exploration.

After differentiating experience, clients need to integrate their experience to make sense of it and develop new gestalts. For example, one client, after exploring the impact of her abusive partner, observed, "The worst of it is that I left myself open to being misused—I need to guard against that in future, but it is difficult to trust myself." This statement indicates that the client has integrated her understanding of what happened and assumes some responsibility for protecting herself in the future. Awareness of what triggered a reaction provides the client with an understanding of how he or she construed and interpreted a situation and what its significance is. As the client attends to and explores experience, new, finer discriminations emerge that result in changes to his or her experiential landscape. Awareness and symbolization of experience in words provides a sense of mastery. No longer is the client puzzled or overwhelmed by feelings; instead, there is a sense of "Oh, that's why I felt this way." Symbolization of one's experience in words gives one a handle with which to grasp it and allows one to work with it to create new meanings and new narratives.

To promote awareness, therapists act as clients' surrogate information processors and emotional regulators. As information processors, therapists reflect clients' experience back to them and help them attempt to process it and find words to express it. As emotional regulators, the validation and support therapists offer provide a soothing balm as they reflect and try to empathically understand their clients' distress and the difficulties they are encountering in their lives. This soothing often engenders a sense of relief in clients as they unburden, without shame, the depth of their hopeless, sad, and negative feelings.

Empathic responses help to promote clients' affect regulation in at least four ways. First, by empathically responding to their clients' pain, experiential therapists provide relief in the moment as their clients feel acknowledged and validated. Second, clients gain knowledge of their feelings, which heightens their sense of mastery and control. Third, in the process of naming and labeling their feelings, clients learn to modulate their level of arousal. As their feelings begin to shift, clients begin to understand that they can acquire some control over their feelings. They gain a sense of perspective as they see that their feelings ebb and flow over time. Finally, the sense of relief and easing of tension that follow from being seen and accepted free energy and resources for clients to explore and problem solve. This freeing of energy is often accompanied by vestiges of hope that they may be able to conquer their feelings of despair.

Therapists move to heighten clients' awareness of their emotional experiencing after the first two or three sessions. If clients are not responsive, therapists pull back and work to solidify the bond by attempting to better understand and validate the clients' experiences. In addition, therapists might explore the reasons behind clients' reluctance to engage in processing their emotional experience more consciously and deliberately. Therapists encourage clients to direct their attention to the immediacy of all the aspects of their experience, including emotional triggers, bodily sensations, feelings, cognitions, needs, and action tendencies, and especially to those that might not be in awareness. For example, if clients are unaware of their bodily felt experience, therapists help them focus on the sensation of tightness in their throats, the numbness in their bodies, or the butterflies in their stomachs. If the label or feeling is missing, therapists help them formulate unformulated experience into words such as *sad, angry, all washed up,* or *despondent*. Once clients are aware of what is happening in their bodies and have labeled their feelings, they are able to recall, report, and reflect on their experience so as to change all or parts of the emotion scheme.

Of the six different aspects of clients' emotion schemes to which EFT therapists attend (emotional triggers, bodily sensations, feelings, cognitions, needs, and action tendencies), clients may be aware of only one or two at a time. Therapists listen to see which aspects of clients' emotion schemes they have not fully represented or described and then focus on helping clients attend to and incorporate these into their narratives. Once clients are fully aware of all the components of their emotion schemes, they are in a better position to make sense of their experience and reflect on it.

Emotional Triggers

It is often important to identify cues or triggers that evoke different emotional states. Sometimes clients with depression are aware that they feel bad but cannot identify the cues they are reacting to. It may seem to them that their depression just descends like a fog out of nowhere. Clarifying triggers is the first step in developing awareness of emotional processes. Therapists help their clients attend to the various stimuli in their environment that spark different reactions. They can attend to clients' reactions in the session as they are describing the events in their lives and help clients establish links between their feelings and specific events. Therapists also can help their clients to be concrete and specific in their descriptions to identify small details in a scene or situation that might have contributed to their clients' feelings. Finally, therapists can encourage their clients to imagine significant others and respond as those significant others to help clients become aware of the others' nonverbal cues and attitudes and ways of responding to or being with the client. All these techniques serve to enhance clients' awareness of their own and others' reactions and of their environment.

Bodily Sensations

When working with clients who are unaware of their feelings, therapists work to help clients increase their awareness by focusing attention on their bodies. Paying attention to and making contact with sensations is a nonverbal form of knowing what one is feeling. Therapists guide clients' attention to their bodies to help them become aware of the sinking sensation in their stomach, or the sadness in their eyes and cheeks, or the tightness in their chests. This awareness of feelings is not an intellectual understanding; clients should not feel that they are on the outside looking at themselves. Rather, they should have a bodily sensed awareness of what is felt from the inside, like the experience of throbbing with a toothache. Clients are directed in the session to pay attention to the quality, intensity, and shape of the sensations at a specific place in their body to help them come to know their bodily felt reactions. For example, a client may become aware that he is experiencing "a hot tight ball" in his chest.

Alternatively, therapists might help clients become aware of incongruities between their verbal and nonverbal behavior. Therapists direct clients' attention to their nonverbal behavior and to the double messages that they are sending. For example, one client would smile brightly while her words conveyed a sense of sadness and distress. When the therapist commented on the discrepancy, the client realized that she did not know how to communicate her feelings openly, partly because she feared being overwhelmed by them and partly because she did not believe anyone would listen. Therapists also have clients attend to other physical movements, such as the clenching of fists, the stroking of an armrest, or the swinging of a foot. By focusing on these nonverbal activities, therapists help clients become aware of different sensations in their bodies and to note areas of tension and relaxation, heightening their awareness of how they are reacting to different situations.

Feelings

We use the words *emotions* and *feelings* in this book interchangeably, although more formally, *emotions* refers to the categorical emotions like anger, sadness, and so forth, whereas *feelings* are the more cognitively and socially differentiated aspects of emotion. An important task in EFT is to have clients become aware of their feelings and emotions. They need to attend to their prereflective reactions and bodily sensations so that they can know the impact and significance of events. Feelings represent the fusion of clients' prereflective reactions and the cognitive meanings attached to these events. To know how they are feeling, clients need to name their subjective experiences. Clients are encouraged to attend to and label their emotions. To fully capture the meaning of their experiences and understand their responses to events, they are encouraged to move beyond general descriptions like "I feel bad" to more differentiated descriptions of their feelings so that they can begin to see what they need in order to feel different about themselves or their situations.

Once clients are aware of their bodies, they can attend to the meaning of the bodily sensations. Some clients do not have easy access to labels for their feelings, and an important task in EFT therapy is to help clients begin to attend to labels and articulate their feelings so that they can share them and use them as a source of information to solve current and future problems. In contrast to other approaches, therapists using EFT do not see feelings as needing to be controlled, dampened, and reined in; rather, clients need to access and attend to their feelings to understand their core beliefs, values, goals, and needs. The process of labeling feelings in conscious awareness serves to modulate arousal so that clients can use the information in a less heated form to inform their decision making and problem solving.

Cognitions

In addition to paying attention to sensations, emotions, and feelings, clients need to become aware of the thoughts accompanying those sensations. All emotions include thoughts as well as feelings. When people feel emotions, an inner dialogue often accompanies the feeling, and images and evaluations of themselves and others may be evoked. For example, if a client is feeling depressed, he or she might think, "I am such a loser" or "I will never get what I need from my husband." Therapists need to guide clients' attention to the thoughts and evaluations that accompany the sensations. Emotional awareness involves awareness of the feelings, thoughts, and images that make up an emotional experience.

Some clients are able to represent their emotional experience in images. These clients may have difficulty describing their experience in words; however, they may be able to represent their experience in pictures or symbols. For these clients, using evocative reflections and coconstructing images of their experience can help them get a better sense of it. For example, Jenny, whose fiancé had recently ended their relationship, was unable to freely talk about her feelings in therapy. She had great difficulty knowing what she felt, but she was able at times to bring up images of her experience. When describing her fear of being alone, she said she felt like she was skating on a pond on which the ice had begun to crack. On another occasion, as she once again contemplated the difficulties of being alone, she presented the image of being caught at sea in a storm. These images provided both her and her therapist with a clearer sense of how she was experiencing the world and allowed the therapist to empathically respond to her sense of vulnerability and helplessness. The focus of therapy was to provide a safe place for her to come to know and express her feelings and reactions to events without fear of judgment so that she could develop a stronger, more effective sense of self to combat her depression.

Needs and Action Tendencies

An important goal of EFT for depression is to help clients identify their needs more clearly. All feelings have implicit needs; feelings inform people about how they need to act to restore a sense of well-being or take care of themselves. Often clients with depression are overwhelmed by feelings of despair and hopelessness, leading them to withdraw from their environments and give up. By this stage they have lost touch with other core feelings and needs that may have precipitated the depression—for example, a sense of vulnerability, fragility, or abandonment and the accompanying needs for support, care, and nurture. Therapists work to help clients heighten and differentiate their feelings in order to become more aware of their needs and explore ways of meeting them in appropriate ways.

Clients' action tendencies associated with the emotion and need can be directed outward and revealed in their behavioral tendencies and interpersonal interactions, or their action tendencies can be inner directed and revealed in their intrapersonal orientation and treatment of themselves. Therapists thus pay particular attention to helping clients become aware of how they treat themselves intrapersonally and others interactionally to help them understand what behaviors their emotions are prompting them to engage in.

Some emotions, like contempt or anger, can be felt toward the self; the action tendency and need in contempt is to diminish or destroy the self. Clients also express disdain for themselves by ignoring themselves. The anxiety and fear of being alone in depression and the need for closeness lead people who are depressed to be clingy and desperate or, as a protection, to be rejecting.

For example, one client, a woman with two young children, came to therapy because she was depressed as a result of her husband's persistent gambling. His behavior meant that he was away from home a lot, leaving her with the burden of caring for the children, and at times his losses caused serious financial distress. In therapy she realized that she had learned not to express her feelings in intimate relationships and that she should subjugate her needs to those of her husband. She realized that she needed to voice her needs more and to find ways that she could be more independent within the marriage. Although this realization did not change her husband's behavior, she felt more in control and more satisfied with her life and thus less stressed by his behavior.

ESTABLISHING COLLABORATION

Before implementing specific interventions to heighten clients' awareness of their emotional reactions, it is important to establish agreement with them on the tasks and goals of therapy. Therapists need to establish a common framework with their clients for thinking about their problems. Clients need to agree that they are having difficulty processing their emotional experience either because it is too overwhelming or because they have difficulty attending to it. If the client does not agree with the therapist's formulation, then the therapist needs to readjust his or her framework and conceptualization to fit better with the client's perspective. Even as therapists try to reframe clients' issues in psychological language, they must not lose sight of clients as the experts on their experience. Once there is a common framework, therapists can focus clients on becoming more aware and tolerant of their emotional experience.

Accepting and Tolerating Emotions

Therapists facilitate not only an awareness of emotions, but also a welcoming of emotional experience; they help clients develop the capacity to tolerate and accept what they feel, rather than avoid it, and to trust that painful feelings will pass. Clients need to understand that they do not have to act on all their emotions but that to avoid or deflect their pain and dreaded feelings is not helpful. With help, clients come to recognize their feelings as an opportunity to gather information about something important to their well-being.

Clients also need to learn that emotions are not reasoned, final conclusions that they must act on. Thus, they can feel them without fear of dire consequences. If clients attend to feelings of hopelessness, this does not mean that things are hopeless, nor does it mean that the next logical step is to give up. A feeling is not a permanent state of being; rather, it is part of a process. Emotion is not about a concluded truth. It provides information about a person's values and judgments in relation to how things are affecting his or her well-being in the moment. An emotion says more about the person than about reality. Anger tells someone that he or she feels violated, not that the other person is a violator. Emotions inform rather than determine. If a client is upset with her partner and feels like saying, "I hate you for what you did," this does not necessarily mean that the relationship must end. Rather, it informs the client about how isolated and enraged she feels. After acknowledging her feelings, the next step in the process is to access her needs by asking herself, "What do I need or want? What do I do?" Becoming aware of their emotions helps clients to understand the impact of events, access their needs, and solve problems in a meaningful way.

Emotions are not actions. People may want to control their actions, but they do not need to control their primary internal experience. Anger is not aggression. People can feel angry at a friend without hitting, and even without telling the friend that they are angry. However, they still need to acknowledge and feel their anger. Trying to deny their feelings by saying "I have no right to feel angry" may lead to the anger leaking out at unguarded moments or exploding in a way that is hurtful.

Expressing how one feels out loud, however, must be appropriate to its context and needs to be regulated. Clients learn to express their feelings and communicate effectively if they are first able to understand, feel, and welcome their primary feelings. Rather than suppressing their feelings until they explode or recklessly blowing off steam at any opportunity, clients need to contact and develop their experience and learn ways of expressing it appropriately. Once clients have allowed their feelings to develop and have made sense of them, they can decide when and what they want to tell others about how they feel. This will allow them to express their feelings in the manner most appropriate to the context in which they find themselves.

Once they have attended to an emotion, clients are more able to let it go. In addition, by attending to their emotions, clients learn that emotions follow a natural course of rising and passing away, of swelling and fading. They come and go if clients do not try to block them out or avoid them, but just let them flow through.

Labeling and Describing Emotions

Awareness entails full comprehension, so awareness of a physical or emotional reaction is insufficient; clients need to label it in words to understand it fully. After helping clients pay attention to and tolerate their emotions, therapists help them to describe the emotions in words to fully comprehend them. Naming emotions is particularly helpful when they signal difficulties that need attention or when they require reflection and communication to others. Feelings, even when they are very clear, are also complex. There is always more to a feeling than any one description can capture. For example, a person may be angry, but he or she might also feel sorry about being angry; the place from which the person's anger comes may include either a fear of retaliation or a steely resolve with no fear. Describing a feeling in words also makes emotional experience more available for future recall. For example, once clients know that they are feeling sad, they can reflect on what they are sad about, what this means to them, and what they need to do. Metaphors are also helpful in helping clients symbolize their inner experience. Conventional images such as feeling stuck in the mud, feeling dirty, or swimming against the tide, as well as novel and idiosyncratic metaphors such as "a volcano is erupting in my chest" or "just all prickly and sharp," are helpful in describing sensations.

Naming or labeling emotion is a first step in regulating it. With words, clients can speak it, rather than act it out. Attaching words to feelings gives clients the ability to understand and control their emotions. Being able to describe their emotions allows them to get a handle on what they are feeling and can help them deal with their problems. Thus, one client described a feeling about a difficulty engaging in social conversations with the words "I feel so left out." On exploring this further, he was able to understand the experience in a new way—"I try so hard to keep up with the conversation, but actually I'm often not interested. That's why I've nothing to say; I don't really find it interesting." The client was now in a new place; he realized that he was often not interested in social conversation. A new meaning emerged, and this new perspective no longer focused on feeling left out. New possibilities emerged that were not available in the state called "feeling left out."

In another example, a client described some of the confusion and difficulty she experienced in taking over someone's job as a supervisor of a team. She said, "Whenever I meet with my team, I feel like there's a ghost in the room [the old supervisor], and I can never fill her shoes." The client then moved on to acknowledge, "I can't do what she did. It's crazy trying to be like her. I'm different—I need to focus on my strengths." In these examples, describing feelings in words promoted the generation of new meaning. New meaning does not always arise automatically, but often it does, and therapists need to promote it by helping clients capture the nuances of their feelings in words to differentiate its central meaning and provide clarity about their needs so that new behavior can be generated.

Knowing what they feel also gives clients a sense of control over their experience and strengthens their belief that they have the power to do something about their feelings. By being able to label feelings in words, an act of separation from the feeling occurs. By putting emotion into words, clients simultaneously provide a label for the feeling itself, thereby knowing what they feel, and create a new perspective from which to see the feeling. It is now "I" who feel "worthless," and "worthless" is not all that "I" am. Some distance is created. The client now feels that "worthless" is something he or she is "feeling," rather than the term describing all of him or her. The act of naming also lets clients experience themselves as agents, rather than as passive victims, of the feeling. Feeling is seen as their current reaction instead of as representing reality or truth. The view of the self as an agent in relation to feelings helps establish a sense of distance from the feeling, which provides strength and agency.

Putting experience into language also helps depressed clients with traumatic histories. Therapists can help clients who have suffered trauma or endured deeply painful experiences begin a reconstructive process of dealing with the trauma with the help of language. This therapeutic process allows them to develop accounts of what occurred (Pennebaker, 1995; Van der Kolk, 1994). The capacity to describe emotionally traumatic experience allows clients to make sense of their experience. Unless they can code the experience in language, only sights, sounds, and images are stored in emotional memory. Being able to put their experience into words in a safe environment enables clients to think about and describe their traumatic memories and thereby gain some control over their terrifying experience. They become authors, rather than victims, of their experience. This process of naming emotions helps marry the verbal and nonverbal parts of the brain and creates an integrated experience in which clients can both feel and think about their experience simultaneously.

Identifying Primary Experience

Therapists and clients need to explore whether clients' emotional reactions are their core feelings. Thus, when a client talks about feeling angry when a colleague at work disagrees with her, she needs to explore whether at some level under the anger she feels threatened. Or when a client angrily says his spouse accused him of being inattentive, he needs to explore whether behind his anger he feels unappreciated. Therapists can help a client who is worrying about her child leaving home for university recognize that under the worry, she feels sad. The ability to identify complex emotions is one of the core skills that therapists help their clients to develop. Therapists promote this ability by constantly focusing clients' attention on their bodily felt feelings and empathizing with those feelings. With practice, clients become adept at monitoring their own feelings.

Primary emotions are based on automatic evaluations of the world and of what is happening to the person and his or her body. To know one's self means to know one's core emotions and what one's most basic evaluation and response is to whatever situation one finds oneself in. This may involve hard work. However, only becoming aware of their primary feelings places people in a position to choose whether to follow them or not. With practice and honesty, clients' primary feelings start to come to them more spontaneously. They will feel sadness at loss, anger at violation, and joy at connection or achievement of goals. They will also more easily spot when their anger is covering fear or when their crying is obscuring anger. Therapists know that their clients have reached the necessary level of awareness when they are more easily able to apprehend the complexity of their feelings, are aware that they may be experiencing two different feelings, or realize that what they are feeling at the moment is not really the core. Some clients come to therapy with this skill in place, and therapists are easily able to move into Stage 2 to help them evoke their feelings. However, other clients may need more time to become aware of their emotions. For them, practice and more practice is needed until this skill becomes more automatic.

In addition to becoming aware of the different schematic processing components, it is helpful for clients to become aware of two other major processes: their ways of interrupting their emotions and their style of relating to self and other. These are discussed in the sections that follow.

Undoing Self-Interruptive Processes

Therapists often need to help clients become aware that they are avoiding or interrupting their feelings and then identify the ways they are doing this. Clients who are unaware of their feelings or trying to avoid them often engage in interruptive processes, which may include constricting their breathing, tensing their muscles, holding themselves rigidly, or engaging in distracting activities.

Physical Responses

Many clients who were traumatized early in life restrict their breathing, and this is exacerbated when they are feeling emotional. As clients become more aware of their bodies, therapists can help them focus their attention on their breathing to determine whether they are holding their breath or are breathing very quickly. Helping clients to become aware of and regulate their breathing makes them more aware not only of their breath, but also of how they hold their bodies and where the tension is located. This awareness suggests a way of modulating their affect. As they attend to their breathing, clients may become aware of tension in their shoulders or tightness in their throats and chest as they try to rein in their sadness and feelings of hopelessness. Other clients deliberately try to tune out their feelings by numbing themselves in an attempt to avoid the pain. Most clients developed these strategies when they were much younger, and they now use them without being consciously aware. Once clients become aware of the different ways they regulate their affect, they can decide whether these strategies are effective or contribute to their feelings of depression and hopelessness, and they then can work to develop alternative strategies to process their emotional experience.

Analytical Descriptions

Conceptual and externalized descriptions of events and experience can keep emotional experience at bay. Clients who did not learn to process their emotional experience or who felt overwhelmed by their emotions may suppress them by focusing on external events or by being very analytical in their descriptions. For example, Geoff, a young lawyer with depression, had great difficulty talking about his feelings. He was feeling disengaged at work, where he experienced a lot of stress as he constantly worried that his performance would fall short or he would make some grave error in judgment. Although he was very articulate, he focused his attention on the cases he was working on and his colleagues' reactions and opinions to his work. The therapist attempted to direct his attention to his feelings by asking directly how he felt in certain situations and by trying to imagine what it might be like to be caught in the kind of environment that Geoff described and then tentatively presenting these impressions to see if they resonated with Geoff's experience. Over time, Geoff gradually became more aware and open to his experience.

Therapists work with clients' interruptive processes in a number of ways. They may share their observations with their clients, noting that their descriptions are very analytical or that their breathing seems very shallow. They can suggest that their clients pay more attention to their bodily reactions and become more aware of when they are tuning out or monitor their breathing and breathe more deeply when it is shallow. They may ask clients to be aware of their breathing through the upcoming week and explore with them other points of tension and muscular constriction and any memories that are associated with those sensations. If clients do recall memories of specific events when they realize they constrict their breathing or become very tense, therapists work with them to reprocess these memories by accessing the feelings associated with them that clients might not have had the opportunity to express and process at the time. If clients are very analytical in their descriptions of events, therapists can ask them directly how they feel about the events they are describing. Therapists might offer empathic conjectures to see whether their understanding fits with how clients might be experiencing the events and to make those feelings more explicit.

For example, very soon after Richard sought treatment for his depression, his therapist observed that there were times in the session, especially when he was talking about conflict with his wife, that he seemed to hold his breath as he was talking. After the therapist commented on this and asked him to breathe deeply, Richard became tearful and expressed how sad and dejected he was that he and his wife were constantly quarreling and had so much difficulty being tender with each other. He also realized that it was very hard for him to express his vulnerability and sadness about this. After his therapist asked when he recalled feeling so tense before, he recalled evenings at the family dinner table, when his mother would be depressed and angry. He never knew whether she would find fault with his behavior and ridicule him or not. He recalled that during these times he would become very tense and stop breathing deeply. In fact, he still had difficulty eating with his mother and would lose his appetite entirely after a confrontation with his wife. Once these memories came to light, the therapist suggested that they engage in an empty-chair exercise to help Richard express his feelings of anger and resentment toward his mother so as to release the tension in his chest and help him start breathing more deeply.

Understanding the Style of Relating

Clients with depression are often harsh and punitive with themselves, evident in the way they judge their behavior, the high standards they hold for themselves, or their criticisms of themselves. Alternatively, they may be quite neglectful, forgetting to eat or otherwise not taking care of themselves or not looking out for their own interests. In their interpersonal interactions, clients who are depressed may be clingy or rejecting of others. Some clients may be quite submissive, totally neglecting their own needs and silencing themselves to maintain connection. Alternatively, they may be overly assertive and hostile for fear that their needs will not be met and they will be disappointed. In either case, they are unable to express their need for care and nurturing in a way that others can respond to effectively. Therapists need to help clients become aware of their style of relating to self and other, generally by attending to moment-by-moment experience in the therapy session.

Therapists are attuned to how clients treat themselves and others and the action tendencies implied by their feelings, and they gently share these observations with their clients. The absence of positive behaviors or the presence of negative ones suggests ways that therapists can intervene. For example, highly critical clients or those who are very demanding of themselves can be encouraged to engage in two-chair work to begin to become aware of the felt impact that these demands have on themselves and others. With clients who are more neglectful, therapists focus their efforts on being empathic so that clients become aware of their inner experience. With these clients, it may be necessary to facilitate their awareness of their body sensations before focusing them on their feelings. If clients withdraw from contact with the therapist or feel shame in the moment at something the therapist says or does, these feelings and tendencies are brought to awareness in the session as they occur.

Creating a Collaborative Focus

A collaborative focus is a central component of building a working alliance. While the client and therapist are developing a bond and awareness is being promoted, a third important process—that of creating a treatment focus—is also under way. A focus on the underlying generating conditions of the depression needs to be created and mutually agreed upon in the first three to five sessions. By identifying with sureness and clarity the client's pain producing the depression, therapists facilitate the strengthening of the bond and the formation of goals of treatment. The alliance is consolidated as therapists help their clients articulate their feelings, and a clearer understanding emerges of the processes that are contributing to the clients' depression.

Therapists listen for markers that indicate that their clients are self-critical or very demanding of themselves. Once these have been identified, therapists establish agreement with clients so that they, too, see how these attitudes contribute to their depression, and together they begin to negotiate how to tackle these in therapy. Therapists gently introduce clients to the specific interventions associated with the different conceptualizations. At first clients may feel strange and awkward, but once they gain a sense of how the process works and get a new view of themselves or significant others, they are more willing to participate and overcome their shyness. Some clients may find it impossible to overcome their sense of strangeness at talking to an empty chair, and at these times the therapist may choose to work with the clients without asking them to switch back and forth to maintain the alliance.

9

METHODS FOR
INCREASING AWARENESS

In their developmental model of emotional awareness, Lane and Schwartz (1992) explained that many clients enter therapy with a simplistic understanding of emotions. New clients often report "just feeling bad" or "feeling it in my stomach." In initial sessions, clients may need to work to increase awareness of their bodily sensations, gain comfort with these sensations, and allow flexibility in responding to them. Therapists encourage them to maintain a focus on their bodies without disengaging or trying to control the experience. Body awareness in psychotherapy has taken a number of forms, including mindfulness training (Kabat-Zinn, 1990), focusing (Gendlin, 1996), and progressive muscle relaxation (D. A. Bernstein, Borkovec, & Hazlett-Stevens, 2000). Any of these techniques might be used in this phase of emotion-focused therapy (EFT).

IDENTIFYING TRIGGERS

Therapists can help clients become aware of and understand their feelings by attending to the triggers, or situational stimuli, that spark the feelings. Identifying the triggers helps clients and therapists begin to understand how clients construe the events in their lives and react to those events. Therapists often use evocative responding to help clients identify the triggers for their depressive reactions and to process traumatic events. The purpose of evocative responding is to access clients' episodic memory about particular events to reconstruct them and evoke the feelings that go along with them. Becoming aware of and labeling their triggers help clients identify the links between their environments, their affective responses, and their behavior.

First, therapists ask clients to describe the event or scene in detail, to "play a movie" of what happened, so that therapist and client get a live sense of what it was like for the client. Therapists can help clients construct a concrete and detailed description of the event by helping them track their affective reactions with the intent of pinpointing the moment when the reaction changed so that the trigger or stimulus can be identified. In the case of a traumatic memory, therapists are concerned not so much with identifying the trigger as with helping clients link their affective reactions with the concrete details of the scene so that clients can compose a coherent narrative of what happened to them and reprocess the event. Once clients have identified the triggers that prompted their reactions, they are able to evaluate their reactions and the situations to develop alternative responses.

For example, Paul, a 32-year-old engineer suffering from depression, was uncertain about what triggered his changes in mood. In one session he mentioned that the previous evening he had felt much worse than usual. He agreed to explore the situation to see if he could better understand his reaction.

> *Therapist:* So try to give me a sense of what happened last night. You had left work, you say, at about 6:30; is that right?
>
> *Paul:* Yes. Then I went to pick up some food for dinner and went home. I was feeling really tired, as I have been putting in long hours at the office recently. We have this deadline due next week. I had decided just to stay home and watch some television.
>
> *Therapist:* OK. So you leave work, and you are tired, sort of looking forward to relaxing and resting. So what happens when you get home?
>
> *Paul:* I made dinner, and then I went down to the workshop to my tool bench. I realized I had not finished cleaning up on Sunday, as a number of my tools were lying about, because a friend had dropped by for a visit. I remember putting them away and then going back upstairs and sitting down in front of the television.
>
> *Therapist:* OK. So you get home and have dinner, and how are you feeling?

Paul:	Tired, really tired.
Therapist:	OK. So you are tired, and then you go down to the basement and see the tools lying around. What happens then?
Paul:	Oh, I remember feeling irritated with myself. My Dad always used to be such a stickler about putting his tools away. I don't know what I was thinking; I am usually so particular about those sorts of things.
Therapist:	So you see the tools and feel angry at yourself—this sort of behavior would have been unacceptable to your Dad?
Paul:	Oh, yes, big time.
Therapist:	So is this the point at which your mood changed?
Paul:	No, it was later, when I was lying on the sofa, that I began to feel awful, just useless and lazy.
Therapist:	Oh, so it is when you start to view yourself as useless and lazy that your mood gets really low?
Paul:	Yes, I guess I never really noticed that before, but I guess I feel awful every time I think I have let my Dad down.

The therapist has had the client describe the details of the evening so that they can identify the moment when his mood changed and the event that triggered the change. Paul's trigger is his self-criticism and high expectations that he always do things as perfectly as his father expected when he was a child. The therapist and client are now aware that when Paul sees himself as useless and lazy, he feels depressed.

Subsequently they explored these feelings further. Paul explored why he was so critical of himself. He recalled that his father had been a very busy and successful professional who had lived during the Depression. He would often tell his children tales of how difficult his life had been and how hard he had to work to support his mother and two siblings. He said he had worked at two jobs just to put some food on the table, and this continued while he was at university to pay for his education. He would say that his own children had it too easy and that they expected things to be handed to them. This left the client feeling that if he did not do things as well as his father, he was lazy and useless.

Paul began to question if this was a fair evaluation of himself. He noted that he and his father lived in different times. He acknowledged that his father had to survive a difficult period that he was lucky to have escaped, but he realized that he was productive and successful in his life and need not be so punishing of himself. Later, Paul and his therapist did some two-chair work to resolve Paul's self-criticism and help him develop more self-acceptance. Both focusing and systematic evocative unfolding helped to promote Paul's awareness and understanding of his affective reactions.

HEIGHTENING AWARENESS OF FEELINGS

Clients may need to learn skills to identify, label, and differentiate among different emotional states. Primary emotional reactions are biologically adaptive emotional responses that provide information about action tendencies, associated meanings, and motivations for behavior. These responses include categorical emotions such as fear, joy, anger, and sadness, as well as more complex feeling states like drained, discouraged, or despairing. Because of their informational value, accessing primary emotions is essential to positive affective change and regulation. Differentiating more idiosyncratic feeling helps clients create meaning.

Therapists focus clients on their feelings using simple empathic responses, including affirmations and simple reflections, and exploratory empathy, including empathic conjectures, exploratory responses, and evocative responses. The aim of these responses is to facilitate clients' awareness and expression of their emotional experience that is at the edges of their conscious awareness.

Simple empathic responses convey an understanding of clients' experiences. They are not intended to push for exploration or increase clients' arousal. Rather, they demonstrate that therapists are actively following their clients' narratives and are working to stay present and responsive to their experiences. However, empathic responses sometimes have the paradoxical effect of revealing the subjectivity of clients' perceptions and the alternatives hidden in certain perspectives (Elliott, Watson, Goldman, & Greenberg, 2004; Watson, 2001).

Empathic reflections convey an understanding of what the client has said. These responses attempt to distill the essence of the client's communication. To do this, therapists try to reflect that which is most poignant in clients' statements. For example, a therapist used empathic reflection with a client who was mourning the death of her son:

> *Client:* I feel like my world was plunged into darkness after Bobbie died. Everyone seems to want me to resume my activities, but I feel so lost; nothing seems to mean anything anymore. I know I am letting the others down, but I just can't seem to help it.
>
> *Therapist:* Since Bobbie died, you feel lost in the darkness unable to get out.

The therapist validated the client's experience but held in focus the two possibilities of being stuck and finding a way out. The therapist suggested implicitly that there was a way out that they could find together. This type of response not only indicated understanding of and support for the client in the moment, but also began to frame the tasks and goals of therapy, thus contributing to the development of a bond.

Empathic affirmations convey that therapists fully understand and appreciate just how distressed clients are feeling. They are typically used when clients have shared particularly painful experiences and appear very vulnerable in the session, and they serve to validate the client's experience. For example,

Client: I feel so defective and not worth anything since I was let go at work.

Therapist: The termination and the way it happened have just been so hard. No wonder it has left you feeling so broken.

When clients are feeling intensely distressed, it is important to help them express their pain and have it heard in a way that helps them feel supported and held. The purpose of affirming responses is to strengthen the self, not to provide new information. Thus, with a client who is feeling depressed and experiencing difficulties in day-to-day functioning, it may be most helpful for the therapist to reflect his or her understanding of the terrible feeling of loss of control, rather than to try to get an understanding of what is causing the overwhelmed response. The therapist's ability to understand that clients at times feel like they are drowning and cannot get their head above water will help clients contain this feeling and strengthen their sense of self.

Evocative responses are intended to evoke vivid, pictorial representations of clients' experience to help them access their feelings. Experiential therapists use imagistic and concrete sensory language to try to bring the client's experiences alive. For example, Eric, a 45-year-old client, had difficulty understanding his reactions or knowing what he felt about events. To help him get a better understanding of his reactions, his therapist used an evocative reflection:

Therapist: So how have you been?

Eric: Pretty well the same. I just feel so down.

Therapist: Watching you sit there and hearing you talk, I just have this image of you being pushed down by a lead weight—suffocated almost. Is that how it feels?

Eric: Yes, exactly; it is as if the life is being squeezed out of me.

Empathic exploration responses are intended to encourage clients to explore the edges of their experience, unlike simple reflections, which focus on what has been said. With empathic reflections therapists attempt to capture feelings and meanings that are just outside of clients' awareness. There are several different forms, including evocative responses, growth-oriented reflections, exploratory and "fit" questions, process observations, and conjectures. These responses are used to stimulate clients to explore their experiencing.

Exploratory reflections are helpful when therapists are trying to have clients consider new information, see things differently, or explore the deeper meaning and significance of events. For example, Eric's therapist noticed that his voice changed when he started talking about his brother's death, and she decided to explore this with him:

> Therapist: Eric, I noticed when you mentioned Charles's death that your voice changed. I am wondering what you are feeling . . . sad, wistful?
>
> Eric: I am not sure; I wasn't paying attention, but now that you mention it, I am aware of this hollow feeling in my stomach.
>
> Therapist: So, like, emptiness?
>
> Eric: Yes, it's a sense of loss and regret I have that I did not get a chance to know him better.

The therapist's statement included both a reflection and a process observation in which the therapist observed the change in the client's voice. Process observations can reference a process in the client, in the interaction, or in the therapist.

Empathic conjectures are attempts by therapists to tentatively express what the client may be feeling but not yet saying. The therapist guesses at what the client is feeling or offers a response for the client to try on. For example, Connie, a 45-year-old woman, was struggling to balance the demands of motherhood with rebuilding a life for herself following a divorce:

> Connie: It is just so important to me that the kids do not lose out because of the divorce. I have to focus most of my energies on them. So between hockey, skating, homework, and the house, I am quite exhausted by the end of the week. So that does not leave any time to relax or get together with friends, let alone dating.
>
> Therapist: That sounds like a very demanding schedule. Am I right in getting the sense that you feel squeezed on all sides?
>
> Connie: Yeah! I am just so worried about them in case they slip through the cracks. The divorce has been so hard on them; they lost everything.
>
> Therapist: It almost sounds like you have forgotten to put yourself in the picture. Like your needs don't count.
>
> Connie: Yes, that is quite true. I hadn't realized that, but I guess I don't feel I have a right to ask for anything, seeing I left the marriage.

Alternatively, therapists can help clients become aware of their feelings by posing exploratory questions. In the case of Connie, her therapist might say, "I can hear that you are very busy—what does that feel like?" Or "It is so important to protect the kids, but who is protecting you?" These questions are attempts to direct the client inward to her own subjective experience so that she can begin to articulate how she is feeling about the events that she is describing.

Once therapists begin to focus their clients' attention on their feelings and reactions, clients are in a position to observe their behavior and to reflect on it more. If clients do not begin to do this of their own accord, therapists can suggest to them that they pay attention to their reactions over the course of the week. They can suggest to clients that they observe any shifts in mood or surprising reactions that they have so that they can explore them at the next session. Helping clients to become aware of their reactions and to begin to question them is the first step toward helping them become more reflective about their emotions and behaviors.

WORKING WITH INTERRUPTIVE PROCESSES

An important way therapists work to increase awareness of interruptive processes is to ask clients how they interrupt themselves and what was happening immediately before they went blank. A two-chair exercise can be used to help clients become aware of the thoughts that accompany their interruptions. Clients often interrupt their process with thoughts like "Nobody cares what I think," "What's the point of speaking about it," or "Don't go there; it's too painful." It is important for clients to become aware of how they constrain themselves and to get a clearer sense of what it feels like when they are silencing themselves so that they can access an alternative response. For example, Abbey, a 27-year-old artist who had suffered from depression most of her life was unable to express her experience with chronic depression in the session. She would often hide her face in her hands and look down, away from the therapist. In therapy she had great difficulty sharing what was happening in her life. Her father was a depressed alcoholic who had been emotionally unavailable to her, and her mother was emotionally unresponsive as she tried to deny what was happening. Abbey felt lost and longed for someone to nurture her and help her realize her dreams. She constantly interrupted her emotional experience. The following is an excerpt from one of her sessions:

Therapist: So how are you feeling today?

Abbey: I don't know—the same as usual.

Therapist: Is that good or bad?

Abbey: I don't know, it is hard to know.

Therapist: It seems that it is just so hard to know how you are feeling.

Abbey:	Yes. [*looking down, holding her chin in her hands—she is silent for 2 or 3 minutes*]
Therapist:	What is happening right now?
Abbey:	Oh, I feel blank.
Therapist:	What happened right then? It seems when I ask you about your feelings, you clam up . . . something stops you. Am I right?
Abbey:	Uh-huh . . . I just go blank. I don't know what to say.
Therapist:	So it sounds as if there might be something you are saying or doing to yourself that somehow shuts you down—what do you think?
Abbey:	Perhaps—I do know that I just shut down, and I am not sure why.
Therapist:	How about we try to identify how you shut yourself down? Let's try to separate out the side that interrupts you to see what is going on for you.
Abbey:	OK.
Therapist:	So, what do you say to yourself to keep yourself quiet?
Abbey:	I don't know. Uhmm . . . [*shrugs her shoulders*]
Therapist:	What is the shrug saying? Is it saying who cares?
Abbey:	Yes. What's the point?
Therapist:	So is that what you say to yourself? "What's the point of talking, no one wants to listen?" [*Abbey nods her head*] How does that make you feel?
Abbey:	Hopeless, like there is no point.
Therapist:	So it depresses you? Can you tell this side what it feels like when she says there's no point?
Abbey:	I feel hopeless when you say that. It just makes me give up.
Therapist:	So what does this side need?
Abbey:	I need it to stop . . . stop telling me it's hopeless. I need encouragement—I need you to let me speak.

In this exchange the therapist helps the client articulate her inner dialogue so that she begins to see not only the ways in which she silences herself but also that this process contributes to her depression. Abbey had great difficulty expressing her experience, so the therapist worked gently and patiently, attending to her nonverbal cues, to help her voice her inner dialogue. Toward the end of the exchange, the therapist helped Abbey develop an alternative response as she encouraged her to express her feelings and need to stop the self-interruption.

ACCEPTING FEELINGS

Even after clients have taken the step toward exploring their inner experience rather than expecting the therapist to solve their problems, they still may have difficulty accepting their experience. They may be critical of what they feel, believe that their feelings are wrong, or try to persuade themselves out of their experience. Although clients genuinely try to work on their concerns, they may try molding their experience into what they think it should be. They may say things like "I have to accept the way things are," while denying that it is hard to accept some things (Depestele, 2004). They exhort themselves to do better or be perfect. They reprimand, blame, and punish themselves with harsh critical words. When clients cannot accept some aspects of their experience, they cannot listen to their own experience in an open and receptive manner. Their feelings produce anxiety, so they avoid them.

Therapists help their clients make the passage from talking about their internal experience to making a space for it by focusing clients on their experience. Therapists can bring clients closer to their experience by asking questions that point to inner feelings. Thus, a question like "What happens inside in response to that critical or demanding voice?" focuses clients' attention inside. If clients can wait a little while and let answers come from their experiencing, rather than try to mold their experience to internal or external dictates, then they are engaged in exploration of their inner experience and no longer complaining or simply stating a problem. They are developing an exploratory attitude and manner and are beginning to ask inner-directed questions about their experience, not only "What am I feeling?" but also "How exactly does it affect me? What does it mean?" These questions require clients to be open to their experience and try to attend to the information contained in it. Now the client is experiencing more deeply, inquiring into the meaning of experience, and synthesizing currently available feelings to solve problems (Klein, Mathieu-Coughlan, & Kiesler, 1986).

Clients who are alexithymic or highly avoidant can be given a list of emotions and their corresponding motivations. Using lists and other aids, clients can learn to identify, label, and differentiate various primary emotional experiences, in addition to other emotion-related skills. They can learn how to better understand the motivational information involved in their emotions by identifying needs that they can act on. Therapists can help clients discuss their emotionally salient needs and the difficulty in achieving these, especially in relation to the emotions associated with these needs, and provide more direct methods for communicating their emotional needs. Finally, self-soothing skills related to managing emotional experience when it is overwhelming include increasing one's personal sense of safety and decreasing one's emotional arousal. Skills to decrease emotional arousal include doing breathing exercises, engaging in pleasant imagery, and increasing activity (e.g., running). Another important aspect of emotion regulation is learning when to introspectively deepen attention to one's emotional experience and when this may be counterproductive. Two important awareness tasks that therapists use to promote awareness with clients with depression are focusing and systematic evocative unfolding.

Focusing

Typically therapists use focusing when clients are willing to explore their inner experience but are unclear about what they are feeling. There is a sense of feeling foggy or uncertain or otherwise out of touch with their subjective experience. At these times therapists might suggest to clients that they try to focus on the unclear or absent felt sense. Clients should identify the place in their body where they usually register their feelings. The therapist then asks them to attend to that inner space and name what comes up. Clients are not to reflect on or monitor what they find there, but merely identify it for both themselves and the therapist and then to leave it to one side. Once clients have named all the nuances of their subjective state, therapists ask them to identify one of the feelings or issues to focus on and to merely attend to and concentrate on the feeling to try to see what occurs to them. If it is a label, they are asked to check inside to see whether it fits or not. If the label does not fit, clients should search for one that better captures what they are experiencing. Therapists can help in this process by gently and tentatively offering some alternatives to the original label. Together therapists and clients search until they find a label that fits the experience. Once a label fits, clients may then begin to explore what the feeling means and to identify the issue or situation to which it pertains.

There are a number of steps in guiding clients through a focusing task. First, the therapist identifies the marker that indicates that the client is vague, stuck, or unclear about his or her feelings. Second, the therapist asks the client to attend to the unclear felt sense. Third, the therapist encourages clients to look for possible descriptors, which may include an image of the felt sense or a label for the feeling. At this point, clients may experience a shift in their feeling as it becomes clearer; however, this is not always the case. Fourth, the therapist encourages clients to ask themselves what the feeling is about or to examine whether there is anything else at the core of the feeling that they have not represented. Clients are then encouraged to appreciate and consolidate any shifts in feeling that have occurred as a result of bringing it into awareness and clarifying what it is about. Clients are asked to set aside any critical or negative reactions to the feelings. Finally, clients explore the feelings and the situation to which they are attached (Depestele, 2004; Gendlin, 1996). The therapist can facilitate the focusing process by using specific reflections that guide the client's attention inward to bodily felt feelings. The many microprocesses of focusing on a bodily felt sense involved in moving into deeper experiencing can be woven seamlessly into the therapist's interventions.

For example, Frances came to therapy because she found that she was very depressed but did not understand why. Frances was 37 years old. She had a good job, and she was happily married and had two children. When she began therapy, Frances was very externally oriented; she was able to describe situations and express judgments of other people, but she was unable to articulate what she was feeling. Her only references to her inner experience consisted of descriptions of her physical symptoms, like not sleeping, feeling irritable, and having an increased appetite. She would occasionally refer to bodily sensations like the tightness in her throat or the tension in her shoulders. In an attempt to have her turn her attention inward to begin to get a clearer sense of what she was feeling, her therapist suggested that they try focusing. First, the therapist identified the marker and got the client's agreement to work on the task together:

Therapist:	It seems that it is hard for you to know what you are feeling moment to moment. Am I correct?
Frances:	Yes, I suppose so. Often when you ask me, it seems I go blank—I don't know what you want me to say.
Therapist:	How about we try an exercise to see if we can get a clearer sense of your feelings and what is happening inside?
Frances:	Sure, if you think it will help.

Next, the therapist asked the client to turn her attention inward to focus on her felt sense:

Therapist:	OK. What I am going to suggest is that you shut your eyes and turn your attention inward. What are you aware of as you focus your attention on your body?
Frances:	Uhmm . . . My jaw is clenched; there is tightness around my shoulders.
Therapist:	OK. So right now, you are aware of tightness in your shoulders and your jaw. If you focus on the tension in your shoulders, what does it feel like?
Frances:	Like a lot of needles jabbing into me or string pulled very tight.

Once the client had an awareness of what was happening internally, the therapist began to ask her to symbolize it with a picture or label:

Therapist:	As you attend to the tight painful sensation in your shoulders, does anything come up for you—a picture, a word, a feeling?
Frances:	Tired . . . I just feel so tired.

The client experienced a felt shift. No longer was she aware of an unclear, vague, unpleasant feeling; rather, the feeling had crystallized into a feeling of exhaustion. Now both she and her therapist were in a better position to know what was contributing to her depression and to find ways of alleviating her exhaustion. Therapist and client then explored what the feeling was about:

Therapist:	So your shoulders are telling you how tired you are feeling. What is that tired feeling about?
Frances:	There is so much to do. When I leave here, I have to rush back to work to finish a report that is due. Then I have to pick up the dry cleaning and some books for my son at the library. Rush home and make dinner and go the parents' school council meeting. After the meeting, I have to rush home so that I can prepare our clothes for tomorrow, make the lunches, and tidy the house before I drop into bed.
Therapist:	Wow! That sounds like a very full agenda. It sounds like there is a constant stream of demands on your time and energy. I can imagine that you must feel totally exhausted and drained. It is no wonder you feel depressed.
Frances:	[softly beginning to weep] I do—I feel so tired most of the time; it's like I am dragging myself around, and it's not just today, but every day, pretty well. Even the weekends are packed full of errands and chores and sport meets for the kids. There never seems to be any time to rest.
Therapist:	You do have a lot on your plate—it sounds like it is just all too much. Can you try to stay with the exhaustion and focus your attention on all the chores and demands that you have to meet and see what comes up for you?
Frances:	I just feel this heaviness inside.
Therapist:	Yes, I can see you seem to be almost slumping down in your chair. You look so burdened. Is that how you feel?
Frances:	Yes, exactly. I feel the weight of all the things I have to do just pushing down on me. What am I going to do? I don't have a choice.

As Frances talked of pushing forward under the strain, her therapist heightened the feeling to make the client even more aware of the toll that her demanding schedule was taking and to try to help her connect with her needs so as to alter her action tendency.

> *Therapist:* Frances, I want you to feel the pressure of all those chores bearing down on you, feel that exhaustion. Now, what does the exhausted side need?
>
> *Frances:* Uhmm . . . I don't know . . . uhmm . . . rest, I suppose.
>
> *Therapist:* So your sense is that you need to rest.
>
> *Frances:* Yes, but how?
>
> *Therapist:* How can you give yourself that? Is there anything that you can shift that would allow you some time to relax and unwind?
>
> *Frances:* Uhmm . . . Well, it's not absolutely essential for me to go to the meeting at the school tonight. I just feel guilty and like I am a poor mother when I don't go.

In this response, a marker of self-criticism emerged. The therapist noted it and stored it away to explore later with the client, and she continued to explore ways that Frances could lighten her load and allow more time for rest and self-care in the next few days.

The focusing exercise put Frances in touch with her body in a different way than she was previously. She became more aware of the messages implicit in her body sensations and better able to articulate the feelings that accompanied them. The therapist and Frances were more aware of what was contributing to the client's depression. From the exercise, it became clear that Frances was very driven and demanding of herself. She and her therapist worked to begin to modify the behavior, but this was only the beginning, because Frances needed to become aware of how she drove herself and to develop alternative ways of treating herself to be more nurturing and considerate of her needs. In later sessions, Frances and her therapist explored the origins of this behavior and the process by which she pushed herself so hard. They identified the messages that she gave herself and engaged in two-chair work to try to modify her behavior even more.

Systematic Evocative Unfolding

Systematic evocative unfolding is another important task that can help clients become more aware of their emotional processing. Often clients who are depressed are not able to pinpoint the reason or causes of their despairing feelings. When clients are uncertain about what has caused their feelings or when they consider their feelings disproportionate, therapists can suggest that they try systematic evocative unfolding. This six-step process includes first identifying the depressive reaction that the client feels is puzzling in some way. Second, the therapist asks the client to provide a vivid description of the scene in which the client was a participant when his or her depressive reaction occurred or worsened. Together, the client and therapist work to rebuild and recapture a graphic sense of the situation. Third, once the therapist and client have vividly recreated the scene, the therapist directs the client to search for the particularly salient aspect of the situation that triggered the depressed reaction. Fourth, after identifying what was salient about the situation, the client is able to determine how he or she construed the stimulus so as to arrive at an understanding of its personal meaning, a process known as the *meaning bridge*.

To help clients understand their reaction better, therapists focus clients on qualitatively differentiating their affective reaction to determine the impact of the situation. For example, clients may focus on their sense of feeling humiliated by a person's facial expression without describing the stimulus as scornful. Fifth, the therapist then helps the client to recognize the emotion scheme that was activated by the problematic situation. The client becomes aware of a personal style and general way of responding that he or she can then examine to understand its origins and determine whether it is still useful. Sixth, following the exploration of the emotion scheme, the client comes up with alternative ways of responding or of construing the situation. The aim of using systematic evocative unfolding is to have clients reexperience as fully as possible the problematic situation to symbolize it more accurately in awareness so as to discover the personal impact or meaning of the situation and identify alternative needs and action tendencies (Rice, 1974).

The importance of experiencing one's own affectively laden reactions to inner and outer events as a means of promoting optimal client process is based on two assumptions in EFT: First, human beings are motivated toward growth and wholeness and the development of their full potential, and their growth is best facilitated by attending to their own emotionally laden organismic experience. Second, people have the ability to turn their attention inward to track their own emotionally toned experience and become aware of their emotions, needs, reactions, and perceptions in the moment (Rice & Greenberg, 1992). In other words, people are able to discover the personal meaning of their experience by turning inward and attending to their feelings.

CASE EXAMPLE: PAULA

Paula, a woman in her mid-30s, was an architect by profession, but the firm where she had been working had had to downsize, and she was let go. In addition, she had recently been divorced. When she began therapy, she had decided to return to school to complete a master's degree. It had been difficult to establish a clear focus with her on the precipitants of her depression. Her therapist suggested that she observe her behavior between appointments to identify shifts in her mood so they could explore these at the next session. At the next session, Paula had identified a major shift in her mood the previous week and wanted to explore it to better understand what triggered her depression. The client started out by describing her shift into depression:

Paula: I was really feeling we were getting a handle on things, and then this week it was just—things just disintegrated.

Therapist: What happened this week?

Paula: I had a quiz in one of my classes which I thought I was quite well prepared for, and it was . . . uhmm . . . on expressionism. And what we had to . . . we essentially, we were shown slides— we hadn't seen them before, but we had to identify the artists and . . . uhmm . . . just say something about them. But I don't know whether he thought it was funny or he thought it was amusing, but essentially he put in slides, several of which were completely uncharacteristic of the artist . . .

Therapist: Hmm . . .

Paula: . . . and we were supposed to somehow, you know, to figure this out by the title.

Therapist: Mm-hmm . . .

Paula: . . . and that's fine, you know; everyone in the class, their reaction was "that was a little unfair," but I got extremely angry about it, and then I realized that I was, for the rest of the week after that, I was extremely depressed. I just found it really demoralizing.

Therapist: Uh-huh.

Paula: So that I suspect it has something to do with people who don't play by . . . who don't play fair.

Therapist: You feel it was unfair?

Paula: Yeah, yeah, and I mean, I know that probably in the long run that's not . . . I don't know, you know, it doesn't matter if afterwards he discounts, you know, that slide or whatever, that's not, to me that was not, it was, I can't even quite, I don't know, maybe it was an abuse of power, it was . . . I just found it . . . I found it infuriating.

Therapist: So, somehow, you felt he had broken the rules, or . . .

Paula: Yeah, and worse, they were the rules that he had set up. I mean, it was, you know, he was the one who said that the test was going to be along this format and this is what you

should be trying to do, trying to learn, and then it was something else entirely. I mean, it wasn't something else entirely,
it was just one small piece, but it was, you know . . . and I
just, I find situations like that extreme—I mean, just, they
just send me off the deep end.

Therapist: Somehow he turned the tables, or your expectations were
violated?

Paula: I suppose, yeah, because I know my reaction was out of all
proportion to . . .

Therapist: You feel your reaction was out of all proportion somehow—
like the intensity of it?

Paula: Yeah, yeah, I mean, getting depressed for the rest of the week
is not great, you know, and I mean, I've been trying to deal
with it, but then, I know that's when it started, because before that I was feeling fine.

Therapist: Mm-hm, so the reaction you feel was out of proportion was
the depression? [therapist confirms which reaction the client felt
was problematic]

Paula: [sigh] The fact that I can't shake the depression.

Therapist: Would it be more productive to look at this a little more
closely, you think?

Paula: Yeah, I think so.

In this exchange Paula described her problematic reaction. Unlike previous times when her mood shifted, this time she was able to pinpoint when
it shifted from anger to depression. However, she was perplexed by the intensity of her anger and the fact that she had not been able to shake her depression. The therapist spent some time establishing that the reaction was problematic for the client and then suggested that they explore the event in more
detail, and the client agreed. At this point, the therapist tried to have Paula
remember the events in greater detail. She asked Paula to be concrete and
specific about what happened so as to make the scene become more vivid
and accessible to help the client have better access to her emotional reaction
at the time.

Therapist: OK, so what you find problematic is that you could not shake
the depression. So tell me what happened during the test.

Paula: Uhmm, as I was writing the test and I was giving what I
thought were reasonable, you know, reasonable guesses to it,
then the last one he showed was an abstract slide, so, I mean,
there was no way that we could get it, but we were supposed
to get it. It was kind of a little expressionist joke that he was

playing, and, I mean, I know that's what he was doing, and that's fine, but that made me . . . that made me extremely angry.

Therapist: So somehow . . . uhmm . . . can we just get a better sense of it? Somehow you're sitting in class, and, uhmm, you come upon this, uhmm, this slide, which doesn't fit . . .

Paula: Uh-huh.

Therapist: It kind of violates your expectations and your sense of what the test is about.

Paula: Mm-hm, mm-hm, mm-hm.

Therapist: Uhmm, and—what happens? You don't get angry at that moment because . . .

Paula: No, no, because I didn't know it was—he went over it afterwards and he told us, you know, he essentially gave us the answers to the, to the quiz, and then with the last one, that is when I realized that. Yeah, you know, because everyone said, well, that's not very characteristic of the artist, and he said, "Oh well," you know, "I told you I'd give you the titles, and in most of the cases the titles aren't important, but in this case the title was very important, because it was a little expressionist joke, and you were supposed to understand from the title that this was a play." I mean it was, essentially, "You'd have to know so much more than we know about surrealism to even have a chance of getting this, and I don't think you could even get it, then, unless you knew whose oil it was."

The therapist thus worked with the client to get a better sense of the situation that triggered her anger and then the depression. Then the therapist tried to unpack Paula's construal of the situation to understand how she interpreted it so as to understand its idiosyncratic meaning for the client and its relevance to the way the client operates in the world. The therapist then began to search for what was most salient about the event to try to identify what triggered the client's reaction.

Therapist: So, somehow, there's this question that's so dependent on the title that seems so unfair?

Paula: It wasn't dependent; it was unfair, because there was nothing anybody, unless you knew, unless you'd seen that painting before, which we weren't supposed to have seen any of these before, there was no possible way of getting it, because it was an in-joke.

Therapist: So there's something about it being so hidden that got to you somehow?

Paula: Yeah, and the fact that if anything in life is supposed to be fair and played by the rules, it's supposed to be tests. I mean, that's . . . you know, you're told what you're supposed to study for, and that's fine. I mean, I have no problems with hard tests or the fact that they're extremely difficult or the fact that they're subtle, but when there's no way of knowing the answer without . . . when there's no . . . when there's no way of knowing the answer, I mean, when there's a trick question.

Therapist: So what, there's just something about this—being a trick question—that really annoyed you?

Paula: Yeah! He wasn't playing by his rules. I mean, he's got all the power in this situation; he's the one who sets the rules. I mean, it's not even . . . it's not even that the rules are set outside by somebody else and somebody else sets the exam, and just . . . You know, he's the one who's setting the exam, he's the one who's telling us what we should be studying for, and he cheated on his own rules.

Therapist: So somehow you felt duped.

Paula: Yeah, yeah.

Therapist: Sort of, what, he's taken advantage of you somehow?

Paula: No, like the rug got pulled out from under me. It didn't matter how well I'd prepared for the test.

Therapist: That's what left you feeling angry?

Paula: Oh, I was furious, I was furious. Then right after, almost immediately afterwards, I realized that I was becoming extremely demoralized, and then the whole thing just built up, I mean . . .

The therapist and client had identified what it was that so infuriated the client about the situation. They began to explore Paula's reaction in greater depth. Paula explored how she dealt with difficult situations and examined how difficult it was for her to cope with change and confrontation.

Therapist: So somehow, you're feeling really angry, and a sense of . . . what, defeat, demoralized, like beaten?

Paula: Mm-hm, it was that the problem is that the switchover happens very quickly, and then it's as if tapes, automatic tapes just come on, you know, how if you're just sort of saying the same thing over and over—what I hear myself saying, and I'm not sure if this is it, that it doesn't matter how hard I try, that the rules can get shifted.

Therapist: So it doesn't matter what you do.

Paula:	Yeah, but part of . . . I don't know how far to trust those thoughts, because those are the . . . that's what exacerbates the depression. I mean, that starts in on a whole, you know, that just builds on the sense of defeat.
Therapist:	So it's like, what's the point? The tables are going to be turned on me anyway.
Paula:	Yeah, it's that I make it worse. Then . . . then I have—and I mean, I know I'm doing it—I have a tendency . . . I'm supposed to be doing a presentation in this class and I just, I don't do it, I don't get at it, it's almost as if, well, I'll prove him right, I don't know, by not trying or . . . that all gets mixed into it.
Therapist:	So you kind of give up somehow.
Paula:	Yes, and I can't seem to get . . . if I could stay angry, that would be fine, or if I could hide it instead of getting so quick to feed it—I think that if I could stay angry, that would be better.
Therapist:	Mm-hm. It's somehow hard to stay angry.
Paula:	Yeah, I don't think, I mean, I think I—yeah, I get angry—well, I don't even get angry at myself, because that's not even what it feels like, it's not . . . I get angry at myself afterwards, because it's just, I mean, the sense of defeat is lost. I mean, it's just . . . it becomes a malaise that I can't seem to fight my way out of.
Therapist:	Mm-hm, so you become weighed down by this defeat.
Paula:	Mm-hm, yeah. I find it [*sigh*] extreme—extremely difficult. I mean, I was just, I was—I was really quite shocked at my reaction. I mean, to be . . . it was probably the first time that I've really sort of been watching it. I realize I just don't want to play the game any more.

Paula thus became more aware of how she reacted to events. She was surprised by her reaction. The therapist continued to explore the meaning of her reaction to understand it better.

Paula:	And it's—it is, I suppose it is, it is a real playground reaction . . . and just, you know, saying, well, I'm going home now.
Therapist:	Somehow seeing someone changing their own rules. It's somehow hard to continue playing the game.
Paula:	Yeah, well, what I first want to do is stamp my feet and get really angry and say, "You can't do that!"
Therapist:	Mm-hm.

Paula: Only I don't do that, I mean, I wish [*sigh*]—I think I wish I did more, because I think that would . . .

Therapist: So, you'd like to tell him . . .

Paula: Mm-hm.

Therapist: . . . that it was unfair . . .

Paula: Mm-hm.

Therapist: . . . but somehow you cannot.

Paula: I start getting panicky, because he still has all of the power.

Therapist: You feel panic?

Paula: Yeah, yeah, I get . . . when I get angry, and I do let something like that slip, I start getting really panicky.

Therapist: What, you kind of feel scared?

Paula: Mm-hm.

Therapist: What's that about? [*asks the client to explore the source of her fear about expressing her reactions to others*]

Paula: [*sigh*] Because usually the people who do things like that are . . . now, I don't know whether, and I know where it all comes from, but they're often, they're often nice, decent people. I mean, they're often, you know . . . and I don't know if . . . except I don't know if this is . . . if they [*sigh*] . . . I don't know, I get all confused about my reaction to it. I mean, I should just, you know, I should just . . . or even think to myself, well, you know, "He was being a jerk," and just walk away from it, but I can't.

Therapist: It's really hard for you to say, hey, I don't think that was fair.

Paula: Mm-hm.

Therapist: What's that about?

Paula: [*sigh*] All sorts of things—I mean, it's, it's so confusing. Part of it is that, uhmm, oh well, he's a really nice person, I shouldn't say things like . . . you know, that would be a very hurtful thing to say. It's part of that, sort of an overinflated sense of my own power and importance in all of this.

Therapist: So somehow you feel you have to protect him, or . . .

Paula: Yeah.

Therapist: And it's not fair to kind of catch him out?

Paula: Yeah, yeah, or to say something like that, and part of it is, too, that is, that he's still got—I mean, the game's still going on, and it . . . and I'm afraid that if he's, you know, if he's changed . . . I mean, so part of the fear is that he can change the rules again, and that maybe he isn't really a nice person and maybe he is out to get me and he can just change the rules again.

Therapist: Uh-huh, so there is one part of you that doesn't feel you can express how you feel, because that might hurt the other, . . .

Paula: Mm-hm.

Therapist: . . . and another part that says,

Paula: "It's a real danger," yeah, . . .

Therapist: . . . "If I do express what I feel, then I can place myself in jeopardy," . . .

Paula: Mm-hm, mm-hm.

Therapist: "I could be at greater risk."

Paula: So there's sort of those two, I mean, conflicting things going on at the same time.

Therapist: Mm-hm.

Paula: And then I just—I do end up giving up, and it's as if I'm saying that, "Well, I'm not going to let you hurt me, but I'm going to do it," you know, "I'm going to go home, and I'm not going to play anymore, and I'm not going to . . ." But it still means that I end up losing. I don't know how to deal with this because I can't make life fair.

Therapist: So you know you're not going to be able to change it.

Paula: No, I mean, and that's [*sigh*] well, I find that frustrating, too, but that's . . . but . . . [*begins to weep softly*]

Therapist: What are the tears saying?

Paula: Hmm?

Therapist: What are the tears saying?

Paula: [*sigh*] Because somewhere along the way, I don't know, I think I was told that life would be fair and keep expecting it to turn out that way, and it's—and it doesn't matter how much my rational sense, self, says that it's not fair, I still get, I mean, I become quite—quite affronted by it. But worse is that every time it happens, it feels like it's just a little chip, like I'm just being chipped away a little bit.

Therapist: There's this real sense of being destroyed—whenever someone changes the rules on you, part of you is lost?

Paula: Yeah, because it feels like when things are going all right, it feels like, I say to myself, OK, I'm getting it, like I think I'm finally getting the rules, and—that's why even a little, sort of, what I feel is a transgression on the rules, it just feels like everything shifts on me, and I don't—I don't understand anything anymore.

Therapist: It's really hard for you to cope with change.

Paula: Mm-hm.

The therapist identified a general difficulty the client has. This prompted Paula to look at other occasions in her life when she acted in this way.

Therapist: It's really hard when things shift for you. You end up feeling confused.

Paula: Yeah, and I think that's happened since I was really little. I find change really difficult; I find it, well, I just don't do it. And I mean, the whole thought of things changing just sends me into a panic, and it's—and I think what's triggered all of this, this latest crisis, is the fact that too many things have changed. I mean, over the last two years I've been divorced and I've lost my job, and it's just, it's gotten too much for me.

Therapist: Mm-hm, so a lot of rugs have been pulled out from under you.

Paula: Mm-hm.

Paula finally understood her problematic reaction. She realized that she felt overwhelmed by the numerous changes that had occurred in her life over the previous few years. Part of her would have liked to withdraw and slow everything down, instead of trying to cope and manage all the challenges. The client also realized how she dealt with change. She tried to rein herself in and not allow herself to change in an attempt to minimize its impact. However, in spite of her reluctance, she also pushed herself, indicating that she was not respecting her feelings. Rather than listen to her needs, she forced herself to do things that were overwhelming and difficult. She realized that that left her feeling trapped.

Therapist: So pushing yourself doesn't get things done, either.

Paula: No; in fact, it's counterproductive.

Therapist: Uh-huh. So part of you won't let yourself be pushed.

Paula: No, oh, but—it's just so frustrating, because it's frustrating even to watch the whole thing happening. I mean, to see it happening, to see the anger changing into depression, and not—this is . . . there doesn't seem to be anything that I can do about it.

Therapist:	You don't feel you've got any options?
Paula:	There are options, but I don't know how to do—but I don't know how to—yeah, I don't know how to do that.
Therapist:	You don't feel that you can speak out?
Paula:	I don't feel I can, it's—I don't know how to do that.
Therapist:	You don't feel you know how to express . . .
Paula:	. . . I think so . . .
Therapist:	. . . what's happening for you with others?
Paula:	Mm-hm, mm-hm.
Therapist:	Somehow it just seems too scary.
Paula:	[*sigh*] Yeah, it's usually—it's funny, because I know that people who knew would probably be really surprised if I told them that I have trouble expressing myself, but—there's some, there's some people in some situations that just, I mean, I just can't cope with them at all.
Therapist:	So there's some people it's hard to express yourself with.
Paula:	Yeah, yeah, some people, I find . . . I think . . . I'm trying to—yeah, there are just some people, some situations I find more difficult than others.
Therapist:	Mm-hm, so it's not all situations.
Paula:	I don't think so.
Therapist:	Which situations are hard for you?
Paula:	When the people don't feel straightforward and there is this—they're in a position of power, but I don't feel that I can read them, so it's . . . that's what I find . . . I find that really . . . [*sigh*] Yet it's, it's . . . it's so much more complicated than that, because I usually put myself in those situations, too, and I can't separate, it's as if every situation has the same life-or-death consequences for me. I mean, the . . . it . . . they are not . . . [*sigh*] I can't seem to just say, "Well this . . . what I'm doing here is not that important, so . . ." I mean, "Don't . . . you don't have to become hysterical about this," or "It doesn't matter." I can't. Everything takes on . . . takes on exactly the same proportions for me.
Therapist:	So somehow it's hard for you to keep things in proportion? You always feel like you're going to lose a lot?
Paula:	Mm-hm, I mean, yeah, it really does feel—that's exactly what it feels like. It's that everything has exactly the same weight,

and I think that's why I find decisions difficult, too, because, I mean, everything has—I don't . . . I don't seem to have any way of prioritizing things. It's—things have all the same weight or the same tug on me, or the same [*sigh*]—that doesn't even sound right when I say it, but I know it is. I mean, any prioritizing I've learned to do, I've learned to do really, purely intellectually, and—but I don't emotionally. That's not what anything feels like. Talking on the phone with somebody has the same possible consequences as . . . [*sigh*] It's a—also, things can hurt me, that's what it feels like.

Therapist: So you feel very, very vulnerable.

Paula: Mm-hm.

Therapist: All the time.

Paula: Mm-hm, and . . . [*sigh*] I do, and I . . . I mean, that would surprise people too, because, I mean, I do and I don't—no, I do, I always feel emotionally vulnerable, always.

Therapist: So you feel constantly at risk?

Paula: Partly because I never know what—it could be something really small which triggers off a week of depression, which is just, is devastating. I mean, I have whole weeks taken out of my life when it's just . . . [*crying*] well, this. All I end up doing is crying, like, for days on end [*sigh*]—and the problem with that is that it almost becomes a self-fulfilling prophecy, because when I'm depressed for a week or for two weeks or whatever it is, I mean, I don't get things done, and so it just—it is . . . it is devastating.

Therapist: So, somehow, because you're so sensitive, uhmm, you find yourself getting depressed, and it does have consequences for you.

Paula: Mm-hm, mm-hm.

Therapist: Because you don't achieve your goal?

Paula: Yeah.

Therapist: What's the vulnerability about then?

Paula: I don't know. I mean, I really don't.

Therapist: It's just, what, a sense of always being threatened by others?

Paula: No, of letting others down, more of that.

Therapist: Something about disappointing people.

Paula: Mm-hm, I think more of that than being threatened by people.

Therapist: So you are really concerned about letting other people down. This sounds important and something that might be important to explore further. What do you think? We have to end soon, but perhaps we can look at it more next week.

Paula: Yeah—it does feel important.

This was a breakthrough session for Paula. Before this session she had great difficulty pinning down the conditions that were contributing to her depression. Through exploring her somewhat intense reaction to what seemed initially like a trivial incident without deeper personal meaning, Paula uncovered a significant way of being in the world: that of stifling her own feelings to protect the feelings of others. During the session, Paula became aware that she had difficulty expressing her feelings to others and realized that the reason for this was that she was constantly worried about disappointing them.

Consequently, Paula suppressed her own feelings and needs, and this silencing of herself contributed to her depression. She and her therapist agreed to explore how she silenced herself and what the possible origin of that behavior might be in subsequent sessions. In the sessions immediately following this one, Paula explored how she always felt like she had disappointed her father and that he did not approve of her actions. She also realized that part of her reluctance and difficulty with change was her divorce from her husband, whom she had married believing that nothing could go wrong. Finally, the client began to look at how she silenced herself in her current relationship and was able to acknowledge feelings of being overlooked and to voice them to her partner in a kindly way that respected both his feelings and her own.

By carefully and slowly focusing Paula on her reactions and her construal of events, the therapist was able to help her identify her personal style of being in the world and to better understand what she was doing to herself that caused her to become depressed. Subsequently, they were able to explore why she did this and to reprocess certain events in her life using unfinished business with her father and ex-husband to create new meaning and generate alternative styles of being that were less costly to her own well-being.

10

EVOCATION AND
AROUSAL OF EMOTION

Emotion-focused therapy (EFT) works to evoke clients' experience of their emotions viscerally and to help them express these emotions in the session. Emotion, when evoked, becomes accessible to new input; clients must feel the painful emotion in order to transform it. Therapists help clients distinguish emotions that transform from emotions that need transforming. Thus, secondary (i.e., defensive, reactive, or avoidant) weepiness, blame, and complaint or feelings of global distress need to be explored for more core emotions, and core maladaptive fear and shame need to be transformed.

The visceral experience and expression of secondary emotions is not in and of itself therapeutic. It is only a step along the path to change. In contrast, the visceral experience and expression of core adaptive emotion are therapeutically transformational. When the client experiences core adaptive emotions viscerally and bodily, without avoidance or interruption, change occurs. The flowing experience and expression of core emotion provide access to previously inaccessible memories, fantasies, and untapped inner resources for adaptive action. Access to previously disclaimed action tendencies and the activation of internal resources and strengths based on these adaptive emotional states is one of the most potent therapeutic agents in

EFT. Access to positive emotions, too, promotes more creative problem solving and flexible thinking. Whereas access to distressing and unpleasant emotions promotes deepening and disclosure, positive emotion states arrived at after the deepening and disclosing serve to broaden and build.

The key question that arises in relation to emotional expression is whether expression of emotion is in itself therapeutic, as Reich (1949) proposed, or whether it is the more complex process of bringing a pattern of expression and prevention into awareness and exposing the expressed emotion to new input that is therapeutic. In the latter, the final expression involves an integration of the expressive activity and awareness of the interruptive process and the emotion interrupted, on one hand, and the transformation of the emotion and the creation of new meaning, on the other; it is this integration that is maximally beneficial. Thus, it is not a case simply of getting emotions out. Rather, a complex process of awareness of the interruptive processes and the emotion suppressed, muscular release, and the completion of the psychoaffective motor program is important in expression, followed by exposure to new experience and information and meaning making.

It is important to reiterate that healing occurs when a client experiences primary emotions within a relationship with an affirming, empathic, emotionally engaged therapist. The regulation of emotion provided by an empathic relationship allows core emotional experiences, previously unresponded to and feared to be unbearable, to come to the fore and be soothed and used. Two people are needed to help build the ability to regulate affect so that its transformational potential can be realized (Fosha, 2000). At times, clients also need to be helped to get some distance from emotions that are overwhelming. For the evoking to work, clients have to have sufficient ability to name emotions, tolerate them, and accept them. When clients are overwhelmed by their emotions, this cannot occur, and rather than evoking emotion, a working distance from their emotions needs to be created by teaching and facilitating emotion regulation skills. These methods are discussed more fully in chapters 11 through 13.

Evoking emotion and encouraging the relatively free expression of emotion in therapy are what distinguish psychotherapy from other kinds of relationships, in which emotion is generally more constricted and socially regulated. Learning in therapy is emotional learning, and finding new ways of dealing with emotion is essential in bringing about change in depression. Change in core maladaptive emotional experience is brought about mainly by activating the maladaptive experience of fear and shame underlying the hopelessness and then by accessing adaptive feelings of sadness at what is missed, yearning for closeness, and anger at maltreatment. These adaptive emotions are attended to and validated and are used to vitalize a more resilient sense of self to help transform the client's maladaptive affects.

Finally, it is important to note that emotional expression in therapy is different from emotional expression in day-to-day living. In therapy it is unprocessed, troublesome emotions that are being evoked to be reprocessed, not impulsive emotional reactions. Advocating an important role for the evocation and expression of feelings in therapy is not the same as promoting a "let it all hang out" form of emotional expression in life. Emotional expression in life must take many factors into account and is a current reaction to a situation vastly different from therapy, where emotion is evoked in relation to past situations or present constructions or reconstructions.

Evocation and arousal of emotion in the session go beyond the process of awareness of emotion, discussed in chapter 9, to a more visceral experiencing and expression of emotion. In the evoking process, the therapist encourages awareness and undoing of interruptive processes; the allowing and accepting of painful emotions, adaptive and maladaptive; the use of emotion to inform adaptive action; and access to new adaptive emotions that facilitate growth and change.

A special type of process occurs when moderate to high levels of emotional arousal are reached. When clients allow and express emotion freely, such as when sobbing or expressing previously unexpressed anger, and when they are viscerally experiencing fear, shame, or disgust, a unique set of neurochemical, physiological, and psychological processes occur; emotional expression has been shown to affect neurotransmitters, sympathetic arousal, conscious experience, cognitive processing, and expressive behavior (Ekman & Friesen, 1975; Lane, Sechrest, Riedel, Shapiro, & Kaszniak, 2000; Panksepp, 2001). These processes do not occur when clients do not allow and express the emotion. Many clients in therapy feel a lot of emotion without being able to allow and express it freely; experience and expression seem to be blocked or constricted. It is the ability to freely experience, acknowledge, and express emotion that helps the client feel clearly what is significant to them and to clearly receive the message from the emotion and be organized by it. With expression, control and inhibition are overcome, and the client freely accesses what previously was blocked. It is not that expression leads to the expulsion of emotion; rather, it is through expression that core material and a vast network of associations become available for further processing.

Our research has shown that although rated expressed arousal of emotion in therapy sessions predicted therapeutic improvement at termination, a client's postsession reports of emotional arousal in sessions did not (Warwar & Greenberg, 2000). We found that certain clients reported, on postsession questionnaires, that they often felt intense anger, pain, sadness, and other feelings in the session, without having shown observable signs of these emotions. In other words, for more constricted clients the correlation between self-reported degree of emotional arousal during a session and an observer's rating of the degree of arousal was weak. Given that the degree of observed emotional arousal in the middle of EFT for depression predicted outcome (Warwar, 2003; Warwar & Greenberg, 1999b), it appears that it is the expression of emotion in sessions, and not the covert experience of emotion, that is therapeutic. We also found that clients' ability to make sense of their feelings and to use them to solve problems, especially by the late phase of treatment, added to the outcome variance predicted. It appears, therefore, that it is the use of the expressed emotion in sessions to solve problems, not catharsis, that leads to change.

In EFT we are advocating the expression of emotion in therapy, for therapeutic purposes. We are not suggesting that expressing emotion in day-to-day living is always indicated. Aristotle (in *Rhetoric*) suggested that in real life, it takes wisdom to consider when, to whom, and with what intensity to express anger. In therapy, suppressed, troublesome emotions that have not been processed are specifically evoked to be reprocessed.

Although arousal and expression appear therapeutic, there are different types of arousal and emotional expression in therapy; some are helpful, and others are not. Emotion can be either a sign of distress or a sign of the working through of distress. Arousal can be over- or underregulated, and the emotion can be adaptive or maladaptive, or primary or secondary. Some forms of arousal and expression can be useful for a variety of reasons, whereas some forms can be therapeutically counterproductive, especially for some clients at some times. Thus, a therapist needs to make conscious decisions as to whether the particular type and level of emotional arousal is helpful or hindering for this client at this time. Although we recognize that all forms of arousal are not useful all the time for all types of client, in our study we still found that overall degree of arousal predicted outcome regardless of type of arousal. The arousal measure we used is shown in Table 10.1 (Warwar & Greenberg, 1999a). Thus, even though in this study finer discriminations were not made as to whether the aroused emotion was a core emotion or was adaptive or maladaptive, tolerated or overwhelming, or stuck or being processed, there still was something about global expressive arousal in our emotion-focused treatment that seemed to enhance outcome. Finer discriminations would probably lead to better predictions, but it is clear that emotional arousal and expression in therapy, by therapists trained to evoke emotion and facilitate reflection on it, can be a very important therapeutic process.

THE FUNCTIONS OF AROUSAL

Expression in therapy is a highly interpersonal process. It involves expressing emotions in front of, or to, another person. The emotional expression is received and responded to by another person, so there are important relational processes at work. In addition, the client is processing the emotion, which involves accepting, tolerating, symbolizing, and reflecting on it, so there are important intrapsychic processes taking place. Emotion is aroused and expressed in therapy not for the purpose of venting or getting rid of it, but to promote its acceptance, use, and transformation.

TABLE 10.1
Client Emotional Arousal Scale—III

Score	Level of emotional arousal
1	Client does not express emotions. Voice or gestures do not disclose any emotional arousal.
2	Client may acknowledge emotions, but there is very little arousal in voice or body. • There is no disruption of usual speech patterns. • Any arousal is almost completely restricted.
3	At this level of arousal, as well as at higher levels, the client acknowledges emotions. Arousal is mild in voice and body. • There is very little emotional overflow. • Any arousal is still very restricted. • Usual speech patterns are only mildly disrupted.
4	Arousal is moderate in voice and body. • Emotional voice is present: Ordinary speech patterns are moderately disrupted by emotional overflow as represented by changes in accentuation patterns, unevenness of pace, or changes in pitch. • Although there is some freedom from control and restraints, arousal may still be somewhat restricted.
5	Arousal is fairly intense and full in voice and body. • Emotion overflows into speech pattern to a great extent: Speech patterns deviate markedly from the client's baseline and are fragmented or broken. • Loudness and volume are elevated. • Arousal seems fairly unrestricted.
6	Arousal is very intense and extremely full as the client is freely expressing emotion with voice and body. • Usual speech patterns are extremely disrupted, as indicated by changes in accentuation patterns, unevenness of pace, changes in pitch, and volume or force of voice. • Expression of emotion is spontaneous, and there is almost no sense of restriction.
7	Arousal is extremely intense and full in voice and body. • Usual speech patterns are completely disrupted by emotional overflow. • The expression is completely spontaneous and unrestricted. • Arousal appears uncontrollable and enduring. • There is a falling apart quality: Although arousal can be a completely unrestricted therapeutic experience, it may also be a disruptive negative experience in which the client feels like he or she is falling apart. • The distinguishing feature between Level 6 and Level 7 is that in Level 6, there is the sense that although the client's expression may be fairly unrestricted, the client would be able to contain or control his or her arousal, whereas in Level 7, the client's expression is completely unrestricted, and there is the sense that the client would not be able to control his or her arousal.

The therapeutic relational processes at work include both the dyadic regulation of affect, in which affect is regulated by the soothing presence of the other, and a corrective emotional experience, in which a new experience with the therapist disconfirms prior experience of self and other. With regard to dyadic regulation, acceptance and validation of emotion by the therapist is an important change process in and of itself. Expression of emotion and its acceptance and validation by the other make the experience change producing. Acceptance and validation by another help soothe anxiety; clients internalize the therapist's empathy with painful affect, which, with time, becomes self-empathy and self-soothing. Expressing emotion in the session also helps the client overcome the fear and shame associated with expression, itself a corrective emotional experience. Clients generally fear that their expression will lead the therapist to look down on them or reject them. Clients may also fear that if they cry or express (i.e., "lose control"), they will be diminished in the eyes of the other and the connection with the other will be broken. The opportunity to experience interpersonal acceptance is important as a corrective emotional experience in therapy.

In terms of more intrapsychic aspects of change, arousal of emotion, as noted by Frank (1963) in *Persuasion and Healing,* is an important ingredient in attitude change. Clients fear that expressing will lead them to lose control, that they will be unable to cope, and that their self-cohesion and identity will be shattered. To experience that one survives the allowing of one's dreaded emotion (exposure) is a corrective experience. Arousal also makes cognitive change more possible; an important intrapsychic function of arousal is that it redirects attention. Affective arousal spontaneously mobilizes and monopolizes attention. It interrupts attention and then redirects it, thereby changing a person's ongoing experience. Arousal of emotion signifies that what is occurring is of importance, signals that core concerns are being met or not met, and simultaneously provides access to both core concerns and core meanings. Thus, arousal makes a large amount of material available from memory through associations and makes it available for further processing.

Releasing the constraints against the expression of tears or anger helps clients experience that which they previously found unbearable and allows them to reclaim these feelings as their own. This process provides clarity; it is as if free-flowing emotion lubricates the brain and sets in motion a large variety of connections and associations not previously available. Beliefs become more available, state-dependent memories are stimulated, and important images emerge. Experience provides access to episodic memories, promotes greater specification of the problematic issues, and promotes articulation of core concerns, as well as stimulating links to the origins of feelings. For example, after crying about a remembered childhood scene of abandonment in the basement, a client who had walled himself off from others emotionally said, "I decided to never need again, rather than to experience the pain that there was no one there to respond to me." Another client reaccessed a scene of making a mistake at work and feeling worthless; after tearfully experiencing and expressing that she felt humiliated, she said, "I just feel so exposed, like everyone is looking at me and sees my mistake. It's like I'm a child and my father is standing over me and criticizing the way I do things. I was just never good enough." These statements were not available before arousal and expression. Emotional arousal thus helps clients gain access to and articulate the core organizing principles of their self-organizations and makes these available for conscious symbolization and articulation in words as beliefs. Arousal can be thought of as promoting the accessing of "hot" cognition (Greenberg & Safran, 1984).

Arousal also promotes exposure to and tolerance of the emotion and facilitates the process of completion. Arousal follows a natural process of arising, increasing, decreasing, and passing away. Completion of expression then involves allowing emotion to run its course, thereby overcoming inhibition and leading to a release of tension. No longer is there a conflict between expressive and suppressive tendencies. The psycho–affective–motor program is allowed to run and complete itself, which leads to reduction in the arousal. Rather than being stuck in the emotion, the client experiences and lets go of it.

DIFFERENTIAL INTERVENTION

The goal of the arousal and expression of emotion is to evoke core depressogenic schemes to make them more accessible to new information. Evoking emotion does not involve linear reasoning, the identification of patterns across situations, or behavioral or situational tracking. Rather, it involves attention, awareness, and stimulation of bodily felt experience, as well as the use of evocative language to highlight poignant meanings. Thus, to evoke, the therapist moves between focusing on verbal meaning and nonverbal experience and expression, between past and present, and between bodily sense and visual imagination in a nonlinear manner to prime different nodes of the emotion-generating schemes (Greenberg, Rice, & Elliott, 1993; Greenberg & Safran, 1987).

The type of emotion expressed and its relation to other emotions are, however, important. In depressions characterized by hopeless weeping, it is the evocation of anger and pride that is needed as an antidote, not an intensification of the wallowing in despair. In clients who are angry and blaming, the experience and expression of sadness at loss or the core fear of abandonment or shame at humiliation are important. In the evocation and arousal aspect of EFT, the goal is to evoke previously unexpressed emotion to allow it to flow freely and to open it to further processing. The secondary or symptomatic emotions that clients enter therapy to get rid of, such as feeling upset, hopeless, helpless, resigned, self-blaming, guilty, empty, and confused, are often the first to appear. Although these emotions may need to be evoked initially, they are evoked not because this is in and of itself therapeutic, but to help arrive at depressogenic core emotion schemes. Secondary emotions, if not already present, then are accessed, usually through therapeutic dialogue and exploration, as a step on a path to help get at the more core, primary emotions. Primary and core emotions are often accessed through differentiation and exploration of the secondary emotion, and accessing and arousing the primary emotions is the fundamental aim.

Once accessed, primary emotions either will change the client by themselves, or the client will need to change them. If the primary emotion arrived at is adaptive, it gives useful information, helps the client become more resilient, and combats the depression, thereby changing the client. If the core emotion arrived at is maladaptive, like the fear, shame, anger, and guilt that often are at the center of more chronic depressions, it will need to be transformed.

Therapy involves arriving at core adaptive emotions and using them to help transform core maladaptive emotions. In depression, anger undoes despair, whereas sadness promotes grieving and acceptance and transforms anger. Anger and sadness both undo fear and shame and turn them into more contactful emotional states. Anger that strengthens also transforms weepy, helpless sadness into assertion, and healthy adaptive sadness that reaches out for comfort transforms the expulsive rejection of disgust and contempt into more healthy interpersonal boundary setting.

Anger and sadness often exist in a curious reciprocal relationship in human experience. A person becomes sad at the loss of a desired object and angry at the frustration of having the desire thwarted. Often, in simpler cases of depression, a conflict about experiencing and expressing either anger or sadness is at the core of the depression. Rather than feel the feeling of anger or sadness, the person closes down, and the result is depressive hopelessness and defeat. Mobilization of the lively emotion with its need and action tendency energizes and brings the person back to life. Deep grieving that has been complicated and prevented by anger is allowed to run its course, or empowering anger blocked by guilt or fear of retribution is accessed and promotes assertion.

In more complex instances of depression, it is the maladaptive emotion at the core of the self that must be transformed, such as the fear and anxiety of basic insecurity, the shame of worthlessness, or the rage at being humiliated and treated abusively. The therapeutic task, having worked through the secondary hopelessness, is first to arrive at the dreaded feeling and then to learn to tolerate it and soothe it until it can be transformed by new input. Examples of maladaptive core primary feelings generally evoked in the treatment of clients with depression are a powerless, shamed sense of victimization; anxious feelings of being weak; and invisible or destructive anger or murderous rage. Core depressive experiences involve a deep sense of woundedness, a feeling of vulnerability and fear, a basic sense of insecurity, a core sense of shame, feelings of defectiveness or worthlessness, or feelings of being unloved or unlovable. Often, however, these emotional states are not readily accessible because they are masked by secondary feelings on the surface, such as feeling upset, irritable, or frustrated.

Maladaptive emotion thus needs constantly to be distinguished from healthy adaptive emotion. Destructive anger needs to be distinguished from healthy empowering anger and hopeless sadness from healing grief. Maladaptive fear that is panicky or desperately dependent needs to be distinguished from fear that seeks out safety and protection. Unhealthy fear grips every fiber of people's bodies while they relive something that is no longer present, whereas secondary anxiety about not succeeding dissolves when they stop thinking about tomorrow's exam. Freezing and tensing in response to a consciously desired sexual touch from a loved one is another example of maladaptive fear; based on past sexual trauma the person's brain sends an alarm signal of danger, even though no danger is currently present. Fear is too readily activated by harmless cues because of past traumatic learning. Debilitating shame needs to be distinguished from shame that informs one that one has violated a norm or overexposed oneself. For example, unhealthy primary shame that makes people feel "I am defective to the core" and encompasses the person's total identity differs from healthy guilt about a regretted action or inaction about which reparation can be made. Guilt can motivate a person to atone, whereas an unhealthy sense of primary shame might make the person want to shrink into the ground. Therapists can help clients turn their shame of "I am defective" into guilt, expressed as "I have made a mistake," which they can try to repair.

Dreams are often helpful ways of rapidly identifying the primary emotion at the core of the maladaptive self-organization. For example, one client had a dream that she was trapped in a hole with only her head sticking above the ground. People walked by her, oblivious to her predicament. She tried yelling for help, but her voice remained trapped in her throat. Entering the feeling state in this dream, she contacted her deep sense of feeling helpless and alone. Another woman dreamed that her husband came to kiss her but she had rotten teeth. The therapist asked her to describe herself as her teeth, and this helped her access her sense of being unattractive and defective. Both of these clients thus got in touch with their core maladaptive sense of self through their dreams. Once they symbolized the primary maladaptive emotions in awareness, they were able to transform these experiences of themselves as alone or bad by accessing their healthy feelings of feeling loved, being angry at violation, grieving over loss, and realizing their basic human need to be valued for who they were.

In activating emotion therapists should ensure that all the components of the emotion scheme are attended to: situation, sensory feeling, action tendency, need, and core meaning. Ensuring that all components are focused on helps the client fully evoke the emotion scheme and process it. When clients are experiencing aroused emotion, therapists have to support them in feeling and bearing their humiliating feelings of shame, their unbearable fragility, their fears of abandonment and dissolution, or their fears of annihilation. These emotions have to be felt, not as victimized states for which they blame others, but rather embraced as their own experience that provides information. For example, in shame clients must acknowledge the shame, identify what triggers it, and analyze the meaning of the trigger, and then they must experience the action tendency of wanting to shrink into the ground and disappear. This experience then provides access to what the self palpably needs—to feel better. It is access to the need that makes it possible for clients to experience an in-session corrective emotional experience that will provide new possibilities and add something new to their emotion response repertoires. In shame, the need generally is for validation, and shame can be transformed by accessing assertion, pride, and a sense of entitlement. When clients are blocked in their processing of the emotion, therapists should check which components have not been attended to and focus on them.

EVOKING SPECIFIC EMOTIONS

The sections that follow describe ways of evoking some of the core emotions important in the treatment of depression.

Adaptive Grief and Sadness

Inadequate grieving can lead to depression. Both delayed and distorted grief reactions can be depressogenic. Evoking sadness and grief to promote the mourning of losses is essential in these depressions. Grief must be experienced and expressed—not just talked about, but felt. The visceral experience of unrestricted healthy grief begins with an upwelling of pressure to cry and sob in the chest and head, which immediately comes out as unconstrained sobbing with tears and usually is accompanied by bending forward or doubling over. Often clients cover their face with their hands as they sob. The "lump in the throat" in grief often is a constriction, a tension from interrupting the rising pressure to sob and cry. When clients are experiencing sadness or grief, the therapist can ask, "Are you holding back the full experience of your sadness [or grief] by tightening your throat or chest?" This question often is useful, especially when followed by the encouragement "Don't hold it back; just let it come." Gentle and empathic encouragement often helps clients to allow the full visceral experience of their grief. If clients are tightening their throat when sadness or grief is present, it generally is an interruption of an audible and uncontrollable sob. Some forms of core sadness are experienced with less intensity than grief, but they have some of the same features, and tears also seem to be important in unblocking the sadness.

The experience of a set of related bad feelings, such as guilt or hopelessness, that have some similarity with the sadness of grief but are not adaptive shares certain features such as a lump in the throat and pain in the chest, but they differ in important ways. In deep grief, there is a gut-wrenching kind of sob that comes up from below. It is usually the loss of a loved one, or of what can never be, that is being mourned. In the bad feeling of guilt or despair, the pain is usually caused by the feeling that the self is bad, and this feeling does not come from the same deep, gut-wrenching place. In guilt, people feel bad about their anger at loved ones or at what they have done, and the physiological and visceral experience differs from that of grief. Grief brings release and relief. Bad feelings leave the person feeling bad. It is important to tease these different feelings out and to evoke grief but to avoid evoking more bad feeling. In a study of pain, the primary experience was found to be one of "brokenness," or a feeling of being shattered (Bolger, 1999; Greenberg & Bolger, 2001), and this feeling always referred to the body and to deep, dark, visceral experiences. These clients reported, for example, "I felt torn into pieces," "My heart was broken," "It is as if a big chunk of me had been ripped out and I was left bleeding," and "I shattered into a thousand pieces." The metaphor of the body being ruptured helped capture their experience. When people are in pain, they feel broken, and this is what they face in grief. The goals, then, in promoting grief are to help clients face the loss and the brokenness; to explore feelings associated with the loss, possibly feelings of anger, fear, or guilt; and to discuss the meaning and the consequences of the loss.

Evocation of sadness is often facilitated by focusing on what is missed. Rather than asking clients to say what they are sad about, therapists can ask them what they miss. Responding to this question helps them articulate the longing and the yearning more clearly. For example, a client whose mother had committed suicide when she was a child said, speaking to her mother in an empty chair, "I missed having you to talk to when I needed you. I missed having you there when I came home from school. I missed you there on my birthday." This expression of what she missed opened this client for the first time in therapy to grieving her loss. If clients cry but try to stifle their tears, it is helpful to ask them to give the tears a voice and to ask, "If the tears could speak, what would they say?" This question gives clients permission to cry and helps them put their sadness into words.

Adaptive Anger

Expression of anger toward key figures is sometimes central to the resolution of depression. In many clients, the lifting of the depression appears to require the ability to be angry at those who were hurtful. Some clients with depression can be overreactive and stuck in anger, but many others are underreactive and do not feel entitled to their anger. Often, after anger at violation is accessed, sadness at loss follows, and the client grieves what is missed. This grieving leads to the completion of the emotional processing and the letting go of the unmet need.

Feeling one's anger and venting it are not the same thing. Venting, which usually involves ranting to another person about the injury, is not therapeutic, because the client is not connecting to the anger and feeling its source. Anger in these cases can be as much a prison as a release. Clients must see their anger as their own and take responsibility for it and for what they want to do about it. Speaking the anger out loud to an imagined other in an empty chair, looking at the person and saying "I resent you," and specifying what they resent or the nature of the violation often help clients feel their anger, rather than simply blaming or venting. Having clients talk directly to the empty chair with the therapist guiding them to differentiate what they want or need helps reduce the efforts to change the other person—for, after all, it is apparent that the other is not there. In addition, having clients describe what their anger feels like inside shifts their focus from complaining or trying to obtain something from the other toward differentiating their own experience. When clients allow themselves to feel their anger, they often also break through to the pain and hurt, and then they grieve more fully.

Some clients are initially too fragile to experience and express anger. They cannot get to core anger because of a vulnerability in their sense of self. For these clients, the self first has to be strengthened before anger can be accessed. In working with anger, it often is not the first core emotion that has to be dealt with. For example, a client who revealed memories of a rape by her father when she was a young child was overcome with fear and pain in the first few sessions. This pain and fear had to be dealt with first. With empathic affirmation of these feelings, she eventually got to her rage and finally to her grief. Attempts to access her anger too early would not have been therapeutic, because she did not yet have the strength and internal security to sustain anger, and if she had been encouraged in that direction, she would have become filled with the fear and pain. The painful feelings had to be processed first. After a number of sessions, she came to focus on the fact that she had survived and that the "the worst was over." With this realization, plus the help of a collaborative alliance with the therapist, who offered her the emotional security and protection she needed, she began to access her anger. The therapist helped her continue to express her anger to her father for a few sessions, which led her to access a deep sense of violation, adaptive anger, and empowerment.

Depression often does not lift until the deep-seated anger is accessed and processed. The journey to anger, however, is not always straightforward. Cathartic venting of blaming anger does not result in real change in core problems. In addition, work on strengthening the self, especially work on compassion for the self, discussed in chapter 11, takes time, and it is only after the self has developed and strengthened that therapy can help get to grief over what happened. This preliminary work then often is followed by a real, justifiable outrage at the violation, and it is only then that the depression lifts.

From our point of view, anger against violation is highly adaptive; originally, it is interrupted because of the negative response of the significant attachment figure to the anger. When the full experience of anger is accessed within the safety of the therapeutic situation, however, the adaptive action tendencies can come to the fore and promote access to previously inaccessible emotions such as grief or shame. New memories and meanings can become available. Or the expression of the anger by itself may lead to a shift in self-organization and a strengthening of the self. Therapists need at all times to pay close attention to the client's process, experientially track affective shifts within the client's moment-by-moment experience, stay close to where the client is, and evoke anger only when the client is ready.

A method we have found helpful in evoking blocked anger involves therapists demonstrating to their clients what the emotional arousal feels like in their own bodies. Therapists can say something like, "Have you ever felt like this?" They may raise their fists and look fierce or describe what anger has felt like in their stomach or chest. Therapists tell clients to let the anger flow without constriction and to notice how it feels and wants to move inside their bodies (i.e., encouragement to adopt an observing stance). The therapist thus becomes an active guide. Helpful questions to ask are "What does the anger or rage want to do?" or "What does it need?"

Dealing with narcissistic anger, however, is quite different. This type of anger could go on forever, and generally it is the underlying shame that needs to be experienced and symbolized. These clients seem to need not only to understand their narcissistic vulnerability and talk about it, but also to viscerally experience the associated emotion, usually shame or sadness, but perhaps something else. What these clients need, with the help of an emotional connection to an empathic therapist, is to get beyond the entitled anger to the core shame and help to regulate it by developing self-soothing abilities.

Maladaptive Fear

Fear and insecurity are at the base of some depressions, but often they are locked out of reach in the amygdala and covered by many layers of coping processes. The fear generally is either a deep fear of abandonment and anxiety that the self cannot survive without the lost attachment, or it is a fear of annihilation, danger, and abuse. Clients' core maladaptive fear needs to be activated in therapy to change it. The fear probably was adaptive at the time of its inception, but it is no longer adaptive and needs to be evoked to expose it to new input. Thus, it is important to get back to the core fear and to identify the helpless feelings associated with it. Clients with core fear initially may be more focused on their anger or sadness, but if they do not get to and process their fear in the safety of the present, they will not resolve their core concerns. To do this clients need to relive their core fear and its origins in the present and feel the fear in their bodies.

Fear is often described as being felt in the chest, whereas anxiety is often felt in the stomach, shoulders, or arms. Fear is always at the center of unresolved abuse or trauma, and therapists need to recognize when clients have such a history. Clients who grew up in violent homes often talk about the experience of walking on eggshells, tightening their bodies, holding their breath, and trying to not be seen or heard in order not to rock the boat. Often it is very helpful, when sufficient safety has been created, to ask them to go back and remember and relive the experience of fear. To let them feel it in their bodies and in the present is to help them begin to loosen the tightening in their bodies. They need to let themselves shake all over their bodies if need be, rather than hold tight. This gives expression to a tendency that often is necessary for healing the fear.

Trauma generally has four components, present to differing degrees in different cases: hyperarousal, constriction, dissociation, and freezing. The latter three components protect against the former—they operate to protect against both the external and internal threat when the highly aroused energy is not being used for active defense. In trauma, constriction occurs in the body and also in perception. All efforts are focused on the threat. Breathing, muscle tone, and posture are all changed to support defensive action, while attention is directed toward the threat and awareness constricts. When constriction fails, dissociation and freezing occur to deal with the emergency. The person then disconnects from the body, and a kind of spaciness or floating sensation occurs. Finally, the most profound type of helplessness occurs in the form of freezing, a type of body paralysis.

Transformation of the fear-based traumatic process occurs in the safety of therapy by slowing down the fear response and experiencing all the elements one at a time in awareness. This process helps the client deconstruct the experience, symbolize it in awareness, and assimilate it into his or her ongoing understanding of what is happening at a rate that is tolerable. In addition, the client begins to access other emotional responses. Often anger and sometimes grief emerge. The client becomes unfrozen, and new material and new responses other than fear and helplessness become accessible.

One client came into therapy with depression and bodily pain. She felt no connection between these symptoms and her fear from childhood physical abuse. After a while in therapy, she began to feel the rage that her depression had been containing. She felt rage at how abusive her father had been toward her and her brother and how ineffectual her mother had been in protecting them all from his abuse. Getting to her fear and re-experiencing her anxiety-ridden childhood were crucial in helping her strengthen the self and resiliently overcome her depression. She became aware of how her old feelings of fear were constantly being triggered in present relationships. With the ability to soothe her fear, her rage became not just a helpless response with no possible sense of resolution, but rather gave her access to her core anger at having been violated. This empowered anger acted to help her transform her re-experienced fear into a more assertive sense of self.

Maladaptive Shame and Guilt

Shame generally is bound with fear but is an important emotion in itself, one that often needs to be addressed at the core of depression. Facing shame requires courage and determination, for it requires clients to face the worst they feel about themselves. Worthlessness and shame are highly related. When people's needs are not met, especially as children, they come to believe there must be something wrong with them. When they are treated with contempt, they feel contemptible. The feeling of the self being defective is shame, and to break its hold clients have to feel their worthlessness. As clients connect with their shame and worthlessness, with the support of their therapists they need to connect with their self-compassion and with their sense of worth and pride. They need to admire their damaged part for its ability to survive and to be able to be compassionate to its suffering (this process is discussed further in chapters 11 and 13).

Being in therapy also can be inherently shaming. The mere act of acknowledging that life is too difficult and laying bare one's deepest secrets to a relative stranger is fraught with shame. Therapists must always keep in mind that clients with depression can feel deeply defective and that asking for help is experienced as one more manifestation of that defectiveness. It requires considerable trust for clients to reveal to the therapist what they consider to be their deepest flaws, what is "wrong" with them, and those parts of self they are most ashamed of. The first goal in counteracting shame thus is to develop a supportive, empathically attuned relationship. The focus then needs to shift to helping clients recognize and overcome avoidance to acknowledge painful feelings of shame. Interventions such as evocative imagery or chair work are needed to help clients bring the shame alive in the immediacy of the session and help them stay in touch with their particular experiences of shame long enough to symbolize these feelings in awareness. Activation of the shame exposes it to new information, and this transforms the maladaptive emotion schemes that produce the shame. Counteracting shame thus involves first revealing the shameful material in therapy and sharing the secret with another person, who is experienced as nonrejecting and validating. In addition, anger at the shaming other often is then accessed and used as a healthy resource to hold the other accountable for harm done. The anger then transforms the shame. Strong support from the therapist for the expression of contempt and disgust, directed at the abusive other rather than at the self, helps undo the shame. Sadness at what was lost often follows.

The therapist often can help the client access core shame by empathically highlighting the underlying pain of wounds to self-esteem and the pain of not belonging. Responses that validate how shaming things were, the longing to belong, and the adaptiveness of this need are very helpful. Responses that help evoke the shame a client feels include "Yes, as kids we need so desperately to be accepted, to belong" or "How humiliating to be exposed like that, caught on the toilet, with them laughing at you" or "There is such shame in being an unchosen one." Clients then might disclose how sad and alone they felt, as a child, wishing more than anything that they were liked or loved in spite of their deficits.

Therapy with clients who are depressed needs most centrally to evoke the core feelings of shame that are generated by a sense of not being good enough. When one client talked about feelings of being unacceptable, the therapist responded, "You live with the fear that, no matter how hard you try, that this will never happen, that you will never be completely accepted." This evoked tears of hopelessness and despair, and the therapist helped the client explore the sense of herself as unacceptable or inferior. Clients find this exploration very difficult, and it requires the establishment of considerable trust and unconditional acceptance in the relationship, delicacy, and attention to client vulnerability. Tentativeness in responding and references to the "part" of the self that the client finds unacceptable make it easier for clients to acknowledge feelings of shame and worthlessness, because it opens the possibility that the whole self is not unacceptable.

Sometimes it is necessary to provide a rationale for experiencing and disclosing shame, because it feels like such a self-damaging emotional state. For example, when clients express reluctance to talk about embarrassing or shameful material, therapists can encourage them with responses such as, "I know it's hard, but it's so important to say; otherwise, it eats away at you" or "keeps you so isolated." Clients with a shame-based sense of self often are highly anxious and live in constant fear of being found out and found lacking. Empathic responses can heighten awareness of how the tendency to retreat accompanying shame cuts off social contact and jeopardizes the person's primary needs for belonging and connectedness. This observation helps clients access healthy needs and motivates them to come out of hiding and risk disclosing shameful material.

As a signal to evoke shame, therapists can be attuned and responsive to nonverbal indicators of shame-related experience in the session. Indicators include downcast eyes, squirming or writhing in the seat, and laughter or shrugging off that serves to cover embarrassment. Empathic affirmations, such as "It's hard, feeling somehow foolish talking about this stuff," open the door for further exploration. Also important are inquiries into whether the therapist has unwittingly shamed the client by not being attuned to the client's feelings or by failing to support when support was needed.

Obvious and frequently occurring indicators of underlying shame-related processes include explicit self-critical statements, such as clients calling themselves "fat" or "lazy" or a "screw-up." Therapists' responses need to highlight the affective quality of contempt and disgust in a client's tone of voice, arrogant tilt of the head, or snarl or curl of the lip and, most importantly, to call attention to how it must feel to be the recipient of such contempt. For example, when a client constantly berates himself or herself for not living up to expectations, the therapist can respond, "I hear how much that voice is saying, 'I don't like myself very much.' This must evoke such feelings of shame. It must be so painful to be treated this way."

A powerful intervention for evoking shame consists of a two-chair dialogue in which the client enacts the harshly negative, contemptuous, self-evaluative processes that produce shame. In this intervention therapists ask clients to enact the two parts of themselves—the critic or judge who directs contemptuous statements and the part of themselves that is the recipient of the contempt and disgust. This process heightens awareness of the specific internalized messages, the expressive quality, and the experiential impact of the contempt and disgust; the pain of such wounds; and the damage to clients' self-esteem. Putting shame into words with a trusted other enables the client to step outside it so that shame no longer seems to permeate his or her entire being and so that some self-compassion can emerge.

Positive Adaptive Emotions

In addition to too much negative emotion, depression is characterized by too little positive emotion. So-called negative emotions tend to focus and narrow consciousness on the stimulus (i.e., the person or event evoking the fear, anger, shame) and to take control of actions. In general, positive emotion broadens one's attention, expands consciousness, and evokes the capacity for clarity—to "see the big picture" in a given situation.

Positive emotion is often seen in the wake of a negative feeling like sadness, grief, pain, or anger. There is something positive in having had the feeling; a sense of mastery or of clarity and strength can come from truly feeling one's feelings. In addition, adaptive action tendencies come to the fore when the positive experience is explored. Therapists need to help clients explore and expand the presence of positive feelings. It can be helpful to look for the positive feelings, however brief the glimmer, and to shed light on them, knowing they can lead to important resources in the self.

For example, a client came into his session reporting that he had, for the first time in years, experienced relief from his anxiety and distress. He shared for a moment his sense of relief and then quickly stated, "But . . . I lost it after a few days and got anxious again." Rather than focusing on the anxiety, the therapist focused on the positive experience—the sense of relief he felt. Over the course of the session his positive experience opened up, and he experienced deeper levels of positive feeling and began to see himself differently. This experiencing also gave way to some grief as he mourned for the self he had lost and how he had suffered. The positive feelings, however, continued to expand into a deeper sense and understanding of how things could be, of how he could feel, and of what could happen when he is open to his experience. None of this would have happened had they not explored this positive experience.

Therapists can encourage positive feelings by exploring them, asking about them, and encouraging clients to stay with and experience them. Specific examples of therapist statements to promote positive feelings include, "I notice that you're smiling today," "How do you feel as you smile?" and "How do you experience excitement in your body?" Positive feelings can also be encouraged through nonverbal communication through tone of voice, facial expression, humor, warmth, and slower pace. The therapist also can explicitly encourage the client to experience the positive feeling by saying, "If you just give yourself a moment to have this experience, what do you notice?" "Can you let it develop or intensify?" or "How can you express it?" The therapist also might say how nice it is to see the client in a positive state, appreciate aloud the vulnerability that is likely involved in sharing it, and ask gently what it is like to share the experience. The interpersonal connection usually deepens the positive feeling and counters the anxiety of aloneness or the shame of feeling deflated by lack of recognition or fear of being shot down. Many clients who have a lot of shame hide their strengths and joys, and it is helpful to have them own their strengths and enjoy them. The therapist's focus on a positive feeling will have an effect on the client and will deepen the positive feeling or evoke other feelings attached to it.

Attempting, at appropriate times, to evoke and amplify positive emotions by asking clients to repeat phrases and to elaborate them helps them overcome embarrassment at and constriction of the expression of these feelings. Encouraging clients to boast about their achievements helps them to express pride and gives them permission to feel it. In general, expressiveness training can help clients experience and express positive feelings more exuberantly. It is helpful to ask clients first to let the positive feeling flow in their bodies, to feel the excitement and let it build, and then to show it on their face and in their voice and express it in their bodies. Some of the positive emotions, such as excitement and interest, joy and pride, love and compassion, and finally hope, are touched on briefly in the sections that follow.

Excitement and Interest

The broaden-and-build theory (Fredrickson, 2001) suggests that positive emotions broaden the array of thoughts and actions that come to mind, as opposed to negative emotions, which are associated with narrowed thought and action tendencies. For example, interest broadens by creating the urge to explore and take in new information, whereas fear focuses on the urge to escape. According to the theory, positive emotions trigger "broad-minded coping," characterized by taking a broad perspective on problems and generating multiple solutions to them. Broad-minded coping facilitates coping with negative circumstances and improves the chances of experiencing future positive emotion. As this cycle continues, clients build their psychological resilience and enhance their emotional health.

Interest encompasses experiences of curiosity, intrigue, excitement, or wonder; arises with challenge; and is a source of intrinsic motivation. Interest is an emotion that is experienced very frequently, possibly without being noticed, and it is a baseline emotion of great importance. The action tendency of interest involves attending, orienting, and exploring. Interest generates a feeling of wanting to investigate, become involved, or extend or expand the self by incorporating new information and having new experiences with the person or object that has stimulated the interest, and it is associated with feeling animated and enlivened. Interest is the primary instigator of personal growth, creative endeavor, and the development of intelligence, and its reinstatement is important to a cure for depression. People with depression have lost interest in living. Finding any spark of interest and helping it grow into a flame of excitement is important in overcoming the lethargy and deadness. Interest comes from connecting with the self's true feelings and needs. The therapeutic relationship and being in therapy are important in helping recreate a sense of baseline interest. Contact with and validation of one's feelings, whatever they are, strengthen and energize the self.

Joy and Pride

The action tendency associated with joy is one of free activation; it is in part aimless, unasked-for readiness to engage in whatever interaction presents itself and is in part readiness to engage in enjoyment. Joy creates the urge to play and be playful in the broadest sense of the word, encompassing not only physical and social play, but also intellectual and artistic play. Play involves exploration, invention, and just plain fooling around. Pointing to no single set of actions, play takes many forms. Joy and related positive emotions broaden an individual's thought–action repertoire and promotes skill acquisition. Accessing joy clearly helps undo depressive withdrawal. It is not that therapists can create false joy or tell clients to look on the bright side; rather, they should be sensitive to when joy can be evoked. Feelings of joy arise in contexts tacitly evaluated as safe and familiar and as requiring low effort, and in some cases they are evoked by events construed as accomplishments or progress toward one's goals (Izard, 1991).

Because clients with depression feel that something is wrong with them, joy or happiness, instead of being a normal state of being that they experience, must be activated in therapy and supported. Clients who are depressed need to recognize achievement and to practice feeling good about themselves. When they feel happy, they need to express those feelings to others. When they feel proud, they need to be encouraged to sustain the feeling.

Anhedonia refers to the depressive person's inability to experience joy. Nothing touches people in the depths of major depression, neither the most intensely pleasurable activities nor the most familiar comforts. With depression people can become emotionally frozen. They are resigned to their plight, and nothing seems to make them feel better. A pervasive problem among people with depression is their gradual withdrawal into isolation and indifference. There is a closing down of self and world. In depression, people lose interest or pleasure in ordinary activities, and their range of activities constricts. They stop making changes, avoid stimulation, play it safe, and begin to cut themselves off from anything that might shake them up, including loved ones.

Symptomatic relief of depression through medication or brief therapy often only helps the client regain a previous level of functioning that was without joy, pleasure, and pride. The absence of feeling makes for empty lives. Regulating sadness, anger, guilt, and shame is not enough for recovery from depression; clients also must learn to access good feelings. Many clients with depression fear positive emotions and prefer to play it safe by avoiding or controlling all emotions. Self and relationships deteriorate into brittle, bitter, vulnerable shells. Although learning to feel may be temporarily upsetting for clients who are depressed, it ultimately is the primary source of richness and meaning in their lives. Joy opens people up and leads them to be more social. Joy enlivens and brings happiness to people's faces and bodies and helps undo sadness. People also cry in happiness, which has a root in a sudden gratitude that is deeply felt but not labeled as gratitude. Some people shed tears when experiencing the emotion of reverence. A person with a strong sense of self-esteem will tend to go into happiness without crying, but crying in happiness often is found in people with depression. When happiness is experienced as a gift that is greatly desired but somehow undeserved, rather than as a natural right, people are overcome and cry in happiness.

Contentment is often used interchangeably with other low-arousal positive emotion terms such as *tranquility* or *calm* or *peacefulness*. At first blush, contentment appears to have no real action tendency and is linked with inactivity. Contentment, however, leads people to savor their current life circumstances and recent successes, experience oneness with the world around them, and integrate recent events and achievements into their overall self-concept and worldview. Contentment, then, is not simple passivity, but rather a mindful broadening of a person's view of self and world and is an antidote to the complaint in depression.

In pride, people puff up and feel strong. Pride is what people are supposed to feel when they have accomplished something, but, like joy, it is not something that people with depression experience very often. Depressed people who are perfectionistic rarely feel that anything they have measures up to their own standards, so they do not feel pride. One reason why people with depression are not able to experience the pleasurable feelings of joy and pride is the paucity of such experiences in their lives. Some clients contain these emotions because of their need to remain in control at all times. Intense feelings of any kind are destabilizing and frightening. They also live in fear of retribution for enjoyment. They have learned to expect that something bad inevitably follows something good, so they had better not let themselves feel too good; better to feel numb or neutral than to feel the crushing disappointment they fear will follow good feelings. They may also avoid joy or pride because they evoke painful memories of past disappointments.

Love and Compassion

Evoking love and compassion in therapy often is best done by having clients express their feelings out loud in imaginary dialogues with others. Homework to express love and appreciation in word or deed to the person in the real world also is helpful. Even simply talking about these often not elaborated feelings in a detailed way is helpful. Asking clients what they feel in their bodies when they feel loving and having them describe this often brings tears to clients' eyes. Helping them bask in the warmth and the glow of these positive feelings is very enlivening and inspiring and gives clients a great sense of the worth of life. Asking them to remember this feeling and to try to access it purposefully at times is also helpful.

Most theorists acknowledge that love is not a single emotion and that people experience varieties of love (e.g., romantic or passionate love, companionate love, caregiver love, and attachment to caregivers). Love experiences probably are made up of many positive emotions, including interest, joy, and contentment. Over time the interactions inspired by love help build and strengthen social bonds and attachment. These social bonds are not only satisfying in and of themselves, but also are likely to be the locus of subsequent social support. In this sense, love and the various positive emotions experienced in love relationships (i.e., interest, joy, and contentment) build and solidify an individual's social resources.

Maslow (1971) distinguished between "D" (deficit) love versus "B" (being) love. D love comes out of the need to fill in what was missing, for example, to feel secure or to prove something to oneself or to the world. B love, however, exists as itself: The lover appreciates the other simply for who the other is and what the other represents, regardless of whether it enhances the lover in any way. In B love there is a deep appreciation and understanding untarnished by the needs, doubts, insecurities, and biases of the individual. Depression has been seen as a sickness of love in psychodynamic views. The depressed person feels unloved. An antidote to this feeling is to love. To love invigorates, pulls one up, and promotes well-being. Focusing on the positive in others and on what one loves can help activate love.

Compassion involves feeling the depth of another's experience in a deeply caring way. It implies a deep caring and respect and a desire to reduce suffering. From a Buddhist perspective, *compassion* is defined as the wish that all beings be free of suffering. The three aspects of compassion are the feeling of caring for another person and his or her suffering, the desire to reduce that suffering, and action taken to help reduce the other's suffering. It is not simply a sense of sympathy or caring; it is also a sustained and practical determination to do whatever is possible and necessary to help alleviate the other's suffering. Compassion is not true compassion unless it is active. Compassion can undo anger, and as we have mentioned, accessing sympathy for a person who had insulted them was shown to change people's brain activation associated with approach tendencies in anger (Harmon-Jones, Vaughn-Scott, Mohr, Sigelman, & Harmon-Jones, 2004).

Hope

Finally, some words about hope are essential in relation to work with depression. Demoralization is a major problem in depression. The absence of hope is, of course, symptomatic of depression and is a major obstacle to engagement in treatment. Cultivating hope thus is a major issue in the therapy of depression, especially for some clients. The therapist therefore must both evoke and offer hope and remind the client sometimes, when things are bleakest, that people with depression do get better. The ability to lend hope comes first from confidence that depression can be reversed, perhaps from the therapist's experience of seeing other people or oneself go through the same process. The aspect of hope that affirms a commitment to one's clients is probably not generally communicated in the content of what one says, but rather in the emotional tone and the conviction with which one speaks.

Hope is an antidote to despair. Hope in therapy comes most centrally from developing trust and belief in the potency of the therapist to help, especially early on in the treatment. If clients, early on, can experience concretely their often vague hopelessness and despair and share it with the therapist, hope is generated. The therapist's ability to acknowledge the pain under the hopelessness activates the client's unfulfilled yearnings for connection. This yearning then opens the client to human contact and breaks his or her sense of isolation. Hope then emerges when one's hopelessness is understood. Hope of being able to reconnect to the human race, of being understood, and most of all of being valid and reconnecting then emerges, as does a will to live.

Experiencing hope means allowing desire. Many people with depression avoid experiencing desire. If clients come from backgrounds of abuse, chronic disappointment, exploitation, or traumatic loss, they may experience desire as a frightening vulnerability or a weakness that others will exploit or that will leave them open to being wounded. If clients have experiences in which their own difficulty controlling emotions or impulses has brought them pain, they may experience desire as an overwhelming force to be avoided at all costs. Experiencing desire can feel dangerous to the core of the self. Hope involves allowing one again to feel and to wish.

Hope involves a yearning for a desired outcome. Some writers view hope not as a positive emotion, but rather as a type of wishful thinking for relief from a negative experience. Camus (1955/1975) captured this by suggesting that hope *is* despair, rather than an antidote to it. That hope can lead people astray is captured in sayings such as, "Hope is what dreams are made of" and "false hope." Many, however, view hope as a virtue. Hope probably is not a singular experience, as it varies with the conditions that initiate it. Hope seems to sustain people in times of difficulty and is very helpful to the psychotherapeutic enterprise in engendering motivation to work on overcoming the problem. In therapy, encouraging hope is an important part of forming a working alliance in that hope activates clients' sense of agency, motivates them to work toward agreed-on goals, and helps open up pathways to attain these goals. People characterized as being high in hope when confronted with blockages have been found to come up with alternate pathways to goals (Snyder, 1994), indicating that hope promotes solutions to problems. Hope can be seen as a vital and life-giving principle, as captured in the saying, "Where there is life, there is hope." Studies have suggested that hope may contribute to the maintenance of healthy physiological states, including increased immunocompetence, under the stress of significant loss (Udelman, 1986).

11

EVOKING EMOTION: TWO-CHAIR DIALOGUE AND HOPELESSNESS

Two major methods used to evoke emotional experience in the treatment of depression are the use of psychodramatic enactments, especially chair dialogues, and the use of emotion-evoking imagery. The methods of focusing and evocative unfolding, discussed in chapter 10, also help in evoking emotions; similarly, the evoking methods described in this chapter also help in enhancing emotion awareness.

TWO-CHAIR DIALOGUE FOR SELF-CRITICISM AND HOPELESSNESS

Two-chair dialogue between parts of the self in conflict and between one part of the self and a disowned or disclaimed aspect of self-experience is important in the treatment of depression. In conflict splits of this type, two parts of the self are in opposition. In one type of dialogue, in which part of the self is disowned, a dialogue is set up in which clients enact rejecting a part of themselves as not them and refusing to identify with the disowned part. Although self-criticism is more typical in depression, disowning of experience also occurs and sometimes lies at the core of the depression. In disowning, people despise their own dependence or some other aspect of themselves and disclaim it. This process of disowning experience and disclaiming the action tendency leads to the unintegrated need or resentment breaking out and expressing itself at times in what feels like an out of control manner. People then become depressed because they cannot make sense of themselves and their experience. Therapeutic work with this type of problem involves acknowledging and integrating the disowned feelings and needs.

In the treatment of depression, an intervention that specifically targets the self-criticism and self-contempt so prevalent in low self-worth and hopelessness is the two-chair dialogue. This dialogue is used to bring the whole process of depression and hopelessness alive in the session to make these states amenable to in-session transformation. In this process, when a self-critical marker, such as "I am such a wimp" or "I feel like a failure," appears in the client's presentation, the therapist asks the client to engage in a dialogue between the critical part and the experiencing part of the self (Greenberg, Rice, & Elliott, 1993). In the first few dialogues, the goal is to help the client become aware of the constant presence of a self-critical voice and its depressing and hopelessness-inducing impact.

In two-chair dialogue, which we have described more fully elsewhere (Elliott, Watson, Goldman, & Greenberg, 2004; Greenberg et al., 1993), therapists, having identified the self-critical voice, encourage clients to visualize themselves and to begin criticizing themselves. The critical part is coached to be as specific as possible in expressing its criticisms to evoke the depressive experience more specifically and concretely. Clients are then asked to move to the self chair, which is asked for its affective reaction to the critic—not just a global reaction of a general malaise, like "I feel bad," but a differentiated sense that actually comes alive in the body, in the moment, such as feeling paralyzed or wanting to shrink into the ground. The more the critic can be helped to target concrete instances of experience—for example, weakness or failure at the meeting yesterday—the more episodic, situational, and emotion memories will be evoked.

The exchanges between Debra, a 46-year-old woman in a troubled marriage, and her therapist provide an example of a self-critical split and identification of the critical voice. We will follow Debra's in-session processes throughout this chapter. Debra felt highly controlled by a dominant husband and wished to leave him, but she was afraid to take their children and leave. She was also out of work, and her inability to motivate herself to look for work was the presenting problem. Looking for work in an effort to support herself so that she could be more independent precipitated the depression.

> *Debra:*   I just don't have anything; there's just no little bit of positive
> . . . anything that I can hold onto and say, I did something.
> All that's demonstrated is this inadequate person with no
> spine.

Therapist:	So, sort of what you're doing, you're telling yourself that you're not good enough, you're inadequate.
Debra:	Mm-hm.
Therapist:	Can you imagine her there and tell her, do that some more? Make her feel inadequate—"You're . . . you're not, you can't . . ."
Debra:	I guess it's "You don't live up to what I wish, I expect, and I . . . I know that there could be so much more, but you don't allow . . . you don't . . . it never comes about." I don't know, because, I don't know . . .
Therapist:	"You never . . . you can't do it, you never do it."

The process with clients with depression during this first period of therapy focuses first on evoking the self-critical evaluations, usually accompanied by contempt, and on evoking the negative emotional reaction activated by the criticism, usually hopelessness. It is the contempt toward the self that evokes the depressed feelings of powerlessness, helplessness, and hopelessness and the more primary core shame. Self-critical dialogue goes beyond just accessing negative thoughts. The self-critic is based on a set of cognitive–affective schemes, or a self-organization, that contains its own emotion and motivation. It is important for clients to capture the feeling and motivation in the critic as well as the thought. Clients often don't pay attention to the manner, but only to the content, of the inner dialogues. They concentrate on what is said, but not on the relationship between the parts. By paying special attention to the nonverbal elements of the dialogue, the therapist reflects not just contents, but also the intonation, gestures, posture, and facial expression, thus drawing the client's attention to the affective tone as well as to the content.

Self-critical work does not have to use a dialogue, and it can be done purely conversationally with questions and reflections of feelings. Then one works with the different parts of the self or voices one at a time in sequence. The use of enactment, however, enlivens the conflict and has the added advantage of making the nonverbal elements of the inner dialogue more accessible.

EVOKING THE COLLAPSED, HOPELESS SELF-ORGANIZATION

The next step in the dialogue is developing the experiencing self's response to the criticism. The experiencing self's response in clients with depression generally is characterized by a collapse into a nonresilient state of hopelessness in response to self-criticism. Symptomatic, reactive hopelessness is evoked by the person's critical voice saying, "You are a failure, you have no future, your life is empty, and you will be alone or worthless for the rest of your life." The hopeless state is more of a reactive than a core state. It involves a closing down or giving up, or it is a protection against a core dreaded feeling. Therapy then needs to work through this secondary, reactive hopelessness to access a more core level of distress. Often the core feeling is either shame about the self's deficits or anxiety and fear about the self's ability to be alone.

The two-chair dialogue of one client who was not depressed exemplifies the important role of the self's response to self-criticism as a key component of depression. In the critical chair, this client said, "You don't deserve to occupy the space in this world that could be used by other people. You don't deserve to use the oxygen that others need." This extremely harsh and seemingly annihilating critic seemed positioned to produce an extreme state of despair and hopelessness in the experiencing self. The client, however, on changing chairs, spontaneously said, "That's not true. I do have things to offer. I do community work, and I care for others." This was a resilient self-response. In contrast, a person with depression would have collapsed into depressive hopelessness and worthlessness under such an attack.

In clients with depression, therapists seek to evoke the depressive hopelessness in the session to work through it to generate new responses as an antidote to the hopelessness. It is only when the depressed hopelessness is evoked that it can be processed and transformed. Often the client has to approach and stay with the secondary state of hopelessness to differentiate it and arrive at the core feeling, most often a maladaptive feeling of worthlessness or shame or a deeper core hopelessness of a totally depleted self. Clients in a collapsed, hopeless state are only able to access the response of defeat to the critic's attack or future projections of doom. People with depression feel helpless and resigned, and they often have felt this way for so long that it has become thematic in their lives. Any client strengths that exist lie beyond present awareness. Clients in this state do not respond well to rational alternatives or looking on the bright side. The only way to overcome the depression is to work through it to access the primary adaptive emotions and needs for survival and well-being. Going into the currently felt secondary experience of hopelessness and resignation, rather than fighting against it, does this best. Thus, feelings of helplessness, powerlessness, and hopelessness are accessed, validated, and explored. In an article entitled "The Only Way Out Is Through," Hunt (1998) showed that a group of clients who focused on an aroused negative feeling by writing about it were less troubled by it one week later than another group who combated the feeling rationally in writing. The therapist's goal ultimately is to access clients' resilient feelings as an antidote to the collapse into hopelessness, but we agree that the best way out is through the hopelessness.

In a two-chair dialogue that begins with the critic saying, "You are useless, worthless, a failure," or the like, often the self's response is one of agreement—"You're right"—and a feeling of hopelessness ensues. It is important to help the client and the process not get stuck in a dialogue that is related to the truth or rationality of the criticism. Rather, the goal is to reveal how feelings are produced and to evoke the feeling to make it amenable to change. Rather than responding to the critic either with agreement or by trying to dispute the truth of the criticism rationally or based on evidence, therapists help clients become aware of the emotional impact on them of the criticism. They are asked what it feels like to be told, "You are worthless" and to speak from the bodily felt experience of shame or hopelessness. The client thus experiences the impact of the criticism, rather than agrees or disagrees with the validity of the negative thoughts.

To evoke the experience of depressive hopelessness that the client is often trying to keep at bay, the therapist might empathically observe non-verbal and paralinguistic indicators of the client's current state of defeat, saying, "Just feeling down. I see that you're hunched over in your chair, and your voice has become small, too. I guess you must be feeling pretty defeated." Another possibility to help evoke the hopelessness is for the therapist to offer empathic conjectures that "feel into" the client's experiential state of hopelessness, of which the client may be only minimally aware, by saying, "I guess, then, just this awful feeling of hopelessness comes up." Or the therapist might capture the feeling of resignation with a reflection of "So, it's like, what's the use?"

Dealing with the hopeless state, however, is difficult. Accepting and staying with the collapsed, hopeless sense of self is often the most difficult part of this work. First, the client's tendency is to avoid or escape this awful feeling. The therapist has the same tendency and tends to try and "help" or change the client. However, rather than adopt a modificational stance, the therapist takes a stance of acceptance. The therapist's first actions need to promote staying with the present experience of hopelessness and following the process. This requires both therapist and client to practice an acceptance of "what is." The therapist's goal, then, is to provide a safe, accepting environment; validate the experience; and turn the client's attention inward to the experience of hopelessness. This inward attention helps clients begin to differentiate the hopelessness into the constituent components of situation, appraisal, sensation, action tendency, and need, goal, or concern and develops into more core feelings. The ultimate goal is to help clients find the sources of strength within themselves by focusing them inward with the help of an empathically attuned, emotion-regulating relationship.

The following exchange illustrates how Debra's therapist stayed with and elaborated on Debra's feelings of hopelessness:

> *Therapist:* So, it's like a feeling of, "What's the use?" When you look, it's like if you could find that one thing . . .
>
> *Debra:* Yeah, right . . .

Therapist:	. . . and that's so painful, it's the fear that there may be nothing there.
Debra:	Yeah, it is, it is . . . [*crying*] I can't find anything, I can't find anything to hold onto. I can't see where I've ever been able to do it, be effective. I don't . . . I just don't have any confidence at all. I almost went the other way, like . . . I worry, there are crazy people and people, you know, that never, ever get it together, and those must be people that don't have it inside them. That's how I feel.
Therapist:	It's like you're saying, "I might not have anything inside to draw on. I might be one of them."
Debra:	Yeah, like "Be careful." Yeah, I have looked back and said, "There must be some time when I've done it before." Like, when I've, you know what I mean—sat down and accomplished something, what I wanted to accomplish, and then when I start thinking, it's no. When then, when?
Therapist:	And when you think like that, it becomes completely bleak, completely hopeless.
Debra:	Yeah, and then I don't even want to try.
Therapist:	The worst thing is to try.
Debra:	I'm just not able to—it's very perplexing to me, it's very . . . It's surprising, in a way, because I almost feel inside that I *could* do it, I *can* do it, so it's very surprising.

In another session, Debra was again feeling hopeless:

Debra:	It makes me feel really hopeless; there's no end in sight, you know, there's no happy ending.
Therapist:	A depressing feeling telling you, like . . . that's where the depression is coming from?
Debra:	Yeah.
Therapist:	And those are the feelings, they're telling you, "It's just hopeless. There is no way that you're ever going to do it . . ."
Debra:	Yeah . . .
Therapist:	. . . you never will . . .
Debra:	Yeah . . .
Therapist:	Like, what do you feel? What happens inside?
Debra:	I just feel very hurt, I don't know.
Therapist:	Can you express those feelings? Can you express those feelings in words?

Debra:	Uhh, it puts me in a place where I don't want to be, this feeling of inadequacy, and . . . and I think these feelings are what's holding me back, and . . .
Therapist:	Feelings of inadequacy are very painful. It's hard to stay with those feelings.
Debra:	Mm-hm.
Therapist:	Even just to sit in that chair and try to access those feelings.
Debra:	Yeah, it's really hard.
Therapist:	It's very painful.
Debra:	Yeah.
Therapist:	Can you try a little bit . . . what it is, just to try to see what it is, try to get a little more of a handle—to describe that, to describe out loud what goes on inside when you tell yourself it's hopeless.
Debra:	I just feel really horrible, terrible, awful . . .
Therapist:	Mm-hm.
Debra:	. . . and stuck, I can't ever get away from it, and it's a horrible, awful feeling.
Therapist:	Yeah, it's horrible and awful, and you'd do anything to get away from those feelings . . .
Debra:	Yeah, yeah . . .
Therapist:	Yeah . . . It's just kind of sitting there, like, "I don't want to be here, I don't want to be in this feeling."
Debra:	Mm-hm, and it's a feeling of, like, I deserve something, it, like, it's . . . it's not fair that this should happen to me.
Therapist:	OK, OK . . .
Debra:	It's not fair.
Therapist:	It's not fair, and kind of, "What did I do to deserve this?"
Debra:	Yes, yeah—yeah, and I keep asking myself, like, "Why?"

Debra's therapist did not pull for change, but rather accepted where the client was, and Debra began to mobilize some resilience. Helping clients face hopelessness or helplessness is often key in dealing with depression and in accepting pain that often has been avoided. To differentiate and elaborate on overwhelming hopelessness and get some perspective on it, the therapist might, in addition to focusing on the sensorimotor aspects of the feeling, empathically reflect the meaning of the hopelessness, inquiring into what it is about or what is the worst part of it. Therapists may also, at a teachable moment, teach the client the purpose of "staying with" the hopelessness. The therapist can explain that feelings of hopelessness lead to depression and feelings of helplessness to anxiety. Further, the therapist can point out that the hopelessness often is a reaction to more primary feelings, such as sadness and anger, that have been obscured or blocked and that it is important to discover and give expression to. Such obscured and unresolved feelings need to find expression, and this will ultimately lead to a change in view of self and problems.

The therapist thus might empathically conjecture that there is some real sadness and pain or insecurity or anger underneath the hopelessness. The goal is to access the thwarted emotional response that underlies the sense of collapse or resignation. Sufficient empathic affirmation of core feelings (i.e., sadness, anger, fear, and shame) and continued internal focus on feelings, and ultimately on needs, invariably lead to the emergence of the more proactive, healthy aspects of self, because primary adaptive emotions are naturally self-assertive and constantly try to promote survival and well-being. This is not a simple or Pollyannish process; it involves pain and struggle and courage, but the healthy voice can be found.

Another way of dealing with hopelessness or defeat in two-chair dialogue when resilience does not emerge and the client seems stuck is to move the client back into the critic chair. The therapist encourages the critic to intensify its critical actions and to become more clearly aware of itself as an agent in the creation of the hopelessness. It is useful to help the client become more aware of its contempt and hostility and of the power and superiority the critic feels as it disempowers the self. Such persecutory action paradoxically serves to stimulate the experiencing self to fight back. The person then overcomes the resigned, hopeless position by fighting back against the oppressor. In addition, by activating the person as a whole, physiologically, affectively, and cognitively, by being the aggressor in the critic position, the client's overall level of energy is increased. When the client moves back to the persecuted part in the dialogue, he or she is already aroused, and this "borrowed" arousal works in the service of self-assertion against the critic, thereby lifting the client out of the hopeless state. The following exchange is a simple example of this process with Rachel, a 39-year-old woman who experienced depression and felt overwhelmed by her life situation.

> Therapist: OK, come back over here. [*client moves to critic chair*] So tell her what's wrong with her.
>
> Rachel: Uhmm . . . you don't provide enough for your children. You don't provide enough love, enough attention to your children, your parent, your husband. When they need you, you are not there for them. You're too needy. That's what's wrong with you. You are too needy.

Therapist:	So, it's "you're too needy." Tell her some more.
Rachel:	Yeah, you're pathetic.
Therapist:	Can you tell her what's so pathetic about being needy?
Rachel:	You just need, need, need. You get lots of love and attention, but it's never enough.
Therapist:	OK, try and be more specific. When should she have been satisfied?
Rachel:	OK, yeah. On the weekend when J wanted to go out and you didn't want him to, you were so pathetic not wanting to be alone. You're such a needy baby.
Therapist:	Are you aware of your mouth as you say this? What are you feeling?
Rachel:	Scorn, disgust.
Therapist:	Yeah. Do that some more. Tell her, "You're disgusting."
Rachel:	[*contemptuous tone*] Yeah, you're disgusting. You want too much for yourself; you're selfish and pathetic.
Therapist:	Change. What do you experience?
Rachel:	Well, I don't like it. I feel mad. [*turning to critic chair*] You have no right to treat anybody like that, let alone me.

While Rachel was in the critic chair, the therapist encouraged her to be as specific as possible and also attempted to heighten her emotional awareness by directing her to express her accompanying body language. The therapist also helped the client symbolize and make meaning from her facial expression. In the final exchange, the client's more resilient self-protective response was evoked.

WORKING IN THE PROXIMAL ZONE OF DEVELOPMENT

The overall focus when working to evoke adaptive emotion as an antidote to hopelessness or to a maladaptive state is always on working at the clients' growth edge. Therapist's responses need to be within clients' proximal zone of development, focusing on possibilities within their grasp. For example, if while experiencing hopelessness or worthlessness a client says, in however shaky a manner, "I do count" or shows a flicker of hope or interest, this is to be supported and focused on. Responding in the proximal zone of development means not being too far ahead or behind of the client, and sometimes at the same level. The therapist's response can be a half-step ahead but needs to be sufficiently close to where the client is to provide a stepping stone that he or she can use to step out of worthlessness or hopelessness. Two steps ahead is too much, and being behind is potentially impeding. Thus, to encourage someone to assert "I do count" after he or she has just said "I can't take it any more" would be too far ahead. Saying "It's just so awful to feel so alone and defeated" when the client has just said from this state "I need encouragement" would be too far behind.

Therapists must be aware when a growth edge has begun to emerge, when new and important ways of experiencing have emerged that forecast that a developmental shift to a higher level of organization is possible. The therapist must also be aware that the client may be cautious about moving to a new level of organization out of fear of the unknown. The therapist must therefore provide sufficient support for where the client is and be careful to communicate understanding of the fear of novelty and change and, at the same time, encourage the elaboration and expression of the associated more resilient growth edge.

ACCESSING NEEDS ALONG WITH FEELINGS IN THE STRENGTHENING OF THE SELF

The first sign of resolution of all types of self-critical splits, whether or not they involve hopelessness, is the emergence of new experiencing during the deepening phase of the work (Greenberg, 1984). At this point, it is very important that the therapist empathically affirm the client's emerging new experience; this is the beginning of the emergence of the resilient self. When clients have worked through their hopelessness or worthlessness to reach a more core adaptive emotion, they generally feel sadness or pain, or sometimes anger. With every primary emotion is an associated need (Greenberg, 2002). Needs are associated with action tendencies and often direct clients toward attaining goals that are highly relevant to their well-being. Although it is essential to recognize and affirm the client's underlying feelings, when working with splits the therapist also must listen for associated needs and direct the client to express these to the critical side in an assertive manner. Adaptive needs are at the core of the resilient self's tendency to survive and thrive. At times, the therapist can encourage a statement of need, aiming to heighten emotional arousal and to help the client empower himself or herself, to strengthen the self and promote change.

The accessing of underlying needs (e.g., for love, comfort, recognition, respect), in part affirming and relieving, may also necessitate a working through of the pain of not having had the needs met in the past. Giving them up involves grieving what was lost or was never there. Accessing needs, however, opens pathways in the brain to new emotional states and to ways to attain those states (Davidson, 2000a, 2000b). Accessing needs is a crucial step in mobilizing resilience. Self-critical splits ultimately resolve by a softening of the critical voice into a more compassionate one that acknowledges and integrates the needs, and greater self-acceptance results (see Greenberg et al., 1993).

A self-critical dialogue is helpful when the client is sufficiently integrated and has the possibility of contacting inner resources. With some clients who are highly self-annihilating or who have been severely abused, the critic is often only destructive, lacking any underlying anxiety or value that is motivating it. With such clients it is better to engage him or her in a self-soothing dialogue in which the aim is to evoke compassion for the self. It is more like starting at the dialogue point of the softened critic in the self-critical dialogue and can be necessary to protect the client from a very aggressive critic.

A method to promote self-soothing or protection (Thomas, 2003) is to ask the client to engage in a particular type of soothing dialogue with a wounded child. The therapist might ask clients how they feel toward the child, as well as what they want to say to the child and what they would do with the child if they could be there right now. Or therapists can ask clients what they would do as an adult on the child's behalf (e.g., stand up to the perpetrator, say something to the parent). The most general question to use is, "What do you want to say to that child or do with her or him right now?" The therapist also might coach by saying, "Children have to be protected," "This was not your responsibility," "Together we'll protect the boy, we'll set up a protective wall around your vulnerable self," or "Can you take care of this little girl?" This coaching can be especially important when the client was violated as a child within the family.

Using this intervention, therapists can ask their clients to imagine a child sitting in a chair in front of them, a child who has suffered what that client has suffered in life. To evoke the child's plight, the therapist might describe poignant details of the client's own history and ask, "What would you feel toward that child? What would you want to say to that child?" These questions typically evoke a compassionate response toward the child and his or her circumstances and recognition of what the child needed. The following exchange exemplifies this technique:

Client: [curling her lip] I wish that wimpy part of me would just get over it. So, my mother ignored me and my father emotionally manipulated me. So what? I should just quit whimpering.

Therapist: Imagine a 9-year-old girl sitting there. Her mother hardly ever looks at her, never talks to her. Her father is emotionally incestuous and then rejects her when he doesn't need her. What do you imagine it's like for her? What would you say to her if she was your child?

Client: I would want to comfort her. Tell her I'll protect her. She would feel so alone without anyone. She deserves more.

Therapist: Can you give her some of what she needs?

Once the client recognizes the child's needs and responds in a soothing manner to the child, then the therapist asks the client, "Could you respond to the child in you in this way?" Although clients really are adults and do not have a child within (Bradshaw, 1988), the metaphor of taking care of their "wounded child" can help them access self-soothing responses.

This intervention is best applied when a client is expressing a lot of self-condemnation or self-contempt and appears unable to access any self-soothing capacities. Timing, particularly for the questions regarding how the client feels toward the younger self, is important. It can't be asked too soon. The client needs to be somewhat differentiated from the child to be able to go there. If the feelings have not been disentangled enough, if clients are still distraught about their behavior, still feeling too ashamed, or are not able to differentiate from the parent clearly or from their fear, then they are not yet ready to begin to explore or touch feelings of compassion toward the self. For this reason, often it is better to start with another or a universal child, not with the person's own child within or with the part of the self that needs soothing. When undifferentiated clients start with their own child, the very contempt or destructive impulse that needs to be transformed is often evoked.

Even though clients understand the implication of what they are being asked to do when imagining a universal child, they seem to be better able to soothe a child in general. Once the softening has occurred in relation to a child in need, it is easier to transfer this feeling to the self. The client may, however, feel frightened at seeing a fearful child, because they do not yet have a sense that they can protect, be effective, or not get lost in the fear itself. It is helpful at this time for the therapist to become a surrogate protector. For example, when a client was frightened by the fear she saw in herself as a young child, the therapist and the client went back together to confront the abusive other. The client might imagine the therapist right behind her or even in front stopping the abusive other. The client feels safety in the therapist's presence and draws strength from this.

Practicing this technique, over time and in conjunction with the empathic soothing provided by the therapist's affective attunement, helps the client develop self-soothing capacity. This intervention is a powerful way of engendering self-compassion, which many clients lack, and directly counters self-contempt, guilt, and self-reproach. It is also often very eye-opening for clients to realize how little compassion they have felt toward themselves or were inclined to feel toward their child self in the beginning.

RESOLVING CORE HOPELESSNESS

In our research program we have been studying how clients with depression resolve the states of core hopelessness that they enter into in therapy sessions. Sicoli (2005) examined this process in the context both of chair dialogues and of empathy. *Hopelessness* was defined and rated as involving at least two statements that reflect a collapsing of the self. In these statements, the individual expresses a sense of futility about some aspects of the future and a lack of faith in the self's ability to cope. In the in-session samples collected, the clients stated that they felt such things as despair, a sense of futility, hopelessness, defeat, being beaten down, and a desire to give up or submit without a fight; some expressed suicidal thoughts. These statements were accompanied by a nonverbal collapse that reflected a defeated, depleted physical state, including tears, a lowered voice or head, slumped shoulders, sighs, eyes downcast, or shrugs. Statements in the session also reflected feelings of helplessness and powerlessness and an inability to cope with the situation and change its outcome. These statements indicated a lack of internal resources to cope (e.g., "I don't have it in me to deal with this"); a lack of self-confidence or ability (e.g., "I don't believe I could pull it off"); a lack of strength or power; a lack of control to change one's situation; feelings of being small, suffocated, immobilized, trapped, defeated, crushed, or squashed; and a lack of power or ability to act (e.g., "I can't do it"), as well as feelings of inadequacy or worthlessness. Some clients who were highly suicidal entered a more intense state that was filled with incoherence and confusion and feelings of being overwhelmed and spinning around without a sense of control; these clients require more regulation and management and were not included in our sample.

The process of resolution of the states we studied was characterized by five steps: (a) recognizing personal agency in the construction of hopelessness, (b) acknowledging an emerging new emotional experience, (c) allowing and accepting a new adaptive emotion, (d) expressing wants and needs associated with the new emotion, and (e) emergence of a resilient self-response. The first two steps were the crucial ones, necessary for the essential third step of allowing the new emotion. The latter two steps of need recognition and resilience followed fairly readily from allowing the new emotion. In the following exchange Debra moved through these steps to resolve a hopeless state during the 12th session:

Debra: [*sighs*] I just don't know what to do anymore. I don't know.

Therapist: That's sort of where you're at, right now, is not knowing? Can you tell me where you're sort of at, right in the moment?

Debra: It's just, oh, I just can't see any way out, any of it. [*sniffles*]

Therapist: So, in the sense, kind of, feeling really hopeless, right now.

Debra: Yeah, but if I was really, really hopeless, I guess I would just give up—and I'm not ready to do that, I'm not ready to just . . . [*sniffles*] to say, "I can't deal with this right now."

Therapist:	So there's still some energy in you to . . .
Debra:	Yeah . . .
Therapist:	. . . and where does that leave you?
Debra:	I don't know. I feel like it leaves me with nothing . . .
Therapist:	Yeah . . .
Debra:	. . . I have nothing, and I feel guilty that I deplete myself, and then there's nothing left for my children. I feel guilty that I, like, let that happen to them. It's like I'm pulled from all sides, and I'm stretched, like, to the limit. [*sniffles*]
Therapist:	So you're hurting, yeah. So, you're feeling really at the end of your rope, here.

Step 1: Recognizing Agency in the Construction of Hopelessness

Clients who resolve hopelessness in therapy first need to recognize and explore their own internal processes involved in the generation of hopelessness. In doing this, they move from a passive stance to an active one. No longer are they purely victims, but also agents. Clients begin to understand that they themselves contribute to maintaining their hopeless state and that their hopelessness is not merely a result of an external situation. Ultimately, through an exploration of their negative cognitions (e.g., "Nothing ever works out"), their maladaptive emotional reactions (e.g., fear, guilt), and their behaviors, clients learn how they contributed to making themselves feel hopeless. This exploration of self as agent often involves unpacking how the current action tendency of defeat is maintained by certain behaviors that prevent problem resolution (e.g., avoidance of talking to spouse, withdrawal, procrastination), leading to a hopeless feeling. The major means accessible to consciousness of maintaining hopelessness is negative cognitions, which focus on lack of belief in the self to cope, self-deprecating statements, negative beliefs about the future, perfectionistic values, and standards and self-blame. Activating the negative cognitions in the session helps induce the hopeless state. Two-chair dialogues often are very helpful to clients in experiencing their agency.

Once clients are able to acknowledge the self as an agent in contributing to the production of their hopeless state, they shift from being overwhelmed, complaining, and stuck to being more open to and focused on self-exploration. They become open to elaborating the negative cognitions and maladaptive emotional reactions and are more specific and concrete. For example, one client who had recently not been rehired to a contract position began by making himself feel hopeless in a two-chair dialogue. After the process, he said, "I am now aware of how bad I make myself feel. It is like I am my own persecutor, telling myself that I am a failure and incompetent. It's not them; it's me who is doing this to myself. It's my own expectations and perfectionism."

In the following exchange Debra worked through Step 1:

Therapist: So tell her, make her feel hopeless, tell her what's going to happen.

Debra: I don't know . . . what's happening now, I guess, [*crying*] it'd fall apart and then it would get worse, and you won't be able to handle it.

Therapist: Uhmm, what's sort of the core, the worst of it for you right now? What would you say is the worst, right here, right now?

Debra: [*crying*] I don't know, I couldn't say . . . It's just the world, everything, I don't know what is, it's all—it's all very bad.

Therapist: Yeah, so, feeling very hopeless—OK, I'm just going, we're just going to try this—OK?—for a minute, so come over here . . . It's OK, this chair.

Debra: Yeah . . .

Therapist: OK, I'm just going to ask you, Debra, to try to put yourself in that chair and imagine, you know, this kind of hopeless feeling, this hopeless part of you, this wounded part of you, and we're going to try to see if we could access how that gets going. So, can you kind of imagine yourself there . . . What I'm wondering is, what are the kinds of thoughts that you say to yourself that make you feel hopeless?

Debra: [*breaking up in tears*] Mm-hm, the fact that things keep coming up over and over again, and I think, I think that I'm gaining ground, but then all these weird, awful situations come up again, and I see it again and again, and then I think, like, when is it ever going to end? Is there any end to . . . is . . . maybe there isn't . . . [*crying*]

Therapist: So you're telling yourself it won't end. Tell her.

Debra: You don't really have what it takes to ever win . . .

Therapist: Yeah . . .

Debra: . . . because, I don't know why, but it's just, means that, things are just going to keep coming up, all over and over and over.

Therapist: So tell her, make her feel hopeless, tell her what's going to happen.

Debra: [*crying*] It just looks like these things will come up time and time again, and over and over, and there's so many of them. You won't be able to handle it.

Therapist:	"You won't be able to handle it."
Debra:	[*sniffles*] I feel scared that all these things are pushing me and pushing me down again, and I'm not going to . . . I'm not going to have a little bit of help anymore. [*crying*]
Therapist:	OK, if you could come over here—I think this is actually where you are right now . . . You're just afraid, really frightened. Tell her about your fear.
Debra:	I'm just afraid that it's going to go on and on, and I won't be able to cope with it, and . . . [*sighs*] I know that it's going to go on, there's so much more to deal with, there's so much more ahead of me. [*crying*]
Therapist:	Just so very frightened that you won't have the strength . . .
Debra:	[*sniffles*] I'm scared, and just everything, everything is just . . . it keeps . . . Different things keep coming up, like how the children, [*crying*] sometimes they turn on me, and they talk to me, and I just think, my god, what's it going to be like as they get to be adults? Am I going to have a horrible relationship with them, too? And . . . am I even losing them? I'll have nothing. [*crying*]
Therapist:	OK, come over here. [*Debra switches*] Somehow, making yourself feel like you're going to lose everything . . .
Debra:	Yeah, that you're going to lose everything, it's happening, and, yeah, it's coming from me, I'm causing it, because I can't deal with it.
Therapist:	Tell her what "you're" doing.
Debra:	[*crying*] You're allowing things to happen and . . . You're allowing bad things to happen.
Therapist:	"It's all your fault"—so that's what you tell her—you tell yourself, somehow, that "It's all your fault."
Debra:	You won't be able to deal with any of all of this.
Therapist:	Come over here, Debra. [*Debra switches*] How do you respond to her? How do you respond to that?
Debra:	I don't know. All I can say [*breaking up*] is that, like, I will try again. That's all I can do.

Step 2: Acknowledging New Emotional Experience

In Step 2, clients who progress to resolution then recognize and identify a new emerging feeling other than hopelessness (e.g., sadness, pain, anger, shame, fear). This recognition often occurred in response to identifying agency and negative cognitions. The client initially experiences the new feeling a little, but often not fully. The feeling is undifferentiated, and there is often some confusion about what is being felt. Sometimes, but not always, the first underlying feelings contacted are the maladaptive shame and fear that lie on the edge of the hopelessness. These maladaptive emotions then need to be acknowledged and worked through.

Clients with simpler, reactive depressions do not necessarily go into more core maladaptive emotions but rather arrive directly at an adaptive feeling. Clients with depression, however, must work through hopelessness to arrive ultimately at a more adaptive emotion. The new emotion often emerges in a tentative manner, indicating that the current feeling is new and was not previously accessible to the client. The emerging new emotional way is a core adaptive emotion. The adaptive emotions that emerge are usually sadness and or pain when the hopelessness is in the context of internal conflicts; in the context of interpersonal conflicts, sadness and pain plus anger emerge. The client must experience the emotion, not talk about not wanting to feel it. In the following example, the client does not acknowledge the new emotion:

> Client: It just feels really negative, and all bad feelings, and I just hate to feel like that. I wish I didn't feel like that.
>
> Therapist: You want to escape from this feeling.
>
> Client: Yeah, mm-hm, I just don't even . . . I hate those feelings. I don't want to feel like that. [sniffle]
>
> Therapist: Mm-hm.

In contrast, the following segment shows the client readily acknowledging a new experience:

> Therapist: What do you feel about all this?
>
> Client: [crying] Sad. Very sad. It's been so difficult.

To promote resolution, the therapist needs to help the client stay focused on this emerging feeling and help clarify and develop it. Confirming the validity of clients' hopelessness by acknowledging what it was they feel hopeless about and why helps strengthen them. Therapists' attunement to what the client is feeling and their communication of this understanding and of the validity of clients' feeling is in and of itself strengthening of the self and often is enough to help access clients' resilience. Otherwise, therapists need to work more specifically on accessing new feelings. Focusing clients' attention on possibilities within their proximal zone of development is one important general principle of accessing new feeling (further ways of accessing new feelings are outlined in chapter 12).

In the following exchange, Debra contacted a new emotion through the therapist's focus on her sigh. Debra's acknowledgment and allowing of the feeling, as well as the next step of accessing the need, occurred together, as they often do. At the end of the exchange the therapist shifted the dialogue to a potential for self-soothing.

Debra: I don't know. I don't know how to get the peace I need. . . [*sighs*] I don't know how to do that.

Therapist: There was a big sigh there—what was in that sigh?

Debra: Just the wish that I could get there, and I could get someplace where . . .

Therapist: OK, that's coming from here . . .

Debra: . . . It would be restful. I just need to get somewhere where I can slow down and rest. [*sniffles*]

Therapist: OK, this is the critical side over here. I want you to picture this side over here and tell this side of Debra that you want some rest, you just need—tell her what it is that you're saying now.

Debra: I just need peace. I can't take it anymore. I can't deal with it. I'm not able to cope with it . . . [*tears*] and so I just need it to go away . . . [*sighs*] and it won't go away, so I just have to find some way to . . .

Therapist: I'd like you to stay with the need for some peace. Can you make it a little more concrete and give her something that you need?

Debra: I need all the things that make me able to cope, [*breaking up into tears*] and I don't know where they are anymore, and I can't find them . . .

Therapist: It's hard . . .

Debra: . . . and it's all so far away.

Therapist: You seem lost, really lost, like a piece of you inside is just feeling so lost.

Debra: [*deep sigh*] I just feel now that I'm coming, like, I don't know, I'm afraid I'm coming to a crisis and that something's going to happen. I'm fearful of that, and yet—I don't know.

Therapist: It's scary. Let's just try to stay with that need. I felt that you're . . . you had a little bit of connection there with what you need.

Debra: [*crying*] Well, there feels like there's a me who is very far away and disconnected from all this, and I think that is where my strength is, and that is what I have to find.

Therapist:	Yeah, yeah, yeah, OK, OK—Can you come over here? [*Debra switches*] Can you put that "you," put that part of you in that chair, Debra, that little part of you? Can you imagine that part of you that's so far away? Can you tell me what you see?

Step 3: Allowing and Accepting the New Emotion

In clients who resolve their hopelessness, the next step is a clear allowing and accepting of the new adaptive emotional experience. This step is crucial to resolution. The client experiences and allows the full intensity of the new emotion and differentiates it. Clients shift from a detached, more conceptual description or a partial acknowledgment of their experience to a more focused and authentically felt experience. Feelings of core anger, pain, and sadness are experienced, intermingled with expressions of unmet needs. In essence, clients begin to truly feel and accept the emerging adaptive emotions and are able to express these emotions by both nonverbal and verbal means. Through this more focused contact with the current emotional experience, clients begin to explore its meaning in more depth and with more specificity. Acceptance of these emerging adaptive emotions is expressed in explicit ways, such as by describing a sense of entitlement or stating that the feeling was valuable and important, and in implicit ways, by losing the sense of a collapsing self or by ceasing to interrupt their adaptive emotional experience.

In the following exchange Debra allowed her adaptive sadness and felt compassion, but she also continued to feel her maladaptive fear:

Debra:	[*sniffles, breaking up*] I don't know, I just see a little girl who never really dealt with everything, and she's a really nice girl who's very sensitive, just like nature and sunshine, and I just want so badly . . . [*crying*] to get . . . [*sighs*]
Therapist:	Tell me more.
Debra:	. . . for that part to stand up and . . . [*crying*]
Therapist:	You want her to stand up . . . you want her to be heard, is that it?
Debra:	Yeah.
Therapist:	Can you tell her, "I want you to stand up"? Can you tell her, "I love you, I care about you"? Can you tell her that?
Debra:	I care about you, and I really believe that that's the best part of me that's being lost.
Therapist:	"You are the best part of me, you are being lost, I'm afraid you're being lost." Tell her.

Debra:	I'm afraid you're going to be lost, and I will never be able to find you again.
Therapist:	I want you to come over here. I want you to be that girl, Debra. How does she respond? How does that little girl respond?
Debra:	I feel so sad and alone.
Therapist:	Tell her some more.
Debra:	I don't know. I don't know. She wants to, but she feels all tied up and very, very far away.
Therapist:	Can you tell her that you're very frightened?
Debra:	I'm just really scared . . .
Therapist:	Tell her what you . . .
Debra:	. . . I feel I don't have the strength. I'm just floating around there without support, and . . . [*sighs*]
Therapist:	Tell her what you're afraid of.
Debra:	I'm just afraid that things that will happen today . . . will happen, I guess, to me. I'm afraid that I'll just be, I don't know, I don't know what, I don't know. I feel like she is pulling away.

Step 4: Expressing Wants and Needs Associated With the New Emotion

Step 4 marks the beginning of the emergence of resilience in the self. The wants and needs that begin to emerge with the expression of deeper, often painful feelings are more clearly articulated and more forcefully stated. Clients show acceptance of their emotion and need through the expression of need entitlement. For example, one client, feeling sad about lack of support from his wife, then stated, "I deserve to be supported and cared for." Needs that clients once dismissed or tentatively stated they now express as valid and legitimate in a convincing manner. New emotional experience helps strengthen and consolidate the sense of self, and the self's needs are asserted in a clear and sustained manner. The self feels entitled to have its needs met and begins to move from feeling helpless to feeling empowered. In the following segment, Debra contacted a need to have fun and a sense of deserving this:

Therapist:	Can you come over here, can you just come over here? This is hard, but you're making some good progress here. Can you still picture that little girl here? Can you still picture that little girl here? Can you tell her . . . tell her that you don't want her to go away?

Debra:	I don't want you to go away, because I feel that that's all I have; I need you.
Therapist:	Tell her what you love about her.
Debra:	[*crying*] I just love that you're just a simple loving person, and I . . . [*breaking up crying*]
Therapist:	What does she look like?
Debra:	I don't know. I don't know.
Therapist:	Kind of fuzzy—you don't have a clear sense, but there's something you can see . . .
Debra:	I just see, like, a brightness, dark hair, long dark hair, and just a brightness . . .
Therapist:	. . . and a beautiful great spirit—you long to hold her and have her with you . . .
Debra:	Yeah . . .
Therapist:	. . . you long to be able to speak from her . . .
Debra:	Yeah, I wish I was her, I wish I was that. [*sniffling*]
Therapist:	You are . . . she's . . .
Debra:	I am that . . . I know it is, it's there, but . . . [*sighs, sniffles*]
Therapist:	Is she afraid of something?
Debra:	I don't know. I'm not sure. I guess she is afraid, and she won't come out, and she—I guess it's "afraid," a fear of, like, being, like I always say, pushed over, run over, . . .
Therapist:	Mm-hm . . .
Debra:	. . . stepped on, tread upon, hurt . . .
Therapist:	Can you tell her that you're sorry that you haven't been able to protect her?
Debra:	I am very sorry [*breaking up*] that I haven't been able to protect her.
Therapist:	Can you tell her that you want to be able to hold her and keep her?
Debra:	I do want to nurture you and . . . [*deep breath*]
Therapist:	Can you come over here? What does she have to say?
Debra:	Just the same thing, that she will try again, and she will . . . she's always there, she won't really ever disappear . . . [*breaks up*] but . . .

Therapist:	"I won't disappear, I won't leave you."
Debra:	Yeah—but someday, I know I'm going to be able to get back to her.
Therapist:	Uh-huh.
Debra:	I think it's going to come with age . . .
Therapist:	Uh-huh . . .
Debra:	. . . once I've dealt with other things, I guess . . . [*deep sigh*]
Therapist:	Can you tell me what you're experiencing right now, Debra?
Debra:	I'm just feeling like, yeah, I can try again, and I think I can—when I become really, really quiet, I think I can find her, and I think I really do get strength from her.
Therapist:	Yeah, I do too . . .
Debra:	. . . and I don't even realize that I do . . .
Therapist:	Yeah, yeah, I think you do.
Debra:	I'm so confused that I don't realize that really, I am accessing that part, and . . .
Therapist:	Yeah, yeah, when all the things are rushing around in your head and there's so many things from the outside coming in to hurt you, to wound you, stab you with their little knives, it's so hard to just shut that out and go out into that part of you. Do you think you could try? I mean, is that something you feel a little more confident in?
Debra:	Yeah, I'm going to try and be quiet and access that part of me.
Therapist:	I'm getting the sense that there's a lot there—that you've only, sort of, you've touched the surface of it, but with the picture of her being someone bright with dark hair, there seems like there's a lot there. I've heard a lot in your emotion . . . uhmm . . . and it reminded me of the time before, when you were in that chair talking about things about you that you had as a young person.
Debra:	Like, there is a time of my life when I think that person was much more . . .
Therapist:	. . . predominant . . .
Debra:	. . . predominant, and I think I just have to remember those times and think everything was totally different, and those are things that affected also . . . the way that I feel and . . . I

just long to have fun, too, it's been so long since I've just been playful. [*breaks up in tears*]

Therapist: Can you say more about that?

Debra: I just really . . . that part of me just wants to . . . I'm easily contented, easily happy person, and I long for . . . to be able to just have fun and be carefree, that feeling . . .

Therapist: Yeah, there's that part of you that's just . . .

Debra: . . . and I think I deserve it, I think I should reward myself . . .

Therapist: Yeah . . .

Debra: . . . but I don't know how to do it. I just haven't found how to do that.

Step 5: Emergence of a Resilient Self-Response

In this final step, clients finally express greater optimism about the future and feel more confident in their ability to cope. Clients move from feeling hopeless and helpless to feeling hopeful and empowered. They exhibit more assertion, both verbally and nonverbally, in their ability to refute self-criticisms or negative beliefs. Clients sometimes express a new perspective or way of looking at the situation or self that is positive and growth enhancing.

In this process, clients thus shift from a hopeless and helpless stance to one of hope and strength. This emerging resilient status is usually characterized by several of the following: shift in emotional state, shift in self-belief, emergence of a new perspective, coping possibility, hope for the future, self-soothing behaviors, ability to maintain strength in the face of self-criticism or perceived rejection or criticism from others, a healthy letting go of unrealistic expectations of self or other, and expressed intentions to change. Clients also exhibit a shift in nonverbal behaviors, including assertive voice, change in posture, absence of tears, or renewed energy, and this resilient stance is sustained through to the end of the session. The following exchange shows how Debra completed this step:

Therapist: It doesn't have to be all at once, step by step . . .

Debra: Yeah . . .

Therapist: Could you come over here? We're almost out of time. Could you just imagine that she's there, saying that she wants to have fun—can you give her a little bit of that? What can you offer her right now?

Debra: What I can think of is like—the closest I can come is, like, in my garden, and nature . . .

Therapist:	Mm-hm . . .
Debra:	. . . and putting my hands in the earth and . . .
Therapist:	Mm-hm . . . So you can do that, put your hands in your garden, give yourself, give this joyful, lovely part of you, this beautiful shining light that's inside you, some room to grow, to gain some strength, by going into your garden, by touching nature and feeling the natural earth and the flowers about to grow and so on, and just feeling that that'll give you a little bit of strength . . .
Debra:	Yeah . . .
Therapist:	. . . allow that part of you . . .
Debra:	Mm-hm . . .
Therapist:	You can do that . . .
Debra:	Yeah . . .
Therapist:	Can you tell her that?
Debra:	That is something that I can do, and I will do, and I'll try to pursue the other things, music, and different things that bring me joy . . .
Therapist:	You have a lot of things that you can do, there's a lot there. Right now, you'll start by just allowing Debra some time in your garden, because eventually that's what's going to give you the strength . . .
Debra:	Mm-hm . . .
Therapist:	. . . the armor to arm that wounded animal, to arm yourself so that when you're out in the world, where horrible people exist, in the world, for whatever reason, and somehow have the power to immobilize you . . .
Debra:	Mm-hm . . .
Therapist:	. . . to build that shield to protect you—yeah, I get the feeling, I get—far away, but it's also not that far away that it's impossible . . .
Debra:	Yeah . . .
Therapist:	. . . maybe today, you saw that it is possible to begin to find that side of you, that it's not as far as you thought.
Debra:	Yeah, it is . . . I did get that feeling that it's there, and I will continue to access it, and I do, and I don't even realize that I do.
Therapist:	Mm-hm . . .

Debra:	I just have to consciously, really put an effort in . . .
Therapist:	Yeah . . .
Debra:	. . . to nurture that side of me because . . .
Therapist:	Mm-hm . . .
Debra:	. . . that will be the side that will save me.
Therapist:	Mm-hm . . . yeah.
Debra:	I think I really do have to consciously, now, put away the other things . . .
Therapist:	Mm-hm . . .
Debra:	I think I really have to, I think I—I'm not going to turn the TV on anymore, . . .
Therapist:	Sort of . . .
Debra:	I think anything that I can control, I should control, and . . .
Therapist:	Yeah, yeah, give yourself permission to do that, that's what you're saying, sounds like you can . . .
Debra:	Mm-hmm . . .
Therapist:	You don't have to . . .
Debra:	No . . .
Therapist:	. . . face every single one of those things . . .
Debra:	Mm-hm. . . some I can't control . . .
Therapist:	Right . . .
Debra:	. . . but anything that I think I should consciously think about . . .
Therapist:	Yeah . . .
Debra:	. . . what I do . . .
Therapist:	Sort of, while you're building your strength back up, you don't have to get yourself slapped in the face by every bad thing.
Debra:	Yeah.
Therapist:	Well, I guess this is a good point to stop. I'm glad you were able to make a little bit of connection today . . .
Debra:	Yeah, I feel I did . . .
Therapist:	. . . of this side of you. I think you're a wonderful person, Debra. I just want you to know that I'm sort of there, rooting for you . . .

Debra:	Yeah . . .
Therapist:	. . . as you go through this tough time, very tough time—OK?
Debra:	OK.

ADAPTIVE HOPELESSNESS

It is important to note that some forms of core hopelessness and helplessness are primary adaptive responses, and these need to be accepted as a crucial first step in change. It appears generally that hopelessness is undesirable and that it is good to feel hopeful. Competence is similarly viewed as good and helplessness as bad. In spite of this, giving up a useless struggle against impossible odds produces adaptive feelings of hopelessness or helplessness, and allowing and experiencing adaptive hopelessness or helplessness sometimes is essential to change. These adaptive forms of hopelessness are responses to impossible situations, rather than to fragile self-responses. Facing this form of primary hopelessness, rather than avoiding it, involves a paradoxical change process. If the therapist is able to help such clients give up struggling against the inevitable and accept feeling hopeless or helpless, this will lead them to let go of unworkable strategies or unattainable goals. Acknowledging feelings of hopelessness or helplessness thus involves giving up futile efforts and reorganizing. For example, a client who accessed in therapy for the first time a sense of hopelessness about ever achieving his professional goals decided that it was useless to keep trying to reach the unattainable. At the end of the session, the client remarked that despite the pain of loss, he felt more at peace.

Feelings of adaptive hopelessness or helplessness in these and all situations are not rational statements about reality, but rather feelings. They are not conclusions that will result in action. They do not necessarily mean lasting depression or despair. Rather, to feel them is to accept them and the evaluation that a goal is unattainable. The acceptance of these feelings is the beginning of taking responsibility for new efforts and new goals. Facing hopelessness is not believing "I am hopeless," but rather receiving feedback from one's body that a particular effort is not working and that one's efforts to overcome obstacles are of no avail. Helplessness means recognizing there is nothing one can do. Contacting and accepting the experience of the futility of the struggle is often a critical step in an emotional change process involving facing what has been fearfully avoided, letting go of unworkable solutions, and setting the stage for creative reorganization.

12

EVOKING BLOCKED EMOTION: TWO-CHAIR ENACTMENTS AND UNFINISHED BUSINESS DIALOGUES

Efforts to evoke emotion often bring into focus clients' means of preventing or interrupting emerging experience. We view defenses against or avoidance of emotion as efforts at self-protection. Perls, Hefferline, and Goodman (1951) suggested that by identifying with resistances, they turn into assistances. This process involves acceptance of what is. Thus, it helps to recognize the positive, protective functions of the interruptive process, bring it into awareness, and have the client identify with this process as part of the self.

As blocks to experience and expression emerge, therapists need to focus on them and help clients become aware of and experience how they interrupt their feelings or needs. Interventions need to explore the various ways clients block experience right in the session. Blocks range from dissociation to stifling tears to deflecting conversation. Helping clients first become aware that they avoid their experience, and then of how they avoid or interrupt their experience, helps them become aware of their agency in the process of blocking their emotions. This awareness, in the long run, helps them allow the emotional experience that is avoided.

A major goal of emotion-focused therapy (EFT) is to help clients become aware of how they block (Greenberg & Safran, 1987). There are two different aspects of blocking—blocking of expression, or inhibition, and blocking of experience, or avoidance. Blocking of either type involves an activity, even if it has become automatic. Therapy helps to deautomatize, or disable the automatic nature of, the blocking activity. When clients express an emotion, their musculature participates in the emotion as the physiological aspect of that event. When they block the emotion, they also do so with the complicity of their muscles. The client is all set to express that emotion but holds the expression in check. The "all set" implies a continuing desire to complete. Perpetually stiffened muscles, however, keep the client from feeling the sadness, rage, desperation, or depression. It is important to note that this is different from storing emotion that then needs to be got rid of. Therapists then need to work with both the wish to express and the wish to inhibit and to give both tendencies a voice (verbally or nonverbally).

First comes the awareness of blocking and then deautomatizing by bringing the blocking process more into the foreground, turning it into an activity, and exaggerating it. The therapist's cue for undoing blocks is seeing when a client mobilizes some energy, however slight the degree. For example, a client might look straight into the eyes of the therapist or be able to disagree or say no. The therapist then highlights these moments and leads the client to awareness of the process—how he or she mobilized energy in this specific moment, what helped do it. The client may be able to experience this as a success; it feels more alive and feels good. Slowly, in this way, clients begin to find their own way to mobilize energy, confirm themselves, and take action.

Exploring and overcoming interruptive processes are important subgoals of therapy for depression, and therapist and client need to establish collaboration to do so and to agree on the means by which it will be done. By definition, facing what is dreaded can be threatening. Collaboration to do this provides safety and minimizes the development of opposition, misalliances, or treatment impasses. In EFT for depression, the therapist seeks to be empathically attuned and highly attentive to the core growth-oriented part of the client. It is through the experience of this safety and attunement with the therapist that clients often are able to undo interruption, let down their protective barriers, and access a core affective experience. A client with major interruptions and avoidances often shows little or no emotion with which to empathize. Often, then, it is very difficult to set up the type of intimate therapeutic bond that is essential for treatment with highly avoidant clients, because their ability and desire to bond are not readily available. Methods that help unblock such clients are particularly helpful, because they make a therapeutic bond and connection with the therapist possible.

It is essential, however, to ensure that clients have sufficient internal support for making contact with emotions before the blocks are undone and emotions are evoked and experienced. Some clients become very tense at the prospect of encountering their feelings. The therapist needs to empathize with the fear and understand that the block is a protection and that more support is needed. On one hand, more relational support in the form of validation and trust building is indicated. On the other hand, building of internal supports by a slower, incremental approach to emotion helps clients deal with the anxiety. A type of graded exposure or desensitization process is most useful in helping clients develop support to approach and tolerate their emotions. The therapist also helps clients mobilize internal support by suggesting, for example, that clients breathe, put their feet on the ground, and describe what they are experiencing to increase contact with sensory reality. In addition, therapists can ask clients to judge when they are ready to move forward to make sure they feel in control. The goal is to melt defensive and protective barriers, not tear them down. This melting is done both with a balance of empathic support and awareness of the presence of the block and the manner of blocking. Identifying with the resistances and accepting and re-owning them as a protective activity also help clients gain the support they need to eventually let go of the interruptions.

Another method of dealing with blocks is interpretation or confrontation of the block. Are confrontations helpful in overcoming blocks? It is important to note first that confrontation is not necessarily aggressive, and, similarly, that empathy is not necessarily always safe. Empathy in our view is a very potent, powerful way of relating and can be very confronting at times. Thus, reflecting the affect that is missing can be as powerful as confronting the block that is protecting against it. The focus of the two interventions, empathy for what is blocked and confrontation of the block, however, are very different. Empathy attempts to ally against the resistance through the affirmation of the growth-oriented healthy strivings of the client, whereas confrontation directly challenges the resistance. Confronting resistance tends to raise anxiety and must be used judiciously, as the goal in EFT is to provide safety. Positive confrontations such as "You seem to lose your strength or "It becomes so hard to stay calm" are better than negative confrontations such as "You are crippled" or " You overreact." Complete elimination of confrontation from a therapeutic repertoire, however, can lead to a kind of therapeutic neglect out of a fear of being too challenging.

If the therapist bottles up irritation with the client and then as a last resort confronts, the irritation comes out, and the confrontation may be prematurely challenging. It is better to address issues of interruption of emotion and lack of collaboration as they come up throughout the treatment. Confronting interventions need to be done with appropriate timing and with the client as a partner in a collaborative process, and always with an understanding of the protective function of the block. Also, confrontation should be an intervention of last resort following a sequence. The therapist seeks to promote first awareness of the blocking process, then clarification, and only then challenge, timed appropriately and in partnership with the client. The following exchange occurred with a client who collapsed into a dependent help-less state:

> *Therapist:* What happens? You become a little child; you seem to lose all your power. [*gently confronts because the client seems stuck*]
>
> *Client:* I can't stand up for myself.
>
> *Therapist:* How come? What happens?
>
> *Client:* I don't know.
>
> *Therapist:* It's like you lose your voice, you become little. Can you stand up for yourself?

TWO-CHAIR ENACTMENTS OF THE SELF-INTERRUPTION OF EMOTION

A particularly helpful intervention for working with blocks to emotion is to have clients enact the process of interruption in an imaginary dialogue between both sides of the personality (Greenberg, Rice, & Elliott, 1993). This two-chair enactment of the interruption of emotion is different from two-chair dialogue for self-criticism, which was discussed in chapter 11. A two-chair enactment is best implemented when the experiencing part of the client begins to express an emotion or associated need or action that is inter-rupted by a self-censoring part of the client that attempts to prevent the expression or experience. In comparison to self-critical splits, markers of self-interruptive splits typically have a larger nonverbal, bodily aspect and some-times are expressed purely nonverbally, such as a headache or tightness in the chest. The therapist's goals in self-interruptive work are both to heighten awareness of the interruptive process and to help the client access and allow blocked or disavowed internal experience.

In a two-chair enactment, at a marker of self-interruption, clients are encouraged to enact how they stop themselves from feeling, to verbalize the particular injunctions used, or to exaggerate the muscular constrictions in-volved in the interruption (Greenberg et al., 1993). Eventually this provokes a response, often a rebellion against the suppression, and the experiencing self challenges the injunctions, restraining thoughts, or muscular blocks, and the suppressed emotion bursts through the constrictions. This process helps undo the depression.

Clients also can be helped by use of this intervention to get past sec-ondary emotional reactions that block their more primary feelings to evoke the more primary feelings. Thus, guilt about being angry at a parent may block acknowledgment of anger and leave the client feeling hopeless, and fear of rejection or anxiety over abandonment may interrupt assertive ex-pression. Shame over loss of control or weakness may interrupt adaptive grieving. Therapists acknowledge but do not intensify these secondary bad feelings. Rather, they have clients enact the process by which they interrupt the more core feelings. Clients are asked to provoke guilt or shame in themselves until they access a more core feeling and fight back. Evocation thus always involves attending to and developing the more primary unacknowledged emotions. Adaptive primary emotions like anger need to be carefully distinguished from defensive secondary emotions like anger that covers hurt or unmet longings. Suppressed adaptive primary sadness that promotes the work of grieving must be distinguished from secondary helpless and depressive weeping that exacerbates feelings of hopelessness and victimization.

Self-interruptions are common in depression; clients either hold back the expression and full intensity of their sadness or anger or have trouble accessing or stating needs. Clients with depression interrupt the expression of needs because they are afraid of not having them met and dread the associated feelings of devastation and disappointment. Or they block feelings for fear of their consequences. Men who are depressed often cannot express anger for fear of their own destructiveness, or they see anger as defeat and do not want to acknowledge weakness. They see acknowledging anger as admitting that something got to them and as no longer being in control. Women often fear that their anger will damage relationships or will be seen as not acceptable. Clients also interrupt full expression of their emotions and needs due to fears of loss of approval or of attachments. Overregulation of emotion is common in simple depressions due to catastrophizing about the consequences of expressing emotion or out of guilt about acknowledging or expressing the emotion. Experiencing and expressing anger and sadness are often a cure of more simple reactive depressions.

The most common indicators of self-interruption in depression are resignation, hopelessness, and feeling trapped. These are often accompanied by physical symptoms, such as feeling oppressed, burdened, or blocked, or tightness in the chest or a pain in the neck. In these cases, the primary feelings or needs have been so efficiently interrupted that they are not in awareness. For example, Tony was a 40-year-old man feeling trapped in his marriage and his job. He was evidently angry by the scowl on his face whenever he talked about these situations, but his reported experience was one of lethargy, tiredness, and headaches. He said that maybe it was physical. In the session he said that his neck hurt and that he had a feeling of heaviness in his shoulders, like a large weight that was making him slump. Subsequent two-chair enactment revealed these experiences to be symptoms of the self-interruption process of feeling trapped. He was interrupting his anger. Tony's self-interruption process in a session is evident in the following extract from early in therapy, and the therapist focuses first on simple awareness of the interruption of emotion:

> *Tony:* Well, a lot of times I would literally . . . uhmm . . . look at myself as bad . . .

Therapist:	Uh-huh . . .
Tony:	. . . so that it did hurt. I would literally think of myself . . .
Therapist:	Mm-hm . . .
Tony:	. . . as not so great . . .
Therapist:	Yeah . . .
Tony:	. . . so that I would deserve whatever I was getting.
Therapist:	Un-huh, uh-huh. So, yeah, so yeah, it was, "The treatment was so bad, that for it to make any sense to me, I had to start to feel like I was a bad little boy and that I deserved it." How terrible for a little boy to take that all. [*pause*] How do you feel as you're thinking about all this now?
Tony:	Well, I feel sad.
Therapist:	Yeah.
Tony:	I feel . . .
Therapist:	Yeah, you feel sad . . .
Tony:	But I almost want to cut it off. [*clear marker of interruption*]
Therapist:	Yeah . . .
Tony:	I want to . . .
Therapist:	I imagine the pain starts to come up again, and it's just overwhelming.
Tony:	Yeah.
Therapist:	Right.
Tony:	I don't . . . I don't want to deal with it.
Therapist:	Uh-huh, yeah. So you want to just cut it off. I guess it starts . . . you start to feel it, if the sadness comes up, and as you remember what it was like and how difficult it was not to be loved. All of that pain is just too much, right? You're saying, "I don't want to be me, I don't want to feel it." [*pause*] Yeah, so what happens? Is it like you start to feel a wave of something, and then you . . .
Tony:	Well, I get a headache, I get . . . my eyes become really foggy.

Fear of Emotion

In trauma-related depression, processes such as shutting down, going numb, and dissociating, which were possibly adaptive at the time of the traumatic event, now interfere with the integration of the traumatic experience. These blocks, too, need to be overcome. Such clients are extremely blocked and seem to be unable to respond, no matter what interventions are tried. They remain detached, or their terror at looking at feelings creates an inability to explore further. This seems to occur around exploring the physiology and impulses related especially to anger, but also to sadness and pain that they feel will shatter them (Bolger, 1999).

Weston (2005) conducted a grounded theory analysis of depressed clients' video recall of nine self-interruptive events. Clients reviewed videotape segments of moments of interruption and recalled their subjective experience at the time of interruption. The category "fear of emotion" emerged as a core category describing their experience. All participants recalled the experience of fear of emotion, but the nature and quality of the fear varied across participants. Some feared a particular emotion, such as anger, whereas others feared a number of different emotions, such as anger, hurt, or sadness. Four subcategories were conceptualized to capture different facets of the experience of fear of emotion: fear of the unknown, fear of losing control, fear in the therapy relationship, and fear of self-annihilation.

Three clients expressed a fear of the unknown qualities of emotional experience. For some, it was the unsymbolized nature of emotional experience that was frightening. One participant described fear of an unknown "wave" of feeling or "it" that he needed to "define" before he could allow himself to be "within it." Another woman recalled, "I really wasn't feeling, and that's the thing that frightens me. I know I was feeling, but I was not aware of what I was feeling . . . I'm starting to realize that there are a lot of feelings I can't name and I want to because . . . then they don't frighten me."

For another participant, fear came from not knowing where the experience and expression of emotion might lead. One participant recalled his fear of expressing anger: "I really didn't feel like yelling it . . . I was afraid of something happening. . . . It was still withheld somehow . . . I was afraid to let it go right over the top . . . not knowing what it would do or what it was like."

The experience of emotion was overwhelming for a number of participants, and this was related to their fear of losing control. They recalled the unanticipated and sudden experience of emotion, together with an increase in physiological arousal. One participant recalled his experience of "old reactions to the old hurts, the physical reactions . . . in the chest, occasionally in my stomach, and I feel a flush in the face, and my eyes start to tear a little, and it's also a case of . . . starting to lose control." Another participant recalled the explosive quality of the experience of emotion and the related fear of "being out of control": "I felt it several times . . . the fear that 'Oh my god, it's gonna explode right here in the room, and they're gonna have to take me away in a white jacket.'"

Some participants recalled feeling fear of emotion in the context of the therapy relationship. One woman recalled a fear of experiencing emotional intimacy with her therapist. "Whenever she asks me, 'How are you feeling right now, at this moment?' that's very frightening, threatening." She described the fear as being related to her sense that the therapist "was getting very close to something uncomfortable." Furthermore, the therapist's "close attention" to her was also new, and she felt "frightened and threatened" by it. It was as if by allowing herself to feel close to her therapist, she was also moving closer to her own emotional experience. Other participants also recalled feeling fear or anxiety in response to the therapist's labeling or inquiring specifically about emotional experience. One woman recalled, "It scares me when she says 'hurt'" because "I don't want to go there." Another male participant recalled, "I don't know how to respond when she says, 'Oh, it seems quite sad.' I was just afraid to say, 'Well, yeah, it is sad,' and I caught myself doing that a number of times." Another participant speculated that his feelings of "apprehension and a lot of anxiety" when he felt anger were related to "a want not to have to take it [the anger] out on the therapist."

A fear of dying was a theme in some participants' accounts of their fear of emotion. One woman recalled that while she experienced sadness, "there was a churning in my belly again. . . . My heart was racing. . . . There's a fear there, also, that no one's gonna help me with this. I might be scared to death." Another participant described the fear that she might die if she allowed herself to experience a "very deep sense of pain and grief. . . . My feeling at that time was, if I let this feeling go and I really cry, I will break. I will just break. Like I might die because I won't be able to stand it . . . the pain." A male participant drew on images from the movie *Alien* to describe the potentially destructive force of his anger as he recalled his fear of self-annihilating anger: "That's exactly what it reminded me of. This guy, he's got this thing growing inside of him, and suddenly it destructively chews and gnaws its way out and kills him in the process."

A task analysis of the clients' tape-assisted recall of the moment-by-moment experience of self-interruption events described the steps of the process of interruption, revealing that an initial impulse or expression of emotion was countered by an initial opposition to impulse or expression (Weston, 2005). At this stage in the process of interruption, the desire to express emotion was immediately met by a lack of desire; acknowledgment or expression of emotion was countered by minimization, automatic cessation of feeling, or physical control (e.g., swallowing sadness). Clients were able to report that they were interrupting emotion, indicating that the interruption of emotion was available to awareness. As the clients further differentiated their opposition to emotion in the therapy session, they described an awareness of vulnerable self-experience that they were trying to block, often fear or anxiety and shame or embarrassment.

In response to the experience of fearful or shameful self-experience, clients engaged consciously in avoidant acts of self-protection and acts of self-control. Avoidant acts were characterized by "flight" from the experience, such as telling the self to run and "hide," numbing, or splitting off pain. Acts of self-control involved moving toward emotional experience with the intention of controlling it. Often, acts of self-control involved an invalidating approach to emotion, such as an attacking, critical approach to anger or sadness. Physiological control and beliefs about the need to control emotion also followed from the intention to control emotion. Finally, the result of avoiding and controlling emotion led to an awareness of depleted self-experience. Clients acknowledged a sense of depletion involving one or more of the following: helplessness, resignation, hopelessness, physical pain, tiredness, numbness, withdrawal of attention, emptiness, confusion, bad feeling, negative beliefs about self, and a weakened sense of self. Each client's pattern of interruption was iterative and idiosyncratic.

These analyses showed that avoidance and self-control in the face of fear of emotion rob clients of their vitality and leave them feeling a sense of physical, emotional, and psychological depletion (Weston, 2005). These findings suggest that the resolution of fear of emotion in ways that do not involve avoidant and self-controlling behaviors is an important focus of change.

Two-chair enactment for self-interruption splits is a good means of working with this type of blocked or suppressed emotional expression. A model of the process of resolution (Greenberg et al., 1993) suggests that enacting the interruptive process and becoming aware of how one interrupts help evoke the suppressed emotion and access the unmet need. At the beginning of the enactment, the therapist helps clients become aware of how they interrupt and gets them to actually engage in the interruptive action. Having had the client identify with the interruptive process, the therapist facilitates the expression of what was being interrupted.

An example of a therapist setting up an enactment follows. The client, Joe, was already in a dialogue with a controlling critic, and he felt scared. They clarified that he feared a loss of control and then moved into how he scared himself:

> Joe: I don't know. I see myself as really stupid, because I'm losing control right now. I feel very, very awkward. I feel very scared.
>
> Therapist: Uh-huh.
>
> Joe: And that's why.
>
> Therapist: Uh-huh.
>
> Joe: And it's the weirdest feeling.
>
> Therapist: Weird. So as much as he keeps trying to control, you start feeling out of control.
>
> Joe: Mm-hm. Scared, that's what I started feeling, right away. That same situation right there.

Therapist:	Yeah. So can you tell . . . make him feel scared?
Joe:	I'm not in control anymore.
Therapist:	Mm-hm.
Joe:	That I can't get back the strength that I had before. And I can't resolve these problems. It's like, "get a grip."
Therapist:	So, I think you clamp down on him. That some part of what the fear of being able to discuss all of these things is, it's going to just come and overwhelm you. And so you don't let him. Like, "Don't say all those things. Don't express those feelings about Joe, because they're just going to be overwhelming to you, and you'll be out of control."
Joe:	OK.
Therapist:	Does that make sense to you? [*getting collaboration, identifying an interruptive voice*]
Joe:	Somewhat, yeah.
Therapist:	So what I'm saying is, yeah, do it. Make him feel afraid of being out of control. Tell him what's gonna happen if he loses control. Like in the situation with—tell him what's gonna happen if he loses control.
Joe:	You're gonna embarrass yourself.
Therapist:	Uh-huh. "You're going to make a fool of yourself."
Joe:	Belittle yourself in front of people.
Therapist:	Uh-huh.
Joe:	They will laugh at you.
Therapist:	So "don't express those feelings. Don't express the anger. People are going to laugh at you." [*promoting awareness of interruptive processes*]
Joe:	Mm-hm.
Therapist:	Yeah. So tell him.
Joe:	They'll think you're a fool. They're all going to laugh.
Therapist:	They're all gonna laugh. OK. OK. So, what should we do with those feelings? I guess put them away? [*heightening awareness of the process of interruption*]
Joe:	Get rid of them. Just throw them away.
Therapist:	Throw them away. Get rid of them. Mm-hm. So how could you . . . make them go away? You just, like, stomp them out? push them down? [*promoting awareness of how client interrupts*]

Joe: Just strike them, just throw them to the side.

Therapist: OK. So throw them to the side. How do you do that?

Joe: Take them . . . get rid of them.

Therapist: Yeah. Get rid of them. Push them away. OK, so are you pushing the feelings away?

Joe: I'm sealing them up right now.

Therapist: Mm-hm.

Joe: Straight up, put his head up.

Therapist: So you do have a lot of control. You're the one that seems to push and control him. So do that.

Joe: You've got to get your back up. Your head straight.

Therapist: Good.

Joe: You've got to be stronger.

Therapist: Yeah, yeah. OK, so what should he do with his feelings?

Joe: I'm trying to see the feelings. Right now, I'm trying to find something tangible. To see whether it's a box of feelings. All I keep seeing is, they're inside of him. I can't get to them.

Therapist: Yeah.

Joe: I'm looking for something tangible to grab and to throw away.

Therapist: Mm-hm.

Joe: And I don't see them. I don't see.

Therapist: OK, let's pretend . . . Put his feelings in a box. [*hands him a small box*] Make them go away. How would you do that? 'Cause you see, what I'm trying to give you a sense of is how you . . . you squeeze them back. You control them. Right?

Joe: Yeah.

Therapist: So make them go away.

Joe: OK.

Therapist: Are you doing it? [*promoting experience of interruption*]

Joe: Yeah. Yeah. You take a lot of room.

Therapist: You don't just want to put them in a box. You want to throw them away.

Joe: Probably.

Therapist: Mm-hm. Come back over here. And how do you feel here? [*identifying with the suppressed*]

Joe:	Very strange right now.
Therapist:	Yeah?
Joe:	Very, very strange.
Therapist:	What is the strange feeling you have?
Joe:	Strange feeling that something so stupid as taking that little box would give me a feeling like this. Feel like that I do have control.
Therapist:	Mm-hm. Mm-hm. Yeah, I mean, I don't know, right. Somehow there is a sense of control.
Joe:	Yeah. I feel like I can stand up for myself rather than be afraid. That I don't need to be so afraid of losing control. There's some sort of . . . I don't know. I feel I can stand up for myself.
Therapist:	Gives you some control, some power. What do you feel right now? Tell him about it.
Joe:	Honestly?
Therapist:	Mm-hm.
Joe:	I feel that there's a slight bit of hope.

Expressing the Suppressed

Having deautomatized the interruptive process by bringing it into awareness and enacting it, and having identified the protective aspect of the interruption and experiencing a sense of control, the client now is ready to experience that which has been interrupted. The therapist a few moments later guides Joe to express some of the suppressed feelings toward his stepmother, a person toward whom he had a lot of suppressed anger and by whom he had been physically abused as a child.

Joe:	The feelings I'm trying to make go away are all those feelings toward my mother.
Therapist:	Mm-hm. Could you express some of your feelings toward her?
Joe:	[*long pause*] This is bringing back the stomachache. It's gonna hurt right now.
Therapist:	When I said that? Mm-hm.
Joe:	Uhmm. Uhh, I haven't felt too much hurt. It's more rage.
Therapist:	Uh-huh. Put her here.
Joe:	Yeah.

Therapist:	Tell her.
Joe:	[*long pause*] You really hurt me.
Therapist:	Mm-hm.
Joe:	You really, really kicked me.
Therapist:	Mm-hm.
Joe:	The more I was down, the more you kicked me harder. Stood on my head.
Therapist:	Mm-hm.
Joe:	Can't you see what the fuck you did?
Therapist:	"You really hurt me. Kicked me when I was down." How do you feel toward her right now?
Joe:	A lot of anger.
Therapist:	Yeah. So tell her, "I'm angry at you."
Joe:	I'm angry at you for what you've done. I can't believe you would do these things. That you treated me like this.
Therapist:	Mm-hm. "I hate you for treating me like this." [*amplifying*]
Joe:	I do hate you.
Therapist:	Mm-hm.
Joe:	I really do.
Therapist:	Mm-hm.
Joe:	My stomach's going crazy.
Therapist:	What's your stomach say?
Joe:	[*exhales*] It's a really, really tight knot.
Therapist:	Mm-hm.
Joe:	Knot. It's not a pain anymore. It's a real hurt. [*sighs*]
Therapist:	It's a real deep wound. You feel it now?
Joe:	It's not a knot anymore. It's more a hurting . . .
Therapist:	Uh-huh.
Joe:	. . . feeling.
Therapist:	Uh-huh. You tell her. Tell her, "You're . . . you . . . really, really hurting . . ."
Joe:	The anger that I had is just a hurt.

Therapist:	So it's both. And what are you more in touch with? [*differentiating*]
Joe:	The rage in my stomach.
Therapist:	Mm-hm. OK, so stay with the rage. Tell her about it. "I hate you for . . ."
Joe:	I hate you for lying to me.
Therapist:	Uh-huh.
Joe:	Playing me against my father.
Therapist:	Uh-huh.
Joe:	I wish I could make you feel what I have in my stomach right now.
Therapist:	Uh-huh.
Joe:	I wish you would hurt like this.
Therapist:	Yeah. How could you make her feel as hurt as you feel? "I hate you for . . ." Can you squeeze her, like you're squeezing your stomach?
Joe:	No. I don't want to touch her.
Therapist:	Hmm. "I hate you so much, I don't want to touch you." Tell her.
Joe:	I hate you so much. I don't want to ever touch you again.
Therapist:	Mm-hm.
Joe:	I want you to feel the rage I have for you. The hate I have for you.
Therapist:	Mm-hm. Mm-hm. Say it louder.
Joe:	I want you to feel the rage I have for you. The hate I have for you.
Therapist:	Tell her about it.
Joe:	The hurt I have inside.
Therapist:	Yeah. Tell her about the hurt.
Joe:	You destroyed me.
Therapist:	Uh-huh.
Joe:	When you saw I was down, you stepped on me even more. And you didn't care. You didn't care the slightest.
Therapist:	Right, and that's what really hurts . . . is that "when you saw I was down, you stepped on me more."

Joe:	You didn't care about stepping on me.
Therapist:	"You never cared for me. You never thought of me. And I hate you for that."
Joe:	And I do hate you for that. I deserve better . . . really hate you for that. [*sighs*]

Relief at the Undoing

Having accessed and expressed some of the previously blocked expression, Joe entered a state of reduced tension and a greater feeling of strength.

Therapist:	Where are you at right now? [*focusing on present experience*]
Joe:	[*sighs*] Strangely enough, a little bit of relief. It's, like, in the back of my head. It's like medicine; it doesn't work immediately. It takes time to work. You shouldn't get a reaction all of a sudden and get some sort of . . .
Therapist:	Yeah.
Joe:	But I had this . . .
Therapist:	this . . .
Joe:	. . . really positive feeling today. Feeling stronger. Also tired.
Therapist:	We have to end. Maybe we'll pick this up again, too, and you'll have . . . uhmm . . . see what happens also during the week. What you feel. Like you say, you're in the process of.
Joe:	Mm-hm.
Therapist:	Uhmm . . . but somehow, there's this sort of sense of, "I'm OK" or "I'm stronger." And tired too? Can you check your body? What are you feeling in your body?
Joe:	Yeah, a little tired. For me to get the feelings of my emotions. A better feeling. A kind of calm and excited, all at the same time.

EMPTY-CHAIR DIALOGUE FOR UNFINISHED BUSINESS

Unresolved loss and humiliation centered on unfinished business with a significant other is usually at the base of the unresolved dependence issues in depressive experience. As we have seen, the abandonment–loss process often is more fundamental than the self-criticism so prevalent in depression and is highly intertwined with it. Unfinished business and unresolved grief from the past often appear to be more distal causes of depression, which is triggered by a current failure, abandonment, or loss. The unfinished business often is further from clients' awareness than their presenting problems but more basic. In addition, more evident self-criticism often was developed in the service of trying to resolve the unmet need in the unfinished business. A perfectionistic critic may emerge under the premise that "if I were more perfect, I would get the love [or acceptance, or approval] that I need." It is the feeling of being unloved, however, that is most core. Working with self-criticism in depression thus often leads back to the unresolved feelings of rejection and abandonment and the unmet need for love. Empty-chair dialogue in which the client expresses unresolved feelings to an imagined other in an empty chair has been found to be very helpful in resolving unfinished business and trauma (Greenberg & Malcolm, 2002; Paivio & Greenberg, 1995, 1998; Paivio, Hall, Holowaty, Jellis, & Tran, 2001; Paivio & Nieuwenhuis, 2001). This intervention has been described fully elsewhere (Elliott, Watson, Goldman, & Greenberg, 2004; Greenberg et al., 1993).

Markers of unfinished business emerge often in therapy for depression. The client feels lonely, unloved, and often resigned, as well as rejected by or angry with another person. In depression it is very common for markers of unfinished business to involve the expression of secondary reactive emotions, especially blame or complaint. For example, one client in the first session expressed both blame and resignation about her father, stating, "He was a terrible father. He still is, just never there. I've given up on trying to have a relationship with him. He always told me I would amount to nothing. I have nothing to say to him now." Although her presenting problem had been criticism and abandonment by her older sisters, who had played a maternal role in her life, it was unfinished business with her Eastern European father that emerged as the theme in the treatment of her depression. She put him in the empty chair, and after a number of sessions she contacted her rage and said, "I hate you. You shouldn't have been able to have children. They should have castrated you in the concentration camp you were in; then you wouldn't have been able to have children. I hate you for all the harm you have done to us." After this acknowledgment of her rage and after processing the loss of the father she never had, she began in the dialogue to soften toward him, acknowledging his difficulties and his inabilities, and went on to have a closer relationship with him in life. This resolution of her unfinished business, in combination with overcoming her internalized criticisms from his maltreatment, alleviated her depression. It is not always the case that hate or rage is the unexpressed emotion evoked as an antidote to depression. Sometimes in clients who have adopted a protective barrier of strength, it is the grief and lonely abandonment that are most suppressed. Anger and sadness often are two sides of the same coin, and both need to be expressed, in whatever sequence they emerge.

Trauma-based unfinished business is typically more intense than the unfinished business related to poor parenting. In trauma-based depressions, there often are strong current life difficulties that precipitate the depression, but the current difficulties evoke unwanted memories, emotional pain, and fragility. To promote enduring change, it is important to deal with the source of the disregulated emotion. Clients with this type of depression are often ambivalent about whether or not they want to return to face the source of the trauma or to engage in an empty-chair dialogue. On one hand, they present the issue in an attempt to rid themselves of the intrusive memories, but on the other hand, there is significant pain that threatens to retraumatize the client. As a result, the empty-chair work should be suggested only after a strong therapeutic relationship is secured and when clients feel ready to face their abusers (Paivio et al., 2001).

At the beginning of this intervention, the therapist must ensure that the client is making contact with the imagined other. Evoking the sensed presence of the other and making sure the client is currently experiencing the real or imagined presence of someone or something in a direct and immediate way are important in evoking the troublesome emotion schematic memory. Enacting the other person performing the hurtful behavior also is important in evoking the emotional reaction to the person. The goal of playing the other is to heighten the stimulus value of the other's behavior to evoke in turn the client's affective reaction to it. Once the negative actions and attitudes of the other have been portrayed, the client's affective reaction to this becomes the focus. With the therapist's careful and attuned tracking and reflection, relevant feelings toward the other emerge.

Throughout the dialogue, the therapist focuses on encouraging the expression of the client's concrete experience and emotions toward the other. Once the experience of the other is sufficiently evoked, the goal of the dialogue is to move beyond these reactions into differentiating underlying meanings and feelings and encouraging the expression of primary emotional states. Complaint must always be differentiated into its more fundamental components—anger and sadness. Typical secondary emotions expressed in empty-chair work include hopelessness, resignation, depression, and anxiety. These emotions are often expressed in an outer-directed manner and in a blaming tone. The therapist acknowledges and helps the client work through these secondary emotions but maintains the aim of encouraging the "pure" expression of primary emotion—for example, "I resent you" or "I missed having you around" rather than "You were a bastard" or "Why did you neglect me?" Secondary and primary emotions are often first experienced and expressed in a jumbled manner and all mixed together. For example, complaint that is fused with anger and sadness often comes out in question form—for example, "Why couldn't you be more . . . ?" or "Why did you . . . ? I just want to know why." It is important to help clients move beyond the expression of complaint and secondary reactions to express their primary emotions to the imagined other, feelings such as sadness, anger, fear, and shame. Anger and sadness are often experienced together, and it is helpful to ensure that these two primary emotional states are experienced, symbolized, and expressed separately. In cases of abuse, combinations of maladaptive fear, shame, and disgust have first to be accessed, validated, and reprocessed to the point where the client is ready to access primary anger and sadness (Greenberg, 2002).

In working with anger, it is important to distinguish between secondary and primary anger. Primary anger, or anger in response to violation, is essential and must be validated and its expression encouraged. In unfinished business, this anger may have been disavowed because it was unsafe to express it in the original relationship. In not being able to access primary anger, clients lose access to healthy resources that can promote adaptive behavior. Thus, expression of anger and standing up to the other by saying, for example, "It was wrong for you to hurt me like that; you were sick, and I did not deserve to be treated like that" is empowering and healing. To distinguish primary anger from secondary anger, therapists use the criteria that adaptive anger is in response to violation, involves an assertion of self, and is empowering. In contrast, secondary anger has a more blustery, destructive quality to it and serves to push the other away or obscure the expression of more vulnerable emotion. Its expression does not bring relief or promote the working through of experience. Interruptions to the expression of primary emotions also need to be worked with to access the core emotion and allow its full expression.

Once emotions have been differentiated and interruptions dissolved, the emotional arousal that is a necessary precondition for resolution of this type of problem emerges. Emotional arousal has been found to be an important precursor of the next step, a change in view of the other. Without arousal, this step is far less likely to occur (Greenberg & Malcolm, 2002). In working with emotions at this stage, therapists need to be aware that once primary emotions are fully and freely expressed, they move quickly. Anger and sadness tend to follow each other in sequence. Thus, when primary sadness is fully expressed, primary adaptive anger emerges rapidly, and creation of boundaries occurs. Conversely, the full expression of adaptive anger allows clients to acknowledge the pain of losses and betrayal and grieve for what they missed.

Evoking emotion involves not only expressing emotion, but also expressing and validating the basic unmet interpersonal needs for attachment or separation or validation. These are the needs that were never expressed in the original relationship, because people felt that they were not entitled to do so and that they would not be met. To be productive, these needs must be expressed as belonging to and coming from the self and with a sense of entitlement, rather than as deprivations or accusations of the other. Thus, they are an assertion of entitlement to the need, rather than an expression of desperate neediness. This step is crucial in helping clients establish their sense of the self as an agent, separate from the other, existing in its own right. At this stage the therapist simply follows the client and encourages him or her to express both emotions and needs. In addition, the therapist helps the client to symbolize and assert boundaries, to say "no" to intrusion, for example, or to reassert his or her rights. Therapists are aware that in early experience clients often found it necessary to disavow their basic needs and that as a result, they do not automatically attend to or express those needs. Therapists therefore listen for needs to form and, when they do, quickly validate them and encourage clients to express them. A thorough exploration of feelings is typically followed by a statement of related needs.

In situations where the need cannot or will not be met by the other, clients must still come to recognize their right to have needs met by the other. This often allows the important process of letting go of the unmet need. At this point in the dialogue, the therapist supports and promotes the letting go of the unfulfilled hopes and expectations. When letting go does not naturally flow from the expression of primary emotions, therapists can help clients explore and evaluate whether the unfulfilled expectations can and will be met by the other, and if not, therapists can help clients explore the effects of hanging on to the expectations. In this situation, therapists can consider asking clients to express to the significant other "I won't let you go" or "I won't let go of the hope you'll change." Letting go often produces another round of grief work, in which the client works through mourning the loss of the possibility of getting the need met from the attachment figure. This is often the most poignant and painful stage of the process. Once clients truly can grieve the parent they never had, then they are able to let go and move on.

Through arousal and direct expression of emotions and a strong sense of the legitimacy of their needs, clients begin to let go of previously salient but overly constricted perceptions and to expand their view of the other. Resolution occurs when clients reach a sense that they are worthwhile and are able to let go of the previously unfinished bad feelings. This letting go is accomplished in one of three major ways: through holding the other accountable for the violation experienced and affirming the self, through letting go of the unmet need, or through increased understanding of the other and possibly forgiveness of the other for past wrongs. In nonabuse cases, the client is able to better understand the other and to view the other with empathy, compassion, and, sometimes, forgiveness. In abuse or trauma-related situations, letting go most often involves holding the other accountable and moving on, but empathy and forgiveness may also occur.

For example, a severely depressed 43-year-old man, who mainly wept when he talked about his childhood, experienced extreme self-disgust when he talked about his father. In the course of describing, for the first time, instances of sexual abuse by his father, he began to get angry at his father. The therapist used a form of unfinished business with imagery to help him picture beating up his father. In response to asking how he felt after doing this, he said he felt powerful and victorious. He said that that's why he hated himself, because he had never, ever been able to stand up to his father. With further exploration, this helped him make sense of his self-punishment and self-disgust. The therapist asked him what he would like to say to that abused little boy. He told the little boy, "You were not bad. Fathers are not supposed to treat their sons like that. You did nothing wrong." The therapist asked him to repeat this several times. He wept with relief and felt comforted.

Unfinished business can be worked with by dialoguing in chairs or by using imagery without actually having the client speak to an empty chair. Imagery also can be used in a variety of other ways to evoke emotion. The visual system is highly related to emotion, so imagination can be used to evoke an unresolved emotion, to enact dialogues in imagination, to experience a new emotion, to imagine adding people or resources to situations or scenes, or to experience the scene in a new way. Thus, the therapist can ask the client to imagine restructuring an originally damaging scene by expressing what was needed or by bringing his or her adult self into the scene. The adult protector can offer the protection that was missing or bring in aids that will empower or protect, like a lock and key to secure the room or a cage in which to put the feared person (Greenberg, 2002; Thomas, 2003).

In this type of imaginal restructuring, the therapist might say,

> Close your eyes, and remember the experience of yourself in the situation. Get a concrete image, if you can. Go into it. Be your child in this scene. Please, tell me what is happening. What do you see, smell, and hear in the situation? What is going through your mind?

After a while, the therapist asks the client to shift perspectives and says,

> Now I would like you to view the scene as an adult. What do you see, feel, and think? Do you see the look on the child's face? What do you want to do? Do it. How can you intervene? Try it now in your imagination.

Changing perspectives again, the therapist asks the client to become the child:

> What, as the child, do you feel and think? What do you need from the adult? Ask for what you need or wish for. What does the adult do? Is it sufficient? What else do you need? Ask for it. Is there someone else you would like to have come in to help? Receive the care and protection offered.

This intervention concludes with the therapist asking,

> Check how you feel now. What does all this mean to you, about you and about what you needed? Come back to the present, to yourself as an adult now. How do you feel? Will you say goodbye to the child for now?

A shift in view of the other or a new experience of the other also is a very important part of the change process. This shift can be promoted by contrasting what the child has longed for with what the child actually received, as seen in the following exchange:

Therapist:	What would you have wanted the other to realize?
Client:	That she was so cruel and horrible to me!
Therapist:	How would you want her to feel as she realizes this?
Client:	Pained, guilty, sorry.
Therapist:	And how can she express this pain and guilt and sorrow to you?
Client:	She says, "I'm sorry."

After this imagined compassion in the other, the client experiences relief, soothing, grieving, letting go, and possibly forgiving (Malcolm, Warwar, & Greenberg, in press), as well as compassion for the self. If, on the other hand, the other does not soften and the client says something like "I'd want her to feel sorry but she never would! She'd never get it!" the therapist could say, "How sad it must have been for you that she is so unable to respond" or "that you got so little." This observation helps to get to more feeling to reprocess and provides soothing through therapist empathy. This example indicates how one can engage in unfinished business work in a client–therapist interaction without using an empty chair or imagery.

Unfinished business work, in whatever way it is done, is ultimately about changing emotion schematic memory. Emotions are often embedded in relational contexts. They connect self to other in the memory. Thus, people have memories of feeling shame in the face of a contemptuous parent, anger at an intrusive other, or fear of an abusive other. Accessing views of the other helps evoke emotion, and accessing alternate views of others and mobilizing new responses to others helps change emotion memories.

Personally relevant events are stored in memory at their emotion addresses. Thus, a current disappointment links to other disappointments, and a feeling of shame links to other losses of face. Present emotional experiences thus are always multilayered, evoking with them prior instances of the same or similar emotional experiences. Helping clients have new lived experience in the session helps them restructure their emotion memories. In addition, accessing a new emotion memory is one of the best ways to change an old emotion memory. Once a previously inaccessible emotion memory is evoked, the new memory either dominates, while the old one recedes into the background, or eventually fuses with the old memory and transforms it.

One client had horrifying memories whenever she thought of her mother; this client had discovered the body of her mother, who had committed suicide. Her memory was filled with that terrible picture of her mother as she had found her. Whenever she thought of her mother, it was this image that came to mind. It left her feeling cold and clammy, with awful feelings of fear and empty abandonment. After working through her anger, shame, and sadness, and after finally empathizing with and forgiving her mother, she talked about being able to replace this awful memory with previous happy memories of her mother. These memories, by contrast, left her feeling warm and safe. She reported later that when she thought of her mother, it was this warm loving memory that she now accessed. A full restructuring of emotion memory ultimately occurred, and she thought of her mother as the loving mother she had known before the suicide, and she had good feelings whenever she thought of her.

New emotion memories, however accessed, help change narratives. No important story is significant without emotion, and no emotions take place outside of the context of a story. The stories people tell to make sense of their experience and to construct their identities are to a significant degree dependent on the variety of emotion memories that are available to them. By changing their memories, or by accessing different memories, people change the stories of their lives and their identities.

A MIDTHERAPY DIALOGUE

This section provides an example of an empty-chair dialogue in a midtherapy session with Beth, a client with a major depressive disorder precipitated by the ending of a romantic relationship but related to an abusive and neglectful background. Beth, a 28-year-old woman, had difficulty focusing on her internal experience and often was externally focused, blaming, complaining, or feeling stuck. Therapy focused on her relationship with her adoptive parents. Although the dialogue with her adoptive father ends in the middle of the resolution process, it demonstrates how to work with a more externally oriented client. In addition, it shows that not all dialogues go to resolution each session; rather, each time the unfinished business is worked on, the client takes a step along a path toward an internal focus, evocation, and finally resolution.

Setting Up the Dialogue

The therapist started by ensuring that Beth made contact with the imagined other:

Therapist: Yeah, so you're saying, "He treats me just like a stranger, or sort of an associate" . . .

Beth: Yeah . . .

Therapist: . . . like I want something . . .

Beth: Like a little more.

Therapist: Yeah. I suggest we bring him in here. You can tell him some of this here. You have all these feelings in relation to him that somehow get jumbled. I understand it's complicated dealing with him, but it's also all these feelings. I know it's not easy. Right, let's try. Imagine . . . see if you can actually see him, what's he wearing—can you imagine him?

Beth: Yeah.

Therapist: How do you feel?

Beth: I just feel sad that we're not . . . like, I don't feel like I'm part of his life. [cries mutedly]

Therapist: Tell him what you're missing, what you long for. [evoking sadness]

Beth: I think that . . .

Therapist: Try to imagine he's here, and you're actually speaking to him. Tell him how it feels inside.

Beth: I just need a little more from him.

Therapist: Uh-huh . . .

Beth: I just need you to at least show me some more attention, like even if you're acting like . . . act like you care. Like, what's going on in my life . . . like, what's going on in my life, and how I'm feeling today or during the week. 'Cause I don't feel like I get it, I just feel like because you think that I'm just a strong individual, you just push me aside and just, you know, focus on yourself, or my mom, or whatever, like, the situation of the week or month is. I just . . . I just feel neglected. [crying in a demanding tone]

Therapist: "I do need stuff, I feel neglected because I do need something." [focusing on an initial need to help get at the feeling]

Beth: I just want to feel like I'm not an inconvenience, but like you care what's going on with me.

Therapist: Right, right. Tell him what it's like when you feel neglected . . . and when he doesn't call. It's just, "I feel like I don't count," or something. [focusing on feeling]

Beth: Like [he says], "You can wait." I don't understand, like, if I call and I need you—to wait a couple days, knowing that I'm upset about something, or even if I have good news, like, you put it off, like I'm, like, an appointment or something, like, I don't know. [shifts to an external focus]

Therapist: Uh-huh. "It makes me feel so—unspecial, unimportant to you." [taking an internal focus]

Beth: It's not that big of a deal. Like, "she can wait" . . . type of attitude that you have. [remains external]

Therapist:	Yeah. Try telling him, "I want to be important to you. I want . . ." [*focusing on need, trying to get client to shift internally*]
Beth:	I want him to show that I'm important.
Therapist:	Right, right. Tell him. "I want you . . ."
Beth:	I want to feel that I'm important to you. [*shifts to focusing internally*]
Therapist:	Right, this is what you want. [*5-second pause*] What's happening?
Beth:	Nothing—I just, I think it's just, he can't do that. It's no use trying. [*sigh*]

Shifting to Focus on Self-Interruptive Process

At this point the therapist, noticing the resignation, decided to change the focus to how the client interrupted her emotion and set up a dialogue between the part that was blocking her feelings and needs and the blocked experience. After working on the self-interruption that produced the resignation, Beth reached a point of feeling, "I deserve his attention," saying, "I do deserve it. I don't do anything wrong." The therapist then directed the newly accessed feelings and need toward Beth's father.

Therapist:	Uh-huh, uh-huh. Put him back there. Tell him, "I deserve it. I deserve more from you."
Beth:	[*crying strongly*] I deserve it, and I want it.
Therapist:	Mm-hm, mm-hm. Tell him more about it. Right. Tell him how your life, tell him, all your life, how it's been. [*promoting elaboration of feeling*]
Beth:	My whole—the whole time that I lived with you, even before that, even when I was living in the city and visiting . . .
Therapist:	Right . . .
Beth:	I was—I was always good; there wasn't anything wrong . . . [*sobbing*]
Therapist:	Tell him, "I've always been good."
Beth:	It's like, I don't know how much more . . . I don't know what else I can do.
Therapist:	Right.
Beth:	Like, everybody else is, like, screwing up around you, everyone in my family, and I was always the one . . .
Therapist:	Tell him. Tell him, "I've always been good . . ."

Beth:	I have, I've done good grades, and I've done anything you wanted me to do, and beyond.
Therapist:	Tell him, "Everything you've wanted from me—I've been a model daughter for you."
Beth:	I have . . .
Therapist:	Yeah, yeah . . .
Beth:	. . . and I just I don't feel like I've—I don't even want the same amount of effort that I've put into it, I just want a little effort. And I just haven't seen it.
Therapist:	Right, "I want a little effort from you—I want some recognition from you." Tell him about the hurt of not getting it. "All my life . . ." [*focusing client internally*]
Beth:	It's like I'm waiting for it. [*anger in her voice*]
Therapist:	Uh-huh. Tell him what you're angry about.
Beth:	That he doesn't see it.
Therapist:	Uh-huh. Try actually to see him and tell him, "I'm angry at you." [*promoting contact with the anger*]
Beth:	I'm angry that you just think that everything is fine, and—when it's not, and you—he doesn't know how to give me what I need.
Therapist:	What do you feel?
Beth:	I'm angry—I don't know if it's anger, I don't know what it is. [*looks down, childlike voice*]
Therapist:	Yeah, what happens there? As soon as this anger comes, then it collapses into a hurt. Is that what happens?
Beth:	A little.
Therapist:	Mm-hm. You find it hard to be angry. Tell him. [*identifying reappearance of an interruptive process*]
Beth:	Because I feel more guilty being angry at him.
Therapist:	Yeah . . .
Beth:	But I shouldn't.
Therapist:	OK, come here. Make yourself feel guilty. How do you do that? [*focusing on self-interruption*]
Beth:	I don't, I know I do, because—I just think about all the things he's done for me.
Therapist:	Uh-huh.

Beth:	But I think that I've proven myself as a daughter . . .
Therapist:	Right, this is what's tearing you apart.
Beth:	Yeah.
Therapist:	Let's bring it out in the open, right now. Tell her, "You've got no right to be angry at him." Tell her what he's done for her. This is the one part.
Beth:	He's taken you out of a bad home and . . . very . . . Whatever, he let me live with him in BC. He sent me to school.
Therapist:	Right.
Beth:	He's been there . . .
Therapist:	So, he's been there for you. So therefore . . .
Beth:	You should feel guilty when you say you're mad at him.
Therapist:	Right, "You're not allowed to be mad at him, 'cause look what he's done for you." Right.
Beth:	He took me, he let me live with him.
Therapist:	Yes, yes.
Beth:	He provided me with a pretty stable home.
Therapist:	Right.
Beth:	He sent me to school, for an education.
Therapist:	Are you actually imagining yourself there? Saying this to you? [*checking contact*]
Beth:	I could totally . . .
Therapist:	Yeah, what?
Beth:	I could stick up for myself, is what I'm saying inside.
Therapist:	Yeah, yeah. Change. But this is exactly . . . stick up for yourself. [*promoting assertion*]
Beth:	All these things are financial things.
Therapist:	Tell her.
Beth:	That's what it is. It all has to do with money. And that's how he makes me feel guilty.
Therapist:	Right, so what are you saying? That "I want" . . . what?
Beth:	I don't want money.
Therapist:	Right. What do you want? Tell this part of you.

Beth:	I don't want the money; it's not important to me.
Therapist:	Right, "what I *do* want is . . ."
Beth:	I want . . . emotional support.
Therapist:	Right. "And I deserve it."
Beth:	I totally deserve it. I've never gotten it. I have in little ways, but [*crying in an angry way*]
Therapist:	Right. "I really want emotional support." And now, try, "I'm angry at you. For not giving it."
Beth:	Or "thinking that you've given it to me," but that's how he thinks; he thinks he supports me.
Therapist:	Put him there. Tell him, "I'm angry at you. For not having given me emotional support." [*supporting a primary emotion*]
Beth:	[*trying to calm herself down and stop crying*] I hate saying that.
Therapist:	Yeah. It's so hard . . . immediately start to feel guilty?
Beth:	Mm-hm.
Therapist:	Change. And this is the drama, right? . . . inside—it's like, how do you make yourself feel guilty? [*again focusing on the guilt-making process*] Come over here. Now be him. Be him, not you. What does he say?
Beth:	"I love you, look at all I do for you. Look at all the money I give you." He thinks that if he gives me more money, or if he buys me a car, or I take a course and make him pay for it, that's how he shows his love . . .
Therapist:	Right . . .
Beth:	. . . 'cause that's what his parents did to him.
Therapist:	So tell her—"The only way I know how to show love is with money." [*guiding her to be her father*]
Beth:	. . . is with money, and giving—and giving it, giving things.
Therapist:	Right, right . . .
Beth:	. . . and . . .
Therapist:	Right. So tell her, "I show you my love . . ."
Beth:	". . . by giving you money, by making sure you have a house or somewhere to live each month." But he'll be the first to use that over my head, just that little bit . . .
Therapist:	Uh-huh . . .

Beth:	Like, if he's going to use something, it would be because I did something wrong . . .
Therapist:	Yeah . . .
Beth:	. . . you know, he'd be, like, "Well, who's paying for your rent?"
Therapist:	Mm-hm, mm-hm.
Beth:	He would use that against me if anything . . .
Therapist:	Yeah, yeah, yeah. Some of the guilt or the trap.
Beth:	The hold . . .
Therapist:	Yeah, "the hold." Right, right. So do it to her. Tell her— how do you do that, what do you . . . try, "You have no right to complain, look at what I've given you." [*crystallizing the father's position*]
Beth:	You have everything.
Therapist:	Right, tell her, "You have . . ."
Beth:	What more do you want?
Therapist:	Uh-huh, that's . . . "You don't have a right to want anything more. You have no right to complain."
Beth:	I do, though. I do. [*whine in her voice*]
Therapist:	Change. [*client laughs about her sniffling*] What happens, you become a little girl? [*gently confronting because client seems stuck*]
Beth:	Because I can't defend myself with him.
Therapist:	How come? What happens?
Beth:	I don't know.
Therapist:	It's like, you lose your voice, you become little. And so . . . I don't know, what's it feel like?
Beth:	I feel like shit because I can't defend myself. And that's why I totally want to be able to support myself, so then I can totally turn around, and he'll have no hold. So I can turn around and maybe say to him, like, "Listen, buddy . . ."
Therapist:	Yeah . . .
Beth:	". . . you know, you may have, like, supported me throughout the years, whatever, financially, but this is what I wanted." And if he's not willing to give it to me, then I'll understand, do you know what I'm saying? So he can't turn around and use the excuse, "Look what I've done for you."

Therapist:	Mm-hm . . .
Beth:	Or "I'm pulling your rent, so you can pay for your own rent."
Therapist:	"And I feel trapped . . ."
Beth:	I do, it's a total control thing, and it's not nice.
Therapist:	Right, tell him; tell him, not me. I mean here, here, tell him. [*promoting contact*]
Beth:	I feel that he uses that as like, his . . . your control.
Therapist:	Right, make contact with him. "I feel controlled by you." And you're saying, "I hate it."
Beth:	I don't even think about it, but it's always in the back of my mind.
Therapist:	Right . . .
Beth:	You know, like, OK, if you fuck up, you're in trouble.
Therapist:	Mm-hm. Tell him what you resent.
Beth:	I resent that underlying, underlying—I don't even know . . .
Therapist:	. . . that underlying hook, that underlying . . .
Beth:	. . . like, it's there, I just picture him saying, "You'll suffer financial consequences." 'Cause my grandmother was not nice to me at all . . .
Therapist:	Right . . .
Beth:	. . . like, I didn't do anything wrong. I was, like, best grand-daughter in the world, and she used that, and I wanted to tell her, and I told my dad, "I can't handle it anymore."
Therapist:	Mm-hm . . .
Beth:	"I have to tell her." And he goes, "If you tell her, you're go-ing to suffer financial consequences." And I was just, like, what the fuck is that!
Therapist:	Right, tell him how angry you are. Tell him, "I resent you controlling me in that way."
Beth:	It's no way to control somebody—it's not nice.
Therapist:	Uh-huh, uh-huh. But it's hard to be angry, still, right? You feel . . . you feel the hurt of it. That's where you become . . .
Beth:	Because he makes me feel that I have no right to be angry. Really.
Therapist:	I understand. Do you have a right to be angry?

Beth:	I think I do, 'cause I am.
Therapist:	I agree. Tell him.
Beth:	I'm furious. I can't stand the way you manipulate me. I can't stand it.

Beth struggled with her anger, her need for love and approval, and her guilt. The therapist stuck with her, helping her try to focus on and differentiate her feelings and the different aspects of her conflict. Beth made small steps toward self-assertion, and she did get to some anger expression, but she was unable to let go of the need for his approval and the desire for him to change. Hanging on to wishes that others will change keeps people stuck in a dependent position in a relationship. Eventually, after a number of dialogues of this type, Beth grieved for the father she never had and would never have, and she began to let go of her need for him to be the father she wished for. She let go of her anger, held him accountable for being an unavailable alcoholic father, understood his limitations, and accepted him for what he had given and still could give her. He had been the only one in her life who had given her some support and love as a child, and she appreciated him for that.

13

TRANSFORMATION: THE CONSTRUCTION OF ALTERNATIVES

The transformation process involves both generating new, more resilient emotional responses and validating the new feelings and the emerging
self-organization. Once clients have accessed core dysfunctional emotion
schemes at the base of the depression, such as feeling shamefully worthless or
helplessly insecure, the scene is set for mobilizing alternate emotional responses based on adaptive needs and goals to expand clients' repertoire and
transform the maladaptive state. Having aroused the maladaptive experience and articulated in words some of the core dysfunctional expectancies;
negative views of self; beliefs about self, world, and other; and negative interpersonal patterns, it is time to leave the maladaptive state and move on.

Transformation occurs most centrally by a dialectical process of accessing the healthy within and having it transform the unhealthy by forming a
new synthesis. Awareness of the healthy resources and strengths promotes a
challenging of the unhealthy from within. Newness emerges by a synthesis of
opposites. A major process of transformation thus involves accessing a more
resilient self-organization and setting this up in opposition to the core depressive organization. The newly accessed alternate organization, say, one of
assertive anger, healthy sadness, compassion, or loving feelings, involves a

state change that results in a change in the client's mode of processing. No longer are the world and the self viewed as hopeless, empty, and isolated, and no longer are core evaluations ones of powerlessness, threat, or diminishment. Now the picture is more hopeful. The self is now experienced as more powerful or vital, as having resources, and as being more deserving or loving, and the world is seen as more manageable or responsive. Core evaluations that result in approach rather than withdrawal now govern the client's processing.

Enduring change, however, requires not only change in momentary state but also change in governing self-organizations. Transformation of self-organizations occurs by constructing new schematic structures through a confrontation between, and synthesis of, two opposing prior organizations—a dialectical process. This confrontation is often between evaluation and need. The evaluation may be, "I am worthless"; the need, "I need to be valued." This need sets in motion a new set of goal-directed feelings, thoughts, and actions that challenge those associated with the "I am worthless" mode of processing. The synthesis that emerges coordinates the two prior schemes, so the client ends up with, "I feel worthless because I was treated so badly, and I deserved better. I am deserving of care." Access to a resilient self-organization is in and of itself helpful, but in addition it is important to have the new resilient responses influence the old depressive views by explicitly challenging them and have a new synthesis emerge. The client's newly mobilized emotions, needs, and resources thus are used to transform the old emotional responses and to confront and challenge the client's negative views and beliefs about self until a new view is formed.

A new construction emerges from synthesis of the common elements in the two schemes that were coactivated and can coapply. Because neurons that fire together wire together (Hebb, 1949), a new organization of neurons (i.e., repertoire of schemes) becomes associated with the activating situation. When this broader associated pairing is activated in the future, it does so as a unified overarching scheme. A new emotion blend, and a new organization that serves to coordinate the two subschemes, thus emerges.

In depression, for example, the withdrawal responses of the collapsed, defeated self that come from the client's core shame or anxious insecurity are now paired with new approach responses associated with empowered anger, comfort-seeking sadness, or expansive pride and their associated tendencies to survive and thrive. A schematically based new self-organization of shy confidence infused with hope or possibility, rather than despair, is synthesized. The earlier depressive subscheme still exists and could be activated under especially stressful conditions. Therefore, the depressive response is not totally extinguished; it recedes into the background, and the new, more adaptive synthesis becomes more figural and dominates self-organization. The old ways are not unlearned, but rather developed, and new ways emerge out of the old. The final product in change and development always involves the synthesis of all one's cognitive–affective learnings built on top of each other.

The alternate voice or new possibilities that emerge to transform the old voice thus come from within, from a new emotional state accessed in the session. It is these new adaptive voices that provide the possibility of a new construction. The focus for the therapist then becomes one of helping generate new possibilities within the personality by promoting the forming of alternate self-organizations that are constructed from a synthesis of newly accessed healthy emotional responses and needs with older, less adaptive responses. Clients are encouraged to use newly accessed emotional resources to transform the maladaptive emotions and to challenge the destructive thoughts in their maladaptive emotional states from the new inner voice, based on healthy primary emotions and needs.

PROMOTING ACCESS TO NEW EMOTIONS

The following are some of the ways therapists can intervene to help clients access new emotions (Greenberg, 2002):

- *validate:* Validation prompts the spontaneous emergence of the more adaptive potential emotion within a facilitative human relationship. Therapists' attunement to what the client is feeling and communication of an understanding of the validity of what he or she is feeling sometimes is sufficiently strengthening of the self to help an alternate more resilient emotional state emerge spontaneously.
- *shift attention:* Shifting clients' focus of attention helps them pay attention to a background or subdominant more adaptive feeling. Shifting is a key method of helping clients change their states. The subdominant emotion is often present in the room nonverbally in tone of voice or manner of expression. What clients attend to in their experience strongly influences the emotion schemes that are activated and therefore what aspects of the self become available for synthesis. Therapists can help clients change their experiencing by helping them attend both to different components of schemes or to different schemes. Paying attention to the bodily felt feeling, rather than to a conceptual explanation, will bring an emotion into the room; likewise, paying attention to another possibility, like attending to primary sadness rather than secondary anger, will bring a new emotion alive.
- *access needs and goals:* Another key method is to ask clients, when they are in their core state or in their pain, what they need. Raising a need or a goal to a conscious self-organizing system activates a sense of agency. If a client in a state of shame

experiences a need for validation, an anger-based sense of pride often emerges at not having the need met. Once clients symbolize what they feel and need, they begin to move toward problem solving to get what they need. Helping clients access their needs and goals is one of the most important ways in which a therapist can facilitate the emergence of new emotional states.

- *positive imagery:* The therapist can ask the client to imagine being in a situation that evokes another emotion, like being in a safe place, or imagine having another feeling in response to a situation, like feeling anger at violation rather than defeat. With practice clients can learn how to generate opposing emotions through imagery and use these as an antidote to negative emotions.

- *expressive enactment of the emotion:* Therapists can ask clients to adopt certain emotional stances and help them deliberately assume the expressive posture of that feeling and then intensify it. Psychodramatic enactments are useful; the therapist instructs the client, "Try telling him, 'I'm angry.' Say it again—yes, louder. Can you put your feet on the floor and sit up straight?" The therapist coaches the client in expressing until he or she experiences the emotion.

- *remember another emotion:* Therapists can ask clients to remember a time when they felt sad or angry. Remembering a situation in which another emotion occurred can bring the memory alive in the present.

- *cognitively create a new meaning:* Therapists can suggest that a client think about or focus on something in a different way, like to focus on what they didn't like about an ex-partner who has rejected them. Changing how one views a situation or talking about the meaning of an emotional experience often helps clients experience new feelings.

- *expressing the emotion for the client:* Therapists might express on behalf of the client the outrage, pain, or sadness that the client is unable to express.

- *using the therapy relationship to generate new emotion:* A new emotion is evoked in response to new interactions with the therapist. The therapist might, for example, self-disclose to create a sense of closeness, challenge to evoke anger, or offer compassion to evoke sadness.

CHANGING EMOTION WITH EMOTION

Transformation involves accessing one's opposing internal emotional resources and using these to transform maladaptive emotions and challenge the dysfunctional beliefs associated with them. Once the client has been helped to arrive at and experience a primary emotion, generally fear or shame, if it is not readily apparent that the emotion is maladaptive, the therapist and client together evaluate whether the fear or shame is an adaptive or maladaptive response to the current situation. Together they explore whether the feeling arrived at can be used to inform action or may be based on a psychological wound of some kind and needs to be changed. If the feelings are maladaptive, they need to be processed further to promote change. If the emotion arrived at is healthy, such as unexpressed adaptive anger or sadness, this adaptive emotion is used as a guide to action. If, however, it is a core, familiar, maladaptive emotion that recurs and never changes, such as shameful inadequacy or fearful insecurity, it needs to be changed. Emotional intelligence involves knowing which emotions to change and which emotions to be changed by.

When clients experience their core maladaptive feelings of primary shame and worthlessness, are able to symbolize them in awareness rather than avoid them, and are able to acknowledge that this is what they feel at core, they begin to gain some reflective mastery over their experience. With the symbolization of their core feeling, they create a separation from it. The feeling is now not simply an overwhelming experience of "I am worthless," but rather an experience of "I feel worthless," which is a feeling I *have*, rather than who I *am*. The feeling becomes an object or product of the self, one that produces distress, rather than being the self, and thus can more easily be regulated. In addition, the supportive therapeutic relationship that is constantly validating and seeing strengths is always there, helping to activate or boost access to more resilient voices within the self. In this context the need to feel loved and accepted becomes much more accessible, and the client begins to feel more deserving of having the need met. The empathic, validating, and supportive therapeutic environment thus is a crucial ingredient of revitalizing and accessing resilience in clients with depression. They are more able to access their inner strengths and soothe themselves when they are actually experiencing their suffering themselves rather than talking about it, focusing on what they need, and exposing their vulnerability to another person and receiving empathy from that person.

Clients thus need simultaneously to experience their distress and to step back sufficiently to see themselves and reflect on their experience. They need to empathize with themselves, symbolize their own pain and suffering, differentiate it, and finally access their adaptive needs. Once they have stepped back and have a place from which to view themselves, they have already begun reorganizing. Now they are ready, with the therapist's help, to construct new alternative responses to the situation to transform the old depressive responses. Now they can, for example, attend to their sense of injustice at having been shamed, begin to shift their attention and feel their anger at the violation, and access their need for inviolability. Access to primary emotion to guide reorganization often is facilitated by verbally symbolizing emerging bodily felt feeling. Describing the physiological sensations involved in the experience of the emotion helps. For example, sadness might be described in terms of a heaviness in the chest, a drooping of the shoulders, and a welling up of tears in the eyes. Anger might be described as an eruption or explosion in the chest, a clenching of the fist, and a tightening of the jaw. An exploration of the motoric action tendency may reveal in sadness a desire to curl up or be comforted, or in anger a desire to strike out. These tendencies can also be given expression in the session psychodramatically or in fantasy enactments. Once the feeling is activated, the evaluation and the need embedded in the emotion can be accessed. When clients have accessed a new feeling, they have now changed their mode of processing and are operating with different core evaluations and needs. The sense of entitlement to needs evokes the more resilient sense of self, which stands up to protect the self. The self, operating as a dynamic self-organizing system, thus reorganizes. With the development of this alternate self-organization, a new voice emerges to challenge the old voice.

The following therapy session excerpt illustrates the activation and transformation of the maladaptive emotion scheme. The client had just begun to access the core depressogenic "bad" self-organization:

Cecilia: Yes. I feel worthless not being all those things.

Therapist: Uh-huh. . . . And this is really the heart of it, right? This painful, awful feeling of worthlessness that makes you live up to somebody's expectation . . . [empathic understanding]

Cecilia: I just can't stand feeling it. [sniffs]

Therapist: What's "it" feel like? [empathic exploration, emotion inquiry]

Cecilia: I just feel so despairing and, like, nothing. I'm just not even a person.

Therapist: Uh-huh.

Cecilia: I'm drowning. [emotion schematic processing]

Therapist: Uh-huh. So, just, your whole self is drowning, and just . . . Tell me more about it. I mean, you're saying, "I just feel so . . ." [emotion inquiry, empathic exploration]

Cecilia: I just feel empty. Like I'm nothing . . . I'm empty. I'm nothing. I'm not worth even . . . I'm not even noticed . . . I'm not even there.

Therapist: Uh-huh.

Cecilia: I'm not even there. I'm not even recognized anywhere without being that.

Therapist:	Uh-huh. So . . . "unless I'm . . . living up to some kind of expectation of . . . perfection . . . I'm nothing. I'm worthless. I don't even exist." [*empathic understanding*]
Cecilia:	That's how I feel inside. And I just get panicky and anxious and afraid . . . [*secondary symptomatic emotion*]
Therapist:	Will you change? Let's make her feel like she is nothing, worthless, unless she lives up to some kind of . . . Tell her, "You're nothing unless . . ."
Cecilia:	Uhmm . . . [*deep sigh*]
Therapist:	There's that heavy, heavy sigh, right, of . . . [*empathic attunement*]
Cecilia:	Yeah. [*softly*]
Therapist:	What it's like to carry all this? [*empathic exploration*]
Cecilia:	Heavy.
Therapist:	Make her feel like she's nothing. Make her disappear. [*process guidance*]
Cecilia:	I mean, she is . . . she's not there . . . I don't have to say anything, 'cause she's just not there anyway.
Therapist:	So, it's like you have no existence. The only way you can be is if you're perfect. [*empathic understanding*]
Cecilia:	Yup.
Therapist:	And as soon as you . . . stop, you don't really exist.
Cecilia:	Hmm.
Therapist:	And then all this terrible painfulness comes up. [*Cecilia sobs*] Can you let some of those tears come? These are the tears you don't want to have, but they're there. [*giving permission*]
Cecilia:	It's too overwhelming. [*sniffs*]
Therapist:	Mm-hm. [*Cecilia sighs*] So, it's just overwhelming to be so wiped out unless you're perfect. [*empathic understanding*]
Cecilia:	Yeah. And I'm supposed to function normally [*sniffs*] and take care of four kids on my own and . . .
Therapist:	Mm-hm. "It's just too much. I can't."
Cecilia:	Yeah, but I expect that of myself. I give, and it's just required, and yet it's . . .

The therapist followed the basic two-step emotion-focused therapy (EFT) approach of first helping the client arrive at the maladaptive core emotion in order, in the second step, to be able to leave it (Greenberg, 2002). In the preceding exchange, the therapist helped Cecilia access the feeling of worthlessness. In the second step, the process shifted to leaving the place arrived at. In the following segment Cecilia, by focusing on her need, began to mobilize some internal resources, and an alternate self-organization emerged with a more resilient voice:

> Cecilia: I used to just so easily be that harsh, mean voice on myself. I don't know why I can't do it today. I just can't. [*sobs*]
>
> Therapist: Mm-hm.
>
> Therapist: Somehow, you're feeling it's too much. [*empathic affirmation*]
>
> Cecilia: I'm just so tired of having this voice in my head all the time. [*sobs*]
>
> Therapist: Uh-huh, uh-huh. "I don't even want to be it."
>
> Cecilia: No. [*crying*]
>
> Therapist: Mm-hm. "I just need something more comforting. More . . ."? [*empathic exploration, focus on need*]
>
> Cecilia: Yes. [*sobbing*]
>
> Therapist: Caring?
>
> Cecilia: [*sobs*] Oh, god . . . [*quiets, breathing deeply*]
>
> Therapist: "I just need rest from that pounding . . ." [*focusing on need*]
>
> Cecilia: Yeah. [*exhales*]
>
> Therapist: Mm-hm.
>
> Cecilia: I'm so tired of always having it attacking me . . .
>
> Therapist: Uh-huh . . .
>
> Cecilia: . . . in such a harsh, harsh way. I just always listen to it so readily and agree with it and lose a sense of myself when I hear it, and I just can't take it today.
>
> Therapist: Uh-huh.
>
> Cecilia: I just don't want to hear it. [*exhales deeply*]
>
> Therapist: Mm-hm, mm-hm. So what do you need? "I just need . . ."
>
> Cecilia: I want to be . . . I just want to be comforted.

In this segment focusing on needs helped Cecilia move on. Based on this need, she eventually got to a place of feeling more worthy and deserving and being able to assert her needs so that she didn't need approval so much. Therapists can generally access a more adaptive emotional response if they help the client articulate a need by asking, "What do you need?" when the client is in his or her pain and has accepted and tolerated it. The process of change is greatly facilitated by accessing the unmet need in the maladaptive emotion, symbolizing it in awareness, and having the client's entitlement to the need supported by the therapist. With the emergence of clear needs or goals, new resources are accessed to meet them. When clients are suffering their pain, usually they know what they need. Once they know what they need in a situation, they often begin to feel like they have some control over it. Raising a need or a goal to a self-organizing system has a number of important effects on the type of processing it induces. At the conscious intentional level, focusing on a need creates a problem space in which to search for a solution. Once clients articulate a need or goal, they begin to ask, "How can I get it met?" At an affective level, identifying a need conjures up a feeling of what it is like to reach the goal and opens up neural pathways both to the feeling and to the goal (Davidson, 2000a, 2000b). People, by saying "I need comfort," remember the feeling of being comforted—they taste it—and this begins to access the emotion itself. By accessing the feeling of the need, the desire to meet it is amplified. Motivation to feel that way again is activated and heightened, and ways of getting to the goal are primed. The self now organizes its agency to meet the goal. The therapist's validation of the need also is an important element in strengthening the self's sense of entitlement to the need. The core of the change process thus involves directing the client's attention to emergent, alternate, emotionally based needs and goals and helping him or her access new more adaptive emotions to meet the need. Once the client experiences the need for boundaries or safety, formerly embedded in shame and fear, anger is mobilized to meet it. Once the need for contact or comfort embedded in abandonment and basic insecurity is contacted, sadness and compassion are experienced at the loss and activate a grieving process.

Maladaptive emotion states are best transformed by undoing them with other, more adaptive emotional states. In time the more adaptive emotion transforms the maladaptive emotion by integrating with it to form a new schematically based self-organization. In more complicated depressions, clients generally contact deep feelings of shame, insecurity, aloneness, and being unlovable or pain at past trauma. These emotions need to be allowed and processed. Adaptive shame will lead to awareness of the desire to belong, grief to the grieving process, insecurity to the recognition of the need to be attached and supported, loneliness to the need to be loved and connect, and pain to the need for release, relief, and reorganization, including a need for inviolability or safety. Attending to these emerging needs and goals precipitates the reorganization, and the client begins to access internal resources to meet the goals and alternate self-views to support their attainment.

At times, construction of alternatives involves explicit discussion of how to meet the newly accessed needs in the outside world and of the difficulties the client might encounter in these attempts. Further work on developing skills to meet needs may be required. When the problem is not skills deficit but lack of awareness, greater awareness and acceptance of emotional experience and needs are required. It is clarifying and confidence building for clients to know what they feel, to know what they need, and to be able to use these as guides to action. Vividly experiencing one's feelings and needs motivates and clarifies, and this overcomes the anxiety and inadequacy that previously impeded action. EFT thus helps clients learn to trust their internal experience and to use their experience to guide them. Validation by the therapist of primary experience is crucial to help clients strengthen their sense of themselves, trust their experience, and act on their own behalf.

PROMOTING THERAPEUTIC RELATIONSHIP AND WORK

Transformation of emotional experience occurs through two major, interacting processes—the therapeutic relationship and therapeutic work. The relationship with the therapist gives clients the opportunity to expose their difficult feelings to their therapists' presence and help. Clients thus have a new affect-regulating emotional relational experience. The new emotional experience can arise relationally in one of two main ways. One involves the disconfirmation of pathogenic expectations or beliefs by a new interactional experience with the therapist. An example is a client expressing for the first time in his or her life a feeling to the therapist, such as anger or disappointment, or disclosing a shameful experience and having the therapist react to it responsively rather than defensively or disapprovingly.

The second way involves the strengthening of the self that occurs by having a core emotion validated or understood by a confirming other. Clients need their therapists to validate and strengthen their emerging new feelings and new sense of themselves. Recognition from others is one of the crucial components in a new sense of a valued self. Clients need to experience and internalize the confirmation of at least one other person to help regulate their own affect and overcome their depression. It is important to recognize that the need for validation is an important ingredient for overcoming the core sense of worthlessness or abandonment in depression.

A validating relationship helps the work aspect of change by providing a safe, facilitative environment for exploratory work. Talking with an understanding therapist helps clients sort out which feelings are healthy and useful and which are problematic and need change. The relationship therefore serves as a facilitator of clarification. The second work aspect of change involves a process in the client of acknowledging new experience and symbolizing the new experience in words so that it exists for consciousness and influences his or her narrative identity. In this process the client has to feel the difficulty and put the difficult feelings into words. Language helps to organize the difficult feelings by symbolizing them in words, where they can better be managed. The client can now speak and explore as needed and can give each nuance of difficult feeling a place to exist, inside, and an opportunity to offer its message. The basic change process in the intrapsychic work of creating new meaning involves progress through the steps of the experiencing process (Klein, Mathieu-Coughlan, & Kiesler, 1986), including approaching a bodily felt sense, experiencing what is new in it, putting this experience into words so that it can exist as a symbolized experience, and using currently accessible feelings to solve problems. Novelty emerges as the result of this process. A new experience arises in the self and offers an alternative to prior experience. Both the experience of new emotion and the designating of language to describe it are essential for the creation of new meaning. Sensation, perception, and affect always exist in the person prior to language, but these are always in search of language to survive. It is their synthesis in novel constructions that produces change.

Thus, one client clearly symbolized in awareness his feeling of not being valuable by saying "I feel so useless, like others are looking down on me"; he sobbed with the full realization of the feeling and its connection to childhood wounds of being devalued by peers and parent alike. After validation and further articulation of his experience at a particular moment, which acted as a dynamic self-organizing system in a process of change, he reorganized, and his survival and attachment-oriented need emerged: "It's not true that I am useless. They were cruel and thoughtless. I was curious, and I cared about people." Once he had accessed his new affectively based adaptive need for survival and well-being, a new self-organization became available. He contacted an inner wellspring of self-worth, and a new voice emerged. At this point he looked up and said, "I am worthwhile. I deserve to be valued" and "I have love to give, and I deserve to be loved."

By acknowledging their primary feelings in a therapeutic environment that both is validating and focuses on their growth-oriented needs, clients with depression are more able to access their organismic strengths and capacities. They are then able to use these to access a new self-view. At this point clients struggling with feeling unlovable or abandoned feel a greater sense of entitlement to having their needs met or being able to support themselves and, no longer feeling shattered, are able to say such things as, "Even if he doesn't respond to me, I still deserve it" or "I can survive." They now also are able to re-evaluate the consequences of their need not being met by the other. They feel they can and will cope. With support from the therapist, clients, feeling more secure, connect with their mastery motivation and their pain avoidance motivation, and this helps them access new resources to cope. In this way, more self-enhancing and self-soothing capacities are available to help the client cope. The client might say, "I do deserve to feel loved. If I can't get it here, now, I can get it from within, or from somewhere else. I can survive if he doesn't respond to me. I know I won't actually fall apart." Clients connect with the fact that they are more than what just happened or what they just felt.

A key process of transformation, then, involves the generation of alternative experiences that transform the person's mode of processing. The generation of alternatives is greatly facilitated by accessing the need or goal within the affect stored in memory. Once the unmet need or desire—say, the need in anger for nonviolation or the need in sadness for comfort or contact—is mobilized and raised to awareness, the client becomes more active. As a dynamic system, once agency is activated, the client begins to reorganize to try to reduce the perceived mismatch between appraisal and desired outcome. Raising the desired goal to awareness opens up pathways to possible solutions in the brain and activates memories of what goal attainment feels like. All this, plus the desire to leave the unpleasant affect, mobilizes clients to begin to transform their experience into something more adaptive and viable. Transformation also occurs, in part, because painful emotions, if endured, subside in intensity by a natural process of rising and falling away.

COMPLETING AND LETTING GO OF GRIEVING AND PAIN

In depression the completion of grieving and pain is also an important change process. Completion is a phenomenon of emergence and transformation. It involves activating a natural process of healing that leads to facing the pain, assimilating the loss, letting go, and moving on. What is pathological is the avoidance of the loss and the pain of grief. Pain essentially is the experience of damage to the self. As such, pain is an adaptive emotion that tells one that damage has occurred. The primary experience of pain involves a feeling of "brokenness," a feeling of the self being broken into pieces or shattered (Bolger, 1999; Greenberg & Bolger, 2001) or a feeling of a bond being broken—one's way of being with another has been shattered. Clients who have had the courage and support to face their pain not only survive, but also grow from the experience if it is completed.

Painful feelings must be approached, then allowed and tolerated, and then accepted as part of the self. The original loss has to be experienced and faced to know experientially that one can survive the pain. People must allow themselves to feel the devastation, the loss, and the powerlessness. The acceptance of the pain helps the client to endure it, and this allows the need or goal associated with the feeling to be recognized and mobilized. Acceptance of pain also empowers clients to combat any dysfunctional beliefs that may be intensifying the pain or that are preventing them from facing it. Allowing oneself to feel pain results in an organismic sense of relief and allows the client to emerge stronger and no longer depressed. When clients are dealing primarily with dreaded painful aspects of themselves, such as feeling defective, rather than with loss, they learn that they can survive what they previously believed was unbearable. They metaphorically face their own existential death and are reborn.

For example, the daughter of one client had disowned her, walking away and refusing ever to see her again. This client had to face in therapy the sense of brokenness caused by this rupture, as well as her shame at having been so rejected. She faced the loss and came to see how her whole life since the rupture had been a protection against the pain. In finally facing her pain, she decided to face life, rather than to protect herself behind a wall of fear and shame. She then let go of the pain and moved on. This process of allowing and accepting therefore requires that the pain be evoked and lived through, and not simply talked about. By experiencing the pain in its actuality, clients are in essence in a novel situation, in which they learn that the pain is endurable and will not destroy them.

The paradox is that avoidance of the pain perpetuates the pain and interferes with the ability to move away from it. Clients need to embrace the pain and face the hopeless, helpless feeling they have been trying to avoid to be able to truly move on by restructuring their experience of the pain. This is what is meant by the terms going "into" or "through" pain, in which the emergence of newness is captured by the image of the phoenix rising from the ashes. In this image, organization emerges out of disorganization and destruction.

For example, a client who, for the first time, accessed in therapy a painful trauma experience associated with sexual abuse felt the intense pain of shame plus the deep sadness at her loss of innocence. Supported by the therapist, she felt empathy for herself as a little girl and quickly switched to intense anger at the perpetrator for violating her. The therapist empathically responded to her vulnerability and validated her experience of being violated. At the end of the session, the client remarked that despite the pain, she felt hopeful "that things will change. I at least feel like these feelings are my own, and I have a right to feel them."

A move to more positive coping after facing pain is in part governed by clients' tendency to "let go," or detach from troubling emotions, and to "go on," or seek more positive, comfortable, healthier states rather than to stay in pain. This process of being able to detach is facilitated by reduction of high arousal by repeated exposure to and processing of the feeling and meaning of the loss and an ability to shift one's focus of attention. The latter process can be helped by working at intentionally shifting one's focus to other aspects of experience, like to one's breathing, to sensory contact with the present sights and sounds of external reality, or to memories of positive aspects of a lost one or love and appreciation for them.

Accessing Positive Emotions

Access to positive emotions also is an important transformation process. As Fredrickson (1998) showed, access to positive emotion counteracts negative emotion and broadens and builds. Emotions like compassion, love, joy, and excitement all interact and rapidly transform clients' state and modes of processing. They produce more hopeful, altruistic, and creative solutions to problems.

Fosha (2004) emphasized the importance of the transformational value of positive affects. She argued that certain transformational affects signal that adaptive change is occurring. For instance, a client was processing some very painful feelings of feeling abandoned or rejected as the therapist empathically reflected these to the client, when suddenly a fleeting look of joy crossed the client's face. The therapist stopped to explore the client's experience in that moment and discovered that in the midst of the client's pain, the fleeting joy signaled a positive feeling of appreciation and connection. The client felt that her pain was understood and recognized, and she felt in harmony with another human being while sharing her painful feelings. These momentary emotions are extremely important, because they signal to both client and therapist that the process of change and healing is on track. Therapeutic work is not only the accessing of core unpleasant maladaptive emotions, but also the accessing of the positive emotion that emerges—love, compassion, excitement, and pride. Clients also feel relieved and calmer after facing painful feelings. Unpleasant emotions need to be faced because they help deepen and disclose, but access to positive emotions serve to broaden and build.

A focus on positive experience is important in promoting change. For example, positive experiences of mastery, of having changed, of being helped, of feeling understood, of feeling unburdened, and of feeling close to another all are important feelings to process. When therapists track experience of a new positive feeling state, the client usually experiences what Fosha (2004) called *healing affects*. She suggested that some healing affects are focused on the experience of transformation of the self: The client feels "moved," "touched," or "emotional." Other healing affects are related to receptive affective experiences, involving feelings of love and gratitude toward the therapist; the client feels helped, seen, or understood. The markers for these experiences often are tears of joy or of being moved. These affects both signal and further the healing process. When clients experience healing affects, they are able to access deeper resources, including calm, wisdom, empathy toward self, and compassion toward others. These affects flow and are fully present to self and other. Transformational affects include expansiveness, the ability to breathe, feeling lighter, feeling electricity coursing through the body, a sense of suddenly feeling alive in the body and not just in the head, and a new sense of body integrity. Therapists need to learn to recognize and accept the healing affects, which let the client and therapist know that a healing impact has occurred.

CHANGING BELIEFS

Constructing alternatives also involves changing cognitive content. Cognitive content is worked on after the affective change has begun by explicitly confronting the articulated dysfunctional belief that has been accessed through emotional arousal. Core beliefs are accessed or articulated more readily and with far greater meaning when arrived at through the arousal of emotion. The conceptual "cold" belief that "I am unlovable" is far different from the experiential "hot" belief that is accompanied by all its visceral components and affective and cognitive associations. It is this hot belief that needs to be accessed for restructuring. Articulation of the maladaptive belief in consciousness and speaking it out loud while it is being experienced in the session then exposes it to reflective re-evaluation and exploration. This is the more explicit conscious aspect of the EFT change process.

Reflective restructuring aids the top-down aspect of the formation of new schemes and serves to consolidate change. Once new, more resilient resources have been accessed in a bottom-up experiential manner, these resources are used explicitly to challenge the negative views of the self. The view of the self as weak or failing is challenged from within by the newly accessed and validated need and by the additional resources mobilized by this need. Thus, the need to be loved or recognized that is at the core of a feeling of worthlessness is accessed and supported by the therapist, and this is used to combat the belief that the client is worthless or unlovable. A client may say, "I deserved more. I was only a child. I needed love" or "I need support, not criticism," thereby explicitly combating beliefs about worthlessness or weakness. With this conscious combating of beliefs, a change in the client's view of self, other, and world is articulated in language, and this consolidates the formation of the newly synthesized self-organization.

The process of accessing and combating self-critical beliefs in this way is self-evidently helpful. Working with beliefs in dependence is not as easy. Dependence fears are more difficult to articulate in words as beliefs than are self-criticisms and therefore are more difficult to challenge. They have more to do with expectations about others' responses than about self. Insecurity cannot be so clearly articulated in words as a belief or activated by saying things to oneself such as "I cannot survive without you or your comfort." Core insecurity and the associated views of self and others generally arise from interpersonal experience and can be seen as parts of a pattern of self–other relating that has been organized into emotion-based self–other relationship schemes in which the way of feeling with another is the core element. Thus, the scheme in which the self is experienced as unlovable or unworthy at the core of the "weak" self-experience is associated with a feeling of being alone, an unmet need for love, and a representation of the other as rejecting, rather than a belief that "I am unlovable." This abandoned and unloved self-organization leads to an expectation that others will reject the person and to a withdrawal from people out of the fear of rejection. The scheme in which the self is experienced as helplessly abandoned simply feels like "I cannot survive on my own." It is this experience that is at the core of the "weak" self-experience, which is associated with a need to be connected and taken care of, an expectation that others will abandon the person, and a response of clinging to others, rather than a more reflective belief about self.

Basic insecurity and anxiety therefore are automatically evoked more in relationship and by interaction than by critical self-talk or belief. It is helpful to articulate the insecure feeling of a fragile, dependent self in words such as "It's as though I will die if he or she doesn't respond to me warmly" or "I feel empty inside without you. Like I don't exist" or "I am afraid you [the other] will disappear, not exist any more, unless I hear your voice." This puts the basic fear into words where it can be reevaluated, but this basic insecurity cannot be changed by rational processes alone. The feeling of insecurity is a pervasive anxiety related to earlier experience of loss of connection and anxiety about being alone and helpless. Here accessing new resilient states and the dyadic regulation of affect are important for change, in addition to conscious re-evaluation of beliefs.

It is through the empathic attunement of another that a core sense of the self as an active agent rather than a passive victim begins to develop and strengthen. Being seen and understood by another helps the self begin to form a sense of itself as separate, as a coherent whole, and as an agent and helps the client experience the bodily experience of new ways of being with the other (Stern, 1985). The client's inability to hold onto his or her sense of connection and loss of a sense of permanence if the other is not immediately present or responsive begin to change when he or she is connected to an empathically attuned other. It is not a rational belief about self that changes, but an affective way of being. A sense of self as an agent able to receive and give love and soothe the self is formed by internalizing the empathic functions of the other. This replaces the other-focused, desperate neediness and yearning for love or comfort. The sense that "I need to please you to be OK" or "I don't exist without you" that leads to the inability to tolerate separation or rejection is transformed by experiencing a new agency in being with the other.

To consolidate this type of change, the therapist initially supports the emergence of the client's internal strengths, competence, and internal resources and then encourages him or her to explicitly combat his or her negative beliefs. Once the client's internal support and self-soothing capacities have been evoked, a sense of vitality and·the will to live are recontacted. Clients who felt vulnerably dependent on others now are able to provide themselves with the support that was not obtained from others, whereas self-critical clients find an inner sense of worth. Now clients can begin to assert themselves and challenge self-denigrating or invalidating beliefs about the self or any catastrophic assumptions concerning separation and abandonment. By developing a stronger sense of themselves as coherent, active agents who endure over time, clients experience greater security or worth. They can experience themselves as being more than what they feel in the moment and therefore less vulnerable to the moment. In response to a threat to security, awareness that the past and future still exist, that all is not destroyed and that "I am more than what just happened" in addition to the client's access to new needs and internal resources and the therapist's support and validation, provide the client with the strength to combat dysfunctional beliefs about the self's ability to survive, separated and autonomous, or to be worthy and lovable.

The EFT approach to working with changing self–other views and dysfunctional beliefs thus is not interpretive, didactic, or disputational. It is not focused on being more logical or on insight or on behavior change per se. EFT does not aim to collect evidence or to reason with clients to see that beliefs are irrational, and it does not focus on identifying or interpreting patterns from childhood or on skill training. EFT does not place a major emphasis on helping clients gain insight into patterns or become more rational or realistic. EFT also does not try to get clients to connect patterns in the present to the past or collect evidence for or against the depressogenic belief. All these processes do occur to differing degrees and can be helpful, but in our view it is not the truth or validity or the origins of patterns or beliefs that is the primary concern, but rather the usefulness of the patterns or beliefs. We take the stance from the outset that the client's articulated patterns or beliefs are probably neither useful nor helpful. Rather, they are generally self-evidently destructive. It is taken for granted that negative views and depressive beliefs are maladaptive if they make people feel bad, and therapists work to demonstrate this by helping clients experience how the beliefs or patterns make them feel. There is no evidence as compelling as feeling something. Awareness of patterns, although useful, does not in and of itself lead to change. *It is the emotional experience of new possibilities that does.* Therapists using EFT thus work to help clients discover how what they feel influences what they are telling themselves and how they interact, and how this then makes them feel, and what these feelings organize them to do. We also do not believe that maladaptive ideas, emotions, or patterns are not known or are unconscious and that making the unconscious conscious sets people free. Rather, avoided experience generally is known but is disclaimed or dissociated—that is, it is not experienced. Reowning experience is an important part of therapeutic work, as well as using or transforming reowned experience.

EFT thus involves exposing clients' unhealthy emotions at the core of their depression to more resilient internal experiences. Helping clients access their feelings of healthy sadness or anger exposes their fear and shame to new input. The maladaptive feelings and the shrinking action tendencies begin to be replaced with thrusting forward, reaching out, or recuperative tendencies, and clients' self-critical views of themselves as bad or worthless are challenged by the sense of worth accessed in healthier emotional states. Clients are thereby helped to integrate all parts of their experience into a new sense of self and to feel more self-accepting. Accessing a new emotional response or a new voice also leads to changes in interpersonal interactions. Once needs are focused on and reclaimed, clients begin to act more assertively to attain their goals.

DEALING WITH IMPASSES

Often clients with depression get stuck in their despair. They see no other possibilities. The construction of alternatives or completion is impeded. They seem unable to make progress, to let go of the bad feeling, and to access their resilience. Half of the battle of change in depression is won when clients see that they are in part authors of their own distress, rather than victims of uncontrollable affect or of abandonment by others. This acknowledgment is a form of taking responsibility for their own experience. Clients are not at fault for their depression; rather, they need to see that they are agents in the construction of their own realities and that they are engaged in a depressogenic process that they can change. Working with how clients interrupt their experience of emotion, discussed in chapter 12, is one important way to deal with blocked emotions. Another is to help clients see that they have many parts and to work together to access another part of the self.

For example, a client was stuck in the maladaptive state of helpless dependence. He entered this state when he met rejection or a challenge to his competence. At times he felt adequate and that he had things to offer, but when he was criticized or rejected, he entered this state and experienced desperate feelings of helplessness and isolation. He panicked and saw people as unsupportive aggressors and himself as lacking any substance. He was sucked into a vortex of maladaptive feelings. In this state, he lacked any solidity; he said he felt like "just an outline of myself, without any substance." The task for the therapist was to help this client get sufficient perspective on this helpless dependent state as a transient, self-created, dysfunctional state and to develop an alternate experience.

Rather than trying to demonstrate to clients with "bad" or "weak" core self-experience and enduring depression that their beliefs are not true, we have found it more helpful to get them to see that this state is one of many states that they enter into and that it is maladaptive; the problem is that they cannot regulate this state and sometimes get stuck rather than that they are making an error. The aim is to create a process sense of self—that it is a state that they enter, in which they get stuck—and that this is only one of a variety of states available to them. It is helpful whenever possible to try and build bridges linking this state to other states by shifts of attention, by changes in meaning, by reminding clients of times they were in other states, or by evoking other states in the session. The purpose is to create the experience of being able to transition between states to be able to shift from hopelessness to anger, sadness to humor, and so on. This activity creates flexibility in emotional style and strengthens links between different states (Greenberg, 2002).

This process of focusing on generating alternatives to despair depends crucially on the therapist maintaining the alliance and on appropriate interactional positioning. Clients have to feel throughout that the therapist is on their side, working with them against this problem state. When the client is feeling the depressive aloneness and insecurity, it is important that the therapist empathize with how painful it is to feel so helpless, fragile, and dependent and how anxiously insecure it leaves one, to feel like one cannot exist without the comfort or presence of another. This empathy with what it is like to feel so unable to exist must come from a place of real understanding and validation in the therapist. "No wonder" responses can be very helpful here; for example, "No wonder you feel so isolated and alone, having struggled all your life to be heard, but never having had a responsive parent or adult in your life." At the same time as validating the client's vulnerability, the therapist needs to hold on to the knowledge of the client's other possibilities and wonder out loud about them, even though the client may not be able to see other possibilities. Thus, the therapist might say, "The issue is how to find your own value when you are feeling so discarded and alone." Or the therapist might say, "The dilemma is how, when in these awful states of abandonment, you can find your own feet, and how I can help you to do that." Clients might insist that this is the way they are and that there is no other reality. The therapist at this point might say, "I know this is a strong part of your experience, and when you are in this state it really feels like this is true and all else is a sham." Rather than disagree, the therapist acknowledges the feeling but leaves open the possibility that other states are possible. The therapist therefore must hold onto the possibility of change even when the client cannot.

These moments when the client feels stuck and has given up are real existential moments of facing an impasse. In these situations it is important both to confront the maladaptive in the client and to support the healthy. It is here that the therapist's seeing of the growth-oriented core of the person—the person's possibilities—is crucial. Buber's (1958) view that in the "I–Thou" relationship it is the seeing of the possibility in others that helps the possibility come into being is important at this point. The therapist also needs to respond in such a way as to set attainable tasks for clients within their motivational reach. The goal is to bump the self-organizing process that cannot be instructed directly to change so that it will jump into a new trajectory. This is not done by explicit information input to try to change the content of clients' processing, but by boosting certain affective elements until a reorganization occurs and a new affectively cued mode of processing emerges. The therapist thus focuses on some elements of experience to amplify them or alludes to other possibilities, all the time engaging clients in the task of finding their strengths and resources while they are in their maladaptive feeling state. In this whole interaction, it is the therapist's valuing of the inner core of possibility in the client that is important. The therapist takes it for granted that there is a will to survive and thrive. The therapist has unconditional confidence in the client's inner core (Lietaer, 1993). The problem is not one of whether the resource is there, but rather of how to promote the type of new experience that will access it. The therapist does not try to prove to clients that their beliefs are not true or provide insight into origins of the problem, but rather works to access alternate emotional experience. This must all be done while the client is feeling the maladaptive feeling, so it is not a conceptual discussion; it is more of an existential experience.

HOMEWORK TO PROMOTE TRANSFORMATION

Homework is used in EFT predominantly to promote emotion awareness, regulation, reflection, and transformation of emotion (Greenberg & Warwar, in press). The main purpose of homework in experiential therapy is to consolidate and reinforce these types of in-session changes through extrasessional practice. Homework can be given to raise awareness of something newly discovered or to promote practice of regulation or transformation that has occurred in therapy. Homework is thus given as a key means to practice and consolidate change (Goldfried & Davison, 1994). Homework in EFT is not standardized and prescriptive, but created responsively. It often is uniquely fashioned to fit the client and circumstance and is designed to be in the client's proximal zone of development (Vygotsky, 1986), something that is not too far ahead but can promote a next step. Homework also is given when the client is in a teachable moment. What is most crucial is that homework suggestions need to fit the situation that is emerging in therapy.

For example, Anna reported in session that she was very uncomfortable in social situations. She complained of feeling lonely and isolated and wished she felt more comfortable interacting socially, but her discomfort and anxiety kept her away from social situations, and she turned down many invitations from friends. They explored this issue experientially in session using two-chair dialogue. Anna was surprised to discover that it was her own critical voice that made her feel that she was not good enough, and she recognized that this was what kept her isolated. Awareness homework was given to have her pay attention in social situations and to become aware of the criticisms that left her feeling unworthy, to write them down, and to allow herself to feel the impact of these criticisms. Change homework, consisting of asking her to practice standing up to this voice or to disagree with the criticisms, might be a helpful proposal at later stages of the therapy process when she has achieved this in a session, but this assignment would not be in her proximal zone at this time.

Homework thus needs to be highly attuned to clients' state and possibilities. Homework designed to prove that despair is unrealistic, offered while clients are feeling despairing, will not be sufficiently validating. It is only when a client has achieved an in-session experience of some resilience or an accessing of some strengths that homework is used to practice and strengthen a new more hopeful response. Then, and only then, might the therapist say, "Notice during the week what happens when you become despairing, and see if you can practice this new way of seeing things by saying, 'I know I have strengths. I am worthwhile.'" Or the therapist might ask the client to write down on cards five strengths and bring them in the next week. Homework thus needs to be in the client's proximal zone of development and is given to practice that which has already been experienced in the session. Therapists also need to be attuned to when they have given their clients homework that is too far ahead of them and correct this by taking responsibility for clients' failure to succeed at their homework.

Awareness of internal processes that interrupt or avoid emotion is one of the important goals of homework. The objective is for clients to come to experience and understand how they stop themselves from experiencing potentially adaptive emotions. Clients need to understand how they suppress their emotions so that the interruption is no longer automatic and they can regain some control or choice in the matter of their feelings. After heightening clients' awareness of an interruptive process in a session, a process such as squeezing back tears or deflecting a feeling, the therapist might have them enact in the session how they do this to themselves. Once the interruption is worked with in the session, then homework is helpful in both heightening awareness of and practicing the interruptive processes outside the sessions. Therapists can ask clients to be aware during the week of when and how they stop themselves from feeling and to actually practice the interruption.

Homework can also be given asking clients to document strengths and resources that were discussed in session. Clients can make this list on a card to keep with them all the time. In addition, they can be asked to add to this list other strengths as they are experienced over the course of the week. This assignment is not a conceptual exercise; rather, clients are to list their strengths as they actually experience them.

14

REFLECTION AND THE
CREATION OF NEW MEANING

The final phase of therapeutic work is the consolidation of new meaning and the reconstruction of narratives that confirm or change clients' identities and the views they have of themselves and their experiences. A primary objective in emotion-focused therapy (EFT) is the dialectical synthesis of reason and emotion, or the integration of head and heart. Emotion-focused techniques help clients to apprehend, symbolize, and integrate information from their rational and experiential systems (Epstein, 1994; Greenberg, Rice, & Elliott, 1993). As clients become aware of their feelings and begin to express their stories in words in the presence of another, they are given the opportunity to reflect on their experience in new ways. During this process, changes occur in clients' experiential knowing, including their immediate sensory experience, their bodily felt experience, and their holistic sense of themselves in the world.

When clients reflect on their experiences, they make connections between different elements of their lives, begin to posit alternative explanations for their experiences, revise their views of themselves or their history, and develop new narratives. This process is often accompanied by a sense of greater connectedness and mastery in their lives. The objective with clients with depression is to help them develop a new set of lenses through which to view themselves, the past, and the future more positively based on a renewed sense of self-worth and the energy to act in ways that are self-enhancing and not self-negating. By reconstructing their views of themselves, clients can develop narratives that emphasize their resiliency and newly acquired sense of agency.

Symbolic representation and reflective examination promote and facilitate each other as they create and transform clients' inner subjective experience and their actions. People's ability to symbolize their environment is one of the primary tools they use to master it and to develop strategies for action (Dewey, 1933; Luria, 1976; C. Taylor, 1990; Vygotsky, 1962). Numerous writers have recognized that it is people's capacity to symbolize their inner experience to know and understand it better that enhances their capacity for self-regulation and control (Harre, 1984; Orlinsky & Howard, 1986; Rennie, 1992). In psychotherapy, the capacity to symbolically represent experience is harnessed in the interest of acquiring self-knowledge and self-regulation so as to formulate more satisfying strategies for acting and living. In the process of symbolically representing their internal and external experience in words, clients objectify it and make it perceptible. Thus, they consciously come to know and understand their experience in ways that were not possible as long as it remained unexpressed.

The symbolic representation of experience results from a dialectical synthesis between language and experience. Thus, conscious experience is constituted by language, such that it is both created and transformed as it is represented in words (Dewey, 1933; Greenberg & Pascual-Leone, 1995; C. Taylor, 1990). Two points need to be stressed. First, inner experience is inchoate and unclear; it is only in the process of expressing it, for example, in words, play, ritual, or various art forms, that it becomes consciously known and understood. Second, the way experience is represented can transform and alter it. For example, there is a great difference between describing the experience of being seen in terms of being "revealed" or "exposed" to the other. The latter connotes a sense of threat that is not suggested by the former. As a result, the emotions and the action tendencies implicit in an experience and its evaluation will be very different depending on how it is described.

This is not to suggest that the meaning of people's experience and the way in which they represent it is entirely arbitrary. Rather, it is a dialectical construction between preconscious emotional experience that has been brought into awareness and the linguistic or other symbols that are used to represent it. The dialectical construction of experience in linguistic symbols is guided by an implicit, albeit inchoate, bodily felt sense and by a choice of words that constitute the best fit for representing the experience and giving it fuller form. The mediation and expression of inner subjective experience in language enhances clients' sense of themselves so that they can better understand their behavior, feelings, needs, and values (Watson & Greenberg, 1996).

EFT emphasizes verbal and nonverbal expression to assist clients in representing their inner experience. In the process of representing their inner experience, clients have the opportunity to come to understand how they construe events and identify patterns of responding or personal styles of behavior that they have developed from emotionally significant past experiences (Epstein, 1994; Greenberg et al., 1993; Watson, 1992). Emotions and actions are automatic, prereflective processes that developmentally precede, and occur independently of, representation and reflection (Luria, 1976; Pascual-Leone, 1991; C. Taylor, 1990; Vygotsky, 1962). As we described in chapter 2, people apprehend, evaluate, and respond to information about their environment at a preconscious level. An inherent difficulty for human beings in knowing and understanding their inner subjective experience and social interactions is that these are continually in flux and are less clearly perceptible than their experience of their physical environment. People's subjective experience and social interactions are potentially less available to conscious awareness, symbolization, and reflective scrutiny (Watson & Greenberg, 1996). As a result, people's perceptions of their inner subjective experience are liable to distortion, misapprehension, and misinterpretation and may be at odds with those of others who hold alternative views of events.

Therapists help clients to become aware of and label their inner subjective experience to create new meaning so that they can reflect on their newly symbolized inner experience and its implicit needs and action tendencies to have more control over their behavior and environments. Once clients have represented their inner experience, its meaning and implicit action tendencies can be more clearly understood. The meaning of their experiences and their action tendencies can subsequently be subjected to reflective examination. Reflective examination involves clients consciously scrutinizing, questioning, and evaluating their experience and behavior in terms of their current needs, goals, values, and social context. Symbolic representation and reflective examination of experience produce moments of insight that can provide understanding about the antecedents and consequences of clients' feelings and behavior. After emotions have been represented symbolically and subjected to reflection, clients are in a position to exercise greater conscious control of their feelings and actions so as to possess them rather than be possessed by them. Thus, clients are provided with a safe environment and encouraged to focus their attention on their internal and interpersonal experiences to symbolize them in language and subject them to reflective scrutiny with the aim of solving the specific cognitive–affective problems that are causing them distress (Greenberg et al., 1993; Greenberg & Pascual-Leone, 1995; J. Pascual-Leone, 1991; Watson, 1992; Watson & Greenberg, 1996; Watson & Rennie, 1994).

Emotional expression facilitates reflection, the construction of narratives, and the creation of meaning. As clients symbolize their feelings and explain themselves and their world, they develop narratives that can potentially allow them to see events differently. Narratives provide a structure for the events in people's lives as they temporally sequence and coordinate actions, people, and events and give perspective and meaning to people's experiences. It is through the stories people tell that they come to understand and incorporate experiences as part of their developing life stories. Reflecting on their narratives allows them to evaluate them and develop alternatives. Pennebaker and Segal (1999) showed that talking and writing about emotionally traumatic experiences immediately caused a drop in skin conductance and blood pressure and improved long-term health and immune functioning. The authors suggested that writing appears to force people to stand back and reorganize their thoughts and feelings in terms of a coherent story in which emotions, thoughts, and actions are organized into a narrative framework with a clear beginning, middle, and end. Subjects commented that the process of writing made them think things through and look at themselves from the outside.

The process of reflecting on experience leading to the creation of new meaning is ongoing throughout treatment and continues beyond any single emotionally laden episode in therapy. However, it is often during episodes of emotional arousal that clients generate core metaphors that capture the complexity and implicit nuances of their experience, giving it a new shape that provides insight into their behavior and the impact of events. These metaphors can subsequently be woven into the fabric of therapy to act as touchstones and beacons of change. At the beginning of treatment, in an attempt to come to fully know the extent of their pain and share it with their therapists, clients might describe their sense of hopelessness. For example, Miriam came to therapy seeking help with her depression. Her mother had died when she was quite young, and she had been raised by her older sister, who had recently died of cancer. Over the past year the client was scattered at work, was unable to concentrate, and was experiencing difficulties with her partner of five years. When she first came to therapy, Miriam described her sense of herself "as sitting in the ashes of a bombed-out city, where nothing could grow." As therapy progressed and she allowed herself to grieve her sister's death and her own childhood losses, she began to speak of planting seeds both metaphorically and in real life, and by the end of therapy she described herself as watching things blossoming and growing all around her.

The distillation of experience in metaphors facilitates the process not only of symbolization but also of reflection; they can lead to new insights and alternative ways of viewing experience. Experientially based metaphors such as being "alone in a vast field," "in a glass cage," "at sea in a rudderless boat," or "thrown on a trash heap" not only symbolize problems, but also contain solutions and provide a sense of what the client needs and clues to how they might meet those needs. In contrast, positive metaphors like "rising out of pit" or "being able to stand firm" or "to freshly see again" capture emergence, development, and the creation of new meanings and solutions. As clients gain insight into their feelings and begin to develop alternative views of themselves, experiences become reorganized so that clients are able to symbolize and organize emotional experience in terms of a new, more resilient sense of self. When this occurs, the self is no longer judged as a failure, but rather as capable of success in the face of obstacles and able to thrive even when confronted with experiences that previously might have been experienced as threatening to survival (e.g., separation from attachment objects). Thus, one's views of the self, the world, and one's experiences are revised and reconstructed as they become illuminated and reflected on in therapy.

THE PROCESS OF REFLECTION

Once clients have symbolized their experience and their personal styles of responding have become clear, they can be subjected to reflective examination. The dialectical synthesis of symbolized experience and reflective scrutiny can result in the creation of new meaning as events acquire altered significance and alternative courses of action are developed. *Reflectivity*, defined as radical self-examination (C. Taylor, 1990), is not merely an intellectual exercise, but rather represents a passionate commitment to the self in an attempt to come to know and realize it in action more fully and completely.

After clients have expressed and clearly articulated their feelings and are aware of their implicit action tendencies, they are in a position to reflect on and evaluate their actions and experiences. Clients' reflectivity reflects their instrumental and moral agency, as well as their ability to think about feelings and actions in the moment-by-moment transactions in therapy. *Instrumental agency* refers to clients' capacity to be goal oriented, independent, and autonomous in their actions, whereas *moral agency* refers to their ability to evaluate the significance of things for themselves in terms of higher-order needs and values (C. Taylor, 1990). The meaning or significance that things have for clients is revealed by their emotions. Once these have been articulated and brought into conscious awareness, clients can begin the process of constructing new meaning as they reflect on and reevaluate the significance of events in the light of current needs, goals, values, and social contexts. Thus, both the instrumental and the moral dimensions of clients' agency are emphasized in a dialectical constructivist perspective of therapy.

These two aspects of clients' agency can be better understood if a distinction is made between first-order and second-order evaluations (C. Taylor, 1990). First-order evaluations are analogous to organismic experience: They are the automatic emotions that the individual experiences and expresses. In contrast, second-order evaluations are the product of subjecting those initial responses to reflective scrutiny and evaluation. The dialectical synthesis of information from both first-order and second-order evaluations is an important process in EFT designed to facilitate enhanced well-being and greater understanding of self and others. If people act on the basis of first-order evaluations only, their behavior remains automatic and outside of conscious control. If they act only on the basis of second-order evaluations, then their actions may become dim reflections of their own innermost needs, desires, and goals. This may have been at the root of Rogers's (1959) observation that accessing values in therapy was unproductive. However, if clients adequately represent both their inner experience and their second-order values, they are in a position to negotiate a satisfying compromise between the two.

In addition to evaluating their experience in terms of its personal significance and meaning, clients also evaluate experience using cognitive abilities that are necessary to solve problems and perform creative acts in other domains. Three important activities have been identified as essential components of clients' reflective self-examination in therapy (Watson & Rennie, 1994). First, clients need to inquire into their inner experience (comprising their emotions, needs, values, and perceptions) and their outer experience (comprising their physical and social environments). Second, clients need to examine and explain their behavior and feelings as they represent them. They begin to see connections between their behavior and external events and their social contexts. Third, clients can evaluate their behavior and experience after they gain an understanding of the antecedents and consequences. Clients continually evaluate their representations of their experience in terms of their goodness of fit and strategic implications. To properly evaluate their experience once it has been adequately represented, clients need to articulate their desires, needs, goals, and values.

If clients are to feel and act differently, they need to acquire a sense of control over themselves and the events in their lives. An important by-product of inquiry is that it provides a sense of control as it allows the relationships among various aspects of experience to be revealed (Dewey, 1933). The thinking through of alternatives and the examination of the possible implications and consequences affords people the freedom of informed choice. Inquiry is often prompted by discord, conflict, perplexity, and doubt. Dewey (1933) saw perplexity and doubt as the motivating force that propels people to seek out or hunt for solutions to resolve dilemmas and ambiguities and to devise methods with which to cope with them. Moreover, the nature of the problem determines its solution, which in turn determines the process of thinking (R. J. Bernstein, 1971).

Negative emotions, in particular, alert people to problematic aspects of experience that require attention, and it is often these that clients bring to therapy. In therapy clients engage in a search motivated by unpleasant affective arousal and a desire to know and understand the significance of their experience to create new meaning. In EFT the questions clients pose about their experience are termed *markers*. Therapists use markers to identify aspects of clients' experiencing that they may be ready to work on. The questions that clients formulate about their experience help therapists to determine the information clients need to access to facilitate the resolution of problematic issues in therapy. For example, with problematic reactions marked by behavioral or emotional reactions that clients see as puzzling or too extreme in some way, therapists promote the recollection and symbolic representation of the problematic situation, whereas with unfinished business marked by the presence of lingering bad feelings toward a significant other, therapists promote the recollection and symbolic representation of the other to facilitate emotional expression (Elliott, Watson, Goldman, & Greenberg, 2004; Greenberg et al., 1993).

For example, a client who felt humiliated and defeated in her marriage began to reevaluate the extent of her husband's power and to question whether he could harm her. After some reflection, she became aware that she had seen him as too powerful and that he was probably more dependent on her than she had realized. In addition, she resolved that she wanted to express her feelings in the relationship and to inform him when his behavior was hurtful to her. Instead of allowing her husband to dictate the rules of the house, she began to stand up to him more and assert her own priorities.

REFLECTING ON REPRESENTATIONS OF EXPERIENCE

An important aspect of EFT for depression is to help clients become more reflective about their inner experience so that they symbolize and examine it to find more satisfying alternatives. The activities that constitute reflection include inquiry, examination, and evaluation. Inquiry is the act of exploring experience and of interrogating it to acquire greater understanding and to access as much relevant information as possible to develop new perspectives and insight into a particular problem area. Once clients have explored and adequately represented a situation or their feelings about it, they can examine it and evaluate whether their perspective is adequate or whether there are alternative explanations, or they can evaluate whether there are other ways of acting and feeling that might be more satisfying and consistent with their goals. Reflection allows people to step back from their experience and to think about what they feel, in relation to whom, and about what personal need, value, expectation, goal, or issue. The reflective differentiation of self and other allows clients to assume different vantages on the problems that they confront and to see alternative perspectives and solutions that can then be incorporated into their life histories.

Many clients with depression seem to have lost touch with the ability to actively explore their feelings and situations to construct alternatives. They feel helpless, defeated, and unable to problem solve. They have lost a sense of perspective and tend to see things as black or white. The capacity to reflect on themselves and their experience is impaired, and they have difficulty planning and maintaining a balanced perspective. They tend to ruminate, have little energy, and are unfocused and at a loss. Thus, their sense of agency is significantly impaired. An important goal is to help them acquire insight into their internal processes so that they can begin to figure out alternative ways of responding or interpreting their experience to feel more effective. As part of this process, clients need to differentiate their inner reactions to recognize the nuances and flow of their feelings that have become swallowed by the black hole of their depression.

Roberta came to therapy because she was feeling depressed. During the course of therapy, she had come to understand that much of her depression was as a result of silencing herself and the expression of her needs in relation to others. One week she came into therapy particularly down. She had just returned from visiting a good friend, who had moved away a number of years ago and whom she had not seen in a while. She reported that she had had a wonderful visit but that she felt very disconnected from her partner since her return and had been feeling irritable and down. She wondered if there was something wrong with the relationship. The therapist began to explore her feelings of sadness. As she spoke, she realized that she had felt very sad leaving her friend but had stuffed it down so as not to be a drag on her partner and spoil their brief vacation. As she explored her feelings, she recalled that she and her friend had separated from their spouses at the same time and had provided each other with support during a very difficult period. They had shared a home for a while and had helped each other parent their children. Her friend's move had left a big hole in her life, and seeing her again had stirred up the painful memories associated with her divorce.

She slowly allowed herself to weep and express the sorrow that leaving her friend had evoked in her. She felt relief as she allowed herself to finally express her sorrow at losing close contact with her friend and the other changes that had resulted from her separation. As she reflected on her sadness, she realized that the reason she had felt so down throughout the week was because she had stifled the feelings. She also realized that her irritability and sense of disconnection had nothing to do with her partner or her feelings toward him and the relationship, but rather were the result of some of the pain she still carried about her marital separation. After fully expressing her feelings and representing her situation, Roberta's feelings of sadness diminished, and she had a new perspective on the events of the last few weeks.

REFLECTION IN THE SERVICE OF REPRESENTATION

Two important processes contribute to the creation of new meaning in EFT—labeling and expressing emotional experience to acquire insight, and then reflecting on those feelings to problem solve and re-examine behavior and feelings to devise alternative ways of acting. To successfully reflect on their experience, clients need to formulate a problem or area of inquiry. Therapists facilitate clients' inquiry into their experience in a number of different ways. To facilitate the task of reflection, they help clients to focus on their inner experience and affective reactions and to examine and explore the origin and personal implications of feelings and behaviors.

Reflecting on Inner Experience

One of the important ways that therapists facilitate and encourage clients' reflective processing is by distilling and reflecting clients' descriptions of their inner experience and sense of the world in a tentative manner. Therapists work to have clients access and reflect on their inner experience. First, therapists teach clients to focus and attend to their inner experience and to represent it in words. While doing so, they encourage clients to find the best fit and to interrogate their experience to ensure that the words they are using to describe it capture its essence and provide the best representation of their inner world. The process of labeling feelings creates new meaning as clients come to see the significance of events for themselves. As clients begin to perceive the significance of events, they are able to see themselves and events differently. For example, Irene had recently become involved with a musician, and she came to treatment because she was experiencing disabling depression. Her boyfriend had been leaving his equipment at her apartment after his performances. His work also took him away a lot, and Irene was left babysitting the instruments. At first she did not appear to mind, but then she found herself becoming irritable and depressed. When she began to explore her feelings with the help of the therapist, she realized that she was feeling crowded out by the equipment in her small apartment. She was resentful because she did not feel that she had agreed to share her space, but the situation had just evolved over time. Once she realized what was the basis for her depression, she was able to think about alternatives that would allow her to reclaim space without jeopardizing the relationship.

As clients represent their experience by speaking aloud or in writing, they are able to evaluate the accuracy and implications of what they are saying. This evaluation reflects the integration of cognition and affect and facilitates affect regulation. The objective is not just to encourage the arousal and expression of feeling, but also, once this is accomplished, to subject the emotions to interpretation and examination to acquire insight into behavior, feelings, and situations. Therapists deliberately offer their reflections and observations in a tentative, inquiring manner to facilitate clients' inquiry into their experience. The tentative style of experiential responses not only functions to facilitate an egalitarian relationship, but is used to stimulate clients' reflectivity. Clients are asked each time to check whether their descriptions really match their inner experience. They are asked to evaluate whether the narrative they are constructing fully captures the complexity of their experience. Tentative reflections help to catalyze clients' reflections on their experience as they become the evaluators of its fit. This prompts them to question whether their experience of themselves—for example feeling very alone, useless, or without support—is accurate or complete.

The manner in which therapists promote a re-examination of experience with EFT contrasts with that of some other therapeutic approaches, which use Socratic questioning or evidence to challenge emotional responses and core beliefs to help clients reevaluate aspects of their experience. Therapists using EFT reflect what their clients have said to hold up a mirror of their experience so that clients can then subject it to scrutiny and evaluation. By responding tentatively, therapists are implicitly asking clients to check whether their descriptions and labels of events fit. The tentative, probing nature of therapist responses helps to slow clients down so that they have the chance to reflect on their experience and see it in new ways. The objective is to move clients out of repetitive thinking grooves and encourage them to explore their experience to see new perspectives or develop emergent ways of thinking. Often therapists model the process of inquiry and exploration in their tone of voice, which can be softened, tentative, and probing. The objective is to unravel rehearsed narratives so that new material can be discovered and incorporated.

The differentiation and expression of feelings in words leads clients to new insights about what they need and how events are affecting them. An important task for therapists is to help clients see how they are treating themselves and what they may be doing that is contributing to their depression. As we noted in chapter 7, often clients with depression have internalized behaviors that may be self-punitive, harsh, and critical, or alternatively they may be neglectful of themselves and their needs. So, for example, therapists work to make clients aware that they are being self-critical or neglectful so that clients can reflect on that aspect of their experiencing. Once clients become aware of their internal dialogue and negative behaviors, they can then think about alternative ways of responding. An active ingredient in the change process is to have clients recognize the emotional impact of their negative behaviors and to express their needs. Once they are aware of their needs, they can reflect on ways to meet them and develop alternative behaviors that are more nurturing and less depressogenic.

Examining the Origins and Implications of Experience

An active ingredient in EFT is to have clients pose questions or define a problem about their emotional experience and behavior that they can purposefully explore and reflect on in the session. Exploration of the problem may be an inquiry into its origins—for example, "Why am I so hard on myself?" or "Why is it so difficult for me to express my needs to my partner?" The problem may also be defined as a proposition that the client then examines and explores to resolve a specific issue or to acquire new insights into ways of behaving. For example, "I have this habit of silencing myself, and it is posing problems for me at work." Alternatively, a client might observe, "I found myself becoming even more depressed after I had dinner with some friends the other night." These statements help clients and therapists define areas of inquiry that they can then pursue in the session to increase understanding of client functioning and to explore alternatives. The exploration needs to be personal and deeply reflective as clients seek to articulate not only their inner feelings, but also their core values and the possible reasons or factors contributing to the development of the behavior or feelings and perceptions that they are investigating.

For example, Erica observed that she silenced herself around people. She realized that doing so contributed to her depression, but she did not understand the trigger. Her therapist used systematic evocative unfolding to help Erica identify the trigger that caused her to shut down her own needs. During the exploration, it emerged that Erica was very concerned about hurting others. After gaining this insight, she began to explore or question how this style had developed. She began to reflect on her childhood and realized that she had always felt the need to take care of her mother. Her mother, who had confided in Erica about her difficulties with Erica's father, seemed very fragile. In addition, her mother constantly threatened abandonment, complaining that she could not cope with the responsibility of four children. Erica came to see that she had suppressed her own needs and desires around her mother to try to ensure that she would not abandon Erica and her siblings and to ease her mothers' difficulties.

FACILITATING REFLECTION WITH TWO-CHAIR WORK

Therapists often help clients develop a focus of inquiry by observing how clients treat themselves. They are attuned to when their clients make self-critical, controlling, and punitive self-statements. Alternatively, clients may be angry or contemptuous with themselves. When this occurs, therapists may gently observe aloud that the client seems angry and self-critical. If a client agrees, the therapist suggests that they focus on working on those intrapersonal processes to try to resolve the anger and to change the self-critical behaviors. Engaging in two-chair work not only heightens clients' awareness of their behavior, but also facilitates the development of new meaning and ways of behaving as clients construct alternative responses and come to understand their experiences differently.

Timothy, who had recently separated and then reconciled with his wife, was depressed and upset. He remained upset about events that had occurred early in their marriage and was unable to let go of them. When he came to therapy, he recalled that during the first years of his marriage, he had been really happy. He and his wife had postponed having children, as they were each building their careers. Although he suggested the idea of children, his wife seemed uncertain, so not wanting to pressure her, he did not suggest it again, preferring to wait until she was ready. In the meantime, his wife started investing in the stock market. Timothy was concerned and asked her to limit her activity, but she persisted, and they subsequently lost a lot of money. This forced them to delay having a family; finally, when they did try, his wife had a number of miscarriages and was advised not to try to conceive again because of her age.

Timothy said that he loved his wife but that he was very angry about what had happened to them. Initially he had been angry with his wife, but later he felt angry with himself. He agreed to engage in a two-chair dialogue to explore the basis of his anger. During the dialogue, Timothy realized that he was disappointed and furious with himself for not taking a stronger stance with his wife. He wished that he had insisted that they have children when they were younger and that he had been more vocal about his reservations about his wife's investments in the stock market. At the beginning of the dialogue, he was quite unforgiving of himself.

Timothy: You failed to take care of your family. You should have made your needs clear, and then you wouldn't be here now.

Therapist: Come over here. [*indicating the self chair*] How does it feel when this side tells you that you failed to take care of your family?

Timothy: I feel terrible . . . so useless.

Therapist: Tell this side about how awful you feel.

Timothy: I feel so bleak and hopeless.

Therapist: What does this side need? [*indicating experiencing chair*]

Timothy: I need you to stop making me feel so bad . . . stop criticizing me.

Therapist: So you need this side to stop. OK. Come over here. [*indicating critic chair*] How does this side respond when the other says, "I feel so useless when you criticize me. Please stop"?

Timothy: Well, it is your fault. If you had been more of a man, you would have intervened and shown some leadership. You got yourself here.

Therapist: So what are you saying? "I am not going to stop criticizing you"?

Timothy: Yeah . . . I guess so. You should have taken care of things.

Therapist:	Come back over here. [*indicating self chair*] How do you feel when this side won't listen and dismisses your request?
Timothy:	Awful. [*slumping further into his chair*] I feel like I don't count; that I am not worth anything.
Therapist:	So it makes you feel awful. What do you need from him?
Timothy:	I need him to understand.
Therapist:	OK. Come back over here. So, how do you respond when this side says, "I feel awful when you don't listen to me, I need you to understand"?
Timothy:	I don't know how to . . . I feel blank . . . I don't know how to respond.
Therapist:	Who is this? Is this you, or did someone else treat you like this?
Timothy:	It's me.
Therapist:	So this is the part that had to take care of you after you lost your parents. It was trying to take care of you and did not want you making any mistakes . . . in case your relatives were angered?
Timothy:	Yes! I guess I did not learn how to be kind to myself. It is hard to listen to myself and allow myself to make mistakes.
Therapist:	So this is what you need to learn. It feels as if you do not have the skills. What would you do if a friend or your wife was upset because they made a mistake?
Timothy:	I would tell them that mistakes happen . . . no one is perfect. Mistakes are learning opportunities.

The therapist stepped back from the process to reflect on the client's way of treating himself and to understand the origins of this behavior. The client began to develop a new view of self as overly harsh and unforgiving. He realized that it was important to treat himself with more care and understanding. As they explored further, the client realized that if he was able to forgive himself, he might be able to forgive his wife.

FACILITATING REFLECTION IN EMPTY-CHAIR WORK

The creation of new meaning in empty-chair work often involves acquiring a new perspective of the other and understanding the other's behavior. Alternatively, clients may develop a new view of self when they learn to recognize that they did not deserve to be treated badly by the other and are able to assert themselves with the other and to set boundaries that may have been violated. Empty-chair work can be suggested to define an area of inquiry when the client expresses a lingering bad feeling or difficulties with a significant other. There are two objectives with this task to create new meaning: to help clients to become aware of and express feelings that have been suppressed and to revise their view of themselves or the other as they take the opportunity to reflect on the others' behavior and response to their feelings. As we have discussed, during this task it is very important that clients use "I" language and express their feelings and the subjective impact of the other's behavior, as opposed to angry blaming statements that accuse the other of wrongdoing. As in marital therapy, accusations typically beget defensiveness in the other, even an imagined other. Dialogue and understanding are promoted by the appropriate expression of feelings.

Clients with depression often carry scars of loss and injury at the hands of others. Therapists help them become aware of their feelings by having them envisage the significant other implicated in the loss or injury. Once clients are in touch with their feelings, they are encouraged to express these to the other; the therapist listens empathically and guides the expression of feelings, ensuring that the client uses "I" language and talks about the subjective impact of events and deeds. Once they have finished expressing their feelings, clients are asked to move to the empty chair and to respond. This is the point at which clients are asked to reflect on the other. As they do this, they may become aware of the other's perspective and develop an understanding of the other's worldview. Thus, the client may realize that her mother's irritability when she was a child was because she was tired from working two jobs to feed and clothe the client and her siblings, and not because she did not love her. The client is ideally able to access or gain a sense that the parent, who initially was perceived as rejecting, did in fact love the client and regrets the pain that the client has experienced. This new view of the other can then be reintegrated into the client's narrative, and a new one, in which she was loved and cared for by her parent, can replace the one in which she felt unloved by her mother. Clients thus are able to throw a gestalt switch and have the opportunity to hear the other's story, which may not have been accessible or obvious to them as children.

However, sometimes the significant other is not able to respond in a positive way. The other may fail to acknowledge or respond to the client's pain. This is an important diagnostic sign that the client does not have a positive introject. Instead of constructing a new view of self by being able to reflect on the other and accessing a positive internal object, such clients need to construct a new view of self and new ways of treating themselves through the empathic therapeutic relationship. With these clients therapists move away from the more active tasks and resort to forms of empathy to strengthen the self.

When clients have been abused, therapists may prefer not to have the other respond. Clients who have been abused have typically suppressed their needs to defer to those of the abusing other; consequently, the objective is not so much to have them throw a gestalt switch and reflect on the experience of the other to understand him or her better, but rather to have these clients assert boundaries. They need to hold others accountable for their behavior and to develop new ways of viewing themselves.

The new view that therapists are trying to help abused clients develop is that they are lovable and did not deserve to be abused. This new view can be facilitated in a number of ways. First, therapists' empathic prizing of clients teaches them that they are worthy of respect and have a right to attend to their inner experience and protect themselves from harm. Second, therapists may ask their clients to imagine how they would respond if they saw another child or someone they loved being abused as they were. This often elicits a protective, caring response to the imagined child that clients can then think about applying to themselves. Once clients have constructed this new view of themselves, they are ready to complete the empty-chair task and tell the abusing other that the behavior was unacceptable, that it caused pain and suffering, that they did not deserve to be treated in this way, and most importantly that they will not let it happen again as they commit to protecting themselves in future and ensuring that their boundaries are not violated. This may prompt another period of reflection and learning as clients begin to identify boundary violations and the behaviors of others that hurt and impinge on them.

FACILITATING REFLECTION IN SYSTEMATIC EVOCATIVE UNFOLDING

A primary objective in resolving or developing an understanding of problematic reactions is to help clients become more reflective about the links among their behavior, their environment, and their feelings. Once clients can see the links among these three aspects of experience, they are in a better position to develop alternative ways of behaving that are more consistent with their needs, values, and goals. The first objective in systematic evocative unfolding is to help clients recall the scenes in which their reactions occurred in a vivid way so as to access and track their affective reaction. This detailed description enables clients and therapists to identify the event or stimulus that triggered the client's reaction. Once they have identified the trigger, therapists focus their clients on identifying their styles of being in the world on which clients can then reflect. For example, Susan, a client who was recovering from depression, did not understand why she had not been able to enjoy herself at a party over the weekend. After exploring the event she realized that she was holding herself back at the party and not joining in because she was trying to keep herself in a neutral zone. She hoped that if she could stay in neutral, not allowing herself to get too happy, then she would not get too depressed. Once she understood her response, she was able to reflect on this solution. She realized that she was paying a high price to protect herself from her depression. As she came to understand the triggers for her depression better, she was able to stop clinging to the neutral zone and to enjoy her family and friends once again.

EVALUATION OF THE SOCIAL CONTEXT, VALUES, AND GOALS

When clients process their emotional experience, they evaluate their responses in terms of their social context, values, and objectives. They evaluate whether their responses are appropriate, whether others will respond positively or negatively, and whether their emotional experiences further their goals and fit with their sense of themselves. If their interpersonal environment is unsupportive, they might deny or distort their experience to win or maintain the approval or sense of belonging with others. In a similar way, if their emotional experience is seen as contrary to their values or self-image, they may also distort or deny it. For example, clients who were subjected to emotional or physical abuse may have difficulty recognizing that they are angry. Anger may be seen as contrary to how they want to appear, and they may view its expression as threatening. These clients need help to deconstruct their worldviews so that they can accommodate a fuller range of emotional experience. This can be a slow process, because clients need to reflect on the costs and benefits of their current ways of being in the world.

Therapists help their clients to see the impact that their current ways of being are having on themselves. This examination helps to generate new narratives of the client's experience that can be reflected on in a different way. However, in addition to becoming more aware of their experiences, clients may need to develop a stronger sense of self before they can generate new meaning systems that they can use to integrate their newly emergent feelings. This type of scenario is often seen when clients feel trapped in partnerships or marriages that are very difficult, but the option of leaving does not fit with their views of themselves, nor is it consistent with the values of their religion and larger social network. These clients may need a lot of time to reconstruct a view of themselves that will accommodate the notion of divorce and themselves as a divorced person, and they may need a lot of time to gather the strength to act contrary to social norms and expectations. Once they have a better sense of their feelings, clients may need to reflect deeply about the choices that face them and weigh the implications of new courses of action very carefully.

DECONSTRUCTING WORLDVIEWS

Therapists use empathic reflection to help clients deconstruct their worldviews and develop alternative perspectives, a crucial aspect of the change process. Clients with depression often feel stuck and unable to envisage alternatives, which can result when there is a clash between their needs and their values. For example, Dennis was very unhappy in his relationship. He found his wife to be critical and unsympathetic to his goals and aspirations. She refused to seek marital counseling or to acknowledge that there was anything wrong with the relationship. Dennis was beginning to feel that he had no option but to leave, but he was having great difficulty accepting this decision. He did not see himself as divorced and felt that it was contrary to his religious views and his social group. Before Dennis was able to leave his marriage, he needed to deconstruct his worldview so as to allow for a wider set of feelings and behaviors. He needed to reflect deeply on his values and to decide how much he was willing to sacrifice to maintain his current image of himself.

Helping clients deconstruct their value systems and reconcile them with their desires and needs can be a lengthy process. They need to develop alternative frameworks or worldviews to accommodate the events that have happened to challenge their cherished view of themselves (K. Clarke, 1989). There is often grief involved as clients let go of cherished perspectives of the world and adopt a different set of lenses to view the events of their lives. Clients often need to develop a stronger sense of self so that they are less threatened by the need to differ from the larger social system of which they are a part and are able to acknowledge and attend to their own needs.

DIFFICULTIES IN FACILITATING REFLECTION

Some clients have great difficulty being reflective. The capacity to reflect on feelings and behaviors requires a certain level of cognitive–affective development. Clients with histories of severe abuse and neglect have difficulty processing their affect. They may be unaware of their affective experience; alternatively, they may be so overwhelmed by their experience that they have difficulty naming and labeling it. These clients have difficulty stepping back and reflecting on their experience. They seem to swing from intense states of arousal to equally intense judgments about their self-worth. Clients may also have difficulty asserting themselves sufficiently to generate new meaning and an alternative narrative; they may not be in touch with their inner experience, or they may be fearful of the consequences of asserting themselves with another to whom they are still attached. Before these clients can engage in reflection, they need to be given the skills to cope with their intense emotional experience. This can be a slow process as therapists help to heighten their clients' awareness and teach them to identify and label their feelings. However, once this has been achieved and they have developed a stronger sense of themselves and a better awareness of their emotional experience, it is possible to start to facilitate their reflection about that experience more directly. Reflection can be facilitated by asking clients questions about the origins of their feelings and helping them to frame their experience in terms of conflict splits, unfinished business, an unclear felt sense, or a problematic reaction.

Another difficulty that can occur is that clients with severe abuse or neglect histories are unable to throw a gestalt switch to shift and imagine themselves in the role of the other. Sometimes the imagined other was disturbed and unpredictable, so that it is hard to know how he or she would respond to requests for comfort. Alternatively, these clients may still be enmeshed with their significant others and may not yet have acquired distinct views of each of them as separate and distinct individuals that would enable them to present differentiated views of the other. Such clients may also be low in empathy and thus have difficulty shifting to take the other's perspective. All these scenarios suggest the need for more relational work to assist clients in building more coherent narratives, differentiating from significant others, learning to manage their affective reactions, and developing positive internal models. The objective is to help clients develop their emotional processing skills so that they are able to get to the point where they can reflect on their experience to effect changes in themselves and their environments.

In emotion-focused psychotherapy, clients are encouraged to be more hypothetical in their approach to the world and to recognize the subjectivity of their experience, which allows them to consider other possibilities both with respect to the interpretation of events and their reactions to those events. In this way experiential techniques serve a dual function of helping clients to express emotion and reflect on those expressions to promote change.

REFERENCES

Abercrombie, H. C., Schaefer, S. M., Larson, C. L., Oakes, T. R., Holden, J. E., Perlman, S. B., et al. (1998). Metabolic rate in the right amygdala predicts negative affect in depressed patients. *NeuroReport, 9,* 3301–3307.

Abramson, L. Y., Seligman, M. E., & Teasdale, J. D. (1978). Learned helplessness in humans: Critique and reformulation. *Journal of Abnormal Psychology, 87,* 49–74.

Adams, K. E., & Greenberg, L. S. (1996, June). *Therapists' influence on depressed clients' therapeutic experiencing and outcome.* Paper presented at the 43rd Annual Convention for the Society for Psychotherapy Research, St. Amelia Island, FL.

Akhavan, S. (2001). *Comorbidity of hopelessness depression with borderline and dependent personality disorders: Inferential, coping, and anger expression styles as vulnerability factors.* Unpublished doctoral dissertation, Temple University, Philadelphia.

Allan, S., & Gilbert, P. (2002). Anger and anger expression in relation to perceptions of social rank, entrapment and depression. *Personality and Individual Differences, 32,* 551–565.

American Psychiatric Association. (1994). *Diagnostic and statistical manual of mental disorders* (4th ed.). Washington, DC: Author.

Arnold, M. B. (1984). *Feelings and emotions: The Loyola symposium.* Oxford, England: Academic Press.

Auszra, L., Herrmann, I., & Greenberg, L. (2004, June). *The relationship between emotional arousal, productivity and outcome in emotion-focused therapy of depression.* Paper presented at the Society for Psychotherapy Research, Rome, Italy.

Avagyan, J. (2001). *Emotional arousal in psychotherapy: An intensive analysis of eight cases.* Unpublished undergraduate thesis, York University, Toronto, Ontario, Canada.

Bargh, J. A. (1982). Attention and automaticity in the processing of self-relevant information. *Journal of Personality and Social Psychology, 43,* 425–436.

Bargh, J., & Chartrand, T. (1999). The unbearable automaticity of being. *American Psychologist, 54,* 462–479.

Barrett, L. F., Lane, R. D., Sechrest, L., & Schwartz, G. E. (2000). Sex differences in emotional awareness. *Personality and Social Psychology Bulletin, 26,* 1027–1035.

Beauregard, M., Levesque, J., & Bourgouin, P. (2001). Neural correlates of conscious self-regulation of emotion. *Journal of Neuroscience, 21,* 6993–7000.

Bechera, A., Tranel, D., Damasio, H., Adolphs, R., Rockland, C., & Damasio, A. R. (1995). Double dissociation of conditioning and declarative knowledge relative to the amygdala and hippocampus in humans. *Science, 269,* 1115–1118.

Beck, A. T. (1983). Cognitive therapy of depression: New perspectives. In P. J. Clayton & J. E. Barrett (Eds.), *Treatment of depression: Old controversies and new approaches* (pp. 265–290). New York: Raven Press.

Beck, A. T. (1996). Beyond belief: A theory of modes, personality, and psychopathology. In P. M. Salkovskis (Ed.), *Frontiers of cognitive therapy* (pp. 1–25). New York: Guilford Press.

Beck, A. T., Rush, A. J., Shaw, B. F., & Emery, G. (1979). *Cognitive therapy of depression.* New York: Wiley.

Benjamin, L. S. (1996). Introduction to the special section on structural analysis of social behavior. *Journal of Consulting and Clinical Psychology, 64,* 1203–1212.

Bergin, A., & Garfield, S. (1996). Introduction and historical overview. In A. Bergin & S. Garfield (Eds.), *Handbook of psychotherapy and behavior change* (pp. 3–18). New York: Wiley.

Berkowitz, L. (2000). *Causes and consequences of feelings.* New York: Cambridge University Press.

Bernstein, D. A., Borkovec, T. D., & Hazlett-Stevens, H. (2000). *New directions in progressive relaxation training: A guidebook for helping professionals.* Westport, CT: Praeger Publishers.

Bernstein, R. J. (1971). *Praxis and action: Contemporary philosophies of human activity.* Philadelphia: University of Pennsylvania Press.

Beutler, L. E., Harwood, T. M., Alimohamed, S., & Malik, M. (2002). Functional impairment and coping style. In J. C. Norcross (Ed.), *Psychotherapy relationships that work: Therapist contributions and responsiveness to patients* (pp. 145–174). New York: Oxford University Press.

Biaggio, M. K., & Godwin, W. H. (1987). Relation of depression to anger and hostility constructs. *Psychological Reports, 61,* 87–90.

Blaney, R. H. (1986). Affect and memory: A review. *Psychological Bulletin, 99,* 229–246.

Blatt, S. (1974). Levels of object representation in anaclitic and introjective depression. *Psychoanalytic Study of the Child, 29,* 7–157.

Blatt, S. (2004). *Experiences of depression: Theoretical, clinical, and research perspectives.* Washington, DC: American Psychological Association.

Bohart, A. C., Elliott, R., Greenberg, L. S., & Watson, J. C. (2002). Empathy. In J. Norcross (Ed.), *Psychotherapy relationships that work* (pp. 89–108). New York: Oxford University Press.

Bohart, A. C., & Greenberg, L. S. (Eds.). (1997). *Empathy reconsidered: New directions in psychotherapy.* Washington, DC: American Psychological Association.

Bolger, E. (1999). Grounded theory analysis of emotional pain. *Psychotherapy Research, 99,* 342–362.

Bonanno, G. A., & Keltner, D. (1997). Facial expressions of emotion and the course of conjugal bereavement. *Journal of Abnormal Psychology, 106,* 126–137.

Bordin, E. S. (1979). The generalizability of the psychoanalytic concept of the working alliance. *Psychotherapy, 16,* 252–260.

Bowlby, J. (1980). *Loss: Sadness and depression: Volume 3. Attachment and loss.* London: Hogarth Press.

Bozarth, J. D., & Wilkins, P. (Eds.). (2001). *Rogers' therapeutic conditions: Evolution, therapy, and practices: Vol. 3: Unconditional positive regard*. London: PCCS Books.

Bradshaw, J. (1988). *Healing the shame within*. New York: Norton.

Brody, A. L., Saxena, S., Mandelkern, M. A., Fairbanks, L. A., Ho, M. L., & Baxter, L. R., Jr. (2001). Brain metabolic changes associated with symptom factor improvement in major depressive disorder. *Biological Psychiatry, 50*, 171–178.

Broman, C. L., & Johnson, E. H. (1988). Anger expression and life stress among Blacks: Their role in physical health. *Journal of the National Medical Association, 80*, 1329–1334.

Brown, G. W., Harris, T. O., & Hepworth, C. (1995). Loss, humiliation and entrapment among women developing depression: A patient and non-patient comparison. *Psychological Medicine, 25*, 7–21.

Buber, M. (1958). *I and thou* (2nd ed.). New York: Charles Scribner's Sons.

Cacioppo, J. T. (2003). Social neuroscience: Understanding the pieces fosters understanding the whole and vice-versa. *American Psychologist, 57*, 819–827.

Campos, J. J., Frankel, C. B., & Camras, L. (2004). On the nature of emotion regulation. *Child Development, 75*, 377–394.

Camus, A. (1975). *The myth of Sisyphus and other essays*. New York: Penguin. (Original work published 1955)

Castonguay, L. G., Goldfried, M. R., Wiser, S. L., Raue, P. J., & Hayes, A. M. (1996). Predicting the effect of cognitive therapy for depression: A study of unique and common factors. *Journal of Consulting and Clinical Psychology, 64*, 497–504.

Cicchetti, D., Ackerman, B. P., & Izard, C. E. (1995). Emotions and emotion regulation in developmental psychopathology. *Development and Psychopathology, 7*, 1–10.

Clarke, D. D., & Blake, H. (1997). The inverse forecast effect. *Journal of Social Behavior and Personality, 12*, 999–1018.

Clarke, K. (1989). Creation of meaning: An emotional processing task in psychotherapy. *Psychotherapy, 26*, 139–148.

Craig, A. D. (2002). How do you feel? Interoception: The sense of the physiological condition of the body. *Nature NeuroScience, 3*, 655–666.

Critchley, H. D., Melmed, R. N., Featherstone, E., Mathias, C. J., & Dolan, R. J. (2001). Brain activity during biofeedback relaxation: A functional neuroimaging investigation. *Brain, 124*, 1003–1012.

Daldrup, R. J., Engle, D., Holiman, M., & Beutler, L. E. (1994). The intensification and resolution of blocked affect in an experiential psychotherapy. *British Journal of Clinical Psychology, 33*, 129–141.

Damasio, A. (1994). *Descartes' error: Emotion, reason, and the human brain*. New York: G. P. Putnam's Sons.

Damasio, A. (1999). *The feeling of what happens*. New York: Harcourt-Brace.

Damasio, A. R. (2003). *Looking for Spinoza: Joy, sorrow and the feeling brain*. Orlando, FL: Harcourt Brace Jovanovich.

Darwin, C. (1998). *Expression of the emotions in man and animals* (3rd ed.). London: Harper Collins. (Original work published 1897)

Davidson, R. (2000a). Affective style, mood and anxiety disorders: An affective neuroscience approach. In R. Davidson (Ed.), *Anxiety, depression and emotion* (pp. 23–55). Oxford, England: Oxford University Press.

Davidson, R. (2000b). Affective style, psychopathology and resilience: Brain mechanisms and plasticity. *American Psychologist, 5*, 1193–1196.

Davidson, R. J., & Irwin, W. (1999). The functional neuroanatomy of emotion and affective style. *Trends in Cognitive Sciences, 3*, 11–21.

Davidson, R. J., Pizzagalli, D., Nitschke, J. B., & Putnam, K. M. (2002). Depression: Perspectives from affective neuroscience. *Annual Review of Psychology, 53*, 545–574.

Davis, M., & Whalen, P. J. (2001). The amygdala: Vigilance and emotion. *Molecular Psychiatry, 6*, 13–34.

Depestele, F. (2004). Space differentiation in experiential psychotherapy. *Person-Centered and Experiential Psychotherapies, 3*, 129–139.

Derryberry, D., & Reed, M. A. (1996). Regulatory processes and the development of cognitive representations. *Development and Psychopathology, 8*, 215–234.

Derryberry, D., & Tucker, D. M. (1992). Neural mechanisms of emotion. *Journal of Consulting and Clinical Psychology, 60*, 329–338.

Dewey, J. (1933). *How we think*. Chicago: Henry Regnery.

Drevets, W. C. (1998). Functional neuroimaging studies of depression: The anatomy of melancholia. *Annual Review of Medicine, 49*, 341–361.

Drevets, W. C. (2001). Neuroimaging and neuropathological studies of depression: Implications for the cognitive–emotional features of mood disorders. *Current Opinion in Neurobiology, 11*, 240–249.

Drevets, W. C., Videen, T. O., Price, J. L., Preskorn, S. H., Carmichael, S. T., & Raichle, M. E. (1992). A functional anatomical study of unipolar depression. *Journal of Neuroscience, 12*, 3628–3641.

Ekman, P., & Friesen, W. V. (1975). *Unmasking the face: A guide to recognizing emotions from facial clues*. Oxford, England: Prentice-Hall.

Elliott, R., & Greenberg, L. S. (1997). Multiple voices in process–experiential therapy: Dialogues between aspects of the self. *Journal of Psychotherapy Integration, 7*, 225–239.

Elliott, R., Watson, J. C., Goldman, R. N., & Greenberg, L. S. (2004). *Learning emotion-focused therapy: The process–experiential approach to change*. Washington, DC: American Psychological Association.

Epstein, S. (1994). Integration of the cognitive and psychodynamic unconscious. *American Psychologist, 49*, 709–724.

Farthing, G. W. (1992). *The psychology of consciousness*. Upper Saddle River, NJ: Prentice-Hall.

Field, T. M. (1998). Massage therapy effects. *American Psychologist, 53,* 1270–1281.

Flack, W., Laird, J. D., & Cavallaro, J. (1999a). Emotional expression and feeling in schizophrenia: Effects of specific expressive behaviors on emotional experiences. *Journal of Clinical Psychology, 55,* 1–20.

Flack, W. F., Jr., Laird, J. D., & Cavallaro, L. A. (1999b). Separate and combined effects of facial expressions and bodily postures on emotional feelings. *European Journal of Social Psychology, 29,* 203–217.

Florence, W. A. (2001). *Emotional arousal in psychotherapy: An intensive analysis of eight cases.* Unpublished undergraduate thesis, York University, Toronto, Ontario, Canada.

Foa, E. B., & Jaycox, L. H. (1999). Cognitive–behavioral theory and treatment of posttraumatic stress disorder. In D. Spiegel (Ed.), *Efficacy and cost-effectiveness of psychotherapy* (pp. 23–61). Washington, DC: American Psychiatric Publishing.

Foa, E. B., & Kozak, M. J. (1986). Emotional processing of fear: Exposure to corrective information. *Psychological Bulletin, 99,* 20–35.

Forgas, J. (2000a). *Feeling and thinking.* Cambridge, England: Cambridge University Press.

Forgas, J. P. (2000b). *Feeling is believing? The role of processing strategies in mediating affective influences on beliefs.* In N. H. Frijda, A. S. R. Manstead, & S. Bem (Eds.), *Emotions and belief: How feelings influence thoughts. Studies in emotion and social interaction* (pp. 108–143). New York: Cambridge University Press.

Fosha, D. (2000). *The transforming power of affect: A model of accelerated change.* New York: Basic Books.

Fosha, D. (2004). "Nothing that feels bad is ever the last step": The role of positive emotions in experiential work with difficult emotional experiences. *Clinical Psychology and Psychotherapy, 11,* 30–43.

Frank, E., Carpenter, L. L., & Kupfer, D. J. (1988). Sex differences in recurrent depression: Are there any that are significant? *American Journal of Psychiatry, 145,* 41–45.

Frank, J. (1963). *Persuasion and healing.* Oxford, England: Schocken.

Frankl, V. (1959). *Man's search for meaning.* Boston: Beacon Press.

Fredrickson, B. L. (1998). What good are positive emotions? *Review of General Psychology, 2,* 300–319.

Fredrickson, B. L. (2001). The role of positive emotions in positive psychology: The broaden-and-build theory of positive emotions. *American Psychologist, 56,* 218–226.

Fredrickson, B. L., & Levenson, R. W. (1998). Positive emotions speed recovery from the cardiovascular sequelae of negative emotions. *Cognition and Emotion, 12,* 191–220.

Freud, S. (1957). Instincts and their vicissitudes. In J. Strachey (Ed. & Trans.), *The standard edition of the complete psychological works of Sigmund Freud* (Vol. 11, pp. 109–140). London: Hogarth Press. (Original work published 1915)

Freud, S. (1961). The ego and the id. In J. Strachey (Ed. & Trans.), *The standard edition of the complete psychological works of Sigmund Freud* (Vol. 19, pp. 1–66). London: Hogarth Press. (Original work published 1923)

Frijda, N. H. (1986). *The emotions*. Cambridge, England: Cambridge University Press.

Geller, S., & Greenberg, L. (2002). Therapeutic presence: Therapists' experience of presence in the psychotherapy encounter in psychotherapy. *Person Centered & Experiential Psychotherapies, 1*, 71–86.

Gendlin, E. T. (1962). *Experiencing and the creation of meaning*. New York: Free Press of Glencoe.

Gendlin, E. T. (1996). *Focusing-oriented psychotherapy: A manual of the experiential method*. New York: Guilford Press.

Gilbert, P. (1992). *Depression: The evolution of powerlessness*. Hove, England: Erlbaum.

Gilbert, P. (1998). What is shame? Some core issues and controversies. In P. Gilbert & B. Andrews (Eds.), *Shame: Interpersonal behavior, psychopathology and culture* (pp. 3–36). New York: Oxford University Press.

Gilbert, P. (2003). Evolution, social roles, and the differences in shame and guilt. *Social Research, 70*, 1205–1230.

Gilbert, P. (2004). Depression: A biopsychosocial, integrative and evolutionary approach. In M. Power (Ed.), *Mood disorders: A handbook of science and practice* (pp. 99–142). Chichester, England: Wiley.

Gilbert, P., & Allan, S. (1998). The role of defeat and entrapment (arrested flight) in depression: An exploration of an evolutionary view. *Psychological Medicine, 28*, 585–598.

Goldfried, M. R. (1991). Transtheoretical ingredients in therapeutic change. In R. Curtis & G. Stricker (Eds.), *How people change: Inside and outside therapy* (pp. 29–37). New York: Plenum Press.

Goldfried, M., & Davison, G. (1994). *Clinical behavior therapy* (exp. ed.) New York: Wiley.

Goldman, R. (1997). *Relating process to outcome in the experiential therapy of depression*. Unpublished doctoral dissertation, York University, Toronto, Ontario, Canada.

Goldman, R., & Greenberg, L. (1997). Case formulation in experiential therapy. In T. Ells (Ed.), *Handbook of psychotherapy case formulation* (pp. 402–429). New York: Guilford Press.

Goldman, R., & Greenberg, L. (in press). Depth of emotional experience and outcome. *Psychotherapy Research*.

Goldman, R., Greenberg, L., & Angus, L. (in press). The effects of adding specific emotion-focused interventions to the therapeutic relationship in the treatment of depression. *Psychotherapy Research*.

Goodwin, G. M. (1996). Functional imaging, affective disorder and dementia. *British Medical Bulletin, 52*, 495–512.

Greenberg, L. (1984). Task analysis of intrapersonal conflict. In L. Rice & L. Greenberg (Eds.), *Patterns of change: Intensive analysis of psychotherapy* (pp. 67–123). New York: Guilford Press.

Greenberg, L. S. (2002). *Emotion-focused therapy: Coaching clients to work through their feelings*. Washington, DC: American Psychological Association.

Greenberg, L., & Angus, L. (2004). The contributions of emotion processes to narrative change in psychotherapy: A dialectical constructivist approach. In L. Angus & J. McLeod (Eds.), *Handbook of narrative psychotherapy* (pp. 331–350). Thousand Oaks, CA: Sage.

Greenberg, L., Auszra, L., & Herrmann, I. R. (2004). *Productivity Scale*. Unpublished manuscript, York University, Toronto, Ontario, Canada.

Greenberg, L. S., & Bolger, E. (2001). An emotion-focused approach to the over-regulation of emotion and emotional pain. *Journal of Clinical Psychology, 57,* 197–211.

Greenberg, L. S., Elliott, R. K., & Foerster, F. S. (1990). Experiential processes in the psychotherapeutic treatment of depression. In C. D. McCann & N. S. Endler (Eds.), *Depression: New direction in theory, research and practice* (pp. 157–185). Toronto, Ontario, Canada: Wall & Emerson.

Greenberg, L., & Geller, S. (2001). Congruence and therapeutic presence. In G. Wyatt & P. Saunders (Eds.), *Rogers' therapeutic conditions: Congruence* (Vol. 1, pp. 73–101). Ross-on-Wye, Herefordshire, England: PCCS Books.

Greenberg, L. S., & Korman, L. (1993). Assimilating emotion into psychotherapy integration. *Journal of Psychotherapy Integration, 3,* 249–265.

Greenberg, L., & Malcolm, W. (2002). Resolving unfinished business: Relating process to outcome. *Journal of Consulting and Clinical Psychology, 70,* 406–416.

Greenberg, L. S., & Paivio, S. C. (1997). *Working with emotions in psychotherapy.* New York: Guilford Press.

Greenberg, L. S., & Pascual-Leone, J. (1995). A dialectical constructivist approach to experiential change. In R. A. Neimeyer & M. J. Mahoney (Eds.), *Constructivism in psychotherapy* (pp. 169–191). Washington, DC: American Psychological Association.

Greenberg, L., & Pascual-Leone, J. (2001). A dialectical constructivist view of the creation of personal meaning. *Journal of Constructivist Psychology, 14,* 165–186.

Greenberg, L. S., & Pedersen, R. (2001, November). *Relating the degree of resolution of in-session self-criticism and dependence to outcome and follow-up in the treatment of depression.* Paper presented at conference of the North American Chapter of the Society for Psychotherapy Research, Puerto Vallarta, Mexico.

Greenberg, L. S., Rice, L. N., & Elliott, R. (1993). *Facilitating emotional change: The moment by moment process.* New York: Guilford Press.

Greenberg, L. S., & Safran, J. D. (1984). Hot cognition–emotion coming in from the cold: A reply to Rachman and Mahoney. *Cognitive Therapy and Research, 8,* 591–598.

Greenberg, L. S., & Safran, J. D. (1987). *Emotion in psychotherapy: Affect, cognition, and the process of change.* New York: Guilford Press.

Greenberg, L. S., & Safran, J. D. (1989). Emotion in psychotherapy. *American Psychologist, 44,* 19–29.

Greenberg, L. S., & van Balen, R. (1998). The theory of experience-centered therapies. In L. S. Greenberg, J. C. Watson, & G. Lietaer (Eds.), *Handbook of experiential psychotherapy* (pp. 28–57). New York: Guilford Press.

Greenberg, L., & Warwar, S. (in press). Homework in experiential psychotherapy. *Psychotherapy Integration*.

Greenberg, L., & Watson, J. (1998). Experiential therapy of depression: Differential effects of client-centred relationship conditions and process experiential interventions. *Psychotherapy Research, 8*, 210–224.

Greenberg, L. S., Watson, J. C., & Lietaer, G. (Eds.). (1998). *Handbook of experiential psychotherapy*. New York: Guilford Press.

Gross, J. J. (2002). Emotion regulation: Affective, cognitive, and social consequences. *Psychophysiology, 39*, 281–291.

Guidano, V. F. (1991). *The self in process*. New York: Guilford Press.

Guidano, V. F. (1995a). Constructivist psychotherapy: A theoretical framework. In R. A. Neimeyer & M. J. Mahoney (Eds.), *Constructivism in psychotherapy* (pp. 93–108). Washington, DC: American Psychological Association.

Guidano, V. F. (1995b). Self-observation in constructivist psychotherapy. In R. A. Neimeyer & M. J. Mahoney (Eds.), *Constructivism in psychotherapy* (pp. 155–168). Washington, DC: American Psychological Association.

Hariri, A. R., Mattay, V. S., Tessitore, A., Fera, F., & Weinberger, D. R. (2003). Neocortical modulation of the amygdala response to fearful stimuli. *Biological Psychiatry, 53*, 494–501.

Harmon-Jones, E., Abramson, L. Y., Sigelman, J., Bohlig, A., Hogan, M. E., & Harmon-Jones, C. (2002). Proneness to hypomania/mania symptoms or depression symptoms and asymmetrical frontal cortical responses to an anger-evoking event. *Journal of Personality and Social Psychology, 82*, 610–618.

Harmon-Jones, E., Vaughn-Scott, K., Mohr, S., Sigelman, J., & Harmon-Jones, C. (2004). The effect of manipulated sympathy and anger on left and right frontal cortical activity. *Emotion, 4*, 95–101.

Harre, R. (1984). *Personal being*. Cambridge, MA: Harvard University Press.

Harter, S. (1998). *The construction of self: A developmental perspective*. New York: Guilford Press.

Hayes, A. M., & Strauss, J. L. (1998). Dynamic systems theory as a paradigm for the study of change in psychotherapy: An application to cognitive therapy for depression. *Journal of Consulting and Clinical Psychology, 66*, 939–947.

Hebb, D. (1949). *The organization of behavior*. New York: Wiley.

Henry, W. P., Schacht, T. E., & Strupp, H. H. (1990). Patient and therapist introject, interpersonal process and differential psychotherapy outcome. *Journal of Consulting and Clinical Psychology, 58*, 768–774.

Hermans, H. J. M. (1996). Opposites in a dialogical self: Constructs as characters. *Journal of Constructivist Psychology, 9*, 1–26.

Holland, P. C., & Gallagher, M. (1999). Amygdala circuitry in attentional and representational processes. *Trends in Cognitive Sciences, 3*, 65–73.

Honos-Webb, L., Stiles, W. B., Greenberg, L. S., & Goldman, R. (1998). Assimilation analysis of process–experiential psychotherapy: A comparison of two cases. *Psychotherapy Research, 8*, 264–286.

Honos-Webb, L., Surko, M., Stiles, W. B., & Greenberg, L. S. (1999). Assimilation of voices in psychotherapy: The case of Jan. *Journal of Counseling Psychology*, 46, 448–460.

Horvath, A., & Greenberg, L. S. (1994). *The working alliance: Theory, research and practice.* New York: Wiley.

Hubble, M. A., Duncan, B. L., & Miller, S. D. (Eds.). (1999). *The heart and soul of change: What works in therapy.* Washington, DC: American Psychological Association.

Hugdahl, K., & Öhman, A. (1977). Effects of instruction on acquisition and extinction of electrodermal responses to fear-relevant stimuli. *Journal of Experimental Psychology: Human Learning & Memory*, 3, 608–618.

Hunt, M. G. (1998). The only way out is through: Emotional processing and recovery after a depressing life event. *Behaviour Research and Therapy*, 36, 361–384.

Isen, A. M. (1999). Positive affect. In M. J. Power & T. Dalgleish (Eds.), *Handbook of cognition and emotion* (pp. 521–539). New York: Wiley.

Izard, C. E. (1991). *The psychology of emotions.* New York: Plenum Press.

James, W. (1890). *The principles of psychology.* Oxford, England: Holt.

Jones, N. A., Field, T., Fox, N. A., Davalos, M., & Gomez, C. (2001). EEG during different emotions in 10-month-old infants of depressed mothers. *Journal of Reproductive and Infant Psychology*, 19, 295–312.

Joseph, R. (1996). *Neuropsychiatry, neuropsychology and clinical neuroscience* (2nd ed.). Baltimore: Williams & Wilkins.

Kabat-Zinn, J. (1990). *Full catastrophe living.* New York: Delta.

Kabat-Zinn, J., Lipworth, L., & Burney, R. (1985). The clinical use of mindfulness meditation for the self-regulation of chronic pain. *Journal of Behavioral Medicine*, 8, 163–190.

Kabat-Zinn, J., Massion, A. O., Kristeller, J., Peterson, L. G., Fletcher, K. E., Pbert, L., et al. (1992). Effectiveness of a meditation-based stress reduction program in the treatment of anxiety disorders. *American Journal of Psychiatry*, 149, 936–943.

Kagan, F. (2003). *Differentiating depression: A qualitative analysis of the depression themes within 36 case studies.* Unpublished honors thesis, York University, Toronto, Ontario, Canada.

Kendler, K. S., Hettema, J. M., Butera, F., Gardner, C. O., & Prescott, C. A. (2003). Life event dimensions of loss, humiliation, entrapment, and danger in the prediction of onsets of major depression and generalized anxiety. *Archives of General Psychiatry*, 60, 789–796.

Kennedy, S. H., Javanmard, M., & Vaccarino, F. J. (1997). A review of functional neuroimaging in mood disorders: Positron emission tomography and depression. *Canadian Journal of Psychiatry*, 42, 467–475.

Kennedy-Moore, E., & Watson, J. C. (1999). *Expressing emotion: Myths, realities, and therapeutic strategies.* New York: Guilford Press.

Kerr, T., Walsh, J., & Marshall, A. (2001). Emotional change processes in music-assisted reframing. *Journal of Music Therapy*, 38, 193–211.

Klein, M. H., Mathieu-Coughlan, P., & Kiesler, D. J. (1986). The experiencing scales. In L. S. Greenberg & W. Pisof (Eds.), *The psychotherapeutic process: A research handbook* (pp. 21–71). New York: Guilford Press.

Klerman, G., Weissman, M., Rounsaville, B., & Chevron, E. (1984). *Interpersonal psychotherapy of depression.* New York: Basic Books.

Korman, L. M. (1998). *Changes in clients' emotion episodes in therapy.* Unpublished doctoral dissertation, York University, Toronto, Ontario, Canada.

Kwan, K., Watson, J. C., & Stermac, L. (2000, June). *An examination of the relationship between clients' social experience of psychotherapy, the working alliance and psychotherapy outcome.* Paper presented at the 31st Annual Meeting of the Society for Psychotherapy Research Conference, Chicago.

Ladavas, E., Cimatti, D., del Pesce, M., & Tuozzi, G. (1993). Emotional evaluation with and without conscious stimulus identification: Evidence from a split-brain patient. *Cognition and Emotion, 7,* 95–114.

Lane, R. D., Quinlan, D. M., Schwartz, G. E., Walker, P. A., & Zeitlin, S. (1990). The Levels of Emotional Awareness Scale: A cognitive–developmental measure of emotion. *Journal of Personality Assessment, 55,* 124–134.

Lane, R. D., Reiman, E. M., Axelrod, B., Yun, L.-S., Holmes, A., & Schwartz, G. E. (1998). Neural correlates of levels of emotional awareness: Evidence of an interaction between emotion and attention in the anterior cingulate cortex. *Journal of Cognitive Neuroscience, 10,* 525–535.

Lane, R. D., & Schwartz, G. E. (1992). Levels of emotional awareness: Implications for psychotherapeutic integration. *Journal of Psychotherapy Integration, 2,* 1–18.

Lane, R. D., Sechrest, L., Riedel, R., Shapiro, D., & Kasniak, A. (2000). Pervasive emotion recognition deficit common to alexithymia and the repressive coping style. *Psychosomatic Medicine, 62,* 492–501.

Lane, R. D., Sechrest, L., Reidel, R., Weldon, V., Kaszniak, A., & Schwartz, G. E. (1996). Impaired verbal and nonverbal emotion recognition in alexithymia. *Psychosomatic Medicine, 58,* 203–210.

Lane, R. D., Shapiro, D. E., Sechrest, L., & Riedel, R. (1998). Pervasive emotion recognition deficit common to alexithymia and repression. *Psychosomatic Medicine, 60,* 92.

Lang, P. J. (1995). The emotion probe: Studies of motivation and attention. *American Psychologist, 50,* 372–385.

Lange, K., Williams, L. M., Young, A. W., Bullmore, E. T., Brammer, M. J., Williams, S. C. R., et al. (2003). Task instructions modulate neural responses to fearful facial expressions. *Biological Psychiatry, 53,* 226–232.

Lazarus, R. S. (1991). *Emotion and adaptation.* New York: Oxford University Press.

Le Doux, J. (1996). *The emotional brain: The mysterious underpinnings of emotional life.* New York: Simon & Schuster.

Leijssen, M. (1996). Characteristics of a healing inner relationship. In R. Hutterer, G. Pawlowsky, P. F. Scmid, & R. Stipsits (Eds.), *Client-centered and experiential psychotherapy towards the nineties* (pp. 225–250). Leuven, Belgium: Leuven University Press.

Leijssen, M. (1998). Focussing microprocesses. In L. Greenberg, J. Watson, & G. Lietaer (Eds.), *Handbook of experiential psychotherapy* (pp. 121–154). New York: Guilford Press.

Levenson, R. W. (1992). Autonomic nervous system differences among emotions. *Psychological Science, 3*, 23–27.

Leventhal, H. (1984). A perceptual motor theory of emotion. In L. Berkowitz (Ed.), *Advances in experimental social psychology* (pp. 117–182). New York: Academic Press.

Leventhal, H., & Scherer, K. (1987). The relationship of emotion to cognition: A functional approach to a semantic controversy. *Cognition and Emotion, 1*, 3–28.

Levinas, E. (1998). *Otherwise than being, or beyond essence.* Pittsburgh, PA: Duquesne University Press.

Levitt, J. T., Brown, T. A., Orsillo, S. M., & Barlow, D. H. (in press). The effects of acceptance versus suppression of emotion on subjective and psychophysiological response to carbon dioxide challenge in patients with panic disorder. *Behavior Therapy.*

Lietaer, G. (1993). Authenticity, congruence and transparency. In D. Brazier (Ed.), *Beyond Carl Rogers: Towards a psychotherapy for the 21st century* (pp. 17–46). London: Constable.

Linehan, M. M. (1993). *Cognitive–behavioral treatment of borderline personality disorder.* New York: Guilford Press.

Linville, P. W. (1985). Self-complexity and affective extremity: Don't put all of your eggs in one cognitive basket. *Social Cognition, 3*, 94–120.

Linville, P. W. (1987). Self-complexity as a cognitive buffer against stress-related illness and depression. *Journal of Personality and Social Psychology, 52*, 663–676.

Lischetzke, T., & Eid, M. (2003). Is attention to feelings beneficial or detrimental to affective well-being? Mood regulation as a moderator variable. *Emotion, 3*, 361–377.

Luborsky, L., Singer, B., & Luborsky, L. (1975). Comparative studies of psychotherapies: Is it true that "everyone has won and all must have prizes"? *Archives of General Psychiatry, 32*, 995–1008.

Luria, A. R. (1976). *Cognitive development: Its cultural and social foundations.* Cambridge, MA: Harvard University Press.

Magai, C., & Haviland-Jones, J. (2002). *The hidden genius of emotion.* Cambridge, England: Cambridge University Press.

Mahoney, M. (1991). *Human change processes.* New York: Basic Books.

Mahoney, M. J. (1995). Emotionality and health: Lessons from and for psychotherapy. In J. W. Pennebaker (Ed.), *Emotion, disclosure, and health* (pp. 241–253). Washington, DC: American Psychological Association.

Malcolm, W., Warwar, S. & Greenberg, L. (in press). Facilitating forgiveness in individual therapy as an approach to resolving interpersonal injuries. In E. L. Worthington Jr. (Ed.), *The forgiveness handbook.* New York: Brunner-Routledge.

Mangina, C. A., & Beuzeron-Mangina, J. H. (1996). Direct electrical stimulation of specific human brain structures and bilateral electrodermal activity. *International Journal of Psychophysiology, 22*, 1–8.

Markus, H., & Wurf, E. (1987). The dynamic self-concept: A social psychological perspective. *Annual Review of Psychology, 38*, 299–337.

Maslow, A. (1971). *The farther reaches of human nature.* New York: Viking.

Mayberg, H., Lewis, P., Regenold, W., & Wagner, H. (1994). Paralimbic hypofusion in unipolar depression. *Journal of Nuclear Medicine, 35*, 929–934.

Mayberg, H., Liotti, M., Brannan, S., McGinnis, S., Mahurin, R., Jerabek, P., et al. (1999). Reciprocal limbic-cortical function and negative mood: Converging PET findings in depression and normal sadness. *American Journal of Psychiatry, 156*, 675–682.

Mayer, J. D., & Hanson, E. (1995). Mood-congruent judgment over time. *Personality and Social Psychology Bulletin, 21*, 237–244.

Myers, D. (1996). *Social psychology.* New York: McGraw-Hill.

Neimeyer, R., & Mahoney, M. (1995). *Constructivism in psychotherapy.* Washington, DC: American Psychological Association.

Nolen-Hoeksema, S. (2001). Gender differences in depression. *Current Directions in Psychological Science, 10*, 173–176.

Norcross, J. C. (2002). Empirically supported therapy relationships. In J. C. Norcross (Ed.), *Psychotherapy relationships that work: Therapist contributions and responsiveness to patients* (pp. 3–16). London: Oxford University Press.

Oatley, K. (1992). *Best laid schemes.* Cambridge, England: Cambridge University Press.

Oatley, K., & Jenkins, J. (1992). Human emotions: Function and dysfunction. *Annual Review of Psychology, 43*, 55–85.

Ochsner, K. N., Bunge, S. A., Gross, J. J., & Gabrieli, J. D. E. (2002). Rethinking feelings: An fMRI study of the cognitive regulation of emotion. *Journal of Cognitive Neuroscience, 14*, 1215–1229.

Öhman, A., & Mineka, S. (2001). Fears, phobias, and preparedness: Toward an evolved module of fear and fear learning. *Psychological Review, 108*, 483–522.

Orlinsky, D. E., & Howard, K. I. (1986). Process and outcome in psychotherapy. In S. Garfield & A. Bergin (Eds.), *Handbook of psychotherapy and behavior change* (pp. 311–381). New York: Wiley.

Orsillo, S. M., Roemer, L., & Barlow, D. H. (in press). Integrating acceptance and mindfulness into existing cognitive–behavioral treatment for GAD: A case study. *Cognitive and Behavioral Practice.*

Paivio, S. C., & Greenberg, L. S. (1995). Resolving "unfinished business": Efficacy of experiential therapy using empty-chair dialogue. *Journal of Consulting and Clinical Psychology, 63*, 419–425.

Paivio, S. C., & Greenberg, L. S. (1998). Experiential theory of emotion applied to anxiety and depression. In W. F. Flack Jr., & J. D. Laird (Eds.), *Emotions in psychopathology: Theory and research* (pp. 229–242). London: Oxford University Press.

Paivio, S. C., Hall, I. E., Holowaty, K. A. M., Jellis, J. B., & Tran, N. (2001). Imaginal confrontation for resolving child abuse issues. *Psychotherapy Research, 11,* 433–453.

Paivio, S. C., & Nieuwenhuis, J. A. (2001). Efficacy of emotionally focused therapy for adult survivors of child abuse: A preliminary study. *Journal of Traumatic Stress, 14,* 115–134.

Palfai, T. P., & Salovey, P. (1993). The influence of depressed and elated mood on deductive and inductive reasoning. *Imagination, Cognition and Personality, 13,* 57–71.

Panksepp, J. (2001). Neuro-affective processes and the brain substrates of emotion: Emerging perspectives and dilemmas. In A. Kazniak (Ed.), *Emotions, qualia and consciousness: Proceedings of the International School of Biocybernetics Casamicciola, Napoli, Italy, 19–24 October 1998* (pp. 160–180). Singapore: World Scientific.

Parrott, W. G., & Sabini, J. (1990). Mood and memory under natural conditions: Evidence for mood incongruent recall. *Journal of Personality and Social Psychology, 59,* 321–336.

Pascual-Leone, A., & Greenberg, L. S. (2004, June). *Resolving emotional distress: An empirical study.* Paper presented at the International Meeting of the Society for Psychotherapy Research, Rome, Italy.

Pascual-Leone, J. (1987). Organismic processes for neo-Piagetian theories: A dialectical causal account of cognitive development. *International Journal of Psychology, 22,* 531–570.

Pascual-Leone, J. (1990). An essay on wisdom: Toward organismic processes that make it possible. In R. J. Sternberg (Ed.), *Wisdom: Its nature, origins, and development* (pp. 244–278). New York: Cambridge University Press.

Pascual-Leone, J. (1991). Emotions, development and psychotherapy: A dialectical constructivist perspective. In J. Safran & L. Greenberg (Eds.), *Emotion, psychotherapy and change* (pp. 302–335). New York: Guilford Press.

Pascual-Leone, J., & Johnson, J. (2004). Affect, self-motivation, and cognitive development: A dialectical constructivist view. In Y. D. Dai & R. J. Sternberg (Eds.), *Motivation, emotion, and cognition: Integrative perspectives on intellectual functioning and development* (pp. 197–236). Mahwah, NJ: Erlbaum.

Pennebaker, J. W. (1990). *Opening up: The healing power of confiding in others.* New York: William Morrow.

Pennebaker, J. W. (1995). *Emotion, disclosure, and health.* Washington, DC: American Psychological Association.

Pennebaker, J. W., & Segal, J. (1999). Forming a story: The health benefits of narrative. *Journal of Clinical Psychology, 55,* 1243–1254.

Perls, F., Hefferline, R. F., & Goodman, P. (1951). *Gestalt therapy.* New York: Dell.

Phan, K. L., Taylor, S. F., Welsh, R. C., Decker, L. R., Noll, D. C., Nichols, T. E., et al. (2003). Activation of the medial prefrontal cortex and extended amygdala by individual ratings of emotional arousal: A FMRI study. *Biological Psychiatry, 53,* 211–215.

Philippot, P., & Schaefer, A. (2001). Emotion and memory. In T. Mayne & G. Bonanno (Eds.), *Emotions: Current issues and future directions* (pp. 82–122). New York: Guilford Press.

Philips, M., Drevets, W., Rauch, S., & Lane, R. (2003). Neurobiology of emotion perception: 1. The neural basis of normal perception. *Biological Psychiatry, 54,* 504–514.

Piccinelli, M., & Wilkinson, G. (2000). Gender differences in depression: Critical review. *British Journal of Psychiatry, 177,* 486–492.

Polster, E., & Polster, M. (1973). *Gestalt therapy integrated.* New York: Brunner/Mazel.

Pos, A. E., Greenberg, L. S., Goldman, R. N., & Korman, L. M. (2003). Emotional processing during experiential treatment of depression. *Journal of Consulting and Clinical Psychology, 71,* 1007–1016.

Prochaska, J. O., DiClemente, C. C., & Norcross, J. C. (1992). In search of how people change: Application to addictive behaviors. *American Psychologist, 47,* 1102–1114.

Rauch, S. L., van der Kolk, B. A., Fisler, R. E., Alpert, N. M., Orr, S. P., Savage, C. R., et al. (1996). A symptom provocation study of posttraumatic stress disorder using positron emission tomography and script-driven imagery. *Archives of General Psychiatry, 53,* 380–387.

Reich, W. (1949). *Character analysis.* New York: Noonday.

Rennie, D. L. (1992). Qualitative analysis of the client's experience of psychotherapy: The unfolding of reflexivity. In S. G. Toukmanian & D. L. Rennie (Eds.), *Psychotherapy process research: Paradigmatic and narrative approaches* (pp. 211–233). Newbury Park, CA: Sage.

Rice, L. N. (1974). The evocative function of the therapist. In D. Wexler & L. N. Rice (Eds.), *Innovations in client-centered therapy* (pp. 289–311). New York: Wiley.

Rice, L. N., & Greenberg, L. S. (1992). Humanistic approaches to psychotherapy. In D. K. Freedheim (Ed.), *History of psychotherapy: A century of change* (pp. 197–224). Washington, DC: American Psychological Association.

Rice, L. N., & Kerr, G. P. (1986). Measures of client and therapist vocal quality. In L. Greenberg & W. Pinsof (Eds.), *The psychotherapeutic process: A research handbook* (pp. 73–105). New York: Guilford Press.

Rice, L. N., Koke, C. J., Greenberg, L. S., & Wagstaff, A. K. (1979). *Manual for client vocal quality* (Vols. 1 & 2). Toronto, Ontario, Canada: Counseling Development Centre, York University.

Riley, W. T., Treiber, F. A., & Woods, M. G. (1989). Anger and hostility in depression. *Journal of Nervous and Mental Disease, 177,* 668–674.

Rimé, B., Finkenauer, C., Luminet, O., Zech, E., & Philippot, P. (1998). Social sharing of emotion: New evidence and new questions. In W. Stroebe & M. Hewstone (Eds.), *European review of social psychology* (Vol. 9, pp. 225–258). Chichester, England: Wiley.

Rogers, C. R. (1957). The necessary and sufficient conditions of therapeutic personality change. *Journal of Consulting Psychology, 21,* 95–103.

Rogers, C. R. (1959). A theory of therapy, personality and interpersonal relationships, as developed in the client-centered framework. In S. Koch (Ed.), *Psychology: A study of a science* (Vol. 3, pp. 184–256). New York: McGraw Hill.

Rogers, C. (1965). *Client-centered therapy: Its current practice, implications, and theory.* Boston: Houghton-Mifflin.

Rolls, E. (1996a). The orbitofrontal cortex. *Philosophical Transactions of the Royal Society of London B, 351,* 1433–1444.

Rolls, E. T. (1996b). A theory of hippocampal function in memory. *Hippocampus, 6,* 601–620.

Ross, R., Smith, G. R., & Booth, B. M. (1997). Treatment outcomes in depressed patients. *Psychiatric Annals, 27,* 119–123.

Rotondi-Trevisan, D., Angus, L., & Greenberg, L. (2004). Autobiographical memory specificity and the York I depression study: An exploratory analysis. Manuscript submitted for publication.

Rousseau, J.-J. (1981). *The confessions* (J. M. Cohen, Trans.). New York: Penguin Classics. (Original work published 1781)

Safran, J. D., & Muran, J. C. (1998). The therapeutic alliance in brief psychotherapy: General principles. In J. D. Safran & J. C. Muran (Eds.), *The therapeutic alliance in brief psychotherapy* (pp. 217–230). Washington, DC: American Psychological Association.

Salovey, P., & Mayer, J. D. (1990). Emotional intelligence. *Imagination, Cognition and Personality, 9,* 185–211.

Salovey, P., Mayer, J. D., Golman, S. L., Turvey, C., & Palfai, T. P. (1995). Emotional attention, clarity, and repair: Exploring emotional intelligence using the Trait Meta-Mood Scale. In J. W. Pennebaker (Ed.), *Emotion, disclosure, and health* (pp. 125–154). Washington, DC: American Psychological Association.

Samoilov, A., & Goldfried, M. (2000). Role of emotion in cognitive behavior therapy. *Clinical Psychology Science and Practice, 7,* 373–385.

Schaefer, S., Abercrombie, H., Lindgren, K., Larson, C., Ward, R., Oakes, T., et al. (2000). Six-month test–retest reliability of MRI-defined PET measures of regional cerebral glucose metabolic rate in selected subcortical structures. *Human Brain Mapping, 10,* 1–9.

Schaefer S. M., Jackson, D. C., Davidson, R. J., Aguirre, G. K., Kimberg, D. Y., & Thompson-Schill, S. L. (2002). Modulation of amygdalar activity by the conscious regulation of negative emotion. *Journal of Cognitive Neuroscience, 14,* 913–921.

Scherer, K. R. (1984). Emotion as a multicomponent process: A model and some cross-cultural data. *Review of Personality and Social Psychology, 5,* 37–63.

Schore, A. N. (2003). *Affect dysregulation and disorders of the self.* New York: Norton.

Segal, Z. V., Williams, J. M. G., & Teasdale, J. D. (2002). *Mindfulness-based cognitive therapy for depression: A new approach to preventing relapse.* New York: Guilford Press.

Seligman, M. E. P. (1975). *Helplessness: On depression, development, and death.* New York: W. H. Freeman, Times Books, Henry Holt & Co.

Shapiro, F. (1995). *Eye movement desensitization and reprocessing: Basic principles, protocols, and procedures.* New York: Guilford Press.

Shapiro, F. (2001). Trauma and adaptive information-processing: EMDR's dynamic and behavioral interface. In M. F. Solomon, R. J. Neborsky, L. McCullough, M. Alpert, F. Shapiro, & D. Malan (Eds.), *Short-term therapy for long-term change* (pp. 112–129). New York: Norton.

Shostrom, E. (Producer). (1986). *Three approaches to psychotherapy* [Motion picture series]. Santa Ana, CA: Psychological Films.

Sicoli, L. (2005). *Development and verification of a model of resolving hopelessness in process–experiential therapy.* Unpublished doctoral dissertation, York University, Toronto, Ontario, Canada.

Siegel, D. J. (2003). An interpersonal neurobiology of psychotherapy: The developing mind and the resolution of trauma. In M. F. Soloman & D. J. Siegel (Eds.), *Healing trauma: Attachment, mind, body, and brain* (pp. 1–56). New York: Norton.

Silberschatz, G., Fretter, P. B., & Curtis, J. T. (1986). How do interpretations influence the process of psychotherapy? *Journal of Consulting and Clinical Psychology, 54,* 646–652.

Smith, T. (1996, July). *Severe life stress: Major depression and emotion related negative memory.* Paper presented at the International Society for Research on Emotions, Toronto, Ontario, Canada.

Snyder, C. R. (1994). *The psychology of hope: You can get there from here.* New York: Free Press.

Spinoza, B. (1967). *Ethics.* New York: Hafner. (Original work published 1675)

Sroufe, L. A. (1996). *Emotional development: The organization of emotional life in the early years.* New York: Cambridge University Press.

Stanton, A. L., Danoff-Burg, S., Cameron, C. L., Bishop, M., Collins, C. A., Kirk, S. B., et al. (2000). Emotionally expressive coping predicts psychological and physical adjustment to breast cancer. *Journal of Consulting and Clinical Psychology, 68,* 875–882.

Stein, K. F., & Markus, H. R. (1994). The organization of the self: An alternative focus for psychopathology and behavior change. *Journal of Psychotherapy Integration, 4,* 317–353.

Stein, K. F., & Markus, H. R. (1996). The role of the self in behavioral change. *Journal of Psychotherapy Integration, 6,* 349–384.

Stern, D. (1985). *The interpersonal world of the infant.* New York: Basic Books.

Stern, D. N. (1995). Self/other differentiation in the domain of intimate socio-affective interaction: Some considerations. In P. Rochat (Ed.), *The self in infancy: Theory and research* (pp. 419–429). Amsterdam, the Netherlands: North-Holland/Elsevier Science Publishers.

Stiles, W. B. (1999). Signs and voices in psychotherapy. *Psychotherapy Research, 9,* 1–21.

Strupp, H. H., & Binder, J. (1984). *Psychotherapy in a new key: A guide to time-limited dynamic therapy*. New York: Norton

Taylor, C. (1990). *Human agency and language*. New York: Cambridge University Press.

Taylor, S. F., Phan, K. L., Decker, L. R., & Liberzon, I. (2003). Subjective rating of emotionally salient stimuli modulates neural activity. *Neuroimage, 18*, 650–659.

Teasdale, J. D., & Barnard, P. J. (1993). *Affect, cognition, and change: Re-modelling depressive thought*. Hillsdale, NJ: Erlbaum.

Teasdale, J. D., Howard, R. J., Cox, S. G., Ha, Y., Brammer, M. J., Williams, S. C., et al. (1999). Functional MRI study of the cognitive generation of affect. *American Journal of Psychiatry, 156*, 209–215.

Teasdale, J. D., Segal, Z. V., Williams, J. M. G., Ridgeway, V. A., Soulsby, J. M., & Lau, M. A. (2000). Prevention of relapse/recurrence in major depression by mindfulness-based cognitive therapy. *Journal of Consulting and Clinical Psychology, 68*, 615–623.

Thase, M. E., & Howland, R. H. (1995). Biological processes in depression: An updated review and integration. In E. E. Beckham & W. R. Leber (Eds.), *Handbook of depression* (2nd ed., pp. 213–279). New York: Guilford Press.

Thelen, E., & Smith, L. B. (1994). *A dynamic systems approach to the development of cognition and action*. Cambridge, MA: MIT Press.

Thomas, P. (2003). Protection, dissociation, and internal roles: Modeling and treating the effects of child abuse. *Review of General Psychology, 7*, 364–380.

Tomkins, S. (1962). *Affect, imagery and consciousness: The negative affects*. New York: Springer.

Tomkins, S. S. (1968). Affects: Primary motives of man. *Humanitas, 3*, 321–345.

Toukmanian, S. G. (1990). A schema-based information processing perspective on client change in experiential psychotherapy. In J. Rombauts & G. Lietaer (Eds.), *Client-centered and experiential psychotherapy in the nineties* (pp. 309–326). Leuven, Belgium: Leuven University Press.

Toukmanian, S. G. (1992). Studying the client's perceptual processes and their outcomes in psychotherapy. In D. L. Rennie & S. G Toukmanian (Eds.), *Psychotherapy process research: Paradigmatic and narrative approaches* (pp. 77–107). Thousand Oaks, CA: Sage.

Toukmanian, S. G. (1996). Clients' perceptual processing: An integration of research and practice. In W. Dryden (Ed.), *Research in counselling and psychotherapy: Practical applications* (pp. 184–210). Thousand Oaks, CA: Sage.

Trevarthen, C. (2000). Intrinsic motives for companionship in understanding: Their origin, development, and significance for infant mental health. *Infant Mental Health Journal, 22*, 95–131.

Troeml-Ploetz, S. (1980). I'd come to you for therapy: Interpretation, redefinition and paradox in Rogerian therapy. *Psychotherapy: Theory, Research and Practice, 17*, 246–257.

Tucker, D. M., Luu, P., Desmond, R. E., Jr., Hartry-Speiser, A., Davey, C., & Flaisch, T. (2003). Corticolimbic mechanisms in emotional decisions. *Emotion, 3*, 127–149.

Tugade, M., & Fredrickson, B. (2000, August). *Resilient individuals use positive emotions to bounce back from negative emotional arousal.* Paper presented at International Society for Research in Emotion, Quebec City, Quebec, Canada.

Udelman, D. (1986). Hope and the immune system. *Stress Medicine, 2*, 7–12.

Van der Kolk, B. A. (1994). The body keeps the score: Memory and the evolving psychobiology of post-traumatic stress. *Harvard Review of Psychiatry, 1*, 253–265.

Van der Kolk, B. A., & van der Hart, O. (1991). The intrusive past: The flexibility of memory and the engraving of trauma. *American Imago, 48*, 425–454.

van Geert, P. (1998). A dynamic systems model of basic developmental mechanisms: Piaget, Vygotsky, and beyond. *Psychological Review, 105*, 634–677.

Vygotsky, L. S. (1962). *Thought and language.* Cambridge, MA: MIT Press.

Vygotsky, L. (1986). *Thought and language.* Cambridge, MA: MIT Press.

Wampold, B. E., Mondin, G. W., Moody, M., Stich, F., Benson, K., & Ahn, H. (1997). A meta-analysis of outcome studies comparing bona fide psychotherapies: Empirically, "all must have prizes." *Psychological Bulletin, 122*, 203–215.

Warwar, S. (2003). *Relating emotional processes to outcome in experiential psychotherapy of depression.* Unpublished doctoral dissertation, York University, Toronto, Ontario, Canada.

Warwar, S., & Greenberg, L. S. (1999a). *Client Emotional Arousal Scale—III.* Unpublished manuscript, York Psychotherapy Research Clinic, York University, Toronto, Ontario, Canada.

Warwar, S., & Greenberg, L. (1999b, June). *Emotional processing and therapeutic change.* Paper presented at the Annual Meeting of the International Society for Psychotherapy Research, Braga, Portugal.

Warwar, S., & Greenberg, L. S. (2000). Advances in theories of change and counseling. In S. D. Brown & R. W. Lent (Eds.), *Handbook of counseling psychology* (3rd ed., pp. 571–600). New York: Wiley.

Warwar, S., Greenberg, L., & Perepeluk, D. (2003, June). *Reported in-session emotional experience in therapy.* Paper presented at the Annual Meeting of the International Society for Psychotherapy Research, Weimar, Germany.

Watson, J. C. (1992, June). *Facilitating affective change processes: Clients' referential activity, experiencing and IPR reports during the resolution of a problematic reaction.* Paper presented to the Society for Psychotherapy Research, Berkeley, CA.

Watson, J. C. (2001). Revisioning empathy: Theory, research, and practice. In D. Cain & J. Seeman (Eds.), *Handbook of research and practice in humanistic psychotherapies* (pp. 445–473). Washington, DC: American Psychological Association.

Watson, J. C., & Bohart, A. (2001). Integrative humanistic therapy in an era of managed care. In K. Schneider, J. F. T. Bugenthal, & F. Pierson (Eds.), *The handbook of humanistic psychology* (pp. 503–520). Newbury Park, CA: Sage.

Watson, J. C., Enright, C., Kalogerakos, F., & Greenberg, L. S. (1998, June). *An examination of therapists' levels of control and affiliation in experiential and client-centered therapies and its relationship to outcome*. Paper presented to the 29th Annual Meeting of the International Society for Psychotherapy Research, Snowbird, UT.

Watson, J. C., & Geller, S. (2005). An examination of the relations among empathy, unconditional acceptance, positive regard and congruence in both cognitive–behavioral and process–experiential psychotherapy. *Psychotherapy Research, 15*, 25–33.

Watson, J. C., Gordon, L. B., Stermac, L., Kalogerakos, F., & Steckley, P. (2003). Comparing the effectiveness of process–experiential with cognitive–behavioral psychotherapy in the treatment of depression. *Journal of Consulting and Clinical Psychology, 71*, 773–781.

Watson, J. C., & Greenberg, L. S. (1994). The working alliance in experiential therapy: Enacting the relationship conditions. In A. Horvath & L. Greenberg (Eds.), *The working alliance: Theory, research and practice* (pp. 153–172). New York: Wiley.

Watson, J. C., & Greenberg, L. S. (1995). Alliance ruptures and repairs in experiential therapy. *In Session: Psychotherapy in Practice, 1*, 19–31.

Watson, J., & Greenberg, L. (1996). Emotion and cognition in experiential therapy: A dialectical–constructivist position. In H. Rosen & K. Kuelwein (Eds.), *Constructing realities: Meaning-making perspectives for psychotherapists* (pp. 253–276). San Francisco: Jossey-Bass.

Watson, J. C., & Rennie, D. L. (1994). Qualitative analysis of clients' subjective experience of significant moments during the exploration of problematic reactions. *Journal of Counseling Psychology, 41*, 500–509.

Weston, J. (2005). *Interruption of emotional experience in psychotherapy*. Unpublished doctoral dissertation, York University, Toronto, Ontario, Canada.

Whalen, P. J. (1998). Fear, vigilance, and ambiguity: Initial neuroimaging studies of the human amygdala. *Current Directions in Psychological Science, 7*, 177–188.

Whelton, W. J., & Greenberg, L. S. (2001). The self as a singular multiplicity: A process–experiential perspective. In J. C. Muran (Ed.), *Self-relations in the psychotherapy process* (pp. 87–110). Washington, DC: American Psychological Association.

Whelton, W. J., & Greenberg, L. S. (in press). Emotion in self-criticism. *Personality and Individual Differences*.

Whelton, W. J., & Henkelman, J. J. (2002). A verbal analysis of forms of self-criticism. *Alberta Journal of Educational Research, 48*, 88–90.

Williams, J. M. G., Stiles, W. B., & Shapiro, D. A. (1999). Cognitive mechanisms in the avoidance of painful and dangerous thoughts: Elaborating the assimilation model. *Cognitive Therapy and Research, 23*, 285–306.

Zajonc, R. B. (2000). Feeling and thinking: Closing the debate over the independence of affect. In J. P. Forgas (Ed.), *Feeling and thinking: The role of affect in social cognition* (pp. 31–58). New York: Cambridge University Press.

Zimbardo, P., Ebbesen, E., & Malasch, C. (1997). *Influencing attitudes and changing behavior*. Reading, MA: Addison-Wesley.

INDEX

and arousal, 206
and awareness of feelings, 178–179
and awareness promotion, 162
and bond creation, 158–160
and bonding, 99
and confrontations, 253
in therapeutic relationship, 121, 130–131
"Emplotted" lives, 42
Empty-chair dialogue
and anger, 212
in midtherapy, 272–280
reflection facilitation with, 315–317
for unfinished business, 270–280
Entrapment, 46, 47
Environment
and bond creation, 158, 159, 161
for bonding, 99
for exploring feelings, 138
of therapeutic relationship, 122–123, 125
Evaluation of response, 39–40
Evocation and arousal of emotion, 201–223
adaptive anger, 211–212
adaptive grief/sadness, 210–211
and differential intervention, 207–210
and expression, 203–204
functions of, 204–207
high levels of, 203
hope, 222–223
interest, 218–219
joy/pride, 219–221
love/compassion, 221–222
maladaptive fear, 213–215
maladaptive shame, 215–217
measure of, 204, 205
positive emotion, 217–218
in therapy vs. day-to-day living, 202–203
Evocation and exploration phase of treatment, 96–97, 107–115
accessing primary emotions, 111–116
problematic feelings, 108–110
support for contacting emotions, 107–108
undoing interruptions, 110–111
Evocative responses, 179
Experience
deepening of, 77
disowning of, 225–226
Experienced emotion, 14
Experiencing the experience, 75

Explicit affect regulation, 22
Exploratory goals, 124
Exploratory questions, 180–181
Exploratory reflections, 180
Expressed emotional arousal, 14
Expressing emotion for the client, 284
Expression
benefits of, 203–204
of emotion, 78, 161
of fear, 89
regulating emotional, 168
of suppressed emotion, 262–265
in therapy vs. day-to-day living, 202–203
Expressive coping, 78
Expressive enactment of emotion, 284
External voice, 154
Eyes, 154

Facial expression, 122–123, 136
Facilitating therapeutic relationships, 93
Facilitative congruence, 128
Failure, fear of, 60, 124
Fear(s), 18, 21, 28
in adults, 46
of anger, 64, 65
and change, 209
of dying, 258
of emotion, 110–111, 256–262
expression of, 89
of failure, 60, 124
maladaptive, 213–215
subcategories of, 60
Feedback, 138
"Feeling knowledge," 20
The Feeling of What Happens (A. R. Damasio), 19–20
Feelings
elements of, 79
fear of, 60
promoting awareness of, 164–165
Film, 113–114, 122
Finkenauer, C., 76
First-order evaluations, 307, 308
Fist clenching, 88
Flack, W., 88
Flashbacks, 26
Flexibility, 85, 87
Focus
on accepting feelings, 184–187
collaborative, 173–174
establishing a, 104–107

core, 70
    identifying, 72
Primary experience, identifying, 170–171
Problematic feelings, 108–110
Problem presentation, 144
Problems in therapy, 133–139
    in constructing narratives, 136–137
    in exploring feelings, 137–138
    of passivity, 135–136
    repairing, 138–139
    of shame, 133–134
    of skepticism, 134–135
Problem solving, 87–88
Process diagnosis, 141
Process experiential therapy, 11–15, 93
Process observations, 180
Process-oriented approach, 95–96
Productive emotions, 73–74
Productivity Scale, 73
Promoting therapeutic work, 93–94
Proximal zone of development, 233–234
Psychoeducation, 82, 101, 135
Punitive self-markers, 150

Rambling, 153–154
Rationale for working with emotion, 100–101
Rauch, S., 22
Reappraisal, 79
Reason, 86, 88
Reflection, 83–85, 157–158
    to deconstruct worldviews, 319
    difficulties in facilitating, 319–320
    empty-chair work to facilitate, 315–317
    on inner experience, 311–312
    on origins/implications of experience, 312–313
    process of, 307–309
    on representations of experience, 309–310
    in service of representation, 310–313
    on social context/values/goals, 318
    in systematic evocative unfolding, 317–318
    of therapist, 130–131
    and transformation, 119–120
    two-chair work to facilitate, 313–315
Reflective awareness, 83, 160
Reflective examination, 305
Reflective restructuring, 295
Reflectivity, 307
Reframing, 85

Regenold, W., 23
Regulation
    affect, 22, 34, 47–49, 102
    emotion, 68
Rehearsed descriptions, 153
Reich, W., 202
Rejection, 45, 51, 52, 60
Relating, style of, 173
Relational empathic treatment, 12
Relational soothing interventions, 25
Relief, 162, 265
Remembering another emotion, 284
Remorse, 62
Repeating family patterns, 60
Repeating the past, 61
Resentment, 64
Resilience, 19, 53, 87, 247–250, 281, 282
Resolution of unfinished business, 269
Resolving hopelessness, 236–250
    acknowledging new experience in, 240–243
    allowing/accepting new emotion in, 243–244
    emergence of resilient self-response in, 247–250
    expressing wants/needs in, 244–247
    recognizing agency in, 238–240
    steps in, 237
Respect, 99, 127
Responsibility
    for felt emotion, 73
    personal, 106–107
    taking, 212
Responsiveness, 95–96
Rice, L. N., 93, 154
Right hemisphere
    and depression, 22, 23, 25, 26
    and empathy, 121
    and therapist's communication, 122
Rimé, B., 76
Rogerian relational qualities, 121
Rogers, C. R., 122, 125, 142, 308
Role-playing, 88
Rousseau, J.-J., 17
Rumination, 24, 77

Sabini, J., 86
Sadness, 25, 28
    in adolescents, 45–46
    and anger, 267, 268
    categories of, 62
    and change, 208, 209

Stability, 41
Steckley, P., 12
Stein, K. F., 85
Stermac, L., 12, 132
Strupp, H. H., 113, 114
"Stuck," 73–74, 298–300
Subjective evaluation of physiological condition, 23
Support
    and bond creation, 158, 159
    for contacting emotions, 107–108
    emotional, 74
    internal, 118
Suppressed emotion
    expression of, 262–265
    as marker, 161
Symbolic representation, 304
Symbolization, 162
Sympathy, 24
Synthetic mode, 160
Systemic evocative unfolding, 187–188, 317–318

Task collaboration, 93
Task completion, 94
Task markers, 105
Thalamus, 21, 22
Themes, 43, 105
Therapeutic congruence, 128
Therapeutic relationship, 94–96, 121–139
    client's contributions to, 132–138
    facilitating a, 93
    generating new emotion through the, 284
    problems in the, 108, 131–132
    repair of, 138–139
    therapist's contribution to, 125–132
    transformation through, 290–292
Therapeutic work, 93–94, 290–292
Therapy
    introducing clients to process of, 124
    shame of being in, 215
Three Approaches to Psychotherapy (film series), 122
Timing, therapist's, 111
Tolerance (of emotion), 81
Tomkins, S., 48, 57
Tone, 123
Top-down processing, 27–28
Transformation phase of treatment, 97, 116–120, 281–301
    and accessing positive emotions, 293

and beliefs, 295–298
changing emotion with emotion, 284–290
encouraging reflection, 119–120
generating new emotional responses, 116–119
homework to promote, 300–301
and impasses, 298–300
and letting go of grieving/pain, 292–294
promoting therapeutic relationship and work, 290–292
supporting emerging sense of self, 120
Transforming emotion, 85–90
Transparency, 127–128
Trauma, 26, 34
    and change, 209
    components of, 214
    and difficulty in constructing narratives, 136
    and exploration of emotions, 108
    and language, 170
    and letting go, 269
    unfinished business based on, 266–268
Triggers, emotional, 163–164, 175–177
Troeml-Ploetz, S., 130
"True self-experience," 41
Trust, 91, 99, 159, 253
Tucker, D. M., 18
Tugade, M., 86
Tuozzi, G., 21
Turvey, C., 77
Two-chair dialogue
    accepting new emotion with, 243–244
    acknowledging new emotions with, 240–243
    agency recognition with, 238–240
    expressing wants/needs with, 244–247
    for hopelessness, 225–233, 238–250
    for interruptive processes, 181–183
    and problematic feelings, 108–109
    reflection facilitation with, 313–315
    resilient self-response emergence with, 247–250
    and self-interruption, 110, 259–265
    and shame, 217

"The Unbearable Automaticity of Being" (J. Bargh and T. Chartrand), 21–22
Undercontrolled emotion, 68
Underregulation, 75, 109–110
Unfinished business, 265–272
    anger in, 268

ABOUT THE AUTHORS

Leslie S. Greenberg, PhD, is professor of psychology at York University in Toronto, Ontario, Canada. He is the director of the York University Psychotherapy Research Clinic, one of the leading authorities on working with emotions in psychotherapy, and a developer of emotion-focused therapy. He has authored the major texts on emotion-focused approaches to treatment of individuals and couples. His latest authored book is *Emotion-Focused Therapy: Coaching Clients to Work Through Their Feelings.* Dr. Greenberg is a founding member of the Society for the Exploration of Psychotherapy Integration and a past president of the Society for Psychotherapy Research, an international interdisciplinary society. He received the 2004 Distinguished Research Career Award of the Society for Psychotherapy Research. He is on the editorial board of many psychotherapy journals, including the *Journal of Psychotherapy Integration* and the *Journal of Marital and Family Therapy.*

Jeanne C. Watson, PhD, is an associate professor in the Department of Adult Education, Community Development and Counselling Psychology at the Ontario Institute for Studies in Education of the University of Toronto, Toronto, Ontario, Canada. She is coauthor of the books *Learning Emotion-Focused Therapy: The Process–Experiential Approach to Change* and *Expressing Emotion: Myths, Realities, and Therapeutic Strategies* and coeditor of *Client-Centered and Experiential Psychotherapy in the 21st Century: Advances in Theory, Research, and Practice* and *Handbook of Experiential Psychotherapy.* In addition, Dr. Watson has written numerous articles and chapters on psychotherapy process and outcome and maintains a part-time private practice in Toronto. She earned her PhD in clinical psychology from York University.